Crisis as Catalyst

A VOLUME IN THE SERIES

Cornell Studies in Political Economy
edited by Peter J. Katzenstein

A list of titles in this series is available at www.cornellpress.cornell.edu.

Crisis as Catalyst

Asia's Dynamic Political Economy

EDITED BY

Andrew MacIntyre, T. J. Pempel,
and John Ravenhill

Cornell University Press
Ithaca and London

First published 2008 by Cornell University Press
First printing, Cornell Paperbacks, 2008

Printed in the United States of America

Library of Congress Cataloging-in-Publication Data

Crisis as catalyst : Asia's dynamic political economy / edited by Andrew
MacIntyre, T. J. Pempel, and John Ravenhill.
    p. cm.—(Cornell studies in political economy)
  Includes bibliographical references and index.
  ISBN 978–0–8014–4714–3 (cloth : alk. paper)—
  ISBN 978–0–8014–7460–6 (pbk. : alk. paper)
 1. Asia—Economic conditions—1945– 2. Asia—Economic policy.
3. Financial crises—Asia. I. MacIntyre, Andrew J., 1960–
II. Pempel, T. J., 1942– III. Ravenhill, John. IV. Title. V. Series.
  HC412.C737 2008
  330.95—dc22   2008014077

Cornell University Press strives to use environmentally responsible
suppliers and materials to the fullest extent possible in the publishing
of its books. Such materials include vegetable-based, low-VOC inks
and acid-free papers that are recycled, totally chlorine-free, or partly
composed of nonwood fibers. For further information, visit our website
at www.cornellpress.cornell.edu.

Cloth printing   10 9 8 7 6 5 4 3 2 1
Paperback printing   10 9 8 7 6 5 4 3 2 1

Contents

Part II. Regional Responses

Part III. National Responses

Preface

In 1997–98 an economic tsunami swept across Asia. The currencies of many East Asian countries depreciated radically; previously sky-high growth rates plummeted; corporations, banks, and other financial institutions shuttered their doors; government budgets were upended; unemployment levels shot up. Numerous political repercussions shook Asia in the wake of these radical economic developments. These often involved dramatic policy shifts or even complete changes in regimes. The economic difficulties faced by Asia, meanwhile, precipitated upheavals in many other parts of the world—from Russia to Brazil. The crisis led to wide-scale and often competing academic and journalistic analyses of its causes. The editors and many of the contributors to this volume were active in these early debates.

The waves that engulfed East Asia in crisis have long since receded. Most of the countries affected have returned to levels of productivity and growth higher than in other developing regions, albeit lower than those they enjoyed in the decade before the crisis. Nonetheless, East Asia a decade after the onset of the crisis is radically different on many dimensions from the region shaken up in 1997–98. The differences, however, are hardly uniform. In some ways, today's Asia shows sharp breaks from prior practices. But in others the shadows of continuity are far more striking than any signs of breaks with the past. Moreover, although certain new trends seem relatively uniform across the region, far more frequently the mixture of change and continuity has differed from one country to the next.

This variance in experience across issues and across countries suggested the need for a project that would provide a systematic review of postcrisis developments in the region. Our preliminary discussions led us to conclude that a decade after the crisis provided enough chronological distance, while simultaneously setting up a convenient benchmark, to allow scholars to think systematically about the crisis and its impacts. We sought to examine what lessons have been learned, how effective the policy responses have been, what institutional changes have occurred, and how well these various changes equip countries to cope with the challenges that they face today and will face in the coming years. In framing our project, we sought to address a number of questions: What has changed due to the crisis? What did it fail to affect? How and why did different actors in various countries use the crisis as a catalyst to promote change? How, cumulatively, is the Asian region different today from what it had been before the crisis struck? To what extent were certain breaks with the past spawning new regional interactions and a new regional identity?

To explore these issues, we held two conferences during 2006. The first took place at the Crawford School of Economics and Government at Australian National University on July 21–22, where we benefited from helpful comments from a number of outside discussants. The second conference was held at the Institute of East Asian Studies (IEAS), University of California, Berkeley, on November 3–4. Generous financial support was provided for the project by the East Asia Forum, the East Asia Foundation, the Crawford School, and IEAS. We thank Taehwan Kim and Hyung Taek Hong for their guidance and help in securing support from the East Asia Foundation, Maree Tait and her colleagues at the Crawford School for managing the initial conference in Canberra, and Martin Backstrom and Kumi Sawada Hadler for their support for the Berkeley conference. Dr. Miwa Hirono of the Department of International Relations, Australian National University, did an outstanding job in assembling and preparing the manuscript to Cornell University Press specifications. Mary-Lou Hickey, of the same department, similarly excelled in coordinating responses from the contributors during the production process.

Roger Haydon of Cornell University Press provided considerable help in shaping the project for eventual publication. Finally, we thank Peter J. Katzenstein and an anonymous reader for exceptionally helpful comments on the individual papers and on the project as a whole.

Andrew MacIntyre
T. J. Pempel
John Ravenhill

Abbreviations

ABF	Asia Bond Fund
ABMI	Asian Bond Market Initiatives
ACU	Asian currency unit
ADB	Asian Development Bank
AFTA	ASEAN Free Trade Agreement
AMF	Asian Monetary Fund
AMU	Asian monetary unit
APEC	Asia-Pacific Economic Cooperation
APT	ASEAN+3
ARF	ASEAN Regional Forum
ASA	ASEAN currency swap arrangements
ASEAN	Association of Southeast Asian Nations
ASEM	Asia Europe Meeting
BA	Barisan Alternatif (Alternative Front) [Malaysia]
BIS	Bank for International Settlements
BN	Barisan Nasional (National Front) [Malaysia]
BSAs	bilateral swap arrangements
CARP	Comprehensive Agrarian Reform Program [Philippines]
CAR	capital adequacy ratio
CBMs	confidence building measures
CDA	Constitutional Drafting Assembly [Thailand]
CDRF	China Development Research Foundation
CGE	computable general equilibrium
CGFS	Committee on the Global Financial System
CFQ	corporate governance quality
CMI	Chiang Mai Initiative

CNOOC	China National Offshore Oil Corporation
CSCAP	Council for Security Cooperation in the Asia Pacific
DAP	Democratic Action Party [Malaysia]
DPP	Democratic Progressive Party [Taiwan]
DPR	Dewan Perwakilan Rakyat (House of Representatives) [Indonesia]
DPRK	Democratic People's Republic of Korea
DRAM	dynamic random access memory
EAS	East Asia Summit
EAVG	East Asian Vision Group
ECU	European currency unit
EFTA	European Free Trade Agreement
EMEAP	Executives' Meeting of East Asia-Pacific Central Banks
EPF	Employees Provident Fund [Malaysia]
ERR	exchange rate regime
ETF	exchange-traded funds
EVSL	Early Voluntary Sectoral Liberalization
FDI	foreign direct investment
FHC	financial holding company
FIDF	Financial Institutions Development Fund
FKI	Federation of Korean Industry
FLAR	Latin American Reserve Fund
FSA	Financial Supervisory Agency (later renamed the Financial Services Agency) [Japan]
FSC	Financial Supervisory Commission [Korea]
FSS	Financial Supervisory Service [Korea]
FTA	free trade agreement
FX	foreign exchange
FY	fiscal year
GATT	General Agreement on Tariffs and Trade
GCF	gross capital formation
GDP	gross domestic product
GLC	government-linked companies [Malaysia]
GOCC	government-owned and -controlled corporations [Philippines]
GSIS	Government Services Insurance System [Philippines]
GW	gigawatt
IAS	International Accounting Standards
IFIs	international financial institutions
ILO	International Labour Organisation
IMF	International Monetary Fund
IPO	initial public offering
JBIC	Japan's Bank for International Cooperation
JSEPA	Japan-Singapore Economic Partnership Agreement
KEB	Korea Exchange Bank
KDIC	Korea Deposit Insurance Corporation
KEB	Korea Exchange Bank
KLSE	Kuala Lumpur Stock Exchange
KMT	Kuomingtang (Nationalist Party) [Taiwan]
KOSPI	Korean Composite Stock Price Index

LDP	Liberal Democratic Party [Japan]
LG	Lucky-Goldstar
M&A	merger and acquisition
MITI	Ministry of International Trade and Industry [Japan]
MNC	multinational corporation
MOFE	Ministry of Finance and Economy [Korea]
MSP	minority shareholder protection
NAFTA	North America Free Trade Agreement
NBFI	nonbank financial institution
NEACD	Northeast Asia Cooperation Dialogue
NEAT	Network of East Asian Think Tanks
NEP	New Economic Policy [Malaysia]
NGO	nongovernmental organization
NIC	newly industrialized country
NPL	nonperforming loan
NYSE	New York Stock Exchange
OECD	Organisation for Economic Co-operation and Development
OTOP	one *tamboon*, one product
PAIF	Pan-Asian Bond Index Fund
PAS	Pan-Malaysian Islamic Party
PDI-P	Partai Demokrati Indonesia-Perjuangan (Indonesian Democratic Party of Struggle)
PBEC	Pacific Basin Economic Council
PECC	Pacific Economic Cooperation Council
PNB	Permodalan Nasional Berhad [Malaysia]
PNS	Pegawai Negeri Sipil [Indonesia]
PRC	People's Republic of China
PPP	purchasing power parity
PTA	preferential trading agreement
PUNB	Perbadanan Usahawan Nasional Berhad [Malaysia]
REMU	Regional Economic Monitoring Unit [ADB]
RIETI	Research Institute of Economy, Trade and Industry [METI, Japan]
ROA	return on assets
ROK	Republic of Korea
SBY	Susilo Bambang Yudhoyono
SCO	Shanghai Cooperation Organization
SDRs	special drawing rights
SEC	Securities and Exchange Commission
SITC	Standard International Trade Classification
SK	SunKyong
SMEs	small and medium enterprises
SOE	state-owned enterprise
SPT	Six Party Talks
SRA	Social Reform Agenda [Philippines]
SSE	Singapore Stock Exchange
SSS	Social Security System [Philippines]
TAC	Treaty of Amity and Cooperation [ASEAN]
TAMC	Thailand Asset Management Corporation

TRT	Thai Rak Thai (Thai Loves Thai) Party
UMNO	United Malays National Organization
UNCTAD	United Nations Conference on Trade and Development
UNIDO	United Nations Industrial Development Organization
UOB	United Overseas Bank [Singapore]
WTO	World Trade Organization
YOY	year-on-year

CHAPTER 1

East Asia in the Wake of the Financial Crisis

Andrew MacIntyre, T. J. Pempel,
and John Ravenhill

The financial crisis that swept across East Asia during 1997–98 had devastating social and political as well as economic consequences.[1] The crisis dramatically interrupted the hypergrowth and sociopolitical modernization that had transformed the region in the previous three decades. A decade later, East Asia not only once again was economically outperforming the rest of the developing world, it was increasingly the central driver of the global economy. Although economic recovery came relatively quickly, the crisis changed East Asia in important ways.

The point of departure for this volume is the conviction that the crisis was historically important in Asia and that its import extended well beyond the short-term impact on macroeconomic performance in a limited number of countries. Just as the crisis had deep roots in noneconomic soil, so its consequences have reached well beyond simple issues of acceptance or rejection of economic policy change. The crisis, as the contributors to this volume show, catalyzed changes across a swath of political, corporate, and social arenas both in the countries hit by the crisis and in many others throughout the region. The central objectives of this book are to assess what has changed (as well as what has not changed) in East Asia since the crisis, to try to explain variations in response to crisis across the region, and to reflect on the longer-term significance of these developments.

---

1. Throughout this volume *East Asia* is used as shorthand for Northeast Asia and Southeast Asia, that is, the ten Association of Southeast Asian Nations (ASEAN) countries (Brunei, Cambodia, Indonesia, Leo PDR, Malaysia, Myanmar, the Philippines, Singapore, Thailand, and Vietnam), China (including Hong Kong and Macau), Japan, the two Koreas, and Taiwan.

Our assessment comes a decade after the onset of the crisis. Although there is nothing magical about "ten years after," any more than there is about the "first one hundred days," it is a convenient and logical time to step back and assess the impact of the financial crisis on the most vibrant economies of the world, the changes that have occurred in the region since the crisis (including the extent to which they were driven by the crisis itself and the extent to which they were responses to global trends), and whether Asian countries remain vulnerable to the type of crisis that hit them in 1997–98 or to other forms of economic crisis. An assessment at this time is logical because it has inevitably taken a period of years before the trends in the policy responses to the chaos in 1997–98 have become clear. Moreover, the tenth anniversary of the crisis attracted a great deal of commentary in official, press, and academic circles, reinforcing our belief that an in-depth review of developments in the region will help to resolve ongoing debates about the contemporary political economy of the region.

The book advances four central arguments. First, the crisis had a profound effect on preexisting patterns of political economy within the region. The natural search to reduce vulnerability to future crises forced a reassessment of many prior patterns of political economy as well as national links to regionalization, globalization, and internationalization. As a consequence of the crisis, the political economy of East Asia changed substantially, reflected particularly in policies regarding banking, corporate regulation, and social protection. In the most severely affected economies, the crisis led to a marked denationalization of ownership in manufacturing and services. For instance, in the automobile industry, the second most important sector in manufacturing across the region after electronics, the crisis caused widespread bankruptcies among locally owned firms. Not only did this lead to the exit of many small and medium-size parts producers from the industry but foreign buyers were able to purchase the assets of larger companies at fire-sale prices (Doner, Noble, and Ravenhill 2004). In Indonesia, the crisis led to the abandoning of statist efforts to build a national automobile industry—regulations that limited foreign auto assemblers to minority shareholdings in joint ventures were removed. In Korea, the only developing country by the mid 1990s that had succeeded in becoming a major player in the international auto industry through the promotion of national champions, three of the five domestic assemblers—Daewoo, Samsung, and Ssangyong—fell into foreign hands.

Yet many anticipated changes, such as those regarding exchange rates (economists expected East Asian governments to abandon the soft pegging of their currencies to the U.S. dollar), did not occur. Overall, the countries of the region showed neither the uniform adoption of any particular mix of economic or political reforms nor any blind recommitment to the continuation of past practices. Interestingly, a reconsideration of policies in response to the crisis also took place in countries that did not suffer the most acute economic consequences during 1997–98. Indeed, countries only indirectly affected economically by the crisis such as China, Japan, and Vietnam, took various steps at the national or regional level to reconfigure important components of their political economies.

The second argument we advance is that, on balance, the widespread East Asian commitment to "growth with equity" that had long been a fundamental component of the economic success of the region was more reasserted than abandoned. Indeed, some of the major social dislocations caused by the crisis, along with the subsequent adoption of more market-based policies, led to the creation of new state-led social programs. Nonetheless, across the region, substantial evidence had accumulated a decade after the crisis to suggest that income disparities had increased substantially.

Changes in ideas provide the third thread throughout the volume. The crisis may have been at least as important in stimulating new perspectives among political and business elites as they were in their impact on the real economies—although, of course, the two were closely related. As Gourevitch (1978, 1986) demonstrated decades ago, severe economic downturns frequently destroy existing equilibria, opening up space for alternative ideas and allowing new battles to be fought by their competing domestic and international advocates.

In particular, the crisis forced a reassessment of the underpinnings of prior East Asian economic successes. Bluntly sketched, economists had generally asserted that the East Asian success had rested on "getting prices right" and adhering to solid economic fundamentals. In contrast, "developmentalists" had long trumpeted the positive role in promoting rapid economic growth played by close government-business relations and selective government interventions. Those who stressed the importance of the developmental state were able to point to investor panic and the activities of international speculators as the causes of the crisis in 1997. Moreover, there was little evidence across the region that crony capitalism had precipitated the upheavals. Nonetheless, the crisis afforded an opportunity for critics of statist approaches to push for greater liberalization.

Fourth and finally, just as individual countries in East Asia went through substantial changes at the national level, so too East Asia as a region changed profoundly following the crisis. Certain responses to the crisis were regional in character, a circling of the Asian wagons in an effort to insulate the region as a whole from potential future crises. Most of these changes were in the vital areas of finance, including the introduction of currency swaps, Asian bond markets, and enhanced accumulation of foreign reserves. Others involved creating such new institutional bodies as the ASEAN Plus 3 grouping,[2] and the East Asia Summit. Moreover, some actions, such as the negotiation of bilateral free trade agreements and enhanced commitments to state-directed social welfare systems, gave a new but relatively common set of characteristics to much of the region. Cumulatively, these changes have left East Asia as a more institutionalized and more "Asian" region than it was at the time of the crisis.

The first part of the volume contains chapters that focus on dimensions of the political economy of the region in which the crisis might have been expected to

---

2. ASEAN Plus China, Japan, and Korea.

promote significant change. Prominent here are exchange rate regimes, domestic regulation of banking and other financial institutions, corporate governance, and social insurance. We then examine developments at the regional level in monetary and financial cooperation, in trade, and in overall linkages among the countries of the region. The last part of the volume examines country-level developments.

Our focus on the crisis and its impact shapes our choice of country studies. The five countries that were the most serious victims of the crisis—Indonesia, Korea, Malaysia, the Philippines, and Thailand—are obvious candidates for detailed scrutiny. We use paired comparisons—with one chapter focusing on Indonesia and Malaysia, and another on the Philippines and Thailand—as a means of highlighting the sources of continuity and change in the domestic political economies of these countries. Korea, the largest of the economies most seriously affected by the crisis, the only one of the original Gang of Four East Asian newly industrializing economies to be so, and the country that most fully embraced an International Monetary Fund (IMF) program that fundamentally challenged its previous political economy configurations, is given a chapter in its own right. Perhaps less obvious is our inclusion of a chapter on China. Yet, as Edward Steinfeld (chap. 9 in this volume) shows, the crisis had a profound impact on the thinking of the Chinese political elites on how to sustain the process of rapid economic growth that was well under way by the time of the crisis.

The editors gave considerable thought as to whether to include a chapter on Japan. In the end, we decided against doing this because the focus of the book is on responses to the crisis rather than on more general changes within the region in the years after 1997. Although Japan remains the most technologically advanced East Asian economy (and its largest, if GDP is measured at current exchange rates), the crisis *itself* had relatively little impact on Japanese domestic political economy. Where the crisis was important for Japan was in prompting changes in Tokyo's policies toward regional collaboration (a topic examined in detail in several chapters in part II).

Economic Crisis and Recovery

At one level of generality, an explanation for the misadventure that befell many East Asian economies in 1997–98 is straightforward. The devastating (although, save for Indonesia, short-term) reversal of economic growth was the product of mutually reinforcing currency and banking crises. These quickly spilled over into the real economy when the collapse of financial institutions led to the nonrenewal of loans and/or to companies being unable to service their debts under a higher interest rate regime. The proximate cause of the crisis was a massive reversal in capital flows, with net international bank and bond finance for the five most severely affected economies (Indonesia, Korea, Malaysia, the Philippines, and Thailand) moving from an inflow of $54 billion in the twelve months from the fourth quarter of 1996 to the third quarter of 1997, to an outflow of $68 billion in the fourth quarter of

1997 and the first quarter of 1998 (Grenville 2000, 42, table 2.3). The turnaround in bank lending between 1996 and 1997 was equivalent to 9.5 percent of the combined GDP of the five crisis economies (Radelet and Sachs 1998, 6).

Looking back on the huge literature that the crisis spawned, there is one point on which substantial consensus existed: the crisis was the product of a flawed process of financial liberalization in East Asia. Financial liberalization facilitated the investment boom that occurred in the crisis economies from the mid-1980s. In the second half of the 1980s, the ratio of investment to GDP was already over 25 percent for all the economies except for the Philippines. In the period 1990–96, the mean figure jumped substantially for all economies, most spectacularly for Malaysia and Thailand, for which the ratio climbed to close to 45 percent (figure 1.1).

By the late 1980s, for all the crisis economies except for Indonesia, levels of domestic savings were insufficient to fully finance the investment boom (figure 1.2). For Korea and Malaysia (except in 1995), the gap between domestic savings and gross fixed capital formation was relatively small as a percentage of GDP; for the Philippines and Thailand, it was much more substantial, averaging over 5 percent for the years from 1990 to 1996.

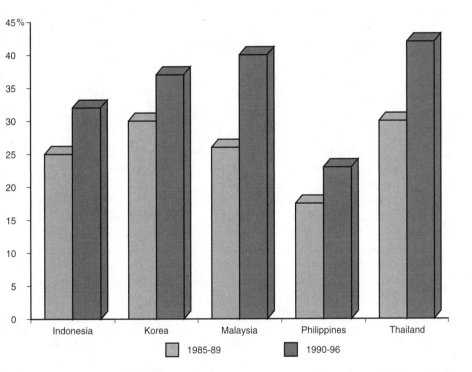

Figure 1.1 Mean investment/GDP ratio, 1985–1989 and 1990–1996 (%).
Source: Calculated from data in World Bank (n.d.).

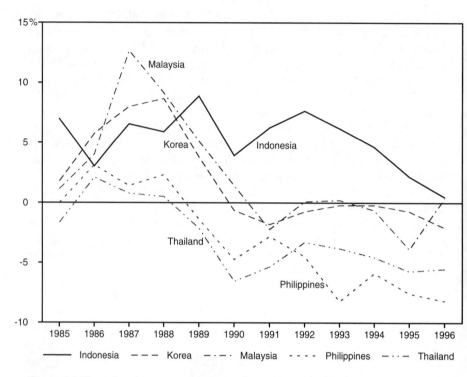

Figure 1.2 The savings-investment gap—the gap between gross fixed capital formation and gross domestic savings, 1985–1996 (percentage of GDP).
Source: World Bank (n.d.).

The investment boom consequently was financed by massive capital inflows. These increased from an annual average of 1.4 percent of GDP during 1986–90 to 6.7 percent during 1990–96. The pace of inflows increased markedly between 1994 and 1996. In 1996, they were equivalent to about 15 percent of GDP for Thailand and the Philippines, 8 percent for Malaysia, and 5 percent for Indonesia and Korea (World Bank 1998a, fig. 1.3). In all of the crisis economies save for Malaysia, the vast majority of capital inflows originated in overseas borrowing by financial intermediaries and by the corporate sector.

From the perspective of both borrowers and lenders, this activity appeared rational. The relative stability of exchange rates in the region (and their seemingly implicit guarantee by governments) reduced the apparent risk for both parties to an easy-to-justify transaction. For borrowers from within the region, foreign loans offered the opportunity to access money at rates lower than those prevailing domestically for lenders and borrowers alike (and, therefore, a chance for financial institutions to profit from intermediation). For financial institutions in high-income economies faced with relatively low interest rates at home, especially for those from

Japan, supplying loans to the rapidly growing economies of East Asia also appeared an attractive proposition, providing them with the opportunity to earn relatively high returns with apparently little risk.

The effects of the investment boom on the financial sector were particularly problematic. One dimension was the misallocation of funds toward largely speculative investments. On the eve of the crisis, it was estimated that the share of bank lending that was directed toward the property sector ranged from 15–20 percent in the Philippines, 15–25 percent in Korea, and 25–30 percent in Indonesia to 30–40 percent in Malaysia and Thailand (Goldstein 1998, 8). In addition, in some countries, notably Korea, banks themselves had substantial investments in stocks.[3] There, the new lending in the 1990s financed the building of massive excess capacity in sectors such as steel and automobiles (Noble and Ravenhill 2000). Risky lending further weakened the balance sheets of the banks, with nonperforming loans (NPLs) estimated as constituting at least 15 percent of total loans in the five economies.[4] Small wonder, then, that by the mid-1990s some financial advisors were warning clients of the vulnerability of the financial institutions of the region.[5] Once the speculative bubble burst, financial institutions quickly found themselves in trouble—and it was the accumulation of NPLs by nonbank financial intermediaries in Thailand that triggered the initial waves of speculation against the baht.

The problems of the financial sector were compounded by what has become known as the "double mismatch" in financial intermediation. The first component was a currency mismatch between financial institutions' borrowing through unhedged loans denominated in foreign currency and their lending of these funds in domestic currencies.[6] The second was a maturity mismatch between the short-term foreign currency borrowing of the financial institutions and their medium-term domestic lending.[7] The double mismatch generated several vulnerabilities. The dependence on short-term loans made the system of investment financing vulnerable to a massive reduction in the availability of funds in a short time period—a reversal of capital flows that could occur for reasons that had little to do with the situation

---

3. An International Monetary Fund (IMF) staff study notes that "While on the whole the Fund and the authorities were aware of the magnitude of these inflows, and some concern was expressed, this concern was tempered by the perception that the inflows were attributable mainly to favorable investment prospects associated with a stable macroeconomic environment and high growth. In hindsight, however, it appears that the inflows were to a considerable extent financing asset price inflation and an accumulation of poor-quality loans in the portfolios of banks and other financial intermediaries" (Lane et al. 1999, 10).

4. During 1996, stock prices fell by more than 20 percent in Korea and by almost one-third in Thailand. Property prices in Thailand also declined before the crisis began (Lane et al. 1999).

5. On private-sector warnings about the health of financial institutions in the crisis countries, see Delhaise (1998) and Hale (2007).

6. On the eve of the crisis, 45 percent of Korean and 50 percent of Thai domestic bank lending to the private sector was funded by borrowing from international banks (Goldstein and Turner 2004).

7. The Financial Stability Forum (2000) estimates that the share of short-term debt to banks in the total external debt of East Asian and Pacific countries rose from 20 to 30 percent from the end of 1990 to the end of 1996.

in the borrowing country.[8] In this context, it is important to remind ourselves of the relatively small size of the financial systems in the crisis economies; decisions by one or two large overseas financial institutions to withdraw from lending could have a disproportionate impact on the local economy.

And any depreciation of the exchange rate generated a gap between the international obligations of the financial institutions and the value of their loan portfolios. Devaluation simply increased the local currency value of the liabilities of the financial institutions. Heavy dependence on unhedged foreign loans also rendered the whole financial system vulnerable to "rational panic" (Radelet and Sachs 1998) if investors became concerned that the foreign exchange reserves of a country were insufficient to meet the foreign currency liabilities of its financial institutions. The situation was ripe for an insolvency crisis driven by self-fulfilling expectations. And, as Grenville (2000, 44) notes, foreign lenders were particularly susceptible to herd-like behavior in a context in which they had little knowledge of and understanding of the local economy.

The trigger for the crisis, then, was the realization by foreign lenders of the dire nature of the relationship between short-term debt and available foreign exchange reserves in Thailand, Indonesia, and Korea (figure 1.3) and the risk that this posed for recovering their loans. By 1995, in all three countries, short-term debts exceeded available foreign exchange—and the ratio rose to as high as 300 percent in Korea. The situation in Korea was made worse by the central bank's lending reserves to commercial banks, and everywhere it was exacerbated by doubts about the accuracy of the asset sheets presented by the central banks.[9]

Once the crisis began, its various elements—in the currency market, the financial sector, and the real economy—became self-sustaining and mutually reinforcing. An attack on the currency took the form of nonrenewal of lending, which caused problems for banks and the corporate sector; currency depreciation increased the local currency liabilities of domestic financial institutions; attempts to stem capital outflows and currency depreciation by raising interest rates caused further corporate defaults; and these defaults in turn further exacerbated the problem of NPLs, generating more concern among foreign investors about the health of the financial sector.

The first manifestation of the crisis was the collapse in the exchange rates of the affected economies (figure 1.4). Indonesia was the most severely affected, with the rupiah losing 80 percent of its value by January 1998. Other crisis economies were less severely affected (with Malaysia, courtesy in part to its capital controls, least badly hit); nonetheless, the extent of depreciation was substantially more than the estimated precrisis overvaluations of the individual currencies.

The currency crisis immediately turned into a banking crisis because of the double mismatch problem. With the banks unable to renew their borrowing, a severe

8. Some observers (e.g., Wade 1998) suggest that problems in the Japanese financial system contributed to decisions by Japanese banks not to renew short-term lending to the region in the second half of 1997.

9. On the Korean situation, see Cho (2002); on the dubious accounting practices of banks in the region, see Delhaise (1998).

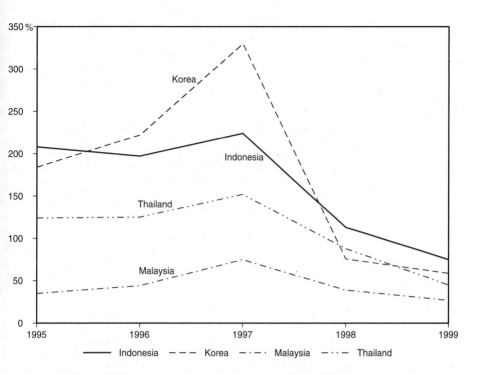

Figure 1.3 Ratio of short-term external debt to foreign reserves, 1995–1999 (%).
Source: Data from Goldstein and Turner (2004, 12, table 2.1).

tightening in domestic credit occurred, a development exacerbated when governments sharply increased domestic interest rates, a move intended to stabilize local
currencies. In turn, the credit squeeze caused a massive increase in bankruptcies.

The severity of the immediate reversal for all the crisis economies except for the
Philippines is evident from figure 1.5, with the Indonesian GDP declining by close
to 15 percent in 1998 and those of Korea, Malaysia, and Thailand falling by close to
8 percent. The Philippines, in contrast, barely ventured into negative territory in
1998 (Hutchcroft 1999). The crisis, however, also spilled over into neighboring
countries enmeshed in the growing regional economic interdependence. Cambodia
and Laos, for instance, both of which depended on Thailand for 30 percent of their
exports and on crisis economies collectively for more than 80 percent of their foreign direct investment, suffered significant currency depreciation and consequent
domestic price inflation (Okonjo-Iweala et al. 1999).

Equally apparent from figure 1.5 is the rapidity of the recovery, denoted by the
pronounced V-shape of the trend lines (the subsequent brief downturn experienced in 2001 primarily reflects the slowdown in the global electronics industry,
on which East Asia continues to depend heavily; see John Ravenhill, chap. 7 in this
volume). Even the Indonesian economy, the one most severely affected by the crisis,
had returned to growth (albeit at a very modest level) by 1999. Looked at from a

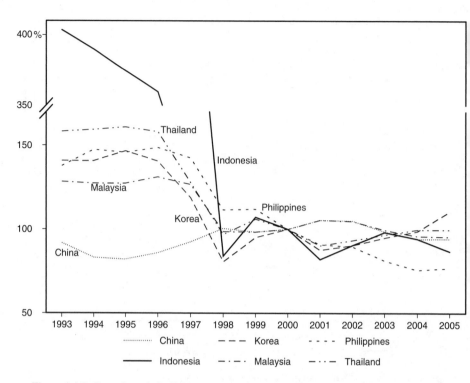

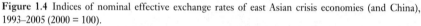

Figure 1.4 Indices of nominal effective exchange rates of east Asian crisis economies (and China), 1993–2005 (2000 = 100).
Source: Calculated from data in IMF, *International Financial Statistics* online database.

medium term perspective (figure 1.6), the crisis does appear to have been no more than a small blip in the overall upward trajectory of East Asian per capita GDP.

The data in figure 1.6, however, do highlight differences between the pre- and postcrisis performances of the five most severely affected economies. Only in Korea has the rate of growth in per capita GDP returned to levels close to that of the pre-crisis decade (the performance of the Philippines is also remarkably constant but with per capita income growing much more slowly than in the other economies). As Jongryn Mo (chap. 12 in this volume) makes clear, Korea presents a striking case study because, of all the countries hit directly and hit hard by the crisis, it was the one that undertook the most extensive set of neoliberal reforms targeted specifically at certain key areas of vulnerability believed to have contributed to the collapse of 1997–98. Although the reform efforts have disappointed in some areas (and in particular have left foreign investors unhappy), overall Korea exhibits the clearest cause-and-effect relationship between the crisis and subsequent efforts to reduce vulnerability to future financial shocks. As Mo shows, the reforms in Korea were heavily contingent on conducive political circumstances, in particular, the election

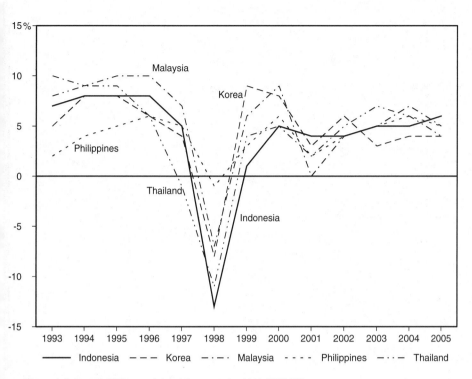

Figure 1.5 Annual GDP growth in crisis economies, 1993–2005 (%).
Source: World Bank (n.d.).

of Kim Dae Jung, whose anticonservative coalition came to power with a mandate to shake up the previously intimate relationships between the giant corporations and government policymakers. A reformist administration, riding a wave of public anger at the economic humiliation of the country, together with pressure from global investors interested in gaining access to Korean assets, made it possible for substantial change to take place.

For Indonesia, Malaysia, and Thailand, the crisis was a disjunction in the trajectory of economic growth, with the growth curve postcrisis much flatter than before. Per capita income in Indonesia did not recover to precrisis levels until 2004. Griffith-Jones and Gottschalk (2006, 19) estimate that the total output loss in the period 1997–2002 suffered by four economies—Indonesia, Korea, Malaysia, and Thailand—as a consequence of the crisis amounted to $917 billion, of which by far the biggest amount is attributable to Indonesia ($346 billion). In addition to this one-off shock, the four Southeast Asian economies experienced ongoing losses because of markedly lower rates of growth. If overall growth had continued at the pace of the two decades before the crisis, the Indonesian GDP in 2007 would have

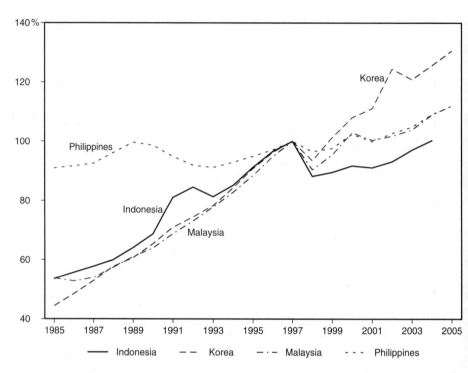

Figure 1.6 Crisis economies index of per capita GDP, 1985–2005 (purchasing power parity, PPP; 1997 = 100).
Source: Calculated from data in World Bank (n.d.).

been one-third higher and that of Thailand would have been one-quarter higher (*Australian Financial Review,* June 18, 2007).

One reason for the postcrisis slowdown in growth is a decline in overall levels of investment in all the economies (figure 1.7). Gross capital formation as a share of GDP fell back to the levels of the late 1980s, substantially below those of the first half of the 1990s. A contributing factor was the postcrisis fall in foreign direct investment inflows, particularly to Southeast Asian economies. For many observers, the high levels of investment in the first half of the 1990s reflected irrational exuberance, were unsustainable, and were responsible for the inflation of asset prices that undermined the competitiveness of exports. For certain commentators, some slowdown in East Asian economic growth was inevitable as these economies acquired middle-income status. This argument may have some plausibility for Korea, but it is more difficult to sustain for Malaysia, Thailand, and especially Indonesia, which still remain a long way from the technological frontier. And it is even less convincing at a time when China continues to enjoy rates of economic growth that are more than 50 percent above those in Southeast Asia. The low rates of investment, in part attributable to a desire to run current account surpluses to minimize vulnerabilities to crisis, are extracting an ongoing toll on economic welfare.

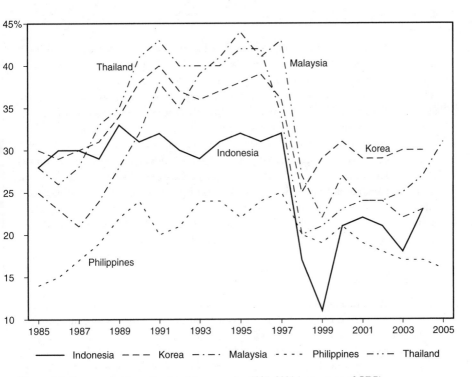

Figure 1.7 Gross capital formation in crisis economies, 1985–2004 (percentage of GDP).
Source: World Bank (n.d.).

The crisis posed a particular challenge to one distinctive feature of the East Asian pattern of economic development—growth with equity. Compared to other developing areas of the world, East Asia managed its rapid economic transformation in ways that were broadly egalitarian in terms of income distribution, educational and health access, gender, employment opportunities, and other areas. The impact of the crisis on low-income groups in Asia is succinctly summarized by Stephan Haggard: capital flight and devaluation combined with the fiscal tightening made obligatory by IMF programs "brought layoffs, declining demand for new entrants into the labor market, real wage declines, and a resultant squeeze on the informal sector" (2000, 190). From 1996 to 1998, the incidence of poverty increased by 80 percent in Indonesia and doubled in South Korea. But the social impact of the crisis was by no means limited to the poor. With a dramatic increase occurring in the number of bankruptcies, there was a huge toll on the owners of small and medium enterprises and (to a lesser extent) on the salaried middle class. Unemployment rates doubled in Indonesia from 1996 to 1998, reaching 10 percent in 1998; in Thailand, the rate increased threefold from 1.5 to more than 5.6 percent, and in Korea, it reached a record level of more than 7.5 percent in 1998 (International Labour Organisation [ILO] 1998).

Responding to the Crisis

The crisis was an intense economic and political shock to the region. Although the most severely affected economies, with the exception of Indonesia, recovered quickly, it was a watershed in the region on at least four fundamental dimensions. The most obvious of these is the changes in domestic economic policies adopted to attempt to reduce the vulnerability of countries to the type of crisis experienced in 1997. Second, important if less conspicuous changes have occurred in poverty, inequality, and social protection policies. Third, moving beyond specific national policy settings, there was also less tangible but nonetheless consequential ideational change about development; challenges to the preexisting patterns of development arose in many countries, pitting reformers against resisters. Finally, governments adopted a changing approach to regionalism in the wake of the crisis. We introduce each of these themes here, but they also flow throughout the chapters of the volume and we return to them in the concluding chapter.

Reducing Vulnerability

In terms of domestic economic policies, combating the sources of vulnerability that led to the crisis in 1997 became a priority throughout the region, including in those countries not severely affected by the crises. A number of reforms were proposed at the time for changing the global financial architecture (notably, Chapter XI mechanisms for countries, bailing the private sector in, etc.). But most of these subsequently stalled (Wade 2007). As a consequence, the main responses to combating vulnerability came at the national and regional levels. At the national level, we see five common trends across the region: (1) the running of significant current account surpluses, (2) the consequent accumulation of massive foreign reserves, (3) ensuring that short-term foreign liabilities are kept well below reserve levels, (4) the greater flexibility in exchange rates, and (5) the strengthening of prudential regulation of the financial system. The emphasis on reducing vulnerability was a significant factor in the lower rates of investment and of economic growth that most countries in the region experienced postcrisis, but preventing any future currency meltdown took priority. Contrary to expectations, for reasons that Benjamin Cohen (chap. 2 in this volume) suggests, East Asian governments have not moved as far as the IMF advocated in freeing their exchange rates; nor have they adopted capital controls, despite the apparent success of China and Malaysia (temporarily) in using them.

Moving beyond these policy commonalities, we also see policy divergence across the region. This, we argue, has to be placed in the context of the historical diversity of the East Asian experience. Despite contentions to the contrary, there had never been a single East Asian model. Accordingly, the political economies of countries across the region were substantially different at the time of the crisis. This diversity was reflected in the specific forms in which the vulnerabilities to crisis were manifested, for instance, with bank lending a particular problem in Korea, corporate debt more of a problem in Indonesia, and the crisis manifesting itself in Malaysia particularly through difficulties in the stock market. And, path dependence arising from this diversity was a powerful shaper of the responses to the crisis. We see this path dependence, in particular, in the postcrisis reform of corporate governance and, to a lesser extent, in reforms to financial system regulation as well as social protection. This theme emerges in Peter Gourevitch (chap. 4), Natasha Hamilton-Hart (chap. 3), and Haggard (chap. 5), respectively.

One of the more widespread and common sets of changes introduced across the region were reforms to domestic banking structures. Thus, Hamilton-Hart shows that the crisis economies, plus Japan, all moved in relatively similar directions to adopt a common set of financial reforms. Collectively, she argues, these effectively extinguished the East Asian predisposition to rely on high debt to ensure high growth. Prudential regulations have been brought closer to international norms. State ownership of banks has declined substantially, whereas the foreign presence in financial systems has increased significantly. In addition, postcrisis reforms of the crisis-affected economies became a means of dealing with broader political economy problems, including cronyism and corruption. Hamilton-Hart concludes that some of the vulnerabilities of the precrisis financial systems have been reduced—most notably related lending, high levels of NPLs, and low capital ratios. Nonetheless, the uneven quality of financial regulation across the region makes any generalizations about the overall soundness of East Asian financial systems somewhat hazardous.

Another dramatic response to the financial weaknesses exposed during the crisis came through unilateral governmental actions aimed at enhancing foreign exchange holdings by most East Asian countries. And these increases were not undertaken only by the crisis economies. Korean reserves have tripled since 1997–98, as might have been expected, but those of Japan have quadrupled and those of China have increased nearly tenfold, despite their having escaped the currency attacks.

Such common and rapid movements toward financial change are congruent with what economists suggest should be logical departures from past practice. But the uniformity of banking reforms found by Hamilton-Hart (chap. 3) and the common expansion of foreign reserves contrast with the absence of an expected move toward a uniform approach to currency regimes (Cohen, chap. 2 in this volume). A number of eminent economists argued that any middle ground—an exchange rate regime of contingent rules or soft pegs—was no longer possible in a world of massive and volatile short-term flows of capital, the kind that beset Asia in 1997–98. Consequently, East Asian governments would be forced to move to one of two corner solutions: to either a free-floating rate or to some form of monetary union (a hard peg). Contrary to these predictions, however, Cohen demonstrates that most East Asian governments, because they see benefits that override the risk, have maintained soft-peg regimes in which the U.S. dollar remains the dominant choice as the anchor currency. Such an approach is a potential source of continued exchange rate vulnerability.

Nor were there any common moves toward pro-market reforms of corporate governance. As Peter Gourevitch (chap. 4 in this volume) shows, on two standard indicators, shareholder concentration and protections for minority shareholder rights, East Asia countries generally continue to rank low. This, he reminds us, is consistent with patterns elsewhere in circumstances of active state involvement in the economy and authoritarian politics. Gourevitch argues that market openness and political openness can be mutually constitutive; if either politics or markets become more open, it becomes harder for the other to remain closed. Korea provides him with one clear example of this phenomenon, an instance of recently opened politics combining with a government with strong reformist credentials pushing significant change. But Korea stands in contrast to other cases such as Malaysia, in which reform to strengthen corporate governance has been slight. Gourevitch argues that whether pushed by market preferences or changes in the political system, across East Asia generally there have been only modest postcrisis changes in shareholder concentration and formal protections for minority investors.

Ironically however, it has been Japan that offers the most profound example of corporate reform within the region (Vogel 2006). A decade of political torpor that began in 1990–91 slowly but eventually drove the Japanese government to become very active in corporate reform by the turn of the century. It made massive revisions to the commercial code, introduced its Big Bang financial reforms, undertook related accounting reforms, and carried out important labor market changes. Inward direct investment was also encouraged, spurring changes in corporate behavior as well as fostering a jump in merger and acquisition (M&A) activities. Such changes were moved even further by the successful campaign to privatize the postal service system by Prime Minister Koizumi Junichiro (Pempel 2006a). Yet there is little to suggest that such changes were in any direct way the outgrowth of the Asian financial crisis.

This is less the case for China. China too undertook reforms in its corporate structures, moving massively to end its heavy reliance on state-owned enterprises, encouraging incoming foreign direct investment, and taking clear steps toward making the country less dependent on state socialism. As Steinfeld demonstrates (chap. 9 in this volume), although the crisis had relatively little immediate economic impact on the Chinese economy, the regional problems and reactions to them profoundly shifted the thinking of political leaders in Beijing. For many, the crisis raised fundamental questions about the relative merits of the preexisting Chinese model of socialist development, the heavy reliance on state-owned enterprises, and the desirability of attempting to emulate the developmental-state approach that up until then seemed to have worked so well for other Northeast Asian economies. It also catalyzed a new interest among Chinese foreign policy circles in the potential to make direct efforts to bolster Asian regionalism as an important complement to previously bilateral Chinese foreign policy approaches.

Social Insurance

Even though economic growth was quickly restored in most countries, as already discussed, the social impact of the crisis was more long term and profound, leaving deep scars in several of the affected countries (in Korea, for instance, they still refer to the "IMF crisis"). Social indicators have been much slower to recover than those for aggregate economic performance. Unemployment is one instance (figure 1.8). Korea and Thailand saw a postcrisis recovery in employment, although in both countries it was not until 2002 that unemployment retreated to approximately its precrisis levels. In the other three countries, unemployment jumped immediately following the crisis and has yet to return to precrisis levels (in Indonesia and the Philippines, it has continued to trend upward in the first half of the first decade of the twenty-first century).

Unemployment data are one of the few indicators available to support impressions that the crisis may have marked a break from the East Asian growth-with-equity model. Although the region as a whole continues to reduce the number of people living in absolute poverty, it seems (although systematic data are not available) that the change in policy direction postcrisis has also led to marked increases in income inequality, not least in China and Japan. Even where postcrisis unemployment levels have been reduced, the East Asian economies have been experiencing a trend similar to their counterparts in North America and Western Europe, namely the casualization of the work force. At the same time, because growth-with-equity

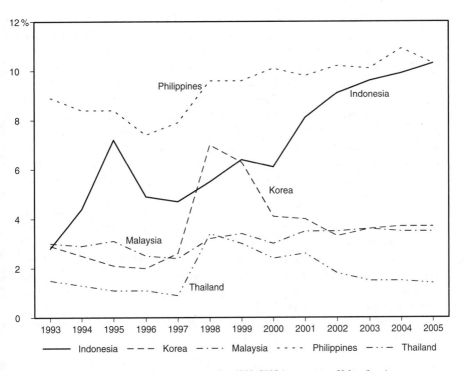

Figure 1.8 Unemployment in the crisis economies, 1993–2005 (percentage of labor force).
Source: Asian Development Bank (2007).

did not depend extensively on massive welfare states, in contrast to many external expectations about rationalizing politics, the crisis did not spur any sweeping dismantling of public programs aimed at slashing social safety nets. Indeed, the social destabilizations caused by the crisis stimulated some countries to take on new state programs. Haggard (chap. 5 in this volume) examines the extent to which the crisis had a lasting impact on the social contract across East Asia.

Ideational Change

The crisis also opened the way for fierce debate about the supposed virtues of patterns of economic development in East Asia, which had only recently received a seal of approval from the World Bank in its East Asian Miracle study (World Bank 1993). As previously noted, severe economic downturns can upset existing equilibria, opening up space for alternative ideas and allowing new battles to be fought by their competing domestic and international advocates. The opening afforded by the crisis was used by various international actors (the U.S. Treasury and IMF) and academic commentators (e.g., Krugman 1998; Corsetti, Pesenti, and Roubini 1999) to assail the moral hazard problems generated by crony capitalism, leading to international demands for significant reform in state-business relations and in corporate governance.

It is easy to exaggerate the extent to which the IMF and its principal Western stakeholders imposed a policy package on recalcitrant governments rather than seeing the crisis as having provided an opportunity for pro-reform domestic elements to advance their own agendas (on Korea, for instance, see Mo and Moon 2003). As Mo (chap. 12 in this volume) shows, the most strikingly successful illustration of domestic actors seizing the opportunity to promote a reform drive was Kim Dae Jung's policies in Korea. Indeed, Rodney Bruce Hall (2003) argues that in Korea the Asian development model was discursively demolished. The case studies by Steinfeld (chap. 9), Allen Hicken (chap. 10), and Thomas Pepinsky (chap. 11) also demonstrate how, in the immediate wake of the crisis, economic reformers in China, Indonesia, and Thailand took advantage of the ideational flux to push their policy agendas forward.

The China case is particularly striking. Even though China had not been directly affected by the crisis, top reformers tapped into the international debate about appropriate relationships between business and government and sought to avoid weaknesses that had apparently left other East Asian countries open to vulnerability. In contrast, in Malaysia Anwar Ibrahim was spectacularly unsuccessful in his campaign to do the same and to use these ideas as a weapon against his political nemesis Prime Minister Mahathir Mohamad (Pepinsky, chap. 11 in this volume). These ideational debates around the region were given an added edge in countries such as Indonesia, Korea, and Thailand because of the lengthy lists of conditions attached to IMF programs, and also fueled the change on the fourth key dimension we highlight—regionalism.

The crisis directly challenged revisionist interpretations of East Asian rapid industrialization (Amsden 1989; Wade 1990). These, in contrast to arguments favored by economists who asserted that the East Asian success had rested on "getting prices right," had long trumpeted the positive role played by selective government interventions. Such revisionist interpretations had gained currency in the years immediately preceding the crisis, with even the World Bank acknowledging at the time that especially in Northeast Asian economies "government interventions resulted in higher and more equal growth than otherwise would have occurred" (World Bank 1993, 6).

The crisis provided substantial ammunition for those who had been critical of these revisionist interpretations of the East Asian miracle. For some commentators, these flaws could be summed up in the concept of crony capitalism. Opaque systems of business-government relations, government-directed financial systems that provided the bulk of business financing through bank loans, and the squandering of public resources through misguided attempts to pick winners were all central elements in this economically flawed syndrome. These characteristics, fundamentalists argued, had handicapped East Asian economies in their efforts to compete in an increasingly liberalized and globalized world marketplace. The much-vaunted partnership between business and government had failed to deliver effective systems of corporate governance or regimes of prudential financial regulation. Crony-driven financial systems consequently could not provide an appropriate response in a timely manner to a rapidly changing global context. Although short-term capital flows may have triggered the economic collapse in 1997, the dramatic downturn reflected a more fundamental economic malaise—East Asia was an economic crisis waiting to happen.

In contrast, East Asian governments and many adherents of the revisionist approach laid the blame for the crisis elsewhere, namely on the international financial system and, in particular, on the speculative flows of hot money. East Asian economies had gotten into difficulties, such analysts contended, because minimally informed speculators had panicked at the first sign of economic downturn. The economic fundamentals of the countries worst hit by the crisis were sound (as the IMF itself had asserted immediately before the crisis). Any flaws in economic policies lay primarily in misguided financial liberalization and the consequent decline in state capacity to shape economics. By opening their economies to speculative flows, East Asian governments had laid the foundations for their becoming victims of "casino capitalism."

Problems in the financial sector, however, did expose several weaknesses of economic governance in East Asia. These included the failure of governments to put in place an effective system of prudential regulation in the face of increasingly volatile capital flows, leaving countries open to the vulnerabilities that grew out of dependence on short-term international borrowing. Prudential lending was further undermined by state pressure to direct financing to preferred clients. Defenders of the developmental-state interpretation of the East Asian miracle consequently soon found themselves fighting a rearguard action. Although many commentators endorsed certain of the criticisms revisionists made of the IMF programs (and the IMF itself conceded that its response to the crisis had been flawed in several ways; Lane et al. 1999), it was difficult to sustain arguments that there were no fundamental weaknesses in relations between the state and the private sector, particularly on matters pertaining to prudential regulation of the financial system or of corporate governance.

Regionalism and Globalism

Since the crisis, the national political economies of East Asia have been connecting to one another as well as to broader global markets in ways strikingly at odds with their precrisis ties. As T. J. Pempel (chap. 8 in this volume) shows, the three most powerful shifts have been: (1) increased governmental activism, in particular, enhanced governmental willingness to create formal and institutionalized regional bodies; (2) more Asian and less pan-Pacific regional ties; and (3) an enhanced China-centric character to the region. At the same time, these trends must be seen as new waves atop powerful countervailing currents. Most notably, (1) the key drivers of Asian regionalization continue to be corporations in search of profits rather than governments in search of institutional ties, (2) pan-Pacific links remain vital to Asia due to the centrality of U.S. and global markets for East Asian exports and the structuring security role played by the U.S. military through bilateral alliances, and (3) any enhanced role for China is counterbalanced by the continuation of Japan as far and away the most sophisticated national economy in East Asia.

In the run-up to the crisis, cross-border production networks were the most critical links binding countries across the region. Formal regional institutions were largely limited to ASEAN in Southeast Asia and the two pan-Pacific regional institutions, the Asia-Pacific Economic Cooperation (APEC) and the ASEAN Regional Forum. Japan, despite several years of desultory economic performance, remained the key national economy driving regional growth, primarily through productive activities by its multinational corporations; financial transactions by its banks; and formal governmental assistance programs, including substantial economic aid packages to China.

The crisis changed all of this. Elite resentment at the perceived lack of sympathetic response from Western governments—particularly in contrast to the Mexican bailout in 1994—was significant in prompting widespread enthusiasm for the creation of new East Asian regional institutions. Governments across the region responded to the crisis by selective increases in their regional activities. The most important developments include enhanced enthusiasm for free trade agreements (FTAs) and a series of new institutional arrangements, most notably the APT, the Chiang Mai Initiative, two separate bond measures, and most recently the East Asia Summit.

Such approaches were most aggressively pursued in the area of finance with a distinct focus on enhancing the use of Asian capital to generate Asian solutions for

Asian problems. Of particular significance have been the new and ever-increasing activities by the APT. As Jennifer Amyx (chap. 6 in this volume) demonstrates, APT put in place a series of bilateral currency-swap arrangements designed to provide an additional buffer against future currency crises. These have gained both in scope and institutionalized intensity, with the latest moves coming in 2007 laying the ground-work for a regional (as opposed to a series of bilateral) swap arrangements.

Equally important, another regional effort to insulate East Asian economies from the vicissitudes of global capital flows can be found in the two regional bond initiatives undertaken in the wake of the crisis. Amyx (chap. 6) and Pempel (chap. 8 in this volume) examine a range of ways in which governments across the region have sought to make better use of their collective financial resources through such new and cooperative regional ventures. These are designed to allow Asian borrowers, primarily governments, to borrow in Asian currencies rather than in dollars, a move that, if successful, will reduce the round-trip borrowing in dollars for use in local currencies, saving perhaps two hundred basis points on such loans.

Trade has always been an integral part of regional ties, although it was more typi-cally the province of corporations rather than governments. Yet, as John Ravenhill argues (chap. 7 in this volume), the pattern of trade relations across East Asia has undergone important change since the crisis. The most striking development has been the emergence of China as an economic hub due to a massive inflow of for-eign investment in manufacturing. Rapid growth in China has been part reflection and part cause of a significant reorientation of regional production networks, with China now at the center of many of these networks. But, although trade within East Asia—particularly with China—has increased, this has taken place against the backdrop of even greater Asian engagement with the global economy. In trade, at least, East Asia is globalizing more than it is regionalizing. Along with the benefits of engagement with global markets, this also brings dependence and potential vul-nerability to trade-related disruptions. As Ravenhill notes, the most striking trade vulnerability arises from the growing regional reliance on exports from a single sector—electronics.

The other marked development in regional trade arrangements since the crisis has been the proliferation of preferential trade agreements. Although this has consumed much policy energy and generated widespread debate, it has had much less impact in actual market outcomes, with the most important actors—the corporations—seemingly showing little interest in the preferential trade arrangements that governments have supposedly negotiated on their behalf. As a result, the preferential trading agreements (PTAs), which had been touted in at least some quarters as a potential tool in limiting vulnerability to trade dimensions of future economic crises, may be significant more for their political-strategic dimensions.

The wave of FTAs has sometimes involved intra-Asian trade and economic partnerships (e.g., China-ASEAN and Japan-Singapore), but equally important have been extra-regional arrangements (Korea–United States, still to be ratified at the time of writing; Japan-Mexico; and Singapore-India). Despite the fact that China has now become the number one trade partner for both Japan and Korea, pan-Pacific markets, particularly in North America, remain vital final destinations for a large amount of Asian production. In short, even as East Asian regionalism deepens, broader ties to global economic processes remain vital; Asian economic linkages continue to be characterized by open regionalism.

China has proven itself better able to enhance its regional influence during and after the crisis than has Japan. Japan made an ambitious, if not fully thought out, proposal for an Asian Monetary Fund that if adopted might well have fended off the worst of the crisis without IMF intervention. But the Japanese proposal was blocked by U.S., Chinese, and IMF resistance, leading to a clear erosion of Japanese regional stature. In contrast, China gained considerable political credit for not revaluing its currency as the crisis countries struggled to regain their monetary footing. Furthermore, China moved much more quickly and effectively to acquire a regional leadership position on trade in the wake of the crisis. Offering the ASEAN countries an FTA, complete with one-sided liberalization of tariffs on imports of agricultural goods, China clearly stole a march on Japan, which was unable to match the Chinese generosity due to resistance from its own farm lobby and their bureaucratic and political supporters.

East Asian regionalism has not taken an exclusive turn, not least because many of the other countries in the region fear the potential Chinese dominance of East Asia. Thus, the East Asia Summit was expanded in membership beyond the APT to include Australia, New Zealand, and India, all countries that presumably might work with Japan, Singapore, and others to counter Chinese regional influence. Such a counterweight is particularly important in the security arena. Important and as institutionalized as increased regional ties have become, they remain almost nonexistent on security affairs, particularly in Northeast Asia.

In the chapters that follow, individual contributors analyze the extent of change and continuities since the crisis, both across the region as a whole and in particular countries. Each author brings something distinctive to the collective analysis of the volume, but our team has been chosen for its ability to integrate the analytical and policy literatures with empirical developments in the region itself. The editorial team for the volume picks up on the overarching themes of change identified in this opening chapter and returns to them in the final chapter to make concluding arguments about the overall shape and significance of change in East Asia a decade after the upheaval of 1997–98.

PART I

Finance, Corporate Governance, and Welfare

CHAPTER 2

After the Fall

East Asian Exchange Rates since the Crisis

Benjamin J. Cohen

The East Asian crisis began with a classic currency collapse—the fall of the baht. Soon nearly every economy in the region came under pressure from investor panic and capital flight—a contagion of "bahtulism," as a few observers grimly quipped. Whereas some governments successfully held firm, others were helpless to prevent massive depreciations. For many, exchange rate instability was a direct cause of the economic turbulence that followed. The experience was searing for all concerned.

A decade after the fall of the baht, what has been learned? This chapter focuses on exchange rate regimes and alignments in East Asia. Governments in the region have made a number of adjustments in their exchange rate regimes designed inter alia to protect their economies from a repetition of the events of 1997–98. The aim of this chapter is both retrospective and prospective: to review what has happened to date and to evaluate prospects for the future. What has (or has not) changed, what is driving currency strategies in the region, and what more, if anything, might governments do to prepare themselves for possible challenges in years to come?

The first two sections set the stage for the analysis. The first section reviews the core factors involved in the choice of an exchange rate regime (ERR), including political and economic considerations. All governments face a number of critical trade-offs in framing their currency strategies; there is no obvious first-best policy for an economy. The second section summarizes the recent history of exchange rate policy in East Asia, focusing on actual behavior as well as official pronouncements. A glance at the record highlights both a considerable diversity of arrangements across the region as a whole and a remarkable continuity of practice in most individual countries. Just as they did before the crisis, most governments continue to practice some form of pegging with a heavy emphasis on stability vis-à-vis the U.S.

dollar. Subsequent sections address a trio of critical questions: (1) What role did exchange rates play in the East Asian crisis? (2) What explains currency strategies in the period since 1997–98? (3) What is the outlook for future ERRs in the region?

Evidence suggests that the role of ERRs in the crisis was more indirect than direct; precrisis currency strategies contributed to events mainly by encouraging risky modes of market behavior that added to the fragility of national economies. In turn, this helps to explain the high degree of continuity of practice in most regional economies since 1997–98. Reforms have been instituted to reduce vulnerability to future shocks—but mainly in related policy areas rather than in the ERRs themselves. The reason is that ERRs are seen as instrumental, not as an end in themselves, and therefore have been adjusted only when change seemed appropriate to serve broader developmental goals. Governments have resisted and are likely to continue to resist more radical innovations in their currency strategies. Despite the popular enthusiasm for new regional initiatives that was prompted by the crisis, authorities have shown little interest in any form of institutionalized exchange rate commitment that would limit their policy autonomy.

Choosing an Exchange Rate Regime

In analytical terms, the choice of an ERR may be framed in a variety of ways. In earlier years, the issue was cast in simple binary terms—fixed versus flexible exchange rates. A state could adopt some form of peg for its currency, or it could allow it to float. Pegs might be anchored to a single currency or to a basket (a weighted average of anchor currencies), they might be formally irrevocable or based on a more contingent rule, and they might crawl or take the form of a target zone. Floating rates, conversely, might be managed (a dirty float) or else just left to the interplay of market forces (a clean float).

More recently, as international capital mobility has grown, the issue has been recast from fixed versus flexible exchange rates to a choice between, on the one hand, contingent rules of any kind (soft pegs) and, on the other hand, the so-called corner solutions of either floating or some form of monetary union (hard pegs). Today, according to a now-fashionable argument known as the bipolar view, no intermediate ERR can be regarded as tenable. Owing to the development of huge masses of mobile wealth capable of switching between currencies at a moment's notice, governments can no longer hope to defend policy rules designed to hit explicit exchange rate targets. The middle ground of contingent rules has, in effect, been "hollowed out," as Barry Eichengreen (1994) memorably puts it. ERRs, it is predicted, will increasingly be driven to one corner solution or the other.

But is that realistic? The bipolar view implicitly assumes that when it comes to choosing an ERR, governments have just one objective—to avoid speculative crises. In effect, no trade-off is considered possible between currency stability and other policy goals. But that hardly seems plausible. In reality, trade-offs are made all the time when currency strategy is decided. No option is ruled out a priori, including contingent rules. As Jeffrey Frankel writes, "Neither [corner solution] sweeps away all the problems that come with modern globalized financial markets. . . . Optimization often . . . involves an 'interior' solution" (1999, 2).

Optimization, of course, implies politics. The core issue is the policy dilemma posed by the familiar Unholy Trinity (Cohen 1993)—the mutual incompatibility of exchange rate stability, capital mobility, and autonomy of national monetary policy. Derived from the well-known Mundell-Fleming model of open economy macroeconomics, the Unholy Trinity suggests that, in an imperfect world, there simply is no perfect solution. Hard pegs, for example, might seem desirable because they reduce uncertainty and lower transactions costs. Their efficiency benefits could be considerable, but with capital free to move, a fixed rate also deprives a government of control over domestic monetary conditions, compromising the management of the national economy. Sensitivity to external shocks is heightened, making the country hostage to policies made elsewhere. Floating, conversely, preserves more of the capacity of a government to manage macroeconomic performance, but it does so at a risk of provoking destabilizing speculation. Moreover, uncertainty is increased, raising transactions costs. The attraction of the middle ground of contingent rules is that they might, in some form, capture the advantages of each corner solution while avoiding their disadvantages.

In all this, governments are essentially on their own. Given the multiple considerations involved, which are as much political as economic, it is obvious that there can be no magic bullet, no single first-best policy that is suitable for all. Quite the reverse, in fact. Ever since the breakdown of the Bretton Woods par-value system in the early 1970s, it has been understood that when it comes to ERR choice, one size definitely does not fit all. Under the amended rules of the International Monetary Fund (IMF), states are now free to make their own choices, depending on the importance each government happens to attach to the benefits and costs of alternative options. States that value certainty more than policy autonomy will be attracted toward some form of pegging; conversely, those that prefer a degree of macroeconomic flexibility, even at the risk of an occasional currency crisis, will move toward some manner of floating.

Few generalizations, however, seem possible. Although there have been many empirical studies of the determinants of ERR choice in recent years by both economists and political scientists, the results have been inconclusive at best and often inconsistent (Rogoff et al. 2004, 17–20). In the end, the trade-offs that states make tend to be designed to accommodate their own unique needs and circumstances.

Recent History

How have policy strategies in East Asia changed since the crisis? A review of available evidence suggests two central observations.

First, reflecting the variety of trade-offs that each state must make, is the considerable diversity of currency policies across the region. ERRs today, a decade after the crisis, run the gamut from independent floating to the hardest of hard pegs. Whatever adjustments governments have made in the last decade, they have not resulted in a closer alignment of exchange rate arrangements.

Second, looking at individual economies, is the relative continuity of currency policies in the region. The crisis was massively disruptive, sending a number of the regional exchange rates into a tailspin. Depreciations ranged in magnitude from some 10–20 percent in Taiwan and Singapore to as much as (at one time) 80 percent in Indonesia. Pressures for reform were enormous. Yet, in response, few East Asian ERRs have undergone radical change, and even fewer have moved in line with the prediction of the bipolar view. Overall, it appears that after a period of upheaval, practice in most cases has returned to something quite like what prevailed before the crisis erupted.

Diversity

Empirically, ERRs can be identified in one of two ways: from official statements or from observations of actual behavior. Either way, the evidence shows a wide diversity of arrangements in East Asia.

Formal exchange rate policies are defined by the pronouncements of central banks or their equivalent. A summary of official policies for the period 1996–2006, as reported by the IMF, is provided in column 1 of table 2.1.

Table 2.1 East Asian exchange rate regimes[a]

	Year	(1) De jure regime	(2) De facto regime
Brunei	1996–2004	Currency board arrangement	Fixed
	2005–2006	Currency board arrangement	—
Cambodia	1996–1998	Managed floating	Float
	1999–2001	Managed floating	Dirty crawling peg
	2002	Managed floating	Inconclusive
	2003	Managed floating	Dirty crawling peg
	2004	Managed floating	Inconclusive
	2005–2006	Managed floating	—
China	1996–1998	Managed floating	Fixed
	1999–2004	Conventional pegged arrangement; flexibility limited to a single currency	Fixed
	2005–2006	Conventional pegged arrangement; flexibility limited with reference to a basket of currencies	—
Hong Kong	1996–2004	Currency board arrangement	Fixed
	2005–2006	Currency board arrangement	—
Indonesia	1996–1997	Managed floating	Dirty crawling peg
	1998	Independently floating	Dirty float (outlier)
	1999	Independently floating	Dirty crawling peg
	2000	Independently floating	Float
	2001	Independently floating	Dirty crawling peg

	Year	(1) De jure regime	(2) De facto regime
	2002–2004	Managed floating	Float
	2005–2006	Managed floating	—
Japan	1996–2004	Independently floating	Float
	2005–2006	Independently floating	—
Korea	1996	Managed floating	Fixed
	1997	Managed floating	Dirty crawling peg
	1998	Independently floating	Dirty crawling peg
	1999–2004	Independently floating	Fixed
	2005–2006	Independently floating	—
Laos	1996	Independently floating	Inconclusive
	1997–1998	Managed floating	Dirty crawling peg
	1999	Managed floating	Dirty float
	2000–2002	Managed floating	Float
	2003	Managed floating	Dirty crawling peg
	2004	Managed floating	Float
	2005–2006	Managed floating	—
Malaysia	1996	Managed floating	Dirty crawling peg
	1997	Managed floating	Float
	1998	Managed floating	Dirty crawling peg
	1999–2004	Conventional pegged arrangement; flexibility limited to a single currency	Fixed
	2005–2006	Managed floating	—
Myanmar	1996–1998	Pegged to a composite of currencies; officially pegged to the SDR	Fixed
	1999–2001	Conventional pegged arrangement; a basket of currencies other than SDR	Fixed
	2002–2004	Managed floating	Fixed
	2005–2006	Managed floating	—
Philippines	1996	Independently floating	Fixed
	1997–2003	Independently floating	Float
	2004	Independently floating	Dirty crawling peg
	2005–2006	Independently floating	—
Singapore	1996	Managed floating	Dirty crawling peg
	1997–1998	Managed floating	Float
	1999–2001	Managed floating	Fixed
	2002	Managed floating	Dirty float
	2003–2004	Managed floating	Fixed
	2005–2006	Managed floating	—
Taiwan	1996–2004	Independently floating	NA
	2005–2006	Independently floating	—
Thailand	1996	Pegged to a composite of currencies	Inconclusive
	1997	Pegged to a composite of currencies; a basket of currencies other than SDR	Dirty crawling peg
	1998	Managed floating	Dirty crawling peg
	1999–2001	Independently floating	Float
	2002–2004	Managed floating	Float
	2005–2006	Managed floating	—
Vietnam	1996–1999	Managed floating	NA
	2000–2001	Pegged exchange rate within horizontal bands	NA
	2002–2004	Managed floating	NA
	2005–2006	Managed floating	—

Sources: International Monetary Fund; Annual Report on Exchange Arrangements and Exchange Restrictions, 1996–2006. Central Bank of China (www.cbc.gov.tw); Levy-Yeyati and Sturzenegger (2005).
[a] NA, not available; SDR, special drawing right.

Formal policy, however, tells only part of the story. Actual behavior, as we know, can diverge significantly from de jure ERRs. For instance, countries that claim officially to maintain a flexible exchange rate may in fact intervene heavily to prevent their nominal rates from moving—a pattern that Calvo and Reinhart (2002) have dubbed "fear of floating." Conversely, others that ostensibly maintain a formal peg may in practice change their parities so often that they more closely approximate a floating regime. Governments do not always act in a manner consistent with their declared ERRs.

To complete the story, therefore, it is necessary also to look at what governments do, not just at what they say. Toward that end, a number of new classification systems have emerged—measures of de facto ERRs—that rely on actual behavior rather than official statements. Among these, the most useful for my purposes are the estimates of Eduardo Levy-Yeyati and Federico Sturzenegger (2005). The Levy-Yeyati and Sturzenegger classification scheme extends through 2004, further than any other study presently available. It also includes the largest number of the economies in the region, thirteen out of fifteen (all but Taiwan and Vietnam).

Levy-Yeyati and Sturzenegger use a cluster analysis to group economies according to the joint behavior of international reserves (a measure of intervention activity) and nominal exchange rates. ERRs are categorized into four distinct types, in order of increasing degree of flexibility:

1. Fixed regimes (high volatility of reserves, signifying extensive intervention, combined with low volatility of the exchange rate).
2. Dirty crawling pegs (stable incremental changes of the exchange rate combined with active intervention).
3. Floating regimes (low volatility of reserves combined with high volatility of the exchange rate).
4. Dirty float (high volatility of both reserves and the exchange rate).

The first two types may be regarded as closely related versions of soft pegs; the last two types may be regarded as alternative versions of floating. A comparison of de facto ERRs with de jure arrangements, based on Levy-Yeyati and Sturzenegger, is provided in column 2 of table 2.1.

A look at the table confirms the diversity of currency arrangements in the region. At one extreme, two economies, Brunei and Hong Kong, maintain currency boards—a particularly hard form of pegging. With a currency board, the local money is firmly tied to a designated anchor currency. The exchange rate between the two currencies is rigidly fixed, ostensibly irrevocably. Most important, any increase in the issue of local money must be fully backed by an equivalent increase of reserve holdings of the anchor currency, making the local currency little more than foreign money by another name. The Brunei currency board, which has existed since 1967, is based on the Singapore dollar. The Hong Kong currency board, dating from 1983, anchors on the U.S. dollar. In neither Brunei nor Hong Kong, evidently, is monetary autonomy a matter of high priority. Being small and very open economies, both place more emphasis on maximizing efficiency benefits and minimizing the risk of adverse speculation.

At the opposite extreme are Japan and Taiwan, which for the most part allow their currencies to float freely. Taiwanese interventions are limited mainly to "leaning against the wind"; Japan, after a period of massive intervention in 2003–4, has largely refrained from active management of the yen. For both countries, control over domestic monetary conditions is obviously the most important consideration. Korea and the Philippines also claim to maintain independent (clean) floats, but in fact they actively manage their exchange rates. Levy-Yeyati and Sturzenegger classify the de facto regime of Korea as fixed (meaning relatively low exchange rate volatility) and that of the Philippines as a dirty crawling peg (meaning stable incremental changes of the exchange rate)—both examples, apparently, of some fear of floating.

Eight countries in the region (Cambodia, Indonesia, Laos, Malaysia, Myanmar, Singapore, Thailand, and Vietnam) are classified by the IMF as having managed floats with no pre-announced path for the exchange rate. In practice, however, several of them—most notably, Cambodia, Myanmar, and Singapore—also appear to exhibit a considerable fear of floating. Until 2002, the same was true of Indonesia, although in the most recent period its behavior seems to have moved more closely in line with its declared policy of a managed float.

Only one country in the region today operates a conventional soft peg—giant, stability-minded China. Previously anchored on the U.S. dollar, the peg for the Chinese yuan was formally switched in 2005 to a basket of currencies. Until 2005, Malaysia also maintained a peg anchored to the U.S. greenback, before changing to a managed float.

Continuity

The diversity of ERRs across the region is matched by their continuity in individual economies. The popular impression is that currency strategies underwent a revolution after the ravages of the crisis, a perception that, in some cases, governments have deliberately fostered. In practice, however, as table 2.1 demonstrates, radical change has been relatively rare and has not always been in the direction predicted by the bipolar view. Some modifications have been introduced. But, contrary to the bipolar view, there has been no broad trend toward one corner solution or the other.

Of the fifteen economies in the region, ten have the same official ERR now that they had prior to the crisis. These include the two with currency boards (Brunei and Hong Kong), three of the independent floaters (Japan, Philippines, and Taiwan), and five with managed floats (Cambodia, Indonesia, Malaysia, Singapore, and Vietnam). For these ten, formally, there has been no change at all.

Moreover, of the remaining five, two have moved in a direction contrary to the prediction of the bipolar view. The one formal pegger in the region, China, officially maintained a managed float before the crisis, whereas Laos has shifted from an independent float to managed flexibility. Both are now further from the corner solution of a pure float than they were a decade ago. Only Korea, Myanmar, and Thailand have formally moved closer to a corner solution. Both Myanmar and Thailand officially abandoned pegging for a managed float—Myanmar in 2002 and Thailand in 1998. Korea shifted from managed flexibility to an independent float in 1998. The Malaysian switch to a managed float in 2005 was simply a return to the ERR that it had maintained before the crisis erupted.

Continuity is also evident in the data provided by Levy-Yeyati and Sturzenegger (2005). Of the thirteen countries included, six show no change of actual practice (Brunei, China, Hong Kong, Japan, Korea, and Myanmar), whereas three others shifted just from one type of soft peg to another (Malaysia, Philippines, and Singapore). Only four made a more radical switch. Cambodia moved from a float to a dirty crawling peg, whereas Indonesia, Laos, and Thailand moved in the reverse direction, from dirty crawling pegs to floating. None of this adds up to the widespread hollowing out that many expected.

Quite the opposite, in fact. Whether we judge from the formal pronouncements or from Levy-Yeyati and Sturzenegger's data, it is evident that most governments in the region prefer to take an active role in managing their currencies and, where possible, to aim for some kind of target, adjusting domestic policy if necessary to limit exchange rate volatility. As one study concludes, "all the concerned countries display some traits of involvement in exchange rate management" (Tiwari 2003, 24). Of the three countries that officially claim to have adopted a policy of floating since the crisis, two (Korea and Myanmar) in practice still seek to keep the movements of their exchange rates as limited as possible, a kind of soft peg. Some version of soft pegging can also be found in Cambodia, Malaysia, Philippines, and Singapore; and of course China still retains its formal peg. Interior solutions based on implicit or explicit contingent rules were common prior to the crisis a decade ago. Apparently, they remain as popular as ever. The overall picture is largely one of continuity rather than discontinuity.

The Crisis

What role did exchange rates play in the events of 1997–98? The crisis was the worst to hit East Asia in generations. Were the ERRs in the region to blame?

There can be no doubt that exchange rates were a central part of the story. Soft pegging was the policy of choice in all the countries worst hit by the fall of the baht. Whether de jure or de facto, currency targets offer a tempting prey for speculators. Once turbulence hit the region, the markets were bound to test the credibility of exchange rate commitments. The rapid spread of bahtulism should have been no surprise.

But that does not mean that exchange rates were the central cause of the crisis. As innumerable sources have noted, the roots of the episode actually go far deeper, drawing nourishment from a variety of sources. In the words of T. J. Pempel, "a complicated multilevel dynamic...was at play" (1999a, 4), involving forces both foreign and domestic, political and economic. Of particular importance were critical defects in the development model favored by most East Asian governments—an export-led model that rested, inter alia, on a foundation of political patronage and close personal connections among powerful politicians, bankers, regulators, and business interests. Although this crony capitalism seemed to work well in good times to promote rapid economic growth, it also proved a barrier to swift and effective policy reform once the clouds began to gather. Also of importance was the spread of economic interdependence across East Asia, a growing web of commercial and investment ties, which made individual economies highly vulnerable to contagion once the storm struck. Nor can we neglect the role of financial liberalization, which opened local capital markets to foreign creditors and investors. The decade prior to the crisis saw a widespread loosening of exchange controls, leading to a marked increase in the degree of capital mobility in the region. The more governments relaxed their vigilance over financial flows, the tighter they drew the noose of the Unholy Trinity around their own necks.

In this complex environment, exchange rates are best thought of as having played the role of catalyst, an indirect rather than direct cause of the crisis. Soft pegs per se were not the culprit; rather, the problem lay in risky modes of behavior that were encouraged by the government stabilization of exchange rates. Pegs appeared to reduce uncertainty for trade and investment decisions, providing an implicit guarantee against exchange risk. But in suppressing volatility, governments also ruled out the disciplinary power of potential rate adjustments. Ultimately, currency stability was to prove illusory. But as long as market actors held faith in the illusion, they felt free to engage in practices that, cumulatively, simply added to the fragility of national economies.

Historically, the economies of the region, like most developing countries, suffered from what has been called "original sin" (Eichengreen and Hausmann 1999), an inability to borrow internationally in their own currencies. With currency rates seemingly stabilized, however, banks and firms felt free to borrow liberally abroad. Massive currency mismatches built up between liabilities denominated in foreign exchange and claims denominated in local money. Yet few saw fit to hedge their debts against the risk of future depreciation. Why buy relatively expensive currency futures or forwards when the outlook was for exchange rate stability? Likewise, much borrowing was done at short term to finance longer-term investment, building up substantial maturity mismatches as well.

The irony is obvious. The longer governments managed to sustain the illusion of currency stability, the more they fed what John Maynard Keynes called the self-destructive "animal spirits" of entrepreneurs and financiers. As Eichengreen comments, "Ironically, Asian governments' very success at pegging their exchange rates was one factor behind the severity of the crisis, for it lulled domestic banks and corporations into a false sense of security" (1999, 163). The easy availability of foreign capital led to exuberant credit expansion, dangerous asset bubbles in real estate and equities, and overinvestment in productive capacity—all factors that contributed to the severity of the crisis once the Thai baht fell. In effect, the ERRs in the region were like an indulgent parent who, by sparing the rod, spoiled the child.

Moreover, the problem was compounded by the choice of anchor for the regional pegs. For all, this was the U.S. dollar. Many of the soft peggers claimed to be linking to a basket of currencies—an effective exchange rate, calculated as a weighted average of several anchor currencies—rather than to any single anchor alone. In practice, however, heaviest weight by far tended to be placed on the U.S. greenback. Even ostensible free floaters such as Japan and Taiwan paid close attention to their dollar exchange rates, using the greenback for intervention purposes. In most cases, currency stability simply meant mooring to the dollar and shadowing it as closely as possible. Currencies tended to be much more volatile in effective terms than they were in relation to the dollar alone (Williamson 1999).

There were two reasons for the choice of the dollar as an anchor. First was the sheer convenience of making use of the predominant international currency, already widely employed around the globe for reserve and intervention purposes. Second was the central importance of the United States as the biggest market for most of the exporters in the region. A stable link to the greenback not only facilitated sales to U.S. consumers; in parallel, dollar pegs also served indirectly to harmonize nominal currency values, thus removing exchange rate variation within the region as a possible threat to relative competitive positions.

Unfortunately, a common alignment of nominal currency values could not prevent the emergence of real exchange rate misalignments, arising from differential inflation rates or other causes. Underlying changes in relative competitive positions across the region were masked so long as the dollar remained comparatively weak, as was the case in the early 1990s. A cheaper greenback meant greater competitiveness for East Asian exports in third markets, supplementing sales in the United States. But once the dollar began to strengthen in the mid-1990s, the growth of export revenues quickly decelerated, worsening trade balances and bringing misalignments to the surface. The impact was particularly sharp in countries such as Indonesia, Malaysia, and Korea. Worst hit was Thailand, whose current-account deficit by the start of 1997 had swollen to nearly 8 percent of GDP, well beyond what might be considered prudent. The fall of the baht was just a matter of time.

In retrospect, it is clear that a different approach to exchange rate policy might well have averted the worst of these fragilities. Soft pegs first encouraged risky market practice while masking accumulating stresses and then, when circumstances deteriorated, proved an easy target for speculation. Hence, it is no surprise that for many observers the policy lesson at the time seemed clear. Soft pegs were out. Corner solutions were in (either hard pegs or floating). The sudden emergence and popularity of the bipolar view can be attributed directly to the East Asian experience a decade ago. If the regional crisis seemed to demonstrate anything, it was the futility of interior solutions based on implicit or explicit contingent rules.

Inertia

How, then do we explain the overall picture of continuity in the decade since the crisis? Contrary to the bipolar view, there has been no rush to the corners in East Asia.

Hard pegs have attracted no new adherents; most governments, even those with ostensibly flexible ERRs, continue to demonstrate a marked fear of floating. Moreover, in almost all cases the U.S. greenback remains the dominant influence on exchange rates. According to one representative study, the predominant weight of the dollar in East Asian currency baskets, following a brief postcrisis hiatus, has largely returned to its precrisis levels, ranging from about 65 percent for Singapore to above 90 percent in Cambodia, Laos, Malaysia, Myanmar, the Philippines, and Vietnam (Volz 2006). Only in Indonesia, Korea, and Thailand has there been a noticeable increase of flexibility vis-à-vis the dollar, and even there the change has been modest at best (World Bank 2006, 9). Even China, despite its switch to a formal basket peg, continues to shadow the greenback closely.

Is there a method to all this inertia, or madness?

Madness?

Many observers would say madness. Soft pegs, critics argue, are an open invitation to speculators. If the Unholy Trinity teaches anything, it is that in an environment of financial openness, market actors sooner or later can be counted on to test exchange rate commitments, as they did in 1997–98. Unless governments are willing to follow the example of Brunei or Hong Kong, abandoning altogether any ambition for a monetary policy of their own, they cannot hope to sustain currency targets indefinitely.

So far, so uncontroversial. The criticism is well understood and helps to explain why even the most determined de facto peggers in East Asia, such as Korea, the Philippines, and Singapore, decline to establish a target de jure. Once a currency gets in trouble, a formal peg offers a one-way option to speculators. Much may be gained by betting on a forced devaluation, whereas little will be lost if the currency is successfully defended. So why tempt speculators unduly? By saying one thing while doing another, governments can hope to increase uncertainty and thus dilute the one-way option. The sole exception in the region, China, feels confident in its ability to maintain a de jure peg only because of the broad panoply of exchange controls that Beijing has long employed to limit the degree of capital mobility across its borders.

But dissembling is not without its own risks. Despite efforts to strengthen local capital markets—including, most notably, the Asian Bond Fund and Asian Bond Markets Initiatives (see Jennifer Amyx, chap. 4 in this volume)—most external borrowing in the region continues to be denominated in foreign currency. East Asia still suffers substantially from "original sin." Soft pegs, therefore, even if no longer de jure, could once again invite a dangerous buildup of unhedged currency mismatches. The risk is less serious at the level of government borrowing; across most of the region, public foreign currency debt has actually fallen sharply in relation to exports and reserves. But as the Bank for International Settlements tactfully puts it, mismatches at the private level "remain significant," suggesting a "need to ensure that the financial sector is taking adequate care to manage the risks associated with these mismatches" (2005, 53).

Worse, dissembling could do serious damage to government reputations, compromising efforts to rebuild confidence in public authority since the crisis. As Eichengreen has suggested, "pretending to float while really attempting to limit the currency's fluctuation...is not a way of building policy credibility" (2004, 62). Quite the contrary, in fact. By openly encouraging disbelief in their own official statements, governments risk cultivating a broader cynicism about their policy intentions in general.

Moreover, critics contend, persistence in targeting most closely on the dollar compounds the problem, by holding regional trade competitiveness hostage to the fortunes of the U.S. currency. Here too would seem to be madness. Anchoring, however informally, to the dollar makes an economy vulnerable to fluctuations between the greenback and other major currencies—what was once known as the "outer exchange rate problem" (Cohen 1977, 183–84). In the most recent years, as in the early 1990s, the outer exchange rate problem has actually worked to the advantage of the region. With the greenback once more weakening under the pressure of accelerating U.S. payments deficits, East Asian economies have ridden the dollar down, regaining a competitive edge in European markets and elsewhere. But the process could also go the other way, as it did in the mid-1990s, again worsening trade balances. Does it really make sense to tie the fate of the region so tightly to the vagaries of currency movements beyond its control?

Method

Such criticisms, however, are myopic, if not outright blinkered. East Asian currency strategies can hardly be described as mad; there is indeed method in their inertia. Regional governments rationally treat their choice of ERR as a deeply political matter, with far more at stake than just the threat of speculation or the outer exchange rate problem. Currency policy is embedded in an optimization process that encompasses a much broader range of issues, including many that are considered vital to government survival or the conception of national interest.

Perhaps most vital is a sustained rate of economic development to absorb surplus labor and lift living standards. For most states in the region, be they democratic or authoritarian, an implicit social contract links the legitimacy of governments directly to their success in promoting rapid growth. Economic progress may not guarantee longevity of office, but its absence will almost certainly make the life of political incumbents more hazardous. Poor economic prospects translate directly into dim career prospects for those in positions of authority.

In turn, growth demands a continued expansion of exports because East Asian governments still rely most heavily on the traditional export-led development model. Trade expansion is valued not only in broad economic terms, for the jobs it creates and the tax revenues it generates; it is also prized in domestic political terms, for the material benefits it brings to specific influential constituencies. Although a number of states have moderated some of the more egregious manifestations of crony capitalism since the crisis (MacIntyre 2006), there can be no doubt that trade interests remain disproportionately powerful in the give and take of domestic politics. Governments have every reason to keep such groups happy.

Finally, trade expansion is valued in national security terms, for its contribution to freeing resources that may be used for military purposes—what Joanne Gowa (1994) has called trade's "security externalities." China is perhaps the most prominent example in the region of a government that has exploited its remarkable trade gains to help modernize its armed forces and enhance its ability to project power beyond its borders. But the Chinese are hardly alone. The neighborhood is one of the most hotly contested areas in geopolitics today. East Asians know that they must do what they can to ensure their own defense.

In this context, the ERR is seen as instrumental rather than as an end in itself, just one more policy tool in service to the objectives of development and trade expansion. And to preserve the usefulness of that tool, most East Asian governments prefer to retain as many degrees of freedom as possible, avoiding corner solutions that might inhibit their autonomy. Fear of floating actually makes sense if an unmanaged exchange rate could result in undue volatility, depressing exports. Conversely, avoidance of a hard peg makes sense as long as governments remain committed to the active management of the development process. The continuity of currency strategies in the region, therefore, is no accident. It is, in fact, part and parcel of the pragmatism that characterizes all dimensions of policy in that part of the world. Soft pegs leave the widest possible latitude to respond to changing circumstances. The result is a compromise—but hardly an unreasonable one.

Nor does the persistence of the dollar anchor seem unreasonable, given the still central importance of the U.S. market for regional exporters. With 30 percent of world GDP, the United States remains the consumer of last resort for the ever-growing output of East Asia. It hardly seems irrational, therefore, for East Asia to seek to preserve a stable relationship with the greenback to sustain sales. In fact, governments have intervened heavily to keep their exchange rates from appreciating significantly in terms of the dollar, accumulating record amounts of reserves in the process—more than $800 billion in China and Japan, and more than $200 billion in Korea and Taiwan. Continued targeting on the dollar is no accident, either.

Does this mean that nothing has been learned from the crisis? Not at all. The risks of inertia, as noted, are widely understood. That is why, China apart, most states in the region now eschew de jure targets that might invite destabilizing speculation. Moreover, even while continuing to attach the heaviest weight to the greenback, some now appear willing to relax the dollar relationship to a considerable extent when conditions warrant (Eichengreen 2004; Fukuda and Ohno 2005). In some cases, such as Japan and Korea, exchange rates have been allowed to appreciate moderately in order to avoid even larger dollar accumulations. In short, much has in fact been learned. It is just that the results of the learning process show up mainly in related policy areas rather than in the ERR itself. Reducing vulnerability to future shocks has obviously become a priority, as the editors of this volume emphasize. But recognizing that exchange rates were at best a catalyst, not a direct cause of the crisis, East Asian nations have directed most of their effort elsewhere, toward reducing the many other fragilities that turned the fall of the baht into such a disaster.

Internally, reforms have been undertaken to improve the prudential supervision of financial markets (Natasha Hamilton-Hart, chap. 3 in this volume). Externally, the enormous new reserve stockpiles in the region, held mainly in the form of U.S. Treasury obligations, provide a more comfortable cushion should another crisis hit. Mainly the by-product of interventions designed to preserve export competitiveness, these reserves are costly in opportunity-cost terms. The interest rate earned on U.S. government debt tends to be far lower than might be earned on more productive investments. But the reserves do also offer the benefit of a kind of insurance policy, a hedge against the risk of future capital outflows. And that hedge, in turn, has been further bolstered by new efforts to cultivate financial collaboration at the regional level, including most notably the Chiang Mai Initiative, intended to provide mutual financial support when needed to combat adverse speculation (Henning 2002; Amyx, chap. 4 in this volume).

In short, there is indeed method in the regional inertia. If currency strategies have been adjusted only marginally, it is in order to best preserve their instrumental role in support of broader developmental goals.

The Future?

What of the future? Inertia in ERR choice may make sense, but does it make the *most* sense? Or are there other strategies that might achieve a more favorable trade-off among policy objectives?

Much depends, of course, on the nature of the threat. Of most salience today is the continued East Asian allegiance to dollar pegging, which for the region as a whole has produced massive trade surpluses matched by corresponding U.S. deficits, a pattern that has been described as a revived Bretton Woods system or Bretton Woods II (Dooley, Folkerts-Landau, and Garber 2003). Much doubt exists about whether the Bretton Woods II pattern is sustainable (Eichengreen 2007). The question on everyone's mind is: What happens if the U.S. deficits trigger a new dollar crisis? Will regional governments be content to go on building up their huge stockpiles of greenbacks, despite low interest rates and significant dollar depreciation? Could new real misalignments be revealed? And what happens if someone then breaks ranks, precipitating a realignment of nominal rates? Turbulence could once again hit the region, as it did in 1997–98.

Asians are acutely sensitive to the dilemma they face. To forestall a repetition of history, myriad alternative strategies have been actively discussed. Broadly, six possible regimes dominate conversation: free floating, currency unification, a dollar standard, basket pegging, a so-called Asian currency unit (ACU), and direct monetary policy coordination. All have their advantages. But each has disadvantages as well, not least, in most cases, a distinct lack of political appeal. Except possibly for some modest version of either of the last two, none is apt to be adopted any time soon, despite the obvious risks of the status quo.

Free Floating

At one extreme are proposals to free exchange rates altogether, the corner solution of an independent float. The case for floating is clear (Goldstein 2002; Eichengreen 2004)—with one stroke, the Gordian knot of the Unholy Trinity is cut, releasing economies from the constraints imposed by any kind of exchange rate rule. If something has to give, advocates argue, it should be the exchange rate, not capital mobility or policy autonomy. Capital mobility is essential to support productive investment; policy autonomy is critical if governments are to sustain the growth process that is so vital to their legitimacy. Exchange rate stability simply represents a lower order of priority.

Most important, floating could help forestall a buildup of real misalignments, thus easing adjustment should the Bretton Woods II pattern prove unsustainable. Regional governments, however, appear to be little convinced. Of much greater concern to them is the risk that unpredictable exchange rate movements could exacerbate rather than inhibit misalignments, disrupting exports and, by implication, growth. They, as well as anyone, know how much nominal currency values can shift even when underlying economic circumstances are relatively stable. Foreign-exchange markets, like all asset markets, are driven by interdependent expectations, which means that multiple equilibria are possible. A glance at the history of major currencies such as the dollar, which have been floating since the early 1970s, shows that medium-term swings of 20–40 percent or more are by no means uncommon. For the currencies of East Asia, where markets are still much thinner than in the more advanced economies, the oscillations could be even more pronounced.

In their pragmatic pursuit of sustained development, few governments in the region have shown an appetite for that much uncertainty. Quite the opposite, in fact. Fear of floating is deeply institutionalized in East Asia. Even Japan, whose yen has been formally floating for decades, intervenes frequently to exercise some degree of control over its exchange rate. A switch to unrestrained flexibility, leaving the determination of currency values more or less to market forces, would be out of character for most states in East Asia. It is not likely that the tigers will change their stripes any time soon.

Currency Unification

What about the other corner solution—currency unification? The case for a common currency is equally clear. If fear of floating is the problem, an East Asian monetary union seems an obvious solution because it would, *ex hypothesi*, eliminate all risk of exchange rate instability in the region. The idea is widely touted (Mundell 2004) and, following the crisis, was even endorsed as a "distinct possibility" by the heads of government of ASEAN (Association of Southeast Asian Nations [ASEAN] 1999).

The reasoning is by analogy with the European Economic and Monetary Union (EMU). At the microeconomic level, a common currency like the euro would reduce transactions costs, thus encouraging intraregional trade. At the macroeconomic level, it would offer insulation against speculative crises by reducing the risk of incompatible exchange rate movements or other negative spillovers of the sort observed after the fall of the baht. A joint money would be easier to manage in the event of a new dollar crisis, compared with a diverse collection of national currencies of differing degrees of credibility.

But is the option realistic? Here too there are problems. Individually, as Natasha Hamilton-Hart (2003) has emphasized, government capacity in many cases may simply be inadequate to carry through such a complex and demanding project. Collectively, there is the challenge of identifying just which economies in the region might become involved. East Asia offers no natural club comparable to the membership of the European Union and is riven with political tensions.

In short, the requisite conditions for a successful monetary union are just not there. This was true before the crisis (Cohen 1993), and it remains true today despite widespread interest in the creation of new regional institutions. Ten years ago, just as the crisis was starting, Joseph Yam, head of the Hong Kong Monetary Authority, threw cold water on the idea when he delivered the prestigious Per Jacobsson Lecture at the annual meeting of the IMF. Regional monetary integration, he declared, "is inappropriate, at least for the time being" (Yam 1997, 21). A decade later, in another Per Jacobsson Lecture by Singapore Second Minister for Finance Tharman Shanmugaratnam, the theme remained much the same. Shanmugaratnam too thought that monetary integration was inappropriate. "Asia's strength is its diversity," he insisted; "That same diversity militates against monetary integration" (as quoted in Primorac 2006, 292). *Plus ça change, plus ça la même chose.*

The reason for the resistance to a monetary union is simple. Governmental monopoly control of the money supply is a source of great power, as I have noted elsewhere (Cohen 1998). East Asian governments, with the exception of the special cases of Brunei and Hong Kong, have shown no inclination to relinquish that power easily. The idea of currency unification may hold a certain appeal as a long-term goal, at least for some, but for the foreseeable future it is fated to remain a nonstarter.

A Dollar Standard

A third possibility, an interior solution between the corners, is to establish a formal dollar standard for the region, a common peg linking all of the currencies of the region to a dollar anchor. The approach has been vigorously promoted by economist Ronald McKinnon (2005). Because most East Asian currencies already share a strong affinity for the U.S. greenback, McKinnon argues, why not take the next step and make the relationship official? A dollar standard, based on a conventional soft peg, would be far less demanding than a monetary union, requiring little in the way of formal institutions or surrender of monetary sovereignty. Yet it would offer all the advantages of more direct exchange rate harmonization. In particular, making a common dollar peg the default position of every economy would reduce the risk of turbulence in the event of a dollar crisis. Moreover, the approach would have the virtue of building on traditional regional practice rather than defying it.

But that would also be its vice because it would preserve and perhaps even amplify the very fragilities that got East Asia into trouble once before. A dollar standard, McKinnon contends, would encourage more foreign borrowing. But that was precisely what led to the massive currency and maturity mismatches that made life so difficult after the fall of the baht. Formal dollar pegs would offer the same tempting target for speculators should new real misalignments emerge. They would also leave the region prey to the same outer exchange rate problem. Even McKinnon concedes that an Asian dollar standard could not survive without a parallel agreement by Japan and the United States to stabilize the yen-dollar rate. East Asian governments, as noted, have taken their cue from the experience of 1997–98 and try to moderate such risks by eschewing de jure targets and, at times, by loosening the dollar relationship. There is little evidence that they might now be prepared to reverse course in a way that, once again, could leave them exposed to financial fragility.

Basket Pegging

A fourth possibility, an alternative interior solution and long advocated by economist John Williamson (1999, 2005), is some form of common basket peg for East Asian currencies. Typically, this means an external basket. Rather than being linked to the dollar alone, as McKinnon would have them do, regional monies would be moored to a weighted average of several major outside currencies. Basket pegging is expressly intended to address the outer exchange rate problem intrinsic to a single-currency peg. Interventions would stabilize exchange rates in effective terms, minimizing vulnerability to fluctuations between the greenback and the currencies of other important trading partners. The benefits of exchange rate harmonization would be gained without the disadvantage of tying the fate of the region to a single anchor. In Williamson's words, "The object of the change would simply be to create an expectation that... variations in the exchange rates among the industrial countries would no longer have major impacts on the relative competitive positions of the East Asian countries" (1999, 342).

In other respects, however, the option shares the same drawbacks as a dollar standard, including, in particular, the same temptation for speculators to exploit any real misalignments that might emerge. Moreover, grave difficulties could be encountered in designing a basket that might suit the circumstances of all the economies in the region. For example, should the Japanese yen or Chinese yuan be included in the basket, alongside the dollar and other logical candidates such as the euro and pound sterling? Japan and China are both major markets for other economies in

East Asia. But, if either of their currencies were included in the basket, they would by definition be excluded from participating in the common peg. A wedge, therefore, could be driven between their exchange rates and the exchange rates of their smaller neighbors, which over time could affect competitive relationships. On the other hand, if their currencies were excluded from the basket so they could share in the common peg, the outer exchange rate problem would no longer be effectively eliminated because the yen or yuan could still fluctuate markedly in relation to the basket components. Similarly, it would be challenging, to say the least, to find a single set of weights for the basket currencies that would satisfy all the governments concerned.

The possibility of basket pegging is currently a focal point for discussion in East Asia, with official studies being commissioned in several countries. Because of the many difficulties involved, however, the probability that a common peg could be negotiated any time soon seems virtually nil. The option requires a good deal more commitment to regional solutions than appears evident in the area at present.

An Asian Currency Unit

Fifth, there is the possibility of an ACU of some kind, inspired by the earlier European experience with the European currency unit (ECU). The ECU was first defined in 1974 as a basket of currencies of the members of the European Community (as the European Union was then known) for purposes of Community accounting. By analogy, an ACU would be defined as a basket of East Asian currencies, an internal basket that might eventually provide a bridge to a common currency for the region. This idea too has become a focal point for discussion and has been actively promoted by the Asian Development Bank (ADB) as a useful first step toward exchange rate harmonization. In May 2006, the approach was formally endorsed by the finance ministers of China, Japan, and Korea in a joint statement (Anand Giridharadas, "Asian Finance Ministers Talk of United Currency," *International Herald Tribune*, May 5, 2006, 12).

How useful would an ACU be? Much depends on how ambitious regional governments wish to be. What the ADB and trio of finance ministers apparently have in mind is something limited to an accounting function, as was the ECU. Such a modest initiative might be politically feasible, but its impact would be correspondingly slight. If they want to heighten the impact of the ACU, East Asian governments would have to go further—to encourage its use not only as a unit of account but for other monetary purposes as well. That would mean, for example, actively promoting the development of markets for privately issued ACU-denominated debt in order to cultivate the role of the ACU as a store of value. It would also mean establishing of an efficient clearing and settlement system for ACU claims and perhaps even endowing the ACU with legal-tender status, to encourage its use as a medium of exchange. In effect, it would mean creating a parallel currency that would circulate alongside national currencies and compete for the favor of market actors.

The idea of a parallel currency has been seriously mooted by Eichengreen (2005), evidently as a second-best alternative should East Asia prove resistant to his preferred solution of free floating. But can anyone really imagine governments in the region creating a potentially attractive rival to their own state-sanctioned monies? The same conditions that are needed for a successful monetary union are demanded by a parallel currency as well; they are equally unlikely to be satisfied any time soon. This option too, for the foreseeable future, is fated to remain a nonstarter.

Monetary Policy Coordination

Finally, there is the possibility of some form of direct monetary policy coordination within the present constellation of soft pegs, as advocated recently by a team of regional specialists led by economist Hans Genberg (Genberg et al. 2005). If the risk of turbulence cannot be suppressed via the reform of ERRs, perhaps it can be subdued instead by some kind of agreement, formal or informal, to collaborate in setting and implementing domestic policy. An institutional framework might be constructed to promote regular consultations and exchanges of information. Monetary authorities might thus be able to avoid new real misalignments by adopting common targets for inflation and credit expansion. Such an approach would hardly be foolproof, of course; in the absence of firm constraints on government autonomy, defection or free riding would always remain a possibility. But at least the chances for monetary stability would be enhanced as compared with totally decentralized decision making. In Genberg's words, "The key is to allow each central bank to implement its own monetary policy...but to agree on a consistent objective to be pursued by all" (2006, 16).

The advantage of the coordination approach is its consistency with the traditional regional pragmatism in policymaking. The process can be pursued experimentally and incrementally, gradually building the institutions and mutual trust needed for more ambitious initiatives. The question, however, is whether even so limited an infringement on national sovereignty is plausible in current circumstances. As I wrote in 1993, several years before the fall of the baht, "a serious and sustained commitment to monetary cooperation requires a real sense of *community* among the countries involved" (Cohen 1993, 155). I suggested then that there seemed little evidence of such a sense of common identity in the East Asian region. Ten years after the events of 1997–98, the necessary degree of mutual commitment still seems most conspicuous by its absence.

Monetary cooperation is not impossible, of course. But as I also wrote back in 1993, it is more likely to emerge during a crisis than before it. At times of speculative pressure, when the benefits of stabilization become paramount, governments may be willing to enter into policy compromises in an effort to restore market confidence. But once the sense of crisis subsides, the desire to exercise monetary autonomy tends to reassert itself, encouraging defection and free riding. The result is a cyclical pattern that provides little assurance of effective coordination over time.

Conclusion

So where does all this leave exchange rate regimes and alignments in East Asia? Answer: Pretty much where they were a decade ago, before the fall of the baht. Currency strategies remain diverse but, in most cases, little changed, despite efforts to reduce vulnerabilities and build regional institutions. Exchange rates are still managed pragmatically in service to broader development goals, and the likelihood of radical reforms is still close to nil. Continuity remains the name of the game. Whether this will be enough to cope with the pressures that might emerge, should the Bretton Woods II pattern prove to be unsustainable, is anyone's guess.

CHAPTER 3

Banking Systems a Decade after the Crisis

Natasha Hamilton-Hart

Banks and the Crisis

The banking industry can be seen as a principal culprit implicated in the financial crises of 1997–98 in that the lending behavior of banks directly contributed to an overindebted corporate sector vulnerable to exchange rate risks. To be sure, many problems besetting crisis-hit economies did not originate in the banking sector; but commercial banks and other financial intermediaries, both foreign and local, played a crucial role in translating a variety of underlying failings into the proximate cause of the crisis—the rapid expansion of credit, much of it foreign currency-denominated, followed by an abrupt reversal of lending (as discussed in Andrew MacIntyre, T. J. Pempel, and John Ravenhill, chap. 1 in this volume). To this extent, the crises suffered by Thailand, Korea, Malaysia, and Indonesia were similar; and the postcrisis trajectories of the banking systems in these countries, the subject of this chapter, can usefully be compared. Postcrisis changes in the Japanese banking system are also discussed here. Although Japan did not suffer a balance-of-payments crisis in 1997–98, long-standing problems affecting its domestic banking system came to crisis point during this period and its reform program shares many similarities with those pursued by the other crisis countries.

Postcrisis reforms in the banking sector in all these countries became a means for dealing with problems that stemmed from broader political economy conditions such as the relationship between business and government (e.g., corruption and cronyism) and issues relating to corporate structure and governance. Not only did the currency crises swiftly manifest themselves in the banking sectors of the affected countries but the extraordinarily expensive public bailouts to deal with bad debt, compensate depositors (and some creditors), and recapitalize banks and other financial intermediaries ensured that the local banking sector became a primary focus of reform.

Even accounts that attribute the crisis largely to other factors agree that not all was well in the banking systems of most Asian countries before the crisis, although there is ongoing disagreement as to the nature of the problems. In one broad camp are those who cite problems relating to too much government intrusion: barriers to entry that created a protected, inefficient banking sector; implicit or explicit guarantees of banks and borrowers that created moral hazard; state-owned banks; and controls on banks such as directed lending and interest rate guidance, which meant that banks did not develop proper risk-management practices (e.g., Haggard, Lim, and Kim 2003). In another broad camp are those who cite the opposite problem: deregulation and the withdrawal of government guidance that opened the door to a banking-sector boom in which banks exploited new freedoms and helped fuel unsustainable asset price inflation in stock and property markets (e.g., Jomo 1998).

In one sense, both camps are correct—all the crisis-affected banking systems suffered from both types of problem, at least to some degree. More pertinently, it was precisely this mixture that produced such potent crises. In Korea, as in Japan, industrial policy supported by a controlled, bank-based financial system had broken down well before the crisis but asymmetric and unbalanced liberalization meant that a market-based financial system failed to emerge. Thus, continuing controls on bank lending and episodic political intervention were combined with the deregulation of corporate issues of commercial paper and the nonbank financial institutions, producing a precarious financial situation (Noble and Ravenhill 2000, 92–95; Hahm 2004, 173–75). In Thailand, the largely family-owned and conglomerate-affiliated banks that had operated with reasonable stability in a system characterized by financial restraint (lack of price-based competition) and little capacity for offshore borrowing proved highly dysfunctional once incentives for competition and offshore borrowing were created by partial liberalization in the early 1990s (Pasuk and Baker 2000). In Indonesia, the previously sluggish banking system dominated by state banks was transformed into a dynamic one after deregulation in the late 1980s, yet the broader context of regulatory failure, corruption, and high levels of particularistic state intervention in the economy remained, producing a particularly toxic mix of incentives (Hamilton-Hart 2002, 45–65). In Malaysia, where the banking sector experienced lower levels of stress in 1998 than in the other crisis economies, a relatively effective regulatory agency was partially successful in containing the problems arising from political intervention, particularistic ties between the government and banks, and banking sector booms following deregulation in the 1980s and 1990s (Hamilton-Hart 2002, 119–27). Nonetheless, the worst problems in the Malaysian banking system can be traced to the combination of de-control and selective state intervention.

Reforms and Outcomes: An Overview

Postcrisis reform programs across the region espouse the creation of market-based, competitive, and internationally open financial systems. For a variety of reasons—the weight of policy orthodoxy, the preferences of the International Monetary Fund (IMF), the political interests involved, and the profound changes in both national and international economic conditions since the heyday of state-led industrial finance systems—policymakers across the region appear to concur that it is impossible and undesirable to put the clock back and return to preregulation policies. Even the Malaysian capital controls, which provided its banking system with temporary insulation, were imposed in a policy context that advocates preparing Malaysian banks for greater international competition. Although government intervention is far from absent (and, indeed, increased as part of crisis management efforts), the direction of movement across the region is toward more competitive, internationally open banking systems.

The other major lesson that emerged from the crisis was that the affected countries suffered from serious problems in policy enforcement, particularly in the area of prudential regulation. The rules that did exist, on issues such as related party lending, concentrated credit risks, financial reporting, provisioning, and capital adequacy, were not enforced consistently. Political interference in the operations of regulatory agencies; regulator unwillingness to recognize the problems in the financial system; personalized and discretionary relations linking regulators, politicians, and bankers; corruption; and technical incapacity have all emerged, in different proportions, as factors behind the regulatory failure in the crisis-hit countries.[1]

As discussed in the third section of this chapter, postcrisis reforms across the region aimed to strengthen banking systems through broadly similar programs of restructuring, recapitalization, and regulatory change. Prudential regulations have been overhauled, and each country has endorsed the major international financial standards governing bank regulation. With the exception of Malaysia and Thailand, the regulatory agencies themselves have been subject to significant reforms. The structure of the banking system in all the countries has also undergone significant change, as outlined in the fourth section of this chapter. There has been considerable consolidation due to mergers and closures of financial institutions, and the structure of ownership has also changed significantly in all the countries except Japan and Malaysia. State ownership rose due to temporary nationalizations of distressed banks and banking assets; and reprivatization has produced a markedly increased role for foreign investors and foreign financial institutions in Korea, Indonesia, and Thailand.

The performance of these postcrisis banking systems has also changed, with a period of credit contractions, fragility, and low profits followed by a resumption of lending, improved nonperforming loan (NPL) ratios, larger capital bases, and a return to profitability, although there is considerable variation across the region. Table 3.1 summarizes the major regulatory and structural indicators in the five Asian countries that experienced a banking crisis in 1997–98. As described in

---

1. This also applies to Japan as well as to the countries that experienced currency crises along with their banking crises in 1997–98; see Amyx (2004b).

Table 3.1 Summary of regulatory and structural changes[a]

	Japan	Korea	Indonesia	Malaysia	Thailand
Financial regulator					
Independence	Medium–high	Medium–high	Medium–high	Low	Low
change from 1996	Increased	Increased	Increased	No change	Planned increase
Powers	Strong	Strong	Medium	Strong	Medium
change from 1996	Increased	Increased	Increased	No change	Planned increase
Unified	Yes	Partially	Planned	Yes	No
change from 1996	Yes	Yes	(Yes)	No	No
Market competition[b]	—	High	Moderate	High	Low
change from 1996	Increased	Increased	Increased	Increasing	Increased
Prudential rules	Tightened	Tightened	Tightened	No change	No change
enforcement	Mixed	Robust	Mixed	Robust	Mixed
State ownership	Low	Low–medium	Medium–high	Low–medium	Medium
change from 1996	No change	Increase	No change	No change	Increase
Foreign ownership	Low	High	Medium	Medium	Medium
increase from 1996	Limited	Major	Major	Limited	Major
Consolidation	Major	Major	Major	Major	Moderate
Bank performance					
Lending growth	Low	Moderate	Rapid	Moderate	Low
Profits (ROA, 2004)	—	0.9	3.5	1.4	1.2
CAR (2004)	—	11.3	19.4	14.3	11.9
Strength[c]	—	18.3	7.3	35.2	15.8

Source: Ghosh (2006, 84–85); International Monetary Fund (2005a, 31).

[a] CAR, capital adequacy ratio; ROA, return on assets.

[b] Competition is based on the *H* statistic, which aims to capture the contestability of banking markets and is computed on the basis of bank responsiveness to changes in factor input prices, as reported in Ghosh (2006, 84–85). These ratings are consistent with the other qualitative measures of competition reported in the same source.

[c] Strength is based on Moody's average bank financial strength index, as reported in IMF (2005a, 31).

more detail in the following two sections, changes have in most cases been in the same direction, but there remains a great deal of variation across countries.

As elaborated in the fifth section in this chapter, the crisis experienced by each country was the initial force precipitating change, although longer-term structural market pressures are also evident. The way the crisis was experienced can also explain some of the similarities and differences in reform programs across the region in that countries that turned to the IMF (Thailand, Indonesia, and Korea) were held to broadly similar commitments whereas Malaysia and Japan, free of IMF conditionalities, were able to chart somewhat different courses. Over the longer term, domestic political forces assume more importance for explaining variance in the implementation of reform programs. The political forces arrayed in support of much of the IMF program in Korea, for example, proved stronger than the pro-reform actors in Thailand. Another important source of variance is that these countries embarked on their reforms from very different starting positions. Malaysia, for example, began with a much stronger financial regulatory agency and a much larger foreign presence in its domestic financial system than any other country discussed here, which helps explain the limited change in Malaysia and puts some of the more dramatic changes in other countries into perspective.

The implications of these changes for the performance and stability of regional banking systems are discussed in the final section. Although some indicators of immediate vulnerability have certainly improved, the effectiveness of significant parts of the reform agenda is largely unknown. Policy reforms pursued across the region have proceeded on the assumption that there are benefits in empowering regulatory agencies and tightening prudential rules. This assumption has become lodged in mainstream policy thinking and, although not new, can be seen as an element of the postcrisis shift in economic policy ideas (discussed in MacIntyre, Pempel, and Ravenhill, chap. 1 in this volume). What is remarkable in this case, however, is how little evidence supports the idea that strengthening the powers of regulatory agencies and adding to the complexity of nonmarket regulations does anything to improve financial-sector performance. A major study of bank regulation in over 150 countries argues that

> [w]e find that empowering direct official supervision of banks and strengthening capital standards do not boost bank development, improve bank efficiency, reduce corruption in lending, or lower banking system fragility. Indeed, the evidence suggests that fortifying official supervisory oversight and disciplinary powers actually impedes the efficient operation of banks, increases corruption in lending, and therefore hurts the effectiveness of capital allocation without any corresponding improvement in bank stability. (Barth, Caprio, and Levine 2006, 12)

Although the benefits of increasing market competition in banking systems stand on less-contested theoretical ground, in practice the consequences of market reforms are not uniform. Overall, political and institutional factors specific to each country are likely to determine whether changes over the last decade will yield positive results in terms of enhancing both financial-sector stability and the ability of banks to contribute to economic growth.

Regulatory Changes

Regulatory change has occurred in all East Asian countries hit by banking crises in 1997–98, but has been most far-reaching in Japan and Korea, and least in Malaysia. Changes in Japan were the result of an extended program of financial liberalization initiated well before the crisis and driven by both long-term structural pressures for a more efficient financial system and a shifting domestic coalition of large internationalized firms, reformist politicians, and, particularly as the crisis unfolded, elements within the finance bureaucracy. In contrast, changes in Thailand, Indonesia, and Korea were set in motion as a result of turning to the IMF in 1997, with the most significant policy changes mandating increased foreign entry dictated by the agreements these countries had with the IMF. The IMF programs also called for wide-ranging institutional reform, strengthened prudential regulation, and regulator independence, but the degree to which these reforms found influential domestic supporters varied. In particular, political opposition in Thailand defeated several key reforms at the legislative stage; and in Indonesia extensive legal and regulatory changes have occurred, but their intent has often been stymied by pervasive problems of policy implementation.

Regulator Status and Structure

Major changes to the structure and status of regulatory agencies have been implemented in Korea, Indonesia, and Japan. The changes were aimed at creating more unified financial-sector supervisory agencies with stronger statutory powers and greater independence than their precrisis predecessors. In Malaysia and Thailand, no major changes to the status and structure of bank regulatory agencies occurred, although some internal reforms to increase capacity were pursued.

In Japan, authority over monetary policy was transferred from the Ministry of Finance to the Bank of Japan in April 1998, making the central bank more formally independent. New laws also broke up the Ministry of Finance and established a separate Financial Supervisory Agency (FSA; renamed the Financial Services Agency in 2000, when it took over another finance-related bureau from the Ministry of Finance). Japan thereby consolidated financial-sector supervision in one agency, which stood apart from the monetary authority. The new FSA showed itself willing and able to take a proactive and resolute approach to banks that were experiencing difficulties, nationalizing two major banks and imposing penalties for regulatory violations (Amyx 2003b). On a number of measures, the FSA has been able to demonstrate that it is decisively more independent from both industry and politicians than the Ministry of Finance had been, although it has also been accused of both forbearance and overzealous enforcement in support of what could be described as political agendas (Amyx 2004a; Chey 2006). FSA staff members have legal immunity from suits by banks or financial institutions (Barth, Caprio, and Levine 2006, database, 2003 survey).

In Korea, a new financial-sector supervisory body, the Financial Supervisory Commission (FSC), was established in 1998. Its executive arm, the Financial Supervisory Service (FSS), was created in 1999. This officially marks a step toward a more consolidated system of financial supervision because, before the crisis, responsibilities had been shared between the Bank of Korea and the Ministry of Finance and Economy (MOFE). However, in practice, the MOFE (itself the result of a merger between the Economic Planning Board and the Ministry of Finance in 1994) had dominated in both monetary policy and financial-sector regulation (including exercising directive oversight of the private commercial banks), and the 1998 reform actually carved up its responsibilities among three agencies. As the MOFE puts it, before the crisis "over-concentration of policy decision-making tended to undermine the checks and balances required for effective government" (Ministry of Finance and Economy [MOFE] n.d). The Bank of Korea also retains the authority to inspect banks, as does the Korea Deposit Insurance Agency, although this is the responsibility of the FSC.

The FSC/FSS were set up to function independently, free of MOFE and political influence. The head of the FSC is appointed by the president for a fixed three-year term and is responsible to the parliament, which can remove the head. Assessing the true independence of the FSC is difficult, in part because the meaning of true independence is hard to pin down. In some accounts, interventions in support of government attempts to promote corporate restructuring or discretionary forbearance in the interests of stability have been considered to be evidence of compromised independence (Walter 2007). But there is more evidence that, on the whole, the FSC did not use its influence over the banks to push for aggressive restructuring in line with government goals but prioritized the preservation of bank balance sheets and capital ratios, often to the detriment of corporate workouts and credit provision (Haggard, Lim, and Kim 2003). The FSC/FSS is empowered by the prompt corrective action framework introduced after the crisis, which allows regulators to mandate management changes or other actions by financial institutions that fail to meet regulatory standards. Its staff members are legally liable for their actions and can thus potentially be sued by banks (Barth, Caprio, and Levine 2006, database, 2003 survey).

In Indonesia, the primary bank regulator before the crisis was the central bank, Bank Indonesia, but it did not have full authority for all financial regulation. Finance companies were regulated by the Ministry of Finance and a separate capital markets authority was responsible for securities firms. The Ministry of Finance also made decisions on the issue of banking licenses. Bank Indonesia was not legally independent of the government; in theory it was governed by a monetary board of cabinet-level officials, and in practice its actions were subject to presidential preferences. Political intervention frequently undermined its regulatory functions and was also blamed for massive issues of emergency liquidity credits to banks during the crisis (Soedradjad 2005; Hamilton-Hart 2002). In 1999, a new Central Bank Act, required under the terms of the Indonesian agreement with the IMF, made Bank Indonesia legally independent. Governors and their deputies are now appointed by the legislature for fixed terms and can be removed only under extreme circumstances. The new-found independence of the bank was dramatically demonstrated in 2000–2001, when the government failed in its efforts to remove the governor, who served out his term despite being convicted in connection with a 1999 banking scandal.[2] Despite facing periodic parliamentary criticism, public differences of opinion with the Ministry of Finance, and calls to lower interest rates, Bank Indonesia has publicly defended its policy and prerogatives (*Jakarta Post*, October 20, 2001; *Kompas*, February 11, 2003; *Kompas*, May 6, 2004). For better or worse, Bank Indonesia appears to enjoy quite a robust level of independence.

The structure of financial supervision in Indonesia was also meant to change according to the 1999 Central Bank Act, which called for an integrated financial-sector supervisory agency to be established as a separate entity from the central bank by 2002. Partly as a result of open opposition by Bank Indonesia to this loss of its functions, later amendments to the law extended this deadline to 2010. There are political and administrative obstacles to the creation of an effective unified financial supervisory agency, and it is not clear how far plans for its establishment have progressed (Siregar and James 2006). In the meantime, bank supervision continues to be the responsibility of Bank Indonesia, which has received technical assistance to improve its capacity from both bilateral and multilateral sources since 1998.

The status of the Thai bank regulator, the Bank of Thailand, has not changed decisively since the crisis. The central bank was found to have suffered from both internal weaknesses and political interference in the years leading up to the crisis, with both factors seriously damaging its performance (Nukul Commission 1998). There is no provision for central bank independence under the terms of the 1942 Bank of Thailand Act, which does not provide for fixed terms of office for the governor or deputy governor, or spell out causes for their removal. A central bank official has noted that, of the previous nine governors, only two had retired from office; "the other seven were either fired or pressured to leave by the Government" (Pakorn 2002). The turnover of governors was especially rapid from 1996 to 2001, during which time five people served, but the governor appointed by Thaksin Shinawatra when he became prime minister in 2001 served until Thaksin's removal by a military coup in September 2006.[3]

---

2. The case against the governor, Syaril Sabirin, dragged on for over two years, during which time he was detained for six months. After his conviction and sentencing in March 2002 (well after President Wahid, who had been suspected of holding a personal grudge against Syaril, had been ousted from office), the head of the parliament's finance commission also called for Syaril's resignation (*Tempo Interaktif*, October 31, 2001; *Business Times*, March 14, 2002.) The conviction was overturned in August 2002, which was seen by some Indonesians as a setback in anticorruption efforts (*Straits Times*, August 31, 2002).

3. Although the governor had been described as a Thaksin ally, this was not the reason for his leaving the central bank; shortly after the coup he was appointed by the military leadership to serve as the Thai finance minister, joining a cabinet made up largely of career bureaucrats.

Under the terms of the IMF program, Thailand was supposed to amend its law to provide for central bank independence, and the Bank of Thailand had by 1999 drafted a bill containing standard provisions such as fixed-term appointments for the governor and deputy governor, as well as other protections and powers. Central bank officials, strong supporters of the bill, had expected it to be enacted in early 2000, but due to "long legal and parliamentary processes" later revised this estimate to mid-2003 (Pakorn 2002; see also Sirivedhin and Hataiseree 2000). Despite the continuing promotion of the bill by the central bank, it had not been passed as of October 2006.[4]

The Bank of Thailand is the primary banking regulator, but it shares some powers with the Ministry of Finance. It also does not have authority over insurance or securities companies or over some specialized government banks. Unlike most other central banks in the region, it has not had its supervisory authority strengthened since the crisis. A Financial Institutions Business bill was proposed after the crisis as part of the reforms agreed to under the IMF program. It would have unified the regulatory framework and strengthened the monitoring and enforcement powers of the central bank. Despite having been "in the final stages of enactment" in August 2002, it was not approved (Chandler and Thong-Ek Law Offices 2006). In May 2005, the Bank of Thailand redrafted the bill after the Ministry of Finance had failed to submit it to the parliament on time, and as of mid-2006 it still had not passed (Chandler and Thong-Ek Law Offices 2006). Bank supervisory staff are legally liable for their actions and can be sued by financial institutions (Barth, Caprio, and Levine 2006, database, 2003 survey).

The Malaysian financial-sector regulator is the central bank, Bank Negara Malaysia. Prior to the crisis, it had already consolidated most financial-sector supervision and is responsible for finance companies, merchant banks, and insurance companies as well as commercial banks. It also advises the Securities Commission on the regulation of securities companies. As a financial supervisor, Bank Negara enjoys robust legal authority, and its staff members are immune from suits arising from their supervisory actions (Barth, Caprio, and Levine 2006, database, 2003 survey). Despite having a reasonable degree of operational autonomy, Bank Negara is not independent. Its website declares that the functions of the bank are to be "carried out within the context of the broader goals of promoting economic growth, a high level of employment, maintaining price stability and a reasonable balance in the country's international payments position, eradicating poverty and restructuring society." According to the central bank act, the governor is appointed (and terminated) by the constitutional head of state and the deputy governor is appointed by the finance minister. In practice, the head of state defers to the prime minister. The Central Bank of Malaysia Act was not changed after the crisis; it underwent its last revision in 1994.

---

4. According to its website, the Bank of Thailand had identified pushing for the formalization of the new law in 2004 as an important task under its Strategic Plan.

Liberalization

The overall direction of policy change in the crisis-affected economies is toward encouraging more competitive banking sectors. Given the degree of precrisis deregulation of banking activities in all the countries except Korea, the aim of increasing competition is largely to be met through allowing greater foreign entry into the banking sector and mandating privatization of state-owned banks. However, as discussed in the next section, actual changes to the structure of ownership in the banking sector have only recently begun to reflect these goals.

In the countries under IMF programs—Korea, Indonesia, and Thailand—limits on the foreign ownership of domestic banks were eliminated during the crisis. However, in the case of Indonesia and Thailand, the elimination of the foreign ownership ceiling was for a ten-year period. After this period, foreign investors in Thailand may not acquire additional shares until the ownership stake is maintained below 49 percent of total shares (Polsiri and Wiwattanakantang 2004, 7). Agreements with the IMF also targeted the early privatization of banks nationalized as a result of the crisis and the eventual privatization of state banks in Korea, Thailand, and Indonesia. Financial-sector plans announced in Thailand and Indonesia set out roadmaps for greater liberalization and competitive performance in the banking sector (Bank Indonesia 2004; Bank of Thailand 2004). Japan has also begun to allow the takeover of domestic banks by foreign institutions and accelerated its earlier financial liberalization program in its 1998 financial-sector reforms (Amyx 2004a).

Policy change in Malaysia has been less dramatic. It did not lift ceilings on foreign ownership of domestic banks in the wake of the crisis and continues to restrict foreign entry into the banking sector. Before the crisis, the foreign presence in the banking sector through foreign bank subsidiaries was already relatively high by precrisis regional standards, although there were limits on foreign bank expansion. Malaysia is working toward promoting a more competitive financial sector, in line with its commitments for liberalization under the World Trade Organization (WTO). In addition to its Financial Sector Master Plan, which largely deals with making domestic banks more resilient and competitive, it has also begun to allow foreign banks more freedom to operate, such as partially lifting branching restrictions (Bank Negara Malaysia 2005, 2006).

Notwithstanding the trend toward liberalization, the governments continue to intervene in the banking sector for other than prudential purposes. Exhortations and guidance with regard to lending targets for small and medium enterprises or specific social groups are common in all the countries discussed here, with the exception of Japan. Although targeted levels of directed lending are generally low and, with the exception of Malaysia, not enforced consistently, they do represent a continued propensity to see the banking system as needing some direction in order to serve social purposes. Again with the exception of Japan, all the countries retain either full or partial state ownership of some financial institutions.

Deposit guarantees for the banking system mark a significant deviation from market-oriented financial policy in most of the countries. It is inherently difficult to eliminate expectations of public support during a crisis and guarantee systems in postcrisis Asia serve more to institutionalize expectations of support. All the countries have moved to create or strengthen deposit insurance systems but they are not adequately funded by industry levies. Precrisis, the guarantee systems tended to take the form of implicit government guarantees, and deposit insurance systems, if in place at all, were drastically underfunded. The Korea Deposit Insurance Corporation (KDIC), for example, was established in 1996 but had not developed anything like sufficient coverage by the time the crisis broke. Early in the crisis, the governments of Korea, Thailand, and Indonesia introduced explicit blanket guarantees of all banking system liabilities. These were later meant to be changed into partial guarantees that would eventually be funded through industry levies. The extent to which this has occurred is limited.[5] In Korea, the blanket government guarantee through the KDIC was lifted in 2001 and replaced with coverage of deposits up to 50 million won. In 2004, credit unions were excluded from coverage, but the system appears to remain government-backed rather than industry-funded. In Indonesia, the blanket government guarantee is to be replaced by new system of deposit insurance, but the system appears to be designed to retain a de facto government guarantee of all deposits; and thus the disastrous overextension of public payments to the banking system in 1997–98 remains very possible in a future financial crisis.[6]

Prudential Regulation

Prudential regulations governing banks have been overhauled across the region; most of the countries have declared an intent to adopt new international standards, including the technically onerous Basel II standards enshrined by the Bank for International Settlements (BIS) bank regulators in 2004. Before the crisis, most regulators had already begun to adopt the 1988 Basel Accord on capital adequacy, but enforcement was highly variable. Mandated capital adequacy ratios in precrisis Malaysia, for example, exceeded the Basel guideline of 8 percent, and, in the case of most banks, reported capital adequacy ratios (CARs) were not significantly compromised by unreported bad loans. In Indonesia and Japan, in contrast, many banks reported that CARs fell below 8 percent and a huge underreported NPL problem meant that actual bank capital was often much lower than reported.

Once the crisis broke, the condition of most banks deteriorated and preexisting hidden problems also came to light. Crisis management measures were broadly similar in all countries, consisting of the injection of public funds to take bad loans off the bank balance sheets and recapitalize the banks. Important differences of scale and detail, however, meant that the process, in fact, varied considerably. Simultaneously, the authorities in these countries embarked on a process of increasing the transparency and effectiveness of prudential standards. Of the crisis countries,

---

5. Ghosh (2006) provides an overview of deposit insurance trends.
6. For scathing criticism of the new Indonesian deposit insurance law, see McLeod (2006).

Korea and Malaysia moved most aggressively to raise bank capital adequacy standards. Korea began to enforce the Basel 8 percent CAR in 1998, closing down five banks that failed to meet it. CARs, calculated according to BIS guidelines, have exceeded 10 percent since 1999 (Hahm 2004, 184).[7] Malaysia forced banks to recognize bad loans and recapitalize if their CARs fell below the minimum as a result. In both cases, forbearance was exercised in the definition of NPLs when conditions were at their worst, but recognition and provisioning requirements were subsequently raised. The risk-weighted CAR for Malaysian banks has remained above 12 percent since 2001 (Bank Negara Malaysia 2006, table A.43).

Given the much worse condition of banks in Japan and Indonesia, authorities were not able to enforce capital-adequacy and loan-reporting standards until much later, and compliance in practice remains incomplete. Although Japan has adopted a much more stringent approach to regulation in line with international rules, some of the changes have been cosmetic, falling short of full substantive compliance (Chey 2006). Bank capital levels remain lower than prescribed by international standards. However, compliance gaps coexist with substantive changes (Kawai 2005). Japan has changed both the rules and the way they have been enforced. As a result of the reorganization of financial regulatory agencies, the Japanese style of financial regulation has changed from a personalized system based on opaque networks and informal guidance to a more transparent and rule-based one (Amyx 2003a).

In Indonesia, in the first phase of bank restructuring the initial minimum CAR was set at 4 percent, and banks below that level were forced to close or recapitalize. After several delays, a large numbers of bank did close or were absorbed by other institutions. By 2006, the average CAR across the banking sector was officially 21.5 percent, far in excess of Basel Accord standards. However, banks continue to hold large amounts of government bonds that are unrealistically valued and therefore inflate their capital ratios (McLeod 2004, 103–4; International Monetary Fund [IMF] 2005a, 30). Nonetheless, real average capital ratios for the private banks still meet or exceed the 8 percent Basel standard. Absolute capital requirements have also been increased, although they remain relatively low. The central bank has stipulated a minimum capital requirement of 80 billion rupiah (approximately $9 million) by 2007. As of 2006, it reported that fifteen banks did not meet this minimum, down from twenty-nine the preceding year (Coordinating Ministry for Economic Affairs 2006). As part of its Indonesian Banking Architecture plan over the next ten years, national banks will be required to have at least 10 trillion rupiah in capital and an international bank at least 50 trillion rupiah. A large number of Indonesian banks are still a long way from reaching this standard.

Indonesia has made many other changes to its prudential framework since 1999. New prudential rules include a requirement for banks to appoint compliance directors responsible for ensuring compliance with regulations, strengthening legal lending limits and increased reporting requirements, applying risk-management

---

7. On Korean postcrisis regulatory reform more generally, see Kim (2003).

principles, and imposing a "fit and proper" test on bank management and major shareholders (Siregar and James 2006, 105). Bank Indonesia has also announced that banks will have to comply with Basel II capital-adequacy and risk-management provisions by 2008, and it has revised its supervision to better assess financial risks. What all these changes mean in practice is not clear, given the long record of failure in actually enforcing prudential rules. Although Bank Indonesia tends to issue up- beat reports about the improved quality of its supervision, others judge that "pru- dential regulation and supervision seems no more effective now than it had been before the crisis" (McLeod 2006, 68). The IMF assessment was that a "significant amount of investment in human capital will be required," along with changes in the supervisory culture and responses from supervised institutions (IMF 2005a, 32). Certainly, there have been ongoing revelations of fraud and violations of the bank- ing law by Indonesian banks. The fact that some of these scandals have resulted in sanctions being placed on the banks—including the closure of two relatively small banks in 2004 (Siregar and James 2006, 104–5)—can be taken as evidence of at least partial enforcement, or as evidence of ongoing regulator failure.

Structural Changes

Structural change in regional banking systems has been driven in part by the exi- gencies of crisis management, which saw an initial increase in state ownership of banks, removal of bad loans from bank balance sheets at public expense, and consoli- dation of financial institutions. Structural shifts have also occurred due to market responses to the changes in regulatory policy already described, as well as to a return to growth across the region.

State and Foreign Ownership

Levels of state and foreign ownership in the banking sector are not transparent, particularly on an aggregate national basis, and sources vary widely in their esti- mates.[8] Despite some uncertainty, however, it is clear that there have been major changes to the structure of bank ownership in Indonesia, Korea, and Thailand, with foreign ownership eventually rising significantly after the crisis and state own- ership first rising sharply and then falling back, but probably still remaining above precrisis levels. Less change has occurred in Malaysia and Japan.

Malaysia has avoided major change to the mix of foreign, state, and local private ownership in the financial sector, although there has been a jump in foreign in- vestment in Malaysian banks, with the average foreign ownership stake in the largest

---

8. Ghosh (2006) and Barth, Caprio, and Levine (2006), for example, rely on different voluntarily disclosed sources and do not appear to include indirect stakes; hence, they underestimate levels of state and foreign ownership in some cases.

ten banks increasing from 16 to 26 percent (Ghosh 2006, 64). More dramatic change was precluded by the prohibition on foreign takeovers and a ceiling on foreign investment in Malaysian banks. However, a new foreign commercial bank, the Bank of China, did enter the market in 2000, and foreign banks continue to account for between 20 and 25 percent of all banking assets. Restrictions on foreign investment in Malaysian banks were later eased slightly, and in early 2007 a foreign investor (Kuwait Finance House) reportedly agreed to buy a controlling stake (32.5 percent) in the fourth largest Malaysian bank (*Business Times*, January 17, 2007). Public-capital injections into the banks through the recapitalization agency Danamodal were comparatively low and were repaid quickly, leaving the state ownership level relatively unchanged.[9]

In Japan, state ownership of banks was already minimal before the crisis and rose only temporarily. The major Japanese banks remain under private Japanese control. However, foreign direct investment in Japanese financial institutions rose from $242 million in 1995 to $8.6 billion in 1998 and has increased at a slower rate since then (Laurence 2001, 183). Foreign-owned banks accounted for a modest 6.7 percent of total bank assets in 2003 (Barth, Caprio, and Levine 2006, 152).

In Indonesia, the state share of the banking market has increased from precrisis levels. Just before the crisis, in July 1997, state banks (including regional government banks) held 38 percent of all bank loans, private Indonesian banks held 53 percent, and foreign banks held 9 percent. By the end of 2005, these figures had changed to state banks holding 43 percent of all bank loans, private Indonesian banks holding 43 percent, and foreign banks holding 14 percent (Pangestu and Habir 2002, 28; Bank Indonesia 2006). Most of the increase in the state bank share is accounted for by the growth in lending by regional government banks after decentralization. Although the government has reprivatized most of its holdings in banks that were nationalized during the crisis, there is no indication of any serious intent to fully privatize the state banks, despite earlier commitments under the Indonesian IMF program.

The foreign presence in the Indonesian banking sector has undergone a much greater increase than the official figures suggest.[10] Before the crisis, foreigners did not hold strategic stakes in Indonesian banks. Since 2002, they have become the controlling shareholders in the largest private Indonesian banks and hold significant stakes in several medium-size banks as well. One estimate is that, at the end of 2005, "41 of Indonesia's 131 banks were under the ownership of foreign investors, representing an overall 48% stake in the banking industry" (Department of

---

9. Danamodal did not inject new capital into any financial institution after December 1999, and its total capital disbursed declined from RM7.5 billion to RM2.1 billion due to repayments by the end of 2001. See Chin (2004, 213). State ownership of commercial banks is often reported as being very low or nil, but this ignores some significant stakes in the largest Malaysian banks held by state investment companies.

10. The central bank statistics continue to classify national private banks as nonforeign, even when foreigners are major shareholders.

State 2006). Given that there were twenty-eight officially recognized foreign banks at this time, this suggests foreign control of another thirteen banks. This fits the announced record of reprivatizations of the banks that were nationalized during the crisis, in which most of the eventual sales (after highly politicized and delayed processes) went to foreign-led consortia. This included the largest private banks, Bank Central Asia and Bank Danamon. In addition, foreign banks became substantial shareholders in some of the medium-size Indonesian banks that were recapitalized without being nationalized during the crisis.

Levels of state and foreign ownership have also increased in Thailand, with one source recording a rise in average state ownership in the ten largest banks from 1 to 29 percent (Ghosh 2006, 64). In 1998, the government took over six of the smaller private banks because they were insolvent or unable to meet recapitalization requirements. These banks were either merged into the three state-owned banks, Krung Thai Bank, Bank Thai, and Siam City Bank, or into a new bank (Radanasin), established to take over the viable assets of the fifty-six closed finance companies. Radanasin was then sold to Singapore United Overseas Bank (UOB) (Polsiri and Wiwattanakantang 2004, 3–4). In 2005, a specialist bank to service small and medium enterprises was opened, with the Ministry of Finance as the largest shareholder, in partnership with Bangkok Bank. The state presence has thus increased over precrisis levels, although its ownership stakes may be reduced in the future.[11]

The situation changed more dramatically for private banks in Thailand. Families or family groups had been the single largest shareholders in twelve of the fifteen banks operating in Thailand in 1996 (Polsiri and Wiwattanakantang 2004, 9). Of those that escaped nationalization, several were forced to invite in foreign investors in order for them to meet recapitalization targets in 1998 and 1999. In 2000, foreign investors held a significant portion (over 30 percent) of the shares in the four largest of the private Thai banks, as well as majority shares in the four smallest (Suehiro 2002, table 3.2).

By 2006, seventeen commercial banks were operating as the result of six new banking licenses having been granted and three banks being merged into others. Two of the new entrants were foreign banks (GE Money and the International Commercial Bank of China). Overall, of the seventeen banks, six had an identifiable foreign investor as the largest shareholder, four were state-owned and seven, including the largest banks (Bangkok Bank, Kasikornbank [then Thai Farmers Bank], and Bank of Ayudhya) were controlled by Thais.[12] Foreign investors as minority

11. In early 2006, the Financial Institutions Development Fund (FIDF) announced it was preparing to publish the requirements for strategic partners interested in buying a stake in state-owned Krung Thai Bank, BankThai, and Siam City Bank. The FIDF said that the central bank would not sell the banks to foreign investors. The FIDF owns 56.4 percent of Krung Thai Bank, 49 percent of BankThai, and 47.6 percent in Siam City Bank; see *Asian Banker,* March 6, 2006.

12. Two of these banks, Bangkok Bank and Kasikornbank, had a foreign investor as the single largest shareholder in 2003, according to Polsiri and Wiwattanakantang (2004, table 7). Family control seems to have been maintained, however, either despite low levels of share ownership or as a result of buying

shareholders, however, held significant stakes (up to 49 percent) in many of the Thai-controlled banks.[13]

Korea followed the same pattern of first a rise in state ownership as a result of nationalization and then foreign ownership as a result of reprivatization. The first sale was something of a showcase for the Korean reform program because the government disposed of Korea First Bank on generous terms to a U.S. investment firm (Newbridge Capital) at the end of 1999 (Yun 2003, 251–55).[14] The next sale of a majority stake to a foreign investor did not occur until 2003, with the sale of Korea Exchange Bank to the U.S. Lone Star Fund (which had lost out on its bid to acquire a different Korean bank in 2002).[15] Before this time, however, foreign investors had been acquiring significant minority stakes in several banks, including stakes of more than 30 percent in Korea Exchange Bank held by Commerzbank and in Koram bank by a U.S. consortium. In 2004, Koram was sold to a single majority foreign investor, Citibank. Of the eight major nationwide banks listed by the FSS as operating at the end of 2004,[16] three were majority foreign-owned and one had a foreign investor as the single largest shareholder.[17] The government no longer held controlling stakes in any of these banks, but it continued to run five specialized development-type banks. By 2006, this had been reduced to four specialized banks, and the government announced plans to reduce its stake in one of them, the Industrial Bank of Korea (*Asian Banker,* March 6, 2006).

Consolidation

The number of banks and other financial intermediaries has been significantly cut since 1998 in all the countries considered here. In almost every case, the closures

---

back into the bank. For example, members of the Lamsam family held positions as CEO, chairman, and another directorship of Kasikornbank in 2006, despite their stake having dropped to less than 6 percent by 2000 (Kasikornbank website, www.kasikornbank.com; Suehiro 2002, table 2). They were not listed among the ten largest bank shareholders in 2006.

13. Ownership details in many cases are obscure. The Stock Exchange of Thailand is listed as the single largest investor in Bangkok Bank, Kasikornbank, and Tisco Bank, and its fully owned subsidiary is also listed as owning significant stakes in several banks. Substantial shareholders are not necessarily revealed because several banks list only their ten largest shareholders, many of which are nominees companies.

14. The bank was later acquired by Standard Chartered in April 2005 and was renamed SC Jeil Eun Haeng (SC First Bank). At this time, it was the seventh largest bank in Korea (Standard Chartered Bank 2005) or one of the smallest of the eight nationwide banks.

15. Before the sale, Commerzbank already held 32 percent of the Korea Exchange Bank, but it did not control the bank. It sold part of its stake to Lone Star in 2003 and disposed of another major block of its remaining shares in 2006 for 703 billion won ($726 million). At the time, press reports suggested that Lone Star Fund would also exit from the bank when it had the opportunity; see *Business Times,* August 27, 2003; *Asian Banker,* March 6, 2006.

16. The government sold Chohung Bank to Shinhan Financial Group in 2003, but the FSS continued to list them separately.

17. Singapore government-owned Temasek Holdings became the single largest owner of Hana Bank shares in 2004, with a 10 percent stake in the bank; see *Business Times,* February 18, 2005.

and mergers of financial institutions required a heavy government hand, due largely to lack of clear exit rules or the failure to enforce them. The crisis decisively strengthened government capacity and incentives to deal with weak financial institutions and overcome resistance to consolidation by bank owners and some politicians (who were either fearful of the costs of bank closure or acting on behalf of bank owners).

Financial stress in Japan before its banking crisis came to a head in late 1997 had already led to a string of closures and takeovers of smaller institutions. Over the decade starting in 1991 more than 170 banks and depository institutions went bankrupt, although 130 of these involved small-scale credit cooperatives (Horiuchi 2003, 89). In 1995, several housing and loan institutions were forced to close and the Ministry of Finance arranged rescues of some larger commercial banks by the major banks from 1996. Since 2000, mergers involving the largest Japanese banks have transformed the financial scene; five new banks have been created from mergers of fourteen of the largest Japanese banks (Amyx 2003b, 2004a).

The number of private banks in Indonesia has more than halved. There were 164 private national banks in January 1997, 130 in mid-1998, 93 in March 1999, and 71 in January 2006. Also, between 1997 and 2006 the number of foreign and joint venture banks was reduced from forty-four in 1997 to twenty-eight, and the number of state banks dropped from seven to five as a result of mergers in 1999 (Bank Indonesia 2006). The fifteen largest banks account for about 70 percent of banking assets (IMF 2005a, 27). The central bank continues to urge smaller banks to merge, but it has had no success in persuading banks to consolidate over the last few years.[18] In 2006, it announced plans to push consolidation through a single-presence policy that would require banks with common ownership to merge. However, if this is enforced, it will almost exclusively affect the larger foreign-invested banks rather than the small banks with low capital levels.

In Korea, of the thirty-three banks operating at the end of 1997, five were closed and mergers reduced the number of commercial banks (including regional and specialized banks) to nineteen as of June 2004. An even larger change occurred in the merchant bank segment, which was responsible for much of the short-term foreign currency debt of Korean firms before the crisis. This category of financial institution has almost been eliminated; from thirty merchant banks at the end of 1999 the number had declined to two in 2004 (Bank of Korea 2004). There has been a corresponding concentration of the banking market. The share of the top three commercial banks rose from 28 percent of total bank assets in 1997 to 53 percent in 2003 (Hahm 2005, 390).

In Thailand, although several banks were closed or merged in 1997–99, new issues of banking licenses have seen the total number of commercial banks rise from fifteen to seventeen (domestic and foreign). The more dramatic consolidation was the closure of fifty-six finance companies early in the crisis.

---

18. About seventy-five small banks have assets of less than 1 trillion rupiah (IMF 2005a, 28).

In Malaysia, consolidation also began with forced mergers among the thirty-nine finance companies, reducing their number to twenty-three by the end of 1999 and to three by 2005. The major phase of consolidation began in July 1999, when the central bank announced a plan to create a radically streamlined financial sector organized around six anchor banks. At the time, there were twenty-one domestic banks, twenty-five finance companies, and twelve merchant banks. Both the time-line for mergers and the selection of the particular six were heavily criticized for being politically motivated, and several bankers tried to resist the forced merger program (Chin 2004, 217–20). Bank Negara then amended its program, announcing minimum capital requirements and allowing financial institutions to identify their own partners with the aim merging the financial sector into ten bank-based groups. The merger program was largely complete by the end of 2001 and finalized in 2002. At the end of 2005, there were ten domestic commercial banks to which were affiliated the three remaining finance companies, two of the six Islamic banks, and all ten merchant banks (Bank Negara Malaysia 2006). In 2006, another bank merger was agreed on, which would reduce the number of domestic commercial banks to nine. Over the whole period, the number of foreign banks remained at thirteen, although this included one new entry and one merger.

Growth and Resilience

All the affected banking systems experienced a slowdown or a reduction in bank lending due to the crisis. The contraction of credit was most dramatic in Indonesia, where total commercial bank lending to the private sector dropped from 360 trillion rupiah at the end of 1997 to 208 trillion rupiah at the end of 1999. The drop in loans by private banks was particularly sharp, from 180 trillion rupiah to a low point of 56 trillion rupiah in November 1999. Loan growth did not pick up until 2001, with banks continuing to hold a high proportion of government securities in their portfolios (Bank Indonesia 2006). Since then, the rate of credit growth to the private sector has increased at an annual average rate of nearly 20 percent, much faster than in the other regional countries (IMF 2005a, 28). However, at end 2005 the banking system loan-to-deposit ratio stood at only 53 percent, although this did mark a major rise from 26 percent in 1999 (*Jakarta Post*, July 1, 2006). Inter-mediation of deposits by banks remains far below the 80–90 percent ratio in other regional countries.

Korean banks also reduced their lending, especially to the corporate sector, and increased their holdings of both government and corporate securities—the former out of preference for safer assets and to support their capital ratios, the latter as a result of debt restructuring deals (Hahm 2004, 179–80). Bank assets returned to faster rates of growth after 2000, and consumer lending, in particular, increased, rising from 20 percent of bank lending in 1996 to 50 percent by 2002 (Hahm 2005, 393).

Both Malaysian and Thai banks heard periodic calls from the government to in-crease their lending to stimulate growth. Although overall bank lending continued to increase at a moderate rate, in Malaysia there has been little growth in loans to enterprises. Instead, growth has been led by a shift in lending to the household sector, which accounted for 43 percent of bank credit in 2001 and 55 percent in 2005, over which time the share of lending to enterprises dropped from 50 to 40 percent (Bank Negara Malaysia 2006, table A.38). Thai banks have been even less responsive to calls to increase lending. Bank credit to the private sector in Thailand remained almost stagnant over 2000–2004, the lowest rate of growth in the region apart from Japan, where loan growth turned positive only in 2005 as NPLs declined (IMF 2005a, 28; PricewaterhouseCoopers 2006, 7). Lending from the offshore banking facility, the Bangkok International Banking Facility (BIBF), which played a major role in channeling foreign loans to the Thai economy before the crisis, has virtually ceased. In 1997, loans from the BIBF made up 23 percent of total bank credit; in 2005, the share was only 1 percent.

Thai banks are still carrying high levels of bad debt, due to a much less aggressive approach to carving out NPLs from the banking system during the crisis. The overall level of NPLs in the Thai banking sector was 8.3 percent at the end of 2005.[19] This was higher than even Indonesia, where net NPLs were at 4.8 percent in 2005, although the ratio rose to 6.4 percent by April 2006 after a change in NPL classification. As of 2005, state-owned bank NPLs accounted for 72 percent of total NPLs in the Indonesian banking industry, a situation that was officially attributed to their limited powers to restructure loans given the legal definition of the debt of a state-owned bank as a state asset, meaning that state-owned banks cannot write off the principal and interest on such loans (Coordinating Ministry for Economic Affairs 2006). Their condition also had a lot to do with their much poorer credit practices and "outside interference" (IMF 2005a, 31). Malaysian NPLs have fallen steadily since 2001 but remain moderately high at 5.7 percent in early 2006. In contrast, banks in Korea are in a much stronger position on this measure. Official NPLs peaked in 1999 at 13.6 percent but had dropped to 3.3 percent in 2001, largely as a result of government purchases of NPLs through the Korea Asset Management Corporation, as well as write-offs and debt restructuring (Hahm 2004, 184, 193). NPLs for the major banks have remained at less than 3 percent since then. NPLs were reduced more slowly in Japan, but by 2006 the net NPL ratio stood at 1.2 percent of total loans, compared to 6.2 percent in 2002 (PricewaterhouseCoopers 2006, 6).

With the increase in the rate of loan growth in most countries, along with lower provisioning levels, banks have returned to profitability. Malaysian banks have maintained positive net growth in profits since 2000 (Bank Negara Malaysia 2006, table A.42). In Korea, average returns for the banking sector turned positive in 2001, after provisioning levels dropped (Hahm 2004, 184). Profits again suffered as a result of a credit card lending crisis in 2003 but rebounded strongly in 2005, when the aggregate profits in the banking sector were expected to increase by over 50 percent (*Asian Banker,* February 13, 2006). Indonesian banks have also reported high profits in recent years and are currently among the most profitable in the region,

---

19. NPLs for Indonesia, Thailand, and Malaysia are as reported by their central banks.

reflecting relatively high growth (IMF 2005a, 29). The large Japanese banks finally returned to profitability during 2004–5, after years of losses.

Although profits and CARs are often taken as indicators of financial health, they do not always correlate with other measures of resilience. For example, Moody's average bank financial strength index rated Indonesian banks the lowest in the region at 7.3, despite their profits and high CARs. This compares to index values of 15.8 for Thailand, 18.3 for Korea, and 35.2 for Malaysia.[20] Singapore banks were rated at 74.7 in the same survey, which shows that the banking sectors of all the crisis countries remain fragile when compared to the strongest in the region.

Actors and Incentives

External and domestic forces have played roles in determining the mixture of change and continuity in the banking sector of each country. External political forces, in the form of pressure by the IMF and other international financial institutions (IFIs), bilateral pressure, and multilateral commitments under the WTO framework, have been pivotal at some decisive moments over the last decade. However, in the absence of either longer-term structural incentives or domestic political support, external political factors have not been able to sustain changes that depend on ongoing domestic implementation efforts. Market forces have played a more insistent role in influencing policy viability, but whether policies respond to market incentives remains subject to the balance of domestic political forces in each country.

The crisis itself represented an acute form of market pressure that forced a policy response in all countries. Some of the commonalities in crisis management across the region, in particular the injection of public funds into the banking sector, reflect the immediate dictates of market pressure. Market-led changes that eroded the viability of earlier bank-based industrial policies by creating alternative channels for investment and savings have also created long-term incentives for policy adjustment. The Japanese extended program of financial liberalization since the 1980s is a partial response to such structural pressures (Laurence 2001). Similarly, the effectiveness of both the earlier Korean system of industrial finance and the Thai family-based bank and conglomerate structure broke down under conditions of capital account openness and access to global financial markets. Because no Asian country has the capacity to significantly alter the international regime that sustains a system of globalized finance, all have faced incentives to adopt domestic policies that take this context into account.

This structural context makes policies of segmented finance and certain types of directive control highly costly and ineffective, but it is not determinative when it comes to the content of policies governing the financial sector (Blyth 2003). Hence,

---

20. Index value as of December 2004. The higher the index score, the higher the financial strength (as cited in IMF 2005a, 31).

although all regional countries have learnt from experience that the risks associated with open financial systems create incentives to develop monitoring systems and prudential standards, the design and content of these standards are politically determined. The bank regulation standards with international status have been determined largely by European and, in particular, U.S. regulators (Oatley and Nabors 1998). Given the status of prudential standards enshrined in agreements such as the first Basel Accord (1988) and the Basel II agreement, the prudential reforms adopted in Asian countries over the last decade have taken these international standards as a template. Even though the standards themselves are as much the product of political expedience as technical rationality, their status ensures that individual countries have little incentive or capacity to develop alternative prudential rules except as add-ons that are consistent with international standards. The ideational context referred to in MacIntyre, Pempel, and Ravenhill (chap. 1 in this volume), therefore, is consequential even though the forces behind current ideas concerning financial regulation are primarily political.

There is little evidence that markets themselves play much of a role in disseminating or enforcing international standards governing banks (Walter 2007). At most, they do so inconsistently. External political actors have played more of a role in this respect in postcrisis Asian countries, particularly because the crisis opened the door to influence via IFI lending programs in Thailand, Indonesia, and Korea. This is another factor behind the degree of uniformity in the direction of change toward greater foreign access, greater liberalization, and enhanced regulator status and independence. These changes were all explicitly mandated by the terms of IMF programs in the region. On occasion, the IMF has been able to sustain its influence beyond the immediate crisis period. For example, in the course of its attempts to remove the central bank governor in 2001, the Indonesian government considered legislation that would have weakened the degree of central bank independence provided for by its 1999 central bank law (a product of its IMF program). In this case, the IMF had the muscle to prevent this attempt from proceeding; it held up funding installments to Indonesia until the issue was shelved (*Business Times*, March 15, 2001, April 17, 2001).

The force of market and external political pressures for change can also be judged by the course charted by Malaysia, where such pressures have been lowest. Although Malaysia has adopted the core international prudential standards and has declared an intention to phase in the Basel II requirements, it has moved the least of any country in the region on foreign entry into the banking market and regulator independence. The degree of protection afforded local banks can be interpreted as a straightforward favor to bank owners, some of whom are personally connected to the ruling party or influential politicians. However, this explanation is not fully convincing because several previously favored local bankers lost their banks, sometimes to government-controlled institutions, in the aftermath of the crisis. Further, the banking market is actually quite competitive (Ghosh 2006, 84–85), which is not consistent with the view that banking policy has been dictated by rent-seeking bank owners. Rather, postcrisis policy reflects the broader political incentives facing the government. The interethnic distribution of corporate wealth remains a highly sensitive issue in Malaysia, and allowing the banking sector to become predominantly foreign-owned would be tremendously politically costly. Although the government bailouts of Malaysian corporations (including two banks) have been unpopular with the electorate, there is no major public discontent with the performance of the banking sector as a whole.

Even in the countries under IMF programs, domestic political factors have been more important in the longer term, particularly on issues that require ongoing enforcement. For example, IMF pressure could help domestic parties in Thailand in their efforts to draft laws to empower the central bank, but it could not force these bills through the Thai parliamentary process. Political fragmentation before 2001 and, after 2001, Thaksin's disinclination to create or strengthen independent centers of bureaucratic power account for a large part of the reform agenda having stalled. Further, as domestic Thai business returned from its temporary period of political disempowerment in the immediate aftermath of the crisis (Allen Hicken, chap. 10 in this volume), government policy has been more accommodating of its interests, taking an avowedly nationalist rather than liberalizing line under Thaksin's leadership from 2001 to 2006. The leading Thai banking families, no strangers to politics, have in several cases made a comeback in terms of exercising control in their banks and have benefited from ongoing limits to competition in the banking market. Although the foreign presence in the domestic market is higher than before the crisis, the equity in Thai banks held by foreigners is in some ways similar to long-standing alliances between domestic and foreign capital elsewhere in the Thai economy, with these investors acting more as white knights than hostile raiders. The increased level of state ownership in the banking sector has offered the government another potentially significant lever to direct resources in support of a more nationalist economic policy, which can explain the lack of urgency to privatize government stakes and the creation of a new state financial institution to direct credit to the small and medium enterprise sector.

Political interests in controlling access to banking resources are also apparent in the evolution of the postcrisis Indonesian banking sector. Compared to the entrenched position of politically influential holders of wealth, domestic players supportive of a competitive economy and rules-based regulation remain relatively weak (Robison and Hadiz 2004). In the realm of electoral politics, calls for clean government resonate and anti-bureaucratic sentiments are often strong, but these are not tied to any coherent agenda for reform in the banking sector or the regulatory agencies. The degree of foreign ownership in the banking sector is already politically unpopular, with the sales of major banks to foreigners having (eventually) gone through as a result of government fiscal needs, IMF pressure, and the lack of acceptable domestic investors. There is little appetite for further privatization. Decentralization has meant the creation of local governments with an urgent need for resources and legitimacy, whose interests have been served by the rapid lending growth by regional development banks since 2001. The central government too shows no sign of carrying out significant privatization of the state banks; these banks continue to provide loans to politically influential corporate players and to provide other opportunities for patronage.

In the case of the extensive Korean reform program, it is clear that the IMF pressure was able to catalyze as much change as it did only because of the reformist commitments and political capacity on the part of the Kim Dae Jung government (Haggard, Lim, and Kim 2003). As a government that came to power on the basis of opposition to the *chaebol*, its own priorities were in line with part of the IMF agenda, and public support for the anti-*chaebol* drive (when it did not involve major job losses) bolstered governmental capacity. Unlike its counterparts in Malaysia, Indonesia, and Thailand, civil society in Korea has also been relatively favorable to foreign capital (Jongryn Mo, chap. 12 in this volume). Given the anti-*chaebol* sentiment and the weakness of alternative Korean investors, it was necessary to find foreign buyers for the stakes in the nationalized banks, if they were to be sold at all. In contrast, the IMF program was not effective in forcing change on issues for which the government was either unwilling or politically unable to implement reform commitments.

Implications

The changes that have occurred in Asian banking systems over the last decade have produced somewhat more efficient, more market-based banks and corporate sectors that are less reliant on bank financing. To the extent that the Asian high-debt, high-growth model was operating before the crisis, the crisis and its aftermath have effectively extinguished it (Wade and Veneroso 1998). Banking systems now have a larger foreign presence, and state ownership of banks has diminished since 2002 from the crisis-related peaks, but it is far from being eliminated, except in Japan. Prudential regulations have been brought closer to international norms. Changes to regulator status and structure have also brought Korea and Japan close to having unified independent regulatory agencies separate from the monetary authority; whereas the Indonesian regulator is independent but not fully unified and not separate from the monetary authority. The Malaysian regulator is unified but not independent and not separate from the monetary authority, whereas the Thai regulator is none of these things.

In terms of their efficiency and strength, regional banking systems have, on the surface, improved their performance. Capital levels are higher, nonperforming loans are lower, profits have returned, and other measures of efficiency have increased, although many domestic banks still score relatively poorly on several tests of efficiency (Williams and Nguyen 2005; Ghosh 2006). In conventional terms, the greater foreign presence and privatization of state banks, to the extent it has occurred, should push banking systems to be more efficient, have better risk management, and, hence, be less vulnerable to instability (Clarke, Cull, and Shirley 2005). Market participants and national regulators share a general confidence that foreign entry has beneficial effects in terms of risk management, technical expertise, and organizational innovation (Committee on Global Financial System [CGFS] 2005).

Certainly, foreign ownership has made a difference to bank performance in some cases in which there have been high-profile takeovers, such as in Korea (Yun 2003, 251–55; Yi and Park 2006).

Against this largely optimistic reading of changes since the crisis, several points of uncertainty make it difficult to conclude that the longer-term efficiency and resilience of regional banking systems have improved. As noted at the start of this chapter, some of the major tenets guiding the reform programs are very far from being well-established facts. Strengthening regulator powers and increasing prudential constraints such as capital ratios do not in themselves improve the efficiency or stability of banks (Barth, Caprio, and Levine 2006). The same authors note that the highly technically complex requirements of meeting Basel II risk-management provisions are likely to exacerbate problems of regulator skills lagging market practices while doing little to improve the prospects for market-based risk management based on disclosure and competition, which they judge the most effective means of regulating bank behavior (Barth, Caprio, and Levine 2006, 69–73).

The changing structure of ownership may have done more to improve banking system performance, at least in some countries, but the benefits of foreign entry and privatization are probably contingent. The big state-owned banks in Indonesia are clearly the worst performers in that country, and it is almost certain that Indonesia would gain economically from their privatization. This, however, remains politically unlikely. In other countries, the benefits of privatization and foreign ownership may be modest. Some state-owned banks in countries such as Malaysia and Singapore have relatively good records. And although foreign entry is associated with more competitive financial systems in advanced countries, some empirical studies have found that in lower-income countries the effects of state ownership are not uniformly negative and that foreign presence is associated with less credit provision to the private sector and not necessarily more efficient financial sectors (Detragiache, Gupta, and Tressel 2005; Detragiache, Tressel, and Gupta 2006).

In some respects, it is too soon to tell what the long-term effects of the changes that have occurred will be. Many of the improved indicators registered by regional banking systems reflect the crisis-related injections of public funds, which cleaned up bank asset sheets, as well as the return to relatively buoyant economic conditions. Whether the improvements will be sustained over the longer term remains speculative. Some vulnerabilities, such as levels of corporate debt and bank exposure to the corporate sector, have clearly decreased. But the household sector, which has taken on a new significance in bank portfolios, is not necessarily more stable in the face of a future economic downturn, particularly as levels of household debt begin to rise. On the other hand, to the extent that levels of related lending were a factor behind the poor quality of bank portfolios before the crisis, banks are less vulnerable now because banks in countries such as Indonesia (and merchant banks in Korea) are no longer part of family-owned conglomerates. This structural change has greatly reduced the potential for related lending, probably more so than the tightened official limits on related lending.

Over the longer term, the changes to the structure and status of the regulatory agencies may in some countries have made them more effective. Japan now has a fully integrated structure of supervision, and Malaysia and Korea have partially integrated supervisors. A recent review of empirical experiences suggests that integrated supervisory structures are associated with higher-quality supervision in some sectors and greater consistency of supervision (Cihak and Podpiera 2006). The transition to an integrated structure is not easy, however, and it does not in itself resolve the underlying issues of regulator capacity or corruption (Siregar and James 2006). Hence, even if the agenda of integrating financial supervision in Indonesia is realized, it is unlikely to redress broader problems in Indonesia with regulatory effectiveness and consistency.

Similarly, formal regulator independence does not appear to be a major determining factor of regulatory effectiveness. Although moves to strengthen the independence of regulatory agencies in Japan and Korea have been associated with better performance, this can also be attributed to the increased political commitment to regulatory integrity. In Indonesia, formal independence does not seem to have decisively affected the performance of the central bank, whereas in Malaysia the clear-cut lack of formal independence of its regulatory and monetary agency has not prevented it from being largely effective in both areas. The wider context of corruption and political commitment to regulatory enforcement, therefore, seems to be more determinative than the formal status of the regulator.

Overall, the changes that have occurred in the regional banking systems over the last decade have reduced some of the specific vulnerabilities they exhibited precrisis; the levels of connected lending, NPLs, and capital ratios have all improved, at least temporarily. Although there is now no longer much scope for connected lending in the countries where it was problematic, the healthier financial ratios that banks are currently reporting could deteriorate. Probably the single greatest factor that has made banking systems slightly less vulnerable over the last decade has nothing to do with regulatory reform at all but, instead, arises from the staggering buildup of foreign exchange reserves by countries in the region. Whether there have truly been improvements in the quality of risk assessment and management processes in the bank remains hard to assess. In some cases, banks that were taken over by foreign institutions appear to have greatly altered their credit culture and internal controls. However, given the role of foreign banks and offshore lenders in oversupplying credit to Asia before the crisis, foreign ownership in itself in no way ensures that credit decisions will be fault-free. The new regulatory context is meant to ensure that both local and foreign suppliers of credit will be held to better practices through new rules on disclosure and risk management, and most large banks in the region are in the process of upgrading their internal systems to meet Basel II requirements. But the new rules themselves are not without critics (Barth, Caprio, and Levine 2006; Wade 2007), and the burden of ensuring compliance continues to rest, ultimately, on national regulators with very uneven capacities.

CHAPTER 4

Containing the Oligarchs

The Politics of Corporate Governance Systems in East Asia

Peter Gourevitch

The Asian financial crisis influenced corporate governance practices and business government relations the way it touched many things in the countries of East Asia. Everywhere politics influenced policy outputs. The common shock of the crisis confronted governments with pressures to change the rules about how firms are run and about investor protections. Countries were not the same going into the crisis in regard to their business-government relationships or their political processes; rather, there are many versions of a stylized Asian model, as Andrew MacIntyre, T. J. Pempel, and John Ravenhill (chap. 1 of this volume) note, with quite distinctive country features, so the common stimulus of the Asian financial crisis led to varying outputs. We can observe changes everywhere, but it is harder to evaluate how deep these are. In his famous essay on the French Revolution, Tocqueville (1856/1998) notes that, although many things surely had changed, many had not—habits, practices, and deeper structures remained the same, in particular the centralization of power and reliance on the state. When asked to evaluate the impact of that same revolution, Zhou Enlai famously remarked, "it is too soon to tell" (Dodd 1989: 290).

The Asian financial crisis lacked the cataclysmic impact of the great revolutions, and our time frame is only ten years, but the comparison is made to note the challenge of measuring, evaluating, and explaining influences of an event on subsequent ones. There have been shifts in corporate governance and business-government relations in East Asia since the Asian financial crisis, but some of these

I thank the editors of the volume and meeting participants, the reviewers for help in developing this material, and Jim Shinn.

are cosmetic—what Walter (2007) calls "mock compliance," changes in the formal rules but not changes in actual practice (which is "substantive compliance"); this distinction is raised by Baskaran (2007) as well. It is a challenge to evaluate which practices remain the same with new labels ("old wine in new bottles") and which practices represent different ways of doing things.

The Asian financial crisis arose out of what MacIntyre, Pempel, and Ravenhill (chap. 1 in this volume) call a double mismatch—unhedged currency borrowing and a spread in the maturity dates of foreign borrowing and domestic lending. To that, we may add a third dimension of mismatch—the lack of transparency about the obligations being incurred not only by governments and financial institutions but also by firms in the private sector. This is when corporate governance becomes an important variable, a cause of the crisis and a target of reform. The vulnerability of the small financial systems grows when the corporate sector allows murky practices to prevail, concealing important information.

Each element of mismatch can attract its own policy response, reflecting different priorities: currency volatility, the strength of financial institutions, and the transparency of corporate governance mechanisms. In the battle over competing models of Asian development—the developmental state versus the Washington consensus—two distinctions about the role of the state are blurred. If an activist state is a key element of the Asian model, one way of being active is by "picking winners"—identifying and promoting in various ways key industries. The other way is through a regulatory apparatus that encourages strong interconnections among the elements of a production system. This is often called the relationship model; in Asia it is exemplified by the Japanese, and in Europe it is exemplified by Germany. Its stylized opposite, "arm's-length" market-driven arrangements, is associated with the U.S. model.

A state can back off from picking winners; it can reform its banks, improve the technical skills of financial regulators, and stabilize currency flows. But it can still have regulatory arrangements that encourage, protect, or at a minimum allow the dense networks of the relationship model to flourish.

There is also a fourth mismatch—the connection between political reform and the economic ones. Can there be transparency in the economy without transparency in political life? To some degree, yes. Singapore runs a pretty effective economy (table 4.1), and although its political system lacks fully free competitive elections, organizations, and media, it is nonetheless ranked as partly free in the Freedom House index of 2007 (see table 4.2), does well in the economic freedom index (table 4.1), and does considerably better on corruption indices than the United States (see the rankings of Transparency International or 2006) where Singapore is tied for fourth place, Hong Kong is in fourteenth place, and the United States in twentieth, the United Kingdom in eleventh, and Finland, Iceland, and New Zealand tied for first place (http://www.infoplease.com/ipa/A0781359.html). The most rapidly growing country in the region, China has the lowest democracy ratings of the countries in our sample. Indonesia, South Korea, and Taiwan are ranked higher on democracy than are the Philippines and Malaysia, with varying growth

Table 4.1 Economic freedom index, 1995–2004

	1995	2004
China	5.20	5.66
India	5.5	6.7
Indonesia	6.6	6.0
Japan	6.9	7.5
Malaysia	7.2	6.7
Philippines	7.2	6.3
Singapore	8.9	8.5
South Korea	6.7	7.1
Thailand	7.2	6.5
Taiwan	7.3	7.3

Source: Gwartney and Lawson (2006).

Table 4.2 Democracy indexes

Country	(1) Overall	(2) Political rights	(3) Civil liberties	(4) Corruption rank number classification
China	Not free	7	6	70
India	Free	2	3	70
Indonesia	Free	2	3	130
Japan	Free	1	2	17
Malaysia	Partly free	4	4	44
Philippines	Partly free	3	3	121
Singapore	Partly free	5	4	5
South Korea	Free	1	2	42
Thailand	Partly free	3	3	63
Taiwan	Free	1	2	34

Sources: For columns 1–3, Freedom House (2007); for column 4, Transparency International (2006).

rates. Such perception indices are vulnerable to news cycles and media influences, but they tell us something.

Economies can run well at times with limited transparency and little democracy. Authority is needed to solve problems, but too much authority opens the country to the risk of predation (Shleifer and Vishny 1997; North and Weingast 1989; Stasavage 2002). MacIntyre (2001) articulates this trade-off between efficacy and predation well in a U-shaped curve applied to policy response to the Asian financial crisis. Strong governments face the challenge of reassuring investors that their funds are safe, even though investors have no formal political means of supervising them, as they would in a democracy. Assurances can be supplied through a bond, or commitment, that substitutes for effective law; authoritarian governments know that the investors will leave if they are not well treated, and investors know the governments know this and take reassurance from that leverage (McMillan and Naughton 1992; McMillan and Woodruff 2002). In stable democracies, the effective rule of law and transparency are enforced via the balance of political forces who demand it. The bond there is the threat of losing the next election if investor flight causes a business downturn. Although economies can attract investment despite weak formal accountability through political transparency, it is likely to have a particular type of corporate governance, blockholding rather than diffuse shareholding. Private bonding occurs as a substitute for weak law, but it takes the form of internal supervision mechanisms, ones that exclude a market for corporate control.

Corporate governance and politics in much of the world involve oligarchs. Firms are controlled by a small number of blockholders, insiders who own enough shares to give them control or coordinate their smaller blocks through cross-shareholding. Governments are controlled by small numbers of officials who restrict access to authority, police, courts, and the media. The two oligarchies interact. The corporate insiders use their special path to political power to get money and contracts and to prevent entry or competition into their business. The state authorities rely on the corporate types for financial and economic resources useful for keeping power and restricting the access of outsiders to political influence. The relationship has acquired the label crony capitalism. Indonesia under Soeharto was a well-known example, one with a relatively clear price, the 10 percent "tax" on the business community (Fisman 2001).

Change in one domain involves change in the other. If either politics or markets become open and competitive, it can be harder for the other one to remain closed. If either is closed, it is easier for the other one to remain closed (North, Wallis, and Weingast 2006). Change in political structures is likely to enable change in market conditions; change in markets can lead to pressure to alter public policy.

In corporate governance we can see this in the interaction between policy preferences and political institutions. All over East Asia, the Asian financial crisis unleashed pressures to change policy toward corporate governance: some pressure from interest groups within each country, some from international investors, and some from international policy institutions such as the International Monetary Fund (IMF). How those preferences actually influenced policy was influenced by the mechanisms of interest aggregation, that is, political institutions. Because these variables differed within each country before the crisis (hence, the variety of Asian models, not a single one), the country responses varied as well.

In some cases, such as Korea, change in political institutions was substantial and had strong effects on economic policy toward corporate governance. Significant democratization altered the power relationship among groups in Korean society. This led to stronger shareholder protections and efforts to limit the authority of the oligarchs. In other countries, political institutions remained the same, but interest-group pressures led to some modification of governance policy and practices; Singapore, Malaysia, and China are examples. Other countries lie someplace in between; Thailand, Philippines, Taiwan, and Indonesia have had partial institutional change, some interest-group pressures, and modest policy shifts. Indonesia has become more democratic, whereas Thailand has become less so.

Since the Asian financial crisis we have seen some evidence of change in areas that affect corporate governance: rapid inflows of foreign money, major acquisitions by foreign firms, adoption of international codes of transparency in governance, reforms of formal financial structures, much talk of unwinding cross-shareholding, and more reporting of information by both private and public sector. The era of crony capitalism is alleged to be ending, if not over.

At the same time, there is substantial skepticism about whether these changes really mark new ways of doing business or whether they are cosmetic changes masking strong continuity with old practices. Shareholding remains concentrated in blocks; law enforcement is weak (Hall 1993). Will backlash (such as Korean reactions to the Lonestar case) cause a reversion of policy to older patterns?

It will take some time to be sure about this—transitional periods are confusing until they are over! But we can do some process tracing of how government rules and practices evolve. Corporate governance outcomes express the interaction of political institutions with preferences. We can explore this interaction by examining process and change in four countries in the region: Korea, Malaysia, China, and Singapore.

To frame the analysis, we can locate these countries in a comparative framework with other countries around the world. The standard instrument for comparing corporate governance systems is shareholder concentration. The more diffuse the shareholding, the more firms are monitored by a mass of minority shareholders via a board of directors that they elect; the more concentrated the shareholding, the more governance is dominated by blockholders, or insiders. A second indicator is the strength of "minority shareholder protections (MSPs), a set of rules and regulations concerning information (disclosure and audit), oversight (board independence), control rules (voting processes), and managerial incentives (executive pay). Countries differ in the strength of their MSPs. A key causal argument in the literature is that the quality of MSPs drives the level of diffusion. The higher the MSPs, the more likely it is that countries have diffuse shareholding; the lower the MSPs, the greater the concentration of shareholding, thus the blockholding pattern. Overall, there is some support for this idea; there is also a lot of variance and strong examples that do not fit (Gourevitch and Shinn 2005).

In comparison with a sample of thirty-nine countries (see Gourevitch and Shinn, 2005), those of East Asia fall toward the middle and the bottom of the shareholder concentration and shareholder protection lists; that is, they have high concentration of shareholding and low MSPs. Hong Kong and Indonesia lie between France and Chile concentration indices; South Korea has a concentration index that is a bit higher than Australia and New Zealand and falls in the upper third; Malaysia, Taiwan, Singapore, the Philippines, and Thailand fall in the middle with Finland, Austria, Sweden, and India. China and Japan do not fit with the other East Asian countries. For China, this is an artifact of the high level of public ownership in the Chinese economy; the data used for the indices include only public firms without a state block holder, which make up only 5 percent of the economy. In Japan, the MSP index is high, but cross-shareholding renders it meaningless because the system is, de facto, bloc-dominated (although some experts argue that this is now changing; Schaefer 2006). On MSP, Singapore is the highest in our group, followed

Table 4.3 Shareholder concentration/diffusion and minority shareholder protections

	Concentration[a]	MSPs[b]
China	5	11
Taiwan	45.5	35
Philippines	46.4	35
Japan	4.1	37
Korea	31.8	37
India	43	39
Venezuela	49	41
Norway	38.6	48
Argentina	72.5	50
New Zealand	27	52
Malaysia	42.6	67
Hong Kong	71.5	70
Australia	27.5	71
Singapore	44.8	84
United States	15	97
Mean	**46.9**	**45.6**

Source: Gourevitch and Shinn (2005, 18, 48).
[a] Concentration tells us the percentage of total shares in publicly traded firms without primary government ownership, held by the top group of owners; thus, a low number means a high degree of shareholder diffusion and a high number means a high degree of shareholder concentration.
[b] Minority shareholder protections (MSPs) are a composite index (out of 100) of several indicators, including control, compensation, and board composition. A higher index means a higher number of MSPs.

by Hong Kong; Indonesia is close to the bottom, with Thailand, Taiwan, and Korea a bit above that, in the 30s (the index is out of 100).

This tells us the East Asian countries lie statistically where the stereotype puts them—in relationship capitalism (or, pejoratively, crony capitalism) rather than in the arm's-length model associated with the United States and the United Kingdom. It would be ideal to track the evolution on these indicators since the Asian financial crisis, but, alas, we do not have the data over time to allow this. Shareholder concentration/diffusion indices are particularly hard to come by; and there have been changes in the formal rules of MSPs in a number of the countries.

A recent IMF study (De Nicolò, Laeven, and Ueda 2006) provides a rough way of tracking changes over time. Instead of looking at MSPs (or other legal regulations), this study looks at indicators of behavior. The authors construct an index, the corporate governance quality (CGQ) index, using three variables: accounting standards (how much information companies report), earnings smoothing (the extent to which managers may obscure earnings by adjustments over time to make them smoother), and stock price synchronicity (the extent to which stock prices vary together or independently). Low amounts of accounting information, obscure earnings reports, and low independence of stock price movements are all behavioral indicators of poor corporate governance patterns. This measure has the advantage of getting past the difficulty of knowing whether the formal MSPs are actually

Table 4.4 Change in the corporate governance index, 1995–2003[a]

	1995	1998	2003	Average growth rate
Korea	0.584	0.615	0.592	0.002
China	0.559	0.547	0.507	−0.012
Hong Kong	0.586	0.568	0.712	0.024
Taiwan	N/A	N/A	N/A	N/A
Japan	0.572	0.620	0.640	0.014
Australia	0.661	0.680	0.727	0.012
Malaysia	0.521	0.529	0.613	0.020
New Zealand	0.470	0.562	0.651	0.041
Singapore	0.605	0.571	0.648	0.009
Argentina	0.523	0.510	0.536	0.003
Venezuela	0.525	0.532	0.487	0.031
Philippines	0.535	0.561	0.663	0.027
Norway	0.698	0.691	0.681	−0.003
India	0.575	0.583	0.603	0.006

Source: De Nicolò, Laeven, and Ueda (2006).
[a] "The CGQ [corporate governance quality] index is a simple average of three proxy measures of *outcomes* of corporate governance in the dimensions of *accounting, disclosure and transparency.*" De Nicolò, Laeven, and Ueda (2006), 4. N/A, not available.

enforced (Berglöf and Claessens 2004). The IMF study finds shifts that are not large but show some change, confirming the impression of modest improvement (table 4.4).

These measurements are supported by experts using analytic observation rather than quantified measurements. Baskaran (2007) sees modest changes, as does Walter (2007) Both see changes in rules, codes, and official practice, but acknowledge that deeper changes in the fundamentals of practice are harder to see.

So some modest change appears to be taking place in East Asian corporate governance. What can we say about the process of change, the causal mechanisms? Shifts in corporate governance policy reflect the interaction of change in political power balance with changes in interest-group preferences connected to economic incentives. All the Asian countries in this set represent a development model with high statist involvement in the economy. In East Asia, as in most of the world, that interaction of strong state action and authoritarian politics produces blockholder-dominant corporate governance. In all of the countries, changes in the global economy create some inducements for reforming the structure of governance toward greater shareholder protections; domestic actors seek to improve their lot by engaging in global capital and trade markets, which starts them down a reformist path. This can generate a bargain among external investors, inside blockholders, and managers to reap the benefits of diffusion (higher share prices and diversification of risk by the investors) and to decrease the level of managerial agency costs. The extent of the change is influenced by both the intensity of the interest-group preferences and the extent of political change; democratization tends to weaken oligarchical power, giving more voice to those shut out of the authoritarian structure. The connection is not automatic. Democracy can also give voice to interest-group coalitions threatened by change. But where economic oligarchy and political authoritarianism have jointly reinforced one another, political changes can produce economic policy ones.

In tracing the impact of the Asian financial crisis, then, we have to triangulate the differences in initial conditions with the outcomes: the differences in preexisting institutions (degree of democracy and corruption), the differences in corporate transparency, and the differences in the impact of the crisis. These are interconnected but autonomous. Singapore ranks as the most democratic and the least corrupt of the mixed systems in our sample. It is oligarchic in elite control but not corrupt; the crisis did not hit it severely; and postcrisis change in corporate governance was limited. The crisis hit Korea hit hard because it was already going through several transitions, perhaps making it more vulnerable: democratization, with an opposition leader recently elected to the presidency; shrinking government oversight of the *chaebol* without clear replacement mechanisms; and continued extensive state action in the economy with a highly charged political atmosphere and considerable personal cronyism. The struggles over the IMF conditions and political change produced visible and controversial responses.

Malaysia had its own strongman democracy before the crisis; despite its vulnerability to finance and currency problems, Mahathir Mohamad used his political authority to stare down the IMF, rejecting its draconian oversight, and Malaysia came out moderately well, with modest pressure and modest reform. China buffered itself from the Asian financial crisis with a nonconvertible currency. The crisis prodded the leadership to accelerate its reform processes in the economic sphere; this is all the more interesting because political reform remains limited.

Despite their differences, all the countries face a common problem. If the lesson of the Asian financial crisis is that more market processes are needed to manage the complexities of a the modern economy, then the problems of oversight increase; as government pulls back its direct supervision, indirect methods are required, and it is not clear how the political systems can manage this. Liberal models take more supervision—not less—and more complex, less personalized supervision. Some of these issues come through in our analytic narrative of the four cases considered next.

Analytic Narratives of Corporate Governance Patterns: Korea, Singapore, Malaysia, and China

Korea: Changing Institutions, Shifting Preferences, and Coalitional Dynamics

Korea illustrates the speed with which a country can shift governance patterns if both preferences and political institutions are changing quickly. Over the past decades, Korea has gone from a military dictatorship to modified authoritarianism to a constitutional democracy, from presidential rule by decree in the 1950s to the generals' junta of the 1960s and 70s to the democratic elections in the 1990s of Kim Young Sam, Kim Dae Jung, and Roh Moo Hyun during the last decade. It has moved from hard authoritarian (not totalitarian but strong military rule) to moderate authoritarian, with limited freedoms and some autonomy for civil society, especially in the economy, to transitional democracy, with free elections, competitive political parties, and a change of leadership from one party to another—the classic indicator of true democratization. The Asian financial crisis may have helped solidify democratization processes by helping to elect Kim Dae Jung, the long-time opposition leader, in that the election happened in December, a few months after the Asian financial crisis began; observers credit the backlash from the economic distress for helping to elect Kim.

The Asian financial crisis hit Korea hard, and the pressure of the IMF demands was felt acutely in both economics and politics. We stress here, as does Jongryn Mo (chap. 12 in this volume) the role of politics in mediating the impact of the Asian financial crisis in Korea and in shaping its response. A particular political hostility to the *chaebol* generated a nationalist sympathy toward foreign capital as a balance, whereas in many countries foreign capital generated a protectionist reaction (although Pinto 2005 argues that the effect turns on whether capital generates jobs) (Haggard, Lim, and Kim 2003).

During these same years, the Korean corporate governance system showed a mixed pattern of change, as Mo (chap. 12 in this volume) notes, shifting in some respects more than others. Korea went from 100 percent blockholder control with effectively zero shareholder protections to a concentration rate of 32 percent in 2000 (which is lower than the mean of the country sample in Gourevitch and Shinn 2005) and a MSP index of 37 (which is close to the sample mean of the thirty-nine countries examined in Gourevitch and Shinn 2005). Indeed, the actual levels for Korea are probably somewhat higher than these data show because the reforms were enacted while those data sets were being constructed. What took almost 150 years in the United Kingdom and at least a century in the United States for governance policy, Korea compressed into a mere four decades; the dramatic Korean economic growth since 1960 compressed into these forty years many of the shifting preferences and governance changes that required far longer to develop in other countries.

With the end of the Korean War, South Korea developed in a classic oligarchy blockholding pattern. The founding fathers of the great firms built their initial fortunes in the heavy manufacturing sectors that powered the rapid Korean economic growth with ample funding through directed lending by the Korean government controlled banking system (rather than through equity markets). Below them on the corporate food chain were dozens of other lesser *chaebol*, also created by a founder-entrepreneur who similarly called the shots.

Political power was concentrated in the military-controlled governments that struck a bargain—the *chaebol* leaders would have a free hand in their economic sphere; workers and professional managerial employees were excluded from having a voice in the firm and the policy, as were smaller owners, regional interests, and religious and other groups. Foreign entry was severely restricted, and antitrust action nonexistent. Concentrated ownership with few MSPs gave the founding families with great power and latitude.

As a result, the Korean blockholder concentration ratio of listed firms was high well into the 1980s, at almost 80 percent (Jang 2003; Gourevitch and Shinn 2005, 123–31). *Chaebol* family owners controlled a horizontal network of firms in diverse industries through a classic pyramid structure, much like the original Japanese *zaibatsu* system. The *chaebol* played a key role in the Korean rapid economic growth period. The Federation of Korean Industry (FKI) served as a classic instrument of top-down economic planning, with instructions flowing from the ministry to the firm. The *chaebol* cooperated with government direction in return for preferential access to capital and protection from market competition.

As a function of increasing scale and technical complexity (Chandler variables), the great *chaebol* owners began to rely more and more on the skills of professional managers, who they gradually absorbed into the system. The criteria for hiring and firing remained opaque; top *chaebol* managers were hand-picked by the office of the *chaebol* chairman, to which they remained beholden.

When democratization began under Roh Tae Woo, the governance pattern shifted. The *chaebol* blockholders gradually wrested control of the FKI away from the state, but kept power in the hands of the very top elite. The concentration index declined somewhat because of some public offerings and the influx of some foreign portfolio investors who relied on an implicit sovereign risk guarantee from "Korea Inc." rather than on financial transparency or shareholder protections. Little change took place in terms of MSPs during the 1980s and most of the decade of the 1990s. The concentration of shareholding could persist because the *chaebol* were able to use domestic capital rather than foreign capital because of their leverage over the banking institutions. The *chaebol* developed a type of merchant bank that by the 1990s rivaled in size the state-controlled commercial banking sector. Almost all the nonbank financial institutions (NBFIs) became insolvent during the Asian financial crisis in 1997–98, and thirty-three were closed in the wake of the crisis. The unhedged foreign exchange liabilities of these NBFIs were one of the prime causes of the crisis in the first place.

Another obstacle to diffusion was the concentration itself, which inhibited the pattern of mergers that generated diffusion in other countries. The sheer size of the *chaebol* gave them autonomy from the need for capital and conferred on them a privileged position in Korean society that they did not wish to dilute by selling shares.

In the 1990s, the pace of change increased. A number of political actors—Korean labor unions, regional groups, smaller businesses, and professionals—began to express demands. The *chaebol* began accommodating partly to foreign investors. On the labor side, massive strikes in the face of state repression led to bargains—*chaebol* control in exchange for employment concessions that made lay-offs difficult and expensive. Rapid economic growth (despite lagging labor productivity), restrictive competition policy, and barriers to foreign entry insulated this convenient arrangement from the chill winds of market forces.

Political democratization, under Kim Young Sam and then Kim Dae Jung, pushed these concessions along. A change in political institutions led to a change in power relations, which in turn caused a shift in policy, which in turn led to changing patterns of corporate governance. The *chaebol* were compromised by complicity with the generals during the long years of repression. Elections brought to power governments that reflected voter concerns about corruption and efficiency. There was substantial political tension between Kim Dae Jung and his center-left support base and the *chaebol* families, especially the owners of Daewoo, as well as an attempt by the Chung family to use control of its Hyundai conglomerate to enter Korean electoral politics.

During the 1990s, with constant media attention and a president in the Blue House seeking to consolidate a new political power base, many of the special deals between the *chaebol* and the banking sector became public. Instances of private benefits of control, outright asset stripping, and high-profile feuds between second-generation members of the *chaebol* family kept corporate governance on the front pages.

In parallel with movement toward democratization in the 1990s, Korea moved to privatize utilities and state-sponsored heavy industrial firms such as Pohang Iron & Steel Company, Korea Electric Power Corporation, Korea Telecom, and Korea Tobacco. These firms accounted for a growing percentage of the total market capitalization of the Korea Stock Exchange, driving the percentage weight of the blockholder-controlled *chaebol* in the market down, thereby increasing shareholding.

The Asian financial crisis arrived, as Mo (chap. 12 in this volume) notes, in a context of contestation and change. The *chaebol* were associated with opposition to reform, both economic and political. The crisis intensified the pressure. With a shift in politics to Kim Dae Jung's presidency, a string of corporate governance reforms were passed. Kim had strong support from all the groups left out of the previous regimes—labor unions, regional groups from Cholla, small owners excluded from the *chaebol* system, civil servants, and reformers of various kinds— all grouped within Kim's reformist Millennium Democracy Party. The coalition of support for corporate governance transparency corresponds to similar political patterns in other countries.

Political openness, embracing a wide range of social groups, generated support against concentrated capital. This produced policies favoring corporate transparency and shareholder rights. Thus, change came not from a private bargain between owners and external investors, as the stylized finance model suggests, but because of bargains and accommodations in the political system. In this regard, Korea carried out in a few years something resembling the process that took a century in the United States.

In 1998, the newly launched Korean Financial Supervisory Commission (FSC), which was struggling to deal with foreign skepticism about the Korean country risk premium, radically overhauled the Korean Financial Accounting Standards to bring them in line with the International Accounting Standards (IAS). External auditors were made mandatory for listed firms. An independent institution for accounting standards, the Korean Accounting Standards Board, was created in June 1999, separating the oversight of accounting standards from the Ministry of Finance and Economy (Kim 2000).

At the same time, new regulations were written to require the detailed disclosure of insider financial transactions between the *chaebol* blockholders and public firms. Korean informal institutions of third-party financial analysis—consisting of the Seoul affiliates of international securities firms—went into overdrive a result of better financial disclosure and more reliable accounting data; there was a panicked concern by global investors that they had miscalculated the underlying business risk in Korea and overestimated the corporate governance good faith of the *chaebol* owners, along with a sinking realization that the implicit state guarantee by "Korea Inc." did not extend to all foreign investors in all firms.

In 1998, the Kim Dae Jung government moved to force the *chaebol* to replace their family-dominated boards, which generally rubber-stamped the orders of the founding blockholders, with increasing numbers of nonexecutive directors. The top five *chaebol* (all still in the hands of the founding families) of Hyundai, Samsung, Lucky-Goldstar (LG), SunKyong (SK), and Daewoo (now bankrupt) were the special targets of these reforms. These firms were required to obtain 50 percent of their directors from outside, with a strict definition of *independence*. Shareholder activists used new regulations to bring derivative suits against firms, some won by the plaintiffs; limits on hostile takeovers were reduced, although none has occurred (Yoo 1999; Yoon 1999; Chang and Kim 2000).

But there were limits to these corporate governance reforms. The banks were effectively bailed out or subsidized when the Asian financial crisis hit, leaving considerable power in the Ministry of Finance. Governance reform was restrained in order to preserve jobs. Worker support for reform derived from the critique of the *chaebol* owners, but was muted by limited share ownership in Korean society.

This is a crucial lesson of the Korean case. The foreign investor–driven model of governance reform frequently assumed in the literature has a thin domestic political base in Korea. The greater mass of Korean citizens stands to benefit little from these reforms, which rebound largely in favor of foreign investors. Koreans do not have the mass of savings that could go into the reorganized firms. Thus, the model lacks one of the key components of the transparency coalition found in other countries—the uniting of workers with pension funds to protect the mass of small external shareholders.

Although Korean institutional investors have accumulated almost $400 billion in assets, the equity portion of these holdings is only about 10 percent. Total South Korean pension assets as a share of GDP are about 13 percent, well below the mean for Organisation for Economic Co-operation and Development (OECD) and developing countries in our sample (Gourevitch and Shinn 2005, table 5.3). Moreover, this asset figure masks the severely underfunded nature of the pension obligations of the Seoul government to its citizens.

Many Korean workers lost their private pension benefits when their employers went bankrupt during the financial crisis; severance benefits from the *chaebol* firms were funded from current operations rather than from external financial assets. When these firms went under, workers' claims on the future cash flows of the firms were written down, along with those of stockholders and external lenders. Failed or tottering firms acquired by foreign direct investors also wrote down or eliminated entirely much of their pension obligations to workers.

Compounding this firm-specific loss, many workers' individually funded pension plans were devastated by huge losses in the postcrisis period. Several funds were bankrupted by ill-advised investments in equity markets urged on them by the finance ministries. In one notable case, several private pension funds made large purchases of securities in Daewoo group companies as part of a government-organized bailout of the struggling firm, a bailout that ultimately failed, wiping out several of the pension funds.

Adding fiscal insult to these economic injuries, the Korean government was so burdened by the mammoth cost of the bailout that its ability to cushion workers' personal losses with a national welfare safety net was severely limited. The Korean government, and every Korean taxpayer by implication, had become an expropriated minority shareholder in the failed *chaebol*.

As a result, Korean workers, and more broadly Korean voters, widely attributed these losses to moral hazard failures in the corporate governance of the *chaebol* firms—a sentiment echoed by the Kim Dae Jung government as it pushed through these reforms over the objections of the *chaebol* blockholders. In Korea, minority shareholders meant foreign shareholders, not Koreans themselves. Thus, in Korea, transparency reforms arrived in a political context that mixed labor power elements and cross-class coalitional features; it was not an investor-led model of change (Yoo 1999; Yoon 1999; Chang and Kim 2000).

China: Seeking Capital without Democracy

In contrast to Korea, the Chinese political system remains closed to competition and it ranks low on comparative democratization. Because it did not have a convertible currency, the Asian financial crisis did not hit China in the same way it did the other countries. Instead, Chinese leaders seem, as Edward Steinfeld (chap. 9 in this volume) notes, to have used the crisis to intensify the process of transition from total state control to market processes while keeping party control of politics. As in all the countries, this leaves complex supervisory relationships with plenty of room for corruption and plenty of room for growth.

China is the most striking example in our cases of the state as oligarch, as opposed to private individuals as founder-blockholders. Now, the government is opening up toward a partial investor model, as the state sells off minority equity holdings in corporatized state-owned enterprises (SOEs) to (mainly) foreign and (a few) domestic individual investors. This transition is built on a thin political coalition. It risks veering off into a form of insider kleptocracy, a sort of managerism with Chinese characteristics, similar perhaps to contemporary Russia or to the United States in the days of the robber barons.

The Chinese experiment with publicly traded firms and stock markets is only a decade old, and the state is the dominant blockholder. The state continues to hold, on average, 65 percent of the equity of traded SOEs, and only 35 percent of the equity is tradable as either A or B shares. Under the threshold of control rules used by various estimates of concentration, China has less than a 5 percent weight of private blockholders, and even this small number is of recent vintage as several entrepreneurial firms from the booming east coast provinces have sought exchange listings in the past few years. This is why China appears quite high on formal lists of MSP and diffusion indices, which obscures the blockholding reality of state control of most firms and the economy.

In parallel, the managers of these SOEs-in-transition, in league with other interested parties (usually local party politicians and bureaucrats who help corporatized the SOEs) have been enriching themselves at the expense of both the nominal state blockholders and the hapless minority investors. As a result, the state lacks the capacity and minority shareholders lack the means to monitor or discipline managers and their insider boards. In one sense, China resembles Russia, without the private oligarchs.

The reasons for this state of affairs lie in politics, whose features are well known. China remains a single-party autocracy, with the Communist Party defending its monopoly on political power, but is slipping gradually into soft authoritarianism. The party has reduced its use of general oppression (it is more selective now, although no less ferocious when challenged by new entrants such as Falun Gong) in a tacit deal with the Chinese people, who now have considerable latitude to organize their own affairs, including business affairs, as long as they leave organized politics to the party. Because the ideological legitimacy of the party has all but evaporated, its right to rule has increasingly turned on its ability to deliver the goods, literally, in terms of providing the background conditions for sustained economic growth and improved living conditions for most Chinese citizens.

Within the party itself, leadership transitions have gradually depersonalized power (from Mao Zedong to Deng Xiaoping to Jiang Zemin and, now, Hu Jintao). This trend makes the leadership more accountable, in an indirect manner, to the preferences of what Shirk (1993) terms the "selectorate"—the few thousand party functionaries at the provincial, city, and national levels; the central state organs (including the state security bureaus); and the People's Liberation Army. The Chinese selectorate has strong preferences for social peace and high economic growth.

Selling off minority shares in SOEs serves several purposes, as least in principle: to provide some degree of outside discipline over the SOEs, which managed to lose billions of yuan (as more SOEs do, East or West); to dilute responsibility for lay-offs from these firms when they do occur; and to raise hard cash as the Chinese government battles to raise revenue in the absence of a well-functioning tax system. Raising cash from outside minority investors (domestic or foreign) does requires at least a modicum of MSPs, starting from, essentially, zero. Thus, the Chinese government began to wrestle with the paradox already noted—how to introduce MSPs with one hand (by state fiat, in the absence of domestic political democracy) and reassure investors that they will not get expropriated with the other hand of the blockholding state oligarchy.

Indeed, in the pursuit of these economic goals, the Chinese government must seek a credible commitment of self-restraint to reassure investors, both Chinese and foreign. Thus, China runs a number of systems in parallel: a core of state-controlled firms (with state as blockholder), another set under partial state control, yet another set with a more distant state role, and a very few almost private. The mechanisms of supervision are complex; ownership patterns and formal rules do not fully capture the role of party- and centrally appointed officials and the capacity of many forms of regulation outside the realm of corporate and securities law that matter. "[S]ome observers have dismissed China's two stock markets in Shanghai and Shenzhen as Potemkin villages. It is perhaps more accurate to refer to them as the tip of the iceberg, that is, as the shiny visible pyramid atop a huge murky mass of informal credit relations" (Naughton 2000, 158; see also Oi and Walder 1999).

In steps toward clearer MSPs, the government formed the China Securities Regulatory Commission and required all listed Chinese firms to adopt Chinese Accounting Standards, replacing an older system focused on monitoring state-owned firms for tax and planning purposes rather than for investment and managerial decision making. The Ministry of Finance retained control over the setting and interpretation of accounting standards (Foley 1998). Despite some official language about directors' responsibility for protecting the rights of shareholders, in fact the supervisory committee of Chinese firms continues to function as a rubber-stamp for the board of managing directors, who are, in turn, all insiders, appointed by the Party, and usually government employees (Xu and Wang 1997).

The rules on voting rights and contests of control profess to protect minority investors, but disclosure, notification, and voting procedures make it difficult in practice for minority shareholders to exercise those nominal rights. Shares held by minority shareholders are placed in a different class with regard to ownership rights than are shares held by state entities. In addition, external and foreign ownership caps effectively rule out the prospect of contests for the control of SOEs.

There are some performance contracts for senior managers, but these are subject to political intervention. Overwhelmingly, Chinese managers are compensated and selected in a manner that ensures their first loyalty is to the state (at least, their first loyalty after looking after themselves and their families) and little loyalty, if any, is to the interests of minority shareholders (Li 2000). But it is likely (although we have few ways of measuring it) that managers' enrichment at the expense of the state (and minority shareholders) has come overwhelmingly from insider transactions involving self-dealing, assets-stripping, and the usual panoply of methods available to managers with poor supervision, corrupt government authorities, and the absence of a monitoring blockholder or institutional investor to keep them honest.

Not all managers of Chinese firms, public or private, are corrupt; nor are their party and state overseers. The system encourages a graduated process of change, to make the politics of adjustment manageable. Many party officials (high and low) undoubtedly see corporatization of the SOEs, and the corporate governance reforms associated with them, as essential to the maintenance of the current regime, as a way to gradually wean these firms from the state, and thus from corruption and mismanagement more generally.

Weak MSPs are part of the investment equation. Individual Chinese investors, with few alternative investment vehicles, may well prefer shares in a corporatized SOE, no matter how poorly run, with dubious MSPs to their only alternatives— cash under the mattress or deposits in the state-owned banking sector.

Foreign institutional investors may also be dubious about the MSPs, but, as in Korea and in Malaysia, the upside is buying into a large economy whose growth prospects are widely believed to range between 8 and 10 percent per annum for the foreseeable future. Rapid growth in firms' aggregate revenues and in earnings can offset many sins, including an expropriation "tax" to corrupt officials and venal managers. These global investors can also reap the portfolio-diversification gains from holdings in overseas stock markets.

The most powerful investment protector is the desire of the Chinese government for stability and growth, to maintain power at home and to project it abroad. Even though it has the capacity to expropriate investors, it must restrain itself. The party pays careful attention to public opinion; signs of unrest among workers, peasants, and pensioners; complaints from urban workers and SOE employees; and, finally, to some degree, the confidence of investors. It does these things in ways that do not look like an OECD democracy and cannot be measured by those institutional indicators.

In sum, China falls midway on a continuum, somewhat more committed to the market than North Korea and Myanmar, and thus with more concern for investor confidence and corporate governance issues, but with fewer restraints on expropriation than in Russia. There is less institutional restraint on its powers than in the advanced industrial democracies and less than in the fully competitive electoral democracies or the mixed regimes of the region.

Singapore: Transparent Governance and Authoritarianism

Singapore is a fascinating case of average ownership concentration, very high MSP, and a soft authoritarian political system (Gourevitch and Shinn 2005, 199–203). How does this balance work? Preferences for corporate governance have changed among the political elite in Singapore, and the state has driven through a set of top-down reforms that resulted in relatively high shareholder protections. Good governance, including economic good governance and especially good corporate governance, happens because it is one of the keys to sustaining legitimacy for what remains essentially a one-party state. It demonstrates the ability of the Singapore government to deliver the goods by providing the highest income levels in Southeast Asia. The formal political institutions in Singapore have changed very little, as in China, with Senior Minister Lee Kuan Yew (and now his son Lee Hsien Loong as prime minister) in control of the parliament, the judiciary, and the organs of executive government since 1959 through the People's Action Party.

At the same, transparency in corporate governance is a monitoring mechanism that allows the government to discipline managers and civil servants and thus avoid the type of corruption and incumbent abuse that usually develops in one-party states. Diffusion via high MSP also prevents the emergence of a potentially dangerous political challenger in the form of a successful and rich blockholder, as happens in other countries.

The Singapore pension system creates the potential for political support for good corporate governance. With growing pension assets, shareholders may want protections, but the democratic processes needed to translate demand into reality are missing because the Singapore rubber-stamp parliament does not provide much direct accountability to its citizens. Nor is there a competitive market for financial services whereby money managers have an incentive to monitor and discipline listed firms in which they invest. The bulk of the Singapore citizens' equity holdings are managed by the Central Provident Fund and Temasek, both virtually branches of the Ministry of Finance. As a result, the government itself is the principal watchdog for ensuring MSPs in Singapore-listed firms. This helps explain the outlier position of Singapore in the comparative data; it has more blockholding than its high ranking on the MSP index predicts.

The weight of private blockholders in Singapore is 45 percent, similar to the mean of the overall sample, above the Asian mean, but typical of other Southeast Asian countries. Family-controlled firms, usually diversified across industries and with deep roots in the Southeast Asian region, exist alongside large corporatized SOEs, the legacy of the rapid industrialization program in Singapore, some of them world-scale listed enterprises, such as Singapore Airlines (Claessens, Djankov, and Lang 2002). As in Malaysia, these firms were privatized during the 1980s and 1990s; several became world-class, extremely well-run firms.

The corporatized SOEs have led the way in adopting good governance practices and enhanced MSPs, with the family firms then complying, somewhat reluctantly, as they are poked and prodded by the regulatory authorities to follow suit. A large number of international high-tech firms have local operations or regional headquarters in Singapore, which has provided a strong learning effect for governance practices.

Singapore has high levels of MSPs, 89 out of 100 on the comparison index, almost double the mean value for the sample overall. The Singapore Generally Agreed Accounting Principles are functionally equivalent to the IAS. All companies in Singapore are required by law to be audited by approved auditors, who in turn must hold a practicing certificate issued by the Public Accountants Board (the regulator). Oversight institutions in Singapore are reasonably fair in protecting the interests of minority investors, and the listing rules of the Singapore Stock Exchange (SSE) include Non Executive Directors (NEDs) on all boards of public firms. Like France, Singapore has a cadre of professional manager-bureaucrats that moves back and forth between the public and private sectors, and many of these individuals can be found on the boards of both private and privatized SOEs on the SSE. Singapore law imposes a strong fiduciary duty on directors, and these are backed up by a court system that is generally fair and fast in cases of financial disputes.

By the same token, Singapore company law provides for a one share–one vote rule, and the Voluntary Code on Takeovers is similar in most respects to the UK City Code and is, by most accounts, reasonably effective in protecting minority rights during changes of control. Contests for control are rare, due to the remaining regulatory caps on foreign ownership (although these are in the process of being removed), the large presence of private blockholders (around 60 percent), the state exercise of informal guidance regarding merger and acquisition (M&A) transactions, and the preponderant position of the state as an institutional investor through Temasek. The market for managers in Singapore is competitive by international standards; the quality is generally high, with quite a bit of turnover and extensive use of incentive compensation, among the highest in the sample. Approximately half of the listed firms on the SSE have a stock option plan.

The government state-controlled pension funds are the largest single investor in the SSE. There are now 3 million beneficiaries with claims on a total $50 billion in assets. In addition, the investment arm of the Ministry of Finance, Temasek, holds an estimated 21 percent of the total Singapore equity market capitalization, including a controlling share in the large corporatized SOEs already noted. The state also holds an estimated $100 billion in offshore assets, including a large block of equity.

The Singapore large net external asset pool, in effect, transformed the state into a large foreign portfolio investor, with similar preferences for improved minority investor protections around the world. Temasek professes a strong corporate governance policy, akin to those of activist institutional investors in the United States, with similar policies with regard to accounting and audit, including the use of economic value-added performance criteria, independent board oversight, and executive compensation.

Singapore politics is centrally controlled. The dominant party directly has it hands on two-thirds of the elected seats in the eighty-three-seat unicameral legislature and strictly controls the rules for electioneering. It is no surprise, therefore, that efforts to enhance shareholder protections stem from the executive and not from the parliament; these are top-down, not bottom-up, reforms.

As with China, Singapore provides a challenge for purely institutionalist interpretations of corporate governance. Concentrated political power and weak formal limits on the government should, according to the dominant view in finance analysis, inhibit investment and growth. What actually happens is that the government curbs political freedoms but encourages economic freedom. To do so, it creates a voluntary restraint; it commits itself to not acting in ways corporate actors find arbitrary. Their guarantee is an assumption that the government seeks to preserve itself through prosperity. There is the possibility of a breakdown. Institutions do not prevent this; only self-restraint does. A government in Singapore has the power to interfere if ever it chooses to do so.

Malaysia: Ethnicity and Democracy in Governance Politics

Malaysia has been a striking case in the importance of politics shaping the response to the Asian financial crisis. Mahathir's political skills in the complex system of ethnic and institutional mixture gave him the leverage, as Thomas Pepkinsky (chap. 11 in this volume) notes, to make the most assertive national response to the

IMF demands. Mahathir moved swiftly to stabilize the economy with currency controls. Malaysia recovered faster than Indonesia, but it has it has not been growing as fast in recent years as before the crisis.

Equity ownership is comparatively widespread (the result of a deep pension plan). Malaysia has high MSPs, a high 52 percent ratio of private pension assets to GDP, and also substantial ownership concentration. Most private blockholders are ethnic Chinese in a body politic controlled by ethnic Malays, the numerical majority, leaving a foundation for tension that has been, mostly, managed successfully. These ingredients create the foundations for broad popular support for MSPs and corporate governance reforms. The large accumulation of domestic capital in Malaysia has made foreign portfolio investors relatively less important in capital market development. As a result, like Chile, domestic private blockholders have entered only slowly into an alliance with these external investors. Malaysia also exhibits the problem of credible commitment to MSPs when the government is a harsh, hard democracy with sometimes questionable allegiance to the rule of law.

The Malaysian weight of private blockholders in total market capitalization is 42.6, slightly below the mean of the sample as a whole, although higher than the average emerging market. Most private blockholders in Malaysia are ethnic Chinese families, with their roots in a wide variety of mining, trade, and financial activities, each with a classic founder-entrepreneur and with active family participation in management. Over the last 50 years of rapid economic growth in Malaysia, some of these have grown into complex networks of firms, such as the Kwok family group, typically a diversified industrial group, sometimes with a house bank (controlled by the blockholder, often indirectly), with close ties across the Association of Southeast Asian Nations (ASEAN) region and investments in China. This pattern reflected a classic oligarchical approach to corporate governance; outside investors were barely tolerated, used as a source of cash but kept largely in the dark. Hired-hand managers and employees were just that—employees, with no voice in governance.

As in many countries, the growth of these firms in terms of scale, complexity, and, important for a relatively small economy such as Malaysia, their international operations led to a gradual transition from oligarchy to greater diffusion. Family members retained control and key management positions, but outsiders were brought inside the tent to help run firm. Despite their frequently opaque financial reporting and susceptibility to insider manipulation, many of these firms became the darlings of foreign portfolio investors, who saw them as an opportunity to participate in the high-growth opportunities provided by the Four Tigers.

The Malaysian pension system is in good condition, due to the farsighted forced savings scheme of the Employees Provident Fund (EPF). Beneficiaries of the EPF receive a detailed summary of their portfolio and the relative performance of the fund on a regular basis. The EPF rapidly became the largest financial institution in Malaysia and continued to occupy that position throughout the high-growth period from the 1970s to the 1990s. By 2002, the EPF had accumulated total assets of ringgit 191.6 billion ($50 billion), accounted for 17 percent of national savings, and held two-thirds of the total government fixed-income debt instruments. More important, the EPF also holds 21 percent of its assets in equities, largely domestic, making EPF the biggest player in the Malaysian stock market. This gave virtually all Malaysian workers a vital interest in the corporate governance of Malaysian firms.

The EPF was periodically tainted by scandals surrounding subsidies to *bumiputra* firms and other *bumi* control transactions, which sometimes involved bribes and dubious political contributions, but, on the whole, it maintained a reputation for honest and reasonably competent investment management. It maintained a relatively passive approach to corporate governance of the firms in which it invested until the late 1990s, stimulated in part by large losses associated with the Asian financial crisis, which hit the Malaysian stock market hard and rapidly engaged the Malaysian government.

Malaysia can be classified as a hard democracy with strong centralizing institutions. The Malaysian government has been dominated by an ethnic Malay coalition since independence in the 1950s. This government pursued a policy of fostering ethnic Malay (or *bumiputra*) blockholders by means of preferential lending, transfers of SOE assets, and other subsidies.

Until his resignation, Prime Minister Mahathir wielded effective control of the policy through his control over the United Malays National Organization (UMNO), which worked in a coalition of smaller ethnic parties. Despite this coalition structure, Malaysia has few veto points, in contrast with Thailand, which lies at the other end of the continuum with many veto points, and the Philippines, which falls in between them but closer to Thailand in terms of the hurdles that governments face in implementing policy reforms (MacIntyre 2001; Hicken 2002). Although Thailand also has a multiparty system, there the parties fight during elections and form volatile coalitions afterward. In contrast, in Malaysia the parties divide the electoral map among themselves before each the election to avoid competing with each. The Barisan Nasional coalition is thus best understood as a unitary actor, or single party, in which the crucial battles are fought not among the parties of the coalition but within the UMNO.

In the wake of the Asian financial crisis, the Malaysian state began a renewed program of enhanced MSPs, promoted as a top-down reforms. These reforms frequently pointed a finger at the governance sins of private blockholders, often a code word for the Chinese. The Kuala Lumpur media (closely monitored by the state) reveled in lurid exposures of insider transactions and self-enrichment by blockholders, which, it was implied, had led to the moral hazard losses associated with the Asian financial crisis. This reflected a conscious argument by the Malaysian government that it had been an example of fiscal rectitude during the late 1990s and that, therefore, the crisis must be laid on the shoulders of evil blockholders and greedy foreign investors.

The top-down reform project began with a High Level Finance Committee on Governance established by the Ministry of Finance in March 1998, which unleashed a series of regulatory changes through the Securities Commission, the Kuala Lumpur Stock Exchange (KLSE), and the Registrar of Companies.

These changes led to the creation of a Malaysian Corporate Governance Code, the Malaysian Institute of Corporate Governance, and the Minority Shareholder Watchdog Group—each of which had strong participation by representatives from the EPF. The motive for these changes was to reassure investors, both domestic and international, to hold and attract capital. Domestic groups had the usual response; blockholders did not like being challenged, yet domestic investors (including the EPF) wanted protections enforced.

As a result, Malaysian shareholder protections climbed to high levels, 67 on our index, placing it well above the total mean of 45 and in the top 5 percent of the distribution. Malaysian information institutions became robust in their MSPs, with important changes concerning the accounting system. Oversight remains a problem because of strong family control of boards. The obligations of directors have begun to be monitored by the Government Minority Shareholder Watchdog Committee, and the courts began to entertain derivative suits for breach of this duty, although class-action suits are not possible. The Malaysian control rules enforced a one share–one vote rule and ensured that minority shareholders have at least a nominal voice in key corporate decisions. The Malaysia Code of Takeovers and Mergers was revised in 1999 to resemble the UK City Code in most respects.

Privatized SOEs account for a sizable portion of the KLSE market cap, thus lowering the weight of private blockholders. These SOEs served as a vessel for implementing schemes for *bumiputra* advancement, as well as garden-variety corruption and a convenient money pot through which to pursue industrial structure (such as the Proton national car) or regional development goals that were important to politicians. The workers (especially *bumiputra* workers, who had hiring preferences in the SOEs) in these firms saw their interests aligned with those of managers—especially *bumiputra* managers—in these firms and not necessarily with those of the faceless minority shareholders.

Shareholder issues enter into intraparty factional disputes to punish party defectors and or cut off financial backers in bitterly contested federal or state elections. For example, several prominent *bumiputra* backers of former Finance Minister Anwar Ibrahim were charged with corporate malfeasance when Anwar was jailed and his political supporters scattered. Domestic and foreign minority shareholders were not encouraged by these examples of government fidelity to good corporate governance when the underlying motives were transparent; and worse behavior was tolerated by other owners and managers who stood (at least temporarily) in better political graces.

Conclusion: Strong States and Permissive Protections

These four countries highlight the direct relationship between political processes and corporate governance choices. Where political systems were politically open and political coalitions changed substantially, as in Korea, policy outcomes changed to reflect the rise and decline of preferences by various groups. In the other countries, preferences by key actors underwent some change in response to shifts in the economy, leading to some change in policy. Overall, corporate governance in the region shows more formal protection of minority investors and some modest behavioral change as well.

The connection among political process, institutions, and economic policy outcomes is not simple. The absence of strong constitutional authority generally seems to favor blockholding over shareholder diffusion as an instrument of corporate governance. Democratic countries vary in the extent of shareholder diffusion, but the nondemocratic ones all have blockholding. Internal mechanisms of supervision, bonding, and control, based on dense networks of relationships, make more senses when external regulatory processes are weak. Adopting formal rules and procedures of transparency is insufficient to provide the guarantees investors want to accept minority shareholder positions. It takes far more extensive political change to support the transplants of codes (Berkowitz, Pister, and Richard 2003).

It is possible to reassure some investors with a variety of techniques. Singapore is able to make credible commitments to investors that substantial property rights will be protected because the political necessity of prosperity to its rulers is so clear. China, Malaysia, and Korea, in varying ways, do the same. MacIntyre's (2001) exploration of the U-shaped curve of the trade-off between efficacy and predation is again most useful in explaining these outcomes. Majoritarian countries such as Malaysia show decisive action, but this may also leave some fear of predation from a government with too much potential power. In weaker democracies (Philippines, Thailand, and Indonesia), the absence of authority leaves another kind of fear, with a similar result in private bonding solutions.

The other relationship to note concerns preferences and coalitions. What kinds of interest-group alignments produce pro–diffusion policies? Shareholder protections in authoritarian regimes require a strong interest by that regime in foreign investment and in private initiatives. China needs investors, but its huge domestic market gives it substantial bargaining leverage toward external investors; it bargains with them to play by Chinese rules concerning technology. In neither Malaysia nor China is there enough democratic politics at work to explore coalitions operating through parliamentary means.

Korea is a good case for comparison because democratization regularizes the checks and balances on the government. Other countries in East Asia have experienced some steps toward democratization; Thailand (until the coup against Thaksin in 2006), the Philippines, Indonesia, and Taiwan have all experienced increased democratization. A fuller country comparison would seek to measure the impact of these partial reforms in political institutions on corporate governance reforms. The logic of inquiry here predicts that greater democratization leads to more transparency in corporate governance; undermining the oligarchy on one side undermines the oligarchy on the other. This does not mean that either the political system or the governance system will converge to look exactly like the United States but, instead, that both will change to some form different from the oligarchic forms of the past. The crisis itself influenced the outcomes by its impact on institutions and preferences. Over time, we could continue to see the rippling effects that the crisis has on demand for change inside each country, among the external pressure groups (foreign capital and international agencies), and on the political institutions and processes that respond to shifting demands.

Do these countries differ in their vulnerability to a future regional financial crisis? In some ways, national and international decision makers have certainly learned lessons and taken some precautions about the most obvious trigger points, such as the liquidity crunch; but the next crisis is likely to be different in some unexpected way. If the next crisis is as expected, policymakers and markets are already correcting for the trigger points. But the unexpected is what detonates storms, and there, countries differ in the various forms of resilience they have: economic (diversification), financial (tougher reporting and transparency), regulatory (rules and structures), and political (responsive to demands). The countries of the region are likely to differ in how they trade off among quick action, preserving the safety net, equality, and long-term growth. Will the most open political systems handle things better? So far, China presses against such a resolute conclusion, its being the most closed of the countries in our sample and the most resilient. South Korea was the most open and hit turbulence. We can project, however, that if countries continue to make their economies more responsive to market signals, the older abilities to contain shocks will diminish and new mechanisms of continuous response and adaptation may prove stronger. We certainly need to continue to work on better categories: evolving versions of an Asian model, different sorts of investors with varying goals, different sorts of markets and technologies with varying requirements, and varying institutional structures and political processes. We will continue to feel pressure in trying to make generalizations and find patterns in the mass of ever more complex detail.

CHAPTER 5

Democratization, Crisis, and the Changing Social Contract in East Asia

Stephan Haggard

The last decade has seen an outpouring of scholarship on the political economy of the East Asian welfare state.[1] This research was initially preoccupied with
the following set of stylized facts on the early period of high growth. In contrast
to other regions, the newly industrializing Asian countries exhibited a pattern of
shared growth, with rapidly rising real incomes, falling poverty, and low to moderate levels of income inequality. An important policy component of this record
was investment in human capital, both through efficient public education systems
and through a variety of vocational training initiatives.[2] Yet governments appeared
averse to the provision of social insurance and redistributive transfers. Subsequent
work has shown that the low level of spending on social insurance holds even when
controlling for a variety of standard determinants, including level of development
(Yang 2006; Rudra 2007; Haggard and Kaufman in press, chap. 1). Despite rising

This chapter is adapted from Stephan Haggard and Robert Kaufman (in press, chap. 6). The research
was supported by the National Science Foundation under Grant no. 0351439 and by the Chiang-ching
Kuo Foundation. The author thanks Jennifer Barrett, Barak Hoffman, and Tanya Lloyd for research assistance and Teri Caraway, Tun-jen Cheng, Peter Gourevitch, Paul Hutchcroft, Byung-kook Kim, Yeun-
wen Ku, Amado Mendoza, John Ravenhill, Nita Rudra, Hokeun Song, and Joseph Wong for comments
on earlier versions. Jinhee Choung provided important insights on the politics of labor market reform.
    1. Comparative efforts to understand social welfare policy in Asia include Dixon and Kim (1985),
but the contributions in Goodman, White, and Kwon (1998) were the first to make the links to the
European literature and offer a theoretical approach. See also Ramesh (2000, 2004); Holliday (2000);
Tang (2000); Gough (2001); Holliday and Wilding (2003); Haggard (2004, 2005). Important country and
comparative monographs include Ku (1997); Kwon (1999b); Aspalter (2002); Wong (2005).
    2. See, however, the skeptical view in Booth (1999).

incomes, public pensions and health insurance were minimal, provided on a defined contribution basis, or characterized by relatively narrow coverage. Unemployment insurance and other forms of social assistance were also small in scope and generosity or lacking altogether.

Just as this literature was taking shape, the region began to democratize. Four countries underwent regime changes prior to the Asian financial crisis: the Philippines (1986), Korea (1987), Thailand (with interruptions, beginning in the mid-1980s), and, more gradually, Taiwan. The Soeharto regime in Indonesia collapsed in the wake of the crisis in 1998. Among the middle-income countries affected by the crisis, Singapore and Malaysia remained semi-authoritarian holdouts.

Democratization had a powerful effect on the nature of the social contract. Despite outward-oriented development strategies and a steady increase in economic openness, factors associated with constraints on social policy commitments,[3] new democracies expanded social insurance and other entitlements, providing at least some support for the proposition that globalization and a robust social policy are not mutually exclusive. In the upper-income democracies of Korea and Taiwan, new entitlements included an expansion of pensions and of health and unemployment insurance, as well as new forms of social assistance. In Thailand and the Philippines, governments innovated or expanded social insurance programs and also focused new attention on persistent problems of rural poverty. The semi-democratic regimes, by contrast, saw much less innovation in this regard and exhibited greater continuity in their more minimalist social welfare models.[4]

A cross-national perspective on the Asian experience suggests that the effects of regime change were partly conditional on the economic circumstances in which democratization occurred. In contrast to the new democracies of Latin America or Eastern Europe, and with the important exception of the Philippines, growth in Asia was robust until the regional financial crisis of 1997–98. New democratic governments also enjoyed strong fiscal positions (figure 5.1). The effects of democratization, thus, must be placed in the context of strong economic performance and government finances. A comparison of the expansive posttransition social policy in the high-growth cases of Korea, Taiwan, and Thailand and the ongoing fiscal constraints on social policy in the Philippines makes these differences clear.

If the effects of democracy on social policy were at least partly contingent on robust growth, the Asian financial crisis of 1997–98 was a rude shock. Two of the new democracies—Korea and Thailand—were among the most-severely affected in the region; both experienced severe contractions in output and were dependent on large International Monetary Fund (IMF) programs as well. The literature on the Asian financial crisis has generally seen the Philippines and Taiwan as exceptions,

---

3. On the demands of an export-oriented growth strategy, see Deyo (1989); Adsera and Boix (2000); Haggard and Kaufman (in press, chap. 1).
4. For a characterization of the liberal welfare model in Singapore and Hong Kong, see, particularly, Ramesh (2004).

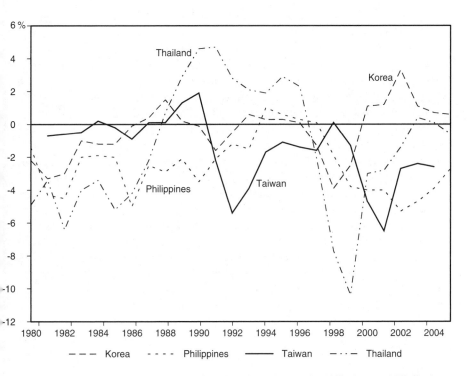

Figure 5.1 Budget balance as a share of GDP in Taiwan, Korea, the Philippines, and Thailand, 1980–2004.

as countries that escaped the regional contagion (see, e.g., Haggard 2000, chap. 3). However, this is true only if compared to the very deep crises in the more seriously affected countries. In the Philippines, the recovery of the Fidel Ramos years ground to a halt in 1998; growth fell from 5.2 percent in 1997 to –0.5 percent in 1998. Despite recovery thereafter, successive Philippine governments have struggled with an almost secular decline in revenue. Taiwan appeared to suffer little more than a slight slowdown in growth during 1998. But this slowdown came on the back of important structural changes in the economy and an outright recession followed in 2001 when GDP contracted by 2 percent. In sum, all four countries have experienced lower and more volatile growth in the decade since 1996 than they did in the decade before it.

Crises have mixed effects on social policy. On the one hand, recession, unemployment, and the informalization of labor markets generate immediate pressures on governments to alleviate distress and to institutionalize more permanent protections against insecurity. On the other hand, social protections in developing countries are typically inadequate to serve the role of automatic stabilizers that they play in the advanced industrial states. To the contrary, fiscal policy in developing countries—and its social policy component—often displays a perverse pro-cyclical pattern (see, in particular, Wibbels 2006). Moreover, the effects of fiscal constraints typically go beyond the immediate limits they place on spending. Crises typically strengthen the hands of technocrats seeking a rationalization or liberalization of social policy commitments and weaken the hand of those committed to increased spending, wider coverage, and the inclusion of new groups.

For the most part, the developing countries of East Asia escaped this pattern. Political support for new entitlements was broad. Moreover, recovery from the crisis was relatively swift. Outside of the Philippines, the crisis did not take place in the context of structural budget deficits or long-standing and highly elaborated social insurance commitments. The new democratic social contracts not only proved compatible with a high degree of economic openness, but were robust even in the face of severe economic shocks.

However, this relatively positive finding with respect to the relationship among economic openness, shocks, and the social contract demands one potentially important qualification, and that has to do with developments in the labor market. As we would expect, democratization in Asia was generally associated with an improvement in *collective* labor rights, such as the right to organize;[5] however, both short-term and longer-term economic circumstances placed increasing pressure on *individual* labor rights. These battles were fought around issues such as the ability of firms to dismiss, the conditions of dismissal, outsourcing, and a variety of regulatory issues surrounding the use of temporary labor contracts, including for foreign workers.

The crisis had an immediate effect on labor markets across the region, increasing unemployment and leading to an expansion of the informal sector. But the crisis also generated pressures from the international financial institutions, foreign investors, and domestic firms to reduce employment protections enjoyed by at least some formal-sector workers. This pressure arose in the context of privatization, in the context of ad hoc restructuring of particular enterprises, and through a more general effort to change labor market regulations to permit greater flexibility. These developments were not simply cyclical in nature. Increased economic openness and corresponding structural changes in industry had generated pressures on labor markets for some time prior to the crisis. These pressures suggest a somewhat more complicated political story about the emergence of unemployment insurance and new forms of social assistance. There is evidence that these policy innovations can be traced to electoral constraints and labor influence, in the context of underlying changes in the nature of Asian labor markets.

The remainder of this chapter explores these issues through two paired comparisons. The two first-generation, newly industrializing countries, Taiwan and Korea, had relatively large industrial sectors at the outset of their political transitions, still

---

5. Although Teri Caraway (2002) argues that the right to strike is a partial—and important—exception.

significant but rapidly declining agricultural sectors, and relatively egalitarian income distributions with low levels of absolute poverty (table 5.1). Korea experienced a very profound crisis in 1997–98, but Taiwan also experienced a slowdown in growth and a short, sharp recession in 2002. Both of these countries, but particularly Korea, also faced strong pressures to maintain or increase the flexibility of the labor market.

Like Taiwan and Korea, Thailand and the Philippines also share a number of features that make a pairwise comparison plausible. The two countries had a nearly identical share of employment in industry, and although Thailand had a much larger share of the workforce in agriculture (68 percent), nearly half of all employment in the Philippines was in agriculture in 1985 as well. Both countries fell at the more unequal end of the Asian cases and had comparable levels of $1-a-day poverty (table 5.1). A noteworthy difference is that growth in Thailand prior to the crisis was much more robust and fiscal circumstances were more favorable. Moreover, although the Philippines is often portrayed as escaping the financial crisis, its lower level of income made the poor highly vulnerable to the recession in 1998.

An important determinant of the demand for both pensions and health care is the demographic profile (table 5.2). The more developed countries in the region show a more marked aging trend that has been a leitmotif of the social policy literature. At the time of their democratic transitions, however, the proportion of the aged did not differ substantially across countries and therefore would not, on its own, constitute an obvious explanation for policy differences with respect to pensions and health.

Table 5.1 Development, economic structure, inequality, and poverty, 1985

	GDP per capita (constant)	GDP per capita (PPP)	Share of workforce in industry	Share of workforce in agriculture	Gini coefficient	$1 per day poverty, 1985
Korea	5,322	5,750	29.5	24.9	34.5	<5 (1984)
Philippines	974	3,266	13.8	49.6	46.1	23 (1984)
Taiwan	7,530[a]	8,000[b]	41.6	17.5	29.2	<2 (est.)
Thailand	1,329	2,751	12.1	68.4	47.4 (1986)	25 (1988)

Source: World Bank (n.d.).
[a] In 1996 dollars.
[b] In 1997 dollars, estimate.

Table 5.2 Aging in Asia: share of population over 65

	1985	1995	2005	2015	2025
Korea	4.3	5.7	8.5	11.5	17.3
Philippines	3.4	3.5	4.0	4.9	6.7
Taiwan	5.1	7.2	8.9	10.3	15.9
Thailand	4.3	5.4	7.5	9.8	13.9

Source: United Nations (2001).

Taiwan

Taiwan differed from the other East Asian democracies in having a long history of social insurance, but both coverage and benefits were limited. Political liberalization changed that. The Kuomintang (KMT) introduced a pilot program in 1985 to extend health insurance to farmers, an electorally important group excluded from the labor insurance scheme (Ku 1997, 82). The government also formed an executive task force in 1988 to investigate the creation of a single-payer national health insurance system (see Lin 1997; Son 2001; Aspalter 2002; Wong 2003, 2005).[6]

In 1988, Lee Tenghui lifted martial law and allowed national-level electoral competition. In the 1991 National Assembly elections, the opposition Democratic Progressive Party (DPP) fared poorly by campaigning on a Taiwan independence platform (Rigger 2001, 125). Prior to the 1992 legislative Yuan elections, the first direct elections for all seats of the major legislative body, more centrist factions of the party sought to rectify this mistake by turning attention to public policy issues, including social welfare (Ku 2002, 159–60; Fell 2004).

The KMT drafted its own policy guidelines for social welfare in 1994. The guidelines struck a more conservative tone than the DPP white paper (Ku 2002, 161), but the KMT accelerated the introduction of its national health program in anticipation of the 1995 legislative elections. The program marked a clear expansion of coverage, which went from 57 percent of the population on the eve of its introduction to over 95 percent within two years of its initiation. Even though Taiwan did not experience substantial difficulties during the financial crisis of 1997–98, emerging fiscal problems did produce efforts to rationalize the new social insurance system through the introduction of private insurers. This effort quickly fell victim to divisions within the bureaucracy, pressures from KMT legislators, and aggressive action by a broad social coalition of over two hundred NGOs (Wong 2003). Both the KMT government and its DPP successor delayed even minor adjustments in premiums until September 2002, and the KMT—now in opposition—sought to mobilize legislative, public, and labor opposition to the move (see, e.g., *Taipei Times*, August 28, 2002).

The national debate over pensions unfolded more slowly. The labor insurance system provided for a modest lump-sum pension payment (core KMT constituents such as civil servants and the military were covered under separate and much more generous systems). Coverage increased gradually during the 1980s, but in the early 1990s, fully a quarter of all people over sixty-five had no retirement income and the maximum payout was extremely modest (Chow 2001, 29; Chen 2004).

In the 1993 elections for mayors and county commissioners, several DPP candidates catapulted the pension issue onto the national stage by promising old-age

---

6. In addition to the benefits of a single-payer insurance system, cost control was to be achieved by a referral system that made primary care clinics important gatekeepers by the gradual introduction of global budgets and by a copay schedule related to the cost of different procedures.

allowances, in effect, a universal, noncontributory pension system. The KMT leadership berated the DPP proposal as blatant vote buying. But in 1997, the KMT candidate for country commissioner of Taipei introduced an old-age allowance proposal backed publicly by President Lee Tenghui. As Christian Aspalter argues, "Lee Teng-hui's proposal triggered a chain reaction in local politics. Other KMT candidates were forced by their voters to either propose similar plans... or to advocate a nation-wide old-age allowance system," which the president ultimately did (Aspalter 2002, 99).

In 2000, the DPP presidential candidate, Chen Shuibian ran successfully on a social welfare platform (the 333 Plan) that included elderly allowances (of NT$3000 per month), subsidized mortgages to first-time buyers (at 3 percent), and government-sponsored health care for children under three. The DPP also promised a national pension proposal after the KMT failed to legislate its own proposal. Consideration of these initiatives took place under quite different political and economic circumstances than those of the past. The new president faced a legislature controlled by a noncooperative opposition alliance (called the Pan-Blues), and the DPP was itself divided on the pension issue between more conservative and more progressive factions.[7] Deadlock ensued.

Economic conditions also changed. Even though Taiwan had survived the Asian financial crisis relatively unscathed, it experienced a sharp recession in 2001, a continual erosion of revenues, and widening budget deficits (figure 5.1). These economic conditions empowered conservatives and technocrats to speak against further social spending (see, e.g., *United Daily News*, April 17, 2001). The Chen government was forced to make overtures to the private sector, back away from its more ambitious national pension proposals, and seek hybrid formulas that would lessen government fiscal commitments. Nonetheless, the expansion of commitments continued. In mid-2001, even as the recession was becoming apparent, the Chen administration forwarded legislation for a nationwide monthly pension for those not covered under the existing system.[8] In 2004, the government succeeded in passing a reform that shifted from an employee-specific nonportable defined-contribution benefit plan to a portable defined-contribution scheme centrally monitored by the government.

Reflecting their reliance on business support and the cross-class nature of their electoral base, both the DPP and KMT initially opposed unemployment insurance. But after 1996, unemployment started to increase, jumping sharply in the recession of 2001 and not declining significantly thereafter. Moreover, unemployment was clearly not cyclical—the Taiwan economy continued to grow, even through the crisis—but structural, reflecting an accelerated outmigration of labor-intensive

---

7. Groups within the DPP believed that the KMT social insurance approach was too conservative and proposed a variety of alternatives, from full-blown tax-financed systems to social insurance systems with greater subsidy components than those proposed by the KMT.

8. The new amendment allowed those already drawing pensions—including government workers—to also avail themselves of this program, and the old-age allowances for farmers were increased 33 percent on the grounds of equalizing benefits to the military and teachers!

manufacturing to China and elsewhere in Asia. In 1998, the KMT passed a modest unemployment insurance scheme and a battery of other policies to assist job-seekers: business loans, allowances for training, and direct subsidies to employers. In the wake of the 2001 recession and substantial protests mobilized by the KMT (which had previously opposed it), the DPP government dramatically expanded unemployment insurance to cover firms with as few as four workers as well as part-time employees. The administration developed both short-term ameliorative mea-sures (such as a major public works programs announced in late 2002) and expanded prior-active labor market policies, increased subsidies to firms hiring unemployed workers, and began a phased reduction in the number of foreign workers.[9]

Despite its ability to navigate through the Asian financial crisis, by 2006 Taiwan was witnessing classic debates over labor market policy that were visible in Korea as well. On the one hand, the relocation of manufacturing jobs to China and other lower-wage locations was resulting in permanent job losses in manufacturing, slug-gish employment and real-wage growth, and increasing informalization of the labor market. On the other hand, employers used these pressures, as well as rising social insurance costs and the introduction of new social insurance legislation, as a reason for holding the line on hiring and wage increases and maintaining or even increas-ing labor market flexibility. Labor-intensive sectors such as textiles and apparel con-tinued to lobby aggressively to maintain access to foreign labor. The share of foreign workers in the workforce had risen sharply in the second half of the 1990s, peaking at 3.3 percent in 2000 but with restrictions following the onset of the recession. In 2003, the government initiated reforms that increased the ability of firms to use dis-patched workers; these workers directly reduced costs to the firm because pension, health insurance, and severance pay requirements are managed by the dispatching agency. Moreover, dispatched workers effectively fell outside the unemployment insurance system because periods of not working are considered voluntary, a per-fect example of how new protections can coexist with new labor market risks and pressures on individual labor rights.

South Korea

Democracy also had a clear and identifiable effect on the expansion of social insur-ance in Korea. As in Taiwan, the social insurance system inherited from the au-thoritarian era was a fragmented and highly unequal one. The Chun Doo Hwan administration expanded the system incrementally by allowing the formation of quasi-public insurance societies or health funds that pooled risk narrowly on an

---

9. The government has allowed firms in certain sectors to hire foreign workers, but they must pay into a vocational stabilization fund that is then used for a variety of passive and active labor market purposes. Also, the hiring of foreign labor is limited to firms of a certain size, and these restrictions are periodically adjusted depending on labor market conditions.

occupational basis (Kwon 2002, 2003). Farmers, the self-employed, and the urban informal sector remained outside the system, leaving total coverage at the end of his administration at about 50 percent.[10] In 1986, as the political battle was joined to define the nature of the transition from authoritarian rule,[11] the Chun administration announced an expansion of health coverage, as well as a national pension scheme and the introduction of a minimum wage. Roh Tae Woo integrated these social policy initiatives into his campaign platform and, after winning a narrow plurality, extended health coverage to the rural and urban self-employed through an expansion and partial subsidization of the funds to cover the previously uninsured (Kwon 2003, 78).[12]

The new pension law passed in 1988 extended coverage to all firms with ten or more workers (lowered to five workers in 1992) through a funded scheme with a mildly redistributive structure.[13] Benefits were kept at a very high level—a replacement rate of 70 percent after forty years—and as a result, the program had financial weaknesses from the outset.[14] Kim Young Sam (1993–98) made further expansion of the pension system part of his election campaign and, in 1995, extended coverage to farmers as compensation for Korean commitments to open the rice market (Yang 2000, 115).

The final component of the new social insurance system was the introduction of unemployment insurance. The Chun administration was actively hostile to unemployment insurance on the grounds of both cost and moral hazard. Nonetheless, policy entrepreneurs within the social policy bureaucracy developed and promoted a program designed to win support not only from labor, which initially lacked any concrete policy proposals on the topic, but from business and the economic technocrats as well (Yoo et al. 2002). Strategically renamed an employment insurance system, the proposal combined a mandatory unemployment insurance scheme with active labor market programs designed to secure wider support. All three major political parties incorporated variants of the proposal into their party platforms prior to the 1992 presidential elections and final legislation passed in 1993.

---

10. As elsewhere, the failure to include these groups can be traced in part to the administrative difficulty of reaching such workers and monitoring their income and contributions. But reluctance to expand coverage was also related to the reliance of the system on mandated employer and employee contributions and to the fiscal conservatism of the government. Farmers and informal-sector workers did not have employers who could match their contributions, and the government was unwilling to use tax receipts to this end.

11. Chun consistently maintained that he would step down at the end of his term in 1987, but sought to control the transition by calling for the indirect election of the president by bodies under his effective control.

12. Efforts by the opposition in the National Assembly to integrate the financial structure of the health insurance system by merging these funds, and thus permitting greater risk-pooling, was vetoed by the president; see Kwon (1999a, 65–67).

13. The initial proposal and the system adopted in 1988 consisted of a basic pension not related to income history and an earnings-related benefit.

14. Although these rates were set to rise gradually and were to be subject to periodic review, the mandated increases would not have left the pension program financially viable even in the medium run. In effect, the political process was simply deferred.

The presidential election that brought the Kim Dae Jung government to office in December 1997 occurred only a month following the onset of the financial crisis in Korea. The new administration faced an immediate dilemma with respect to labor. With a large share of the workforce in the formal sector, unemployment was higher than in the other countries affected by the crisis and there were fewer opportunities for the rural areas to serve as a shock-absorber for displaced urban workers. Although the overall level of unionization was low, the high degree of industrial concentration had resulted in fairly strong and militant unions in the larger enterprises.

But the administration was also under intense pressure from the IMF, the United States, and creditors to increase the flexibility of labor markets to facilitate the corporate restructuring process. To secure agreement to greater labor market flexibility, Kim Dae Jung resorted to a tripartite commission (Kim and Lim 1999). After weeks of intense debate, the government extracted an agreement from labor to permit lay-offs when urgently needed or in case of takeovers and to allow the formation of a worker leasing system for both specialized professions and laborers; as in Taiwan, dispatched workers played an increasing role in the labor market.

In return, the government promised a number of important political reforms of the system of industrial relations: the right for civil servants to form a labor consultative body and for teachers to unionize, and reversal of a long-standing prohibition on labor involvement in political activities. More vaguely, all parties would work to minimize lay-offs and seek alternative solutions such as work-sharing. Management believed it had gained greater freedom to retrench; labor believed that the terms of the bargain were not being enforced. Over the next year, the government intervened to break a number of strikes, leading the more independent Korean Confederation of Trade Unions to pull out of the second tripartite process in February 1999, effectively bringing the tripartite experiment to a close.

Despite the ambiguous reviews of the tripartite experiment, the government did honor its commitment to expand the social safety net. Some initiatives were temporary components of a gradual turn, with IMF acquiescence, to a counter-cyclical fiscal stance. In 1998, 10 percent of the national budget was allocated for short-term ameliorative measures of various sorts: a public works program that supported 437,000 workers by February of 1999; investments and labor subsidies for small and medium-size firms; temporary extension of unemployment benefits; a temporary livelihood program that covered 750,000 people by 1999; and scholarships for children of the unemployed.

But the Kim Dae Jung government response to the crisis was not just short term; rather, the government expanded coverage of all of the major social insurance programs—pensions, health insurance, and unemployment insurance—while fundamentally changing the principles guiding social assistance. With respect to pensions, the new government explicitly rejected reform proposals made at the end of the Kim Young Sam administration (Yang 2000). The administration sought to put the pension system on a sounder financial footing through regularly scheduled increases in both premiums and the retirement age and a new benefit formula that lowered the average replacement rate (from a relatively high 60 to 55 percent). Yet the plan rejected proposals to separate the redistributive from the earnings-related portion of the scheme and took the difficult step of extending coverage to the heterogeneous urban self-employed, a sector that included professionals such as doctors and lawyers as well as informal-sector workers.[15]

In the health sector, the administration had a mixed record. Efforts to control health-care costs by separating prescriptions and the dispensing of drugs and by reforming the payment system confronted stiff and effective resistance from providers, including a succession of crippling doctors' strikes (Kwon 2003). Nonetheless, the government did manage a major consolidation of the geographically based funds covering the rural areas and self-employed. Market-oriented economists wanted to use the funds to introduce more competition, but progressive academics, fund workers, and farmers' organizations pressed for the integration of the funds and wider-risk pooling (Kwon 2002). With physicians indifferent to the reform (because regulation, in any case, occurred at the national level) and business in a weakened position, the latter approach won out. In October 1998, the regional insurance societies and administration of the funds for public employees and teachers were subsumed into a National Health Insurance Corporation; the remaining company associations followed in July 2000.

With assistance from the World Bank and the Asian Development Bank, the Kim Dae Jung government expanded eligibility and coverage of its unemployment insurance (Korea Labor Institute 1999; Yoo et al. 2002). The administration effectively expanded mandatory unemployment insurance from firms with thirty or more employees to all firms, making it a universal program. These benefits were not particularly generous, and they retained productivist biases; benefits were only 70 percent of the minimum wage, which was itself just 25 percent of average earnings, and claiming benefits was tied to work and training requirements. Business support was also bought by coupling the unemployment insurance with wage subsidies that went straight to the bottom line of the firm. Nonetheless, no such protections had existed in Korea in the past. The change in principles associated with the new administration was even more clear in the reform of social assistance. The legislation of a National Basic Livelihood Security Law in 1998 used an income test to target the poor and allowed for cash benefits in addition to noncash assistance, resulting in a dramatic increase in eligibility for assistance and in spending on it. The country also came under close monitoring with respect to collective labor standards as a result of its membership in the Organisation for Economic Co-operation and Development (OECD) and undertook a number of reforms to bring national

15. Because it required the self-employed (and unemployed) to report their average income to determine the level of monthly premiums, there were strong incentives to underreport income. Formal-sector workers balked at their payroll taxes effectively subsidizing the self-employed. The government compromised by exempting a number of workers from paying, either because they could not pay (students and the military) or because payment was deferred due to unemployment or business failures. Salaried workers, meanwhile, feared that the inclusion of a large number of new subscribers would cause the fund to run out of money. All workers were concerned about plans to raise premiums from 3 to 9 percent.

legislation into conformity with both International Labour Organisation (ILO) and OECD expectations (Kim and Kim 2003).

The transition to democratic rule in Korea was associated with a quite dramatic change in social policy; interestingly, the first stages of this expansion were driven by conservative politicians seeking to offset their other political liabilities. The Kim Dae Jung government maintained the extension of benefits that occurred prior to the crisis and moved quickly to provide a social safety net and to initiate broader reforms of the social contract. These reforms expanded social insurance, changed the terms of social assistance, and allowed greater labor participation in both government and management decision making.

As in Taiwan, however, these gains in the range and de jure coverage of social protections came in the context of policy changes that increased the flexibility of labor markets. A curious feature of authoritarian rule in Korea was the existence of a relatively elaborate set of individual labor rights, enjoyed primarily by workers in the *chaebol* sector (Lee 2002). Dismissal was difficult and had to be justified through tripartite bodies overseen by the Ministry of Labor. The crisis was followed by important changes in the law governing dismissal—which could now be undertaken for "managerial" reasons—and a sharp increase in the role of contract or contingent workers, an outgrowth not only of the crisis itself but of legal changes introduced with the grand tripartite bargain of 1998. Contract workers replaced regular workers at some of the larger *chaebol* with little significant difference in terms of workload or duties but at wages that were substantially lower (Caraway 2002; Kim and Kim 2003, 356–57). Moreover, these contract workers were concentrated in smaller firms at which organization was low and collective bargaining limited. Jae-jin Yang has shown that the coverage of the major social insurance programs—pensions, health insurance, unemployment, and disability insurance—were effectively bounded by the inability or unwillingness of workers and management in these enterprises to make the required contributions (Yang 2006, 223).

As a result, the question of informalization has been one of the most important and contentious industrial relations issues in the country. As early as 2000, the Kim Dae Jung government was forced to revisit the problem of dispatched workers because of abuse of the terms of the 1998 agreement, particularly with respect to social insurance payments. Battles over protections for irregular workers continued into the Roh Moo Hyun administration. Although legislation passed in 2006 required firms to shift irregular workers to regular status after two years of employment, both employers and some unions recognized that the legislation could have the perverse consequence of increasing rather than reducing the share of informal workers as firms avoided longer-term contracts.

Thailand

As in Taiwan and Korea, social initiatives in Thailand were not a monopoly of opposition politicians and nongovernmental organizations (NGOs) (Heaver 2002).

The military initiated a number of antipoverty programs in line with a changed strategy toward the rural insurgency in the early 1980s, including a health card scheme that became a template for future health insurance initiatives (Samudavanija, Snitwongse, and Bunbongkarn 1990; Donaldson, Pannarunothai, and Tangcharoensathien 1999, chap. 5, 38–39; Pannarunothai et al. 2000, 303–11; Ramesh 2000, 104). Nonetheless, the politics of social policy changed quite dramatically in the mid-1980s. In 1983, a coalition of political parties defeated efforts by the military to maintain a number of political prerogatives, political competition became more open, and an influx of office-seeking provincial elites and businessmen transformed the political parties. In 1988, Prem was forced to call a general election that brought Chatichai Choonhaven, a retired general, to office as the first popularly elected prime minister. Almost immediately on taking office, Chatichai's cabinet endorsed a contributory social insurance scheme that provided health insurance and maternity and death benefits for workers in firms with twenty or more employees. The parliamentary bill also promised to introduce pensions and family allowances within six years and called on the king to introduce an unemployment scheme.

It is important to underline the modesty of this social insurance scheme when compared with those introduced in Korea and Taiwan; because Thailand was a largely rural country, Thai social policy focused largely on antipoverty efforts targeting the rural poor (Warr and Sartinsart 2004). In 1993, the social insurance system covered only 2.5 percent of the population, overwhelmingly urban and therefore overwhelmingly in Bangkok.[16] After the return to democracy in 1992, following a brief authoritarian interlude, however, the scheme continued to undergo incremental expansion by allowing the self-employed to join the system on a voluntary basis and by making contributions compulsory for firms with more than ten employees (Pannarunothai et al. 2000, table 8, 309). The health card system underwent a much more dramatic expansion after 1993 when the government moved to directly subsidize the purchase of health cards.[17] A series of initiatives in the early 1990s also expanded the scope of the Low Income Card Scheme, beginning with a Free Medical Care for the Elderly Scheme (1992) for those not covered under any other insurance program. On the eve of the financial crisis, the various targeted health card schemes provided at least some coverage to about 70 percent of the population (Supakankunti 2000).

As with health insurance, the pension system in Thailand has also been highly fragmented and expanded more slowly. The major public pension development for

16. Dependents were not included except for the maternity component of the scheme. The capitation approach to reimbursement meant that those covered did not have to make copayments, but it also required the insured to seek treatment only from hospitals to which they were registered by employers. As a result, beneficiaries often met their needs through out-of-pocket payments. See Tangcharoensathien, Supachutikul, and Letiendumrong (1999, 913–23).

17. This subsidy was undertaken with the assumption that costs would be recovered at the point of delivery, but, in fact, the cards ran a deficit; see Donaldson, Pannarunothai and Tangcharoensathien (1999, chaps. 5, 39).

private-sector workers was the introduction of the defined-benefit pension scheme mandated by the 1990 Social Security Act.[18] As late as 2004, only 22 percent of the private-sector workforce was covered and only 5 percent enjoyed the private provident funds to which the public effort was presumably supplementary. However, prior to the expansion of the 1980s, only the public sector enjoyed mandated coverage.[19]

Thailand differs from the other newly industrializing East Asian countries in being a relative laggard with respect to education (see, e.g., Kuhonta 2003). At the outset of the transition in 1980, the Primary Education Act finally made six years of primary education compulsory, and in 1987 the Prem government initiated a controversial subsidy scheme to increase secondary school enrollments in rural areas through tuition exemptions, scholarships, and various supports for transportation, including bicycle loans. Measured by both spending and results, however, education did not receive sustained attention during the early transition period. Between 1980 and 1990, the population without schooling actually increased (from 20 to 22 percent) and both the share of the population that had attended primary school or completed secondary school fell (Witte 2000, 225).

Education policy changed dramatically following the return to democratic rule in 1991, when a confluence of political forces including not only politicians but also the international financial institutions, technocrats, and portions of the private sector combined to push a dramatic expansion of education spending.[20] Several wide-ranging reviews of the educational system undertaken in conjunction with the drafting of the Seventh National Economic and Social Development Plan underlined the deficiencies in the primary, secondary, and vocational training systems. The Thai gross secondary school enrollment ratio increased by one-half from 1993 to 1998, rising from 40 percent to nearly 75 percent. Although increased enrollment undoubtedly reflected rising incomes and increasing returns, government spending was rising as well. This process of expanding educational entitlements was capped in the 1997 constitution (described in more detail later), which expanded compulsory education to twelve years.

18. As in Korea, benefits accrued only after a stipulated payment period, and as a result, no benefits were payable until 2014; consequently, even though doubts were raised about the long-term viability of the scheme, the Old Age Pension Fund initially accrued substantial surpluses.

19. Public-sector workers enjoyed a generous defined-benefit pension program financed directly out of the budget, justified in part by low public-sector salaries. As in several other Asian countries, teachers also operated under a preferential pension scheme. In 1996, the government system underwent a moderate rationalization. The original pension benefits were reduced somewhat but, in the context of introducing a defined-contribution second pillar, mandatory for those entering the system after 1997. However, the government matched employee contributions in the second pillar and, in combination, the replacement rate for government workers actually rose (Kanjanaphoomin 2004).

20. The following is based in part on United Nations Educational, Scientific and Cultural Organization ([UNESCO] 2000a).

Prior to the financial crisis, the expansion of social services and insurance in Thailand lagged behind both Korea and Taiwan. The piecemeal expansion of the system implied inequality in coverage, and there is ample evidence of inequality in financing, patronage, and leakage through the targeting of politically significant constituencies (Warr and Sarntisart 2004).

Nonetheless, the gradual transition to democratic rule saw a renewed attention to rural poverty, expansion of coverage of basic social services, and fundamental changes in principles with respect to the financing of social insurance, most notably in expanded fiscal support for health insurance. Between 1993 and 2000, the full panoply of poverty-oriented programs—cash transfers from the Ministry of Labor and Social Welfare, the health card schemes, income generation programs, and the education loan scheme—increased sevenfold in terms of baht, or from 1.1 to 4.6 percent of central government expenditure (Warr and Sartinsart 2004, 15). Moreover, these initiatives provided the basis for a further expansion of coverage following the Asian financial crisis.

As in Korea, the crisis had powerful political consequences (Haggard 2000; MacIntyre 2003). Not only did the economic collapse of 1997 lead directly to the fall of the Chavalit government, but it also influenced the passage of a wide-ranging constitutional revision that had important implications for subsequent social policy. Much of the constitution is devoted to political reform, but it also included important social initiatives enshrined as citizen rights: free education through twelfth grade (Section 43; legislated in 1999); an "equal right" to standard health services and free care for the indigent (Section 52); assistance for elderly people without adequate income (Section 54); and more vaguely worded commitments to maintain a public health-care system and provide social security (e.g., Sections 82 and 86). A sweeping commitment to decentralization also had important implications for social policy, particularly because the Thaksin Shinawatra government sought to dramatically expand transfers to lower levels of government (Kuwajima 2003; Warr and Sartinsarts 2004).

Like the Kim Dae Jung government, the Democrat government under Chuan also faced a variety of social pressures on coming to office, including from the stronghold of the opposition in the poor and rural northeast, organized labor, and grassroots organizations; unlike Kim Dae Jung, the Chuan administration did not enjoy close ties with these groups. By summer 1998, however, the fourth letter of intent with the IMF codified a relaxation of fiscal policy and loans from the World Bank, Asian Development Bank, and Japan provided the basis for an expansion of social policy commitments. Given the weakness of the existing administrative machinery for managing social safety nets, the loans generally supported or expanded existing programs rather than launching altogether new ones (World Bank Thailand Office 1999a, 1999b; World Bank 2002): increased funding for the low-income health card scheme and a student loan program to keep children in school, an increase in social assistance via cash transfers targeting the poor and the elderly and disabled without other means of support, increased funding for employment services and job training, and the creation of a Social Investment Fund similar to those in Latin America to support the decentralization process.

Despite these externally funded initiatives, the increase in spending on the poor was concentrated largely on the controversial education loan program, which was not unambiguously pro-poor. Expenditures on school lunches, housing assistance, and job creation actually contracted. The World Bank concludes that the government relied on temporary employment-creation programs and informal mechanisms rather than on formal social safety nets (World Bank 2002). Although the Chuan government did ultimately introduce the pension and child-allowance scheme contained in the 1990 social security law, the administration clearly favored productivist programs such as job training and placement, and it was openly reluctant to expand the existing social insurance system or to consider more permanent innovations such as the introduction of unemployment insurance.

This reluctance can be traced in part to fiscal constraints and the ascent of the technocrats under Chuan, but it can also be traced to the relatively conservative political orientation of the Democrat Party leadership on social issues. In the words of one government official referring to short-term assistance, "The reason behind giving them such a tiny amount of money is to create an incentive for them to look for jobs; otherwise they may want to live on social security for the rest of their lives and take advantage of others" (*Bangkok Post,* June 7, 1998). The important point for our purposes is not the merits or demerits of the Chuan government social policy but its political vulnerability. Although the Democrat Party had initially benefited from the crisis, it gradually became associated with the IMF and austerity and ultimately spawned a political alternative in Thaksin's Thai Rak Thai (TRT, or Thai Loves Thai) party. The TRT won a large plurality in the 2001 elections and an outright majority in the elections of 2005 on a platform that combined support for domestic business and opposition to a number of reforms associated with the IMF, with a mildly populist economic platform that promised greater attention to social welfare (Hewison 2003).

In fact, a gradual return to fiscal health permitted the government to pursue a wide-ranging social program with a strong populist flavor. One important and contentious social initiative was a dramatic expansion of health insurance in the Health Security for All program based on a 30-baht health card (Hewison 2003; Kuhonta 2003; Towse, Mills, and Tangcharoensathien 2004). The new scheme involved (as the name suggests) a card that granted fixed, low-fee access to contractor units designated by the province with which an individual must register. In contrast to the social security system, which relied on hospitals, the new approach was anchored by public primary health-care units. The system faced a number of political as well as administrative problems in implementation, including controversy over capitation rates and the long-term financial viability of the system; resistance from doctors and nurses, who complained of increased workloads, and a resulting exit to private practice; and concerns about creeping socialization from private-sector providers who were almost entirely excluded from the program. Yet, as in Korea, the new government had taken initiatives that increased coverage, particularly with respect to health and education, and did so on the basis of a universal rights-based approach. A number of other initiatives targeted more narrowly the rural constituency that had elected him, although not necessarily sharply. A debt-suspension program for farmers was introduced in 2001, and a wide-ranging Village Fund program combined outright transfers to village governments with the microfinance approach visible in other settings.

In sum, democracy seemed to matter. With respect to labor market issues, Thailand did not have the same level of individual protections enjoyed by Korean or Taiwanese workers going into the crisis, and Andrew Brown and Kevin Hewison (2005) and Teri Caraway (2002) have documented the ongoing difficulties with respect to establishing basic collective labor rights as well as individual rights. Still, there seems little doubt that the democratic period was characterized by a much more robust approach to social policy than had been the case in the prior period.

The Philippines

A major difference in the context of social policymaking in Thailand and the Philippines has to do with economic circumstances during and following the transition to democratic rule. Thailand went through a slowdown in growth during the first half of the 1980s but did not experience a crisis of the magnitude as those in Latin America and the Philippines. Growth, although slowing, remained positive throughout the first half of the decade and exploded thereafter, contributing to the accumulation of large fiscal surpluses (figure 5.1). The Philippines, by contrast, underwent the people-power transition to democracy under Corazon Aquino in 1986 in the aftermath of a profound debt crisis that not only forced difficult economic policy reforms on the new government but also saddled it with a highly controversial foreign and domestic debt burden. Growth at the end of the Aquino administration was also interrupted by another political-economic crisis, rapidly increasing fiscal deficits, and another stabilization episode (1990–92). Even under the Ramos recovery, growth rates did not equal those elsewhere in Asia and were interrupted by the effects of the Asian financial crisis and the political crisis that surrounded the ouster of President Joseph Estrada in 2000–2001. The results of this more erratic growth record were two; economic constraints were evident in episodic shifts in overall economic policy priorities toward stabilization and structural adjustment measures (in 1990–91, at the time of the Asian financial crisis in 1997–98, and again in the early 2000s) and in recurrent limits in the capacity of both the national and local governments to finance new initiatives.

Given the high incidence of rural poverty, as well as the rapid growth and spread of the armed insurgency in the mid-1980s (Kessler 1989; Riedinge 1995), it is not surprising that the Aquino government (1986–92) and those of her successors, Ramos (1992–98), Estrada (1998–2000), and Gloria Macapagal-Arroyo (2000–present), placed particular emphasis on the countryside (Reyes 2002). The first major social initiative of the Aquino administration was a temporary antipoverty program, the

Community Employment and Development Program, that used local infrastructure spending to create jobs in rural areas. The central social policy initiative of the Aquino years was the controversial Comprehensive Agrarian Reform Program, but the new administration also emphasized an expansion of basic social services. Dramatically increased external funding from international financial institutions supported a variety of basic health initiatives that carried over into subsequent administrations, including a renewed effort to achieve universal childhood immunization. The administration also took a number of initiatives with respect to urban housing.

Education saw a particular increase in spending. The constitution, drafted by Aquino appointees and ratified in 1987, stipulated that education should receive the largest share of the budget and made secondary education free. Secondary school enrollments jumped rapidly following this initiative in 1988. Yet the emphasis on increasing enrollments also had significant drawbacks. The nationalization of the secondary schools, popular as a status and pork-barrel issue with legislators but opposed by education planners, actually shifted the allocation of basic education spending away from primary and toward secondary education.[21] The Aquino government initiated a number of complementary programs to monitor and improve the quality and efficiency of primary education, including national testing and an expansion of early-childhood development programs. But these efforts, too, were affected by both the level and allocation of spending, and evaluations reveal a failure to meet targets or to substantially improve the quality of education (UNESCO 2000b).

Beginning at the close of 1989, the Aquino administration was hit by a near-perfect storm of political crises: a serious coup attempt in December that year, a succession of natural disasters (earthquakes, typhoons, and the eruption of Mt. Pinatubo), and a spike in oil prices associated with the Gulf War. These problems only compounded a more basic macroeconomic dilemma (de Dios n.d.). In the face of low tax collections and a large debt service overhang, the government could pursue a more expansive social agenda only at the cost of more borrowing, confrontation with lenders, or monetization of the deficits and inflation. During its last two years, the Aquino administration generated new rural development and targeted anti-poverty programs, but they were not implemented because of lack of funding.

The Ramos administration saw a gradual return to growth, an easing of fiscal constraints, and a number of important social policy innovations. However, the initial policy focus of the new administration was rectifying the deteriorating fiscal position of the country by restraining expenditures and focusing on a number of major economic policy reforms aimed at reviving economic growth.[22] Not

21. Many secondary schools had previously been run by local governments and financed in part through tuition.

22. These included a complete restructuring of the central bank; a number of privatization schemes; introducing competition into previously monopolized sectors, including telecomm, banking, and interisland shipping; and liberalization of both trade and foreign investment. The poverty impact of the structural reforms is discussed in Balisacan (1995).

coincidentally, the early years of the Ramos administration were also taken up with institutional rationalization designed to improve efficiency, including redefining the role of the Departments of Health and Social Welfare and Development in the wake of a decentralization under Aquino and breaking up ("trifocalization") the sprawling Department of Education, Culture and Sports into component parts.

The passage of more expansive social policy legislation occurred as the economy began to recover after 1992. With the presidential elections conducted in the midst of an economic downturn, all candidates had emphasized social policy issues in their campaigns; in his inaugural, Ramos promised a war on poverty. One of his first acts as president was the appointment of presidential commissions to fight poverty and to develop the countryside; the latter focused on the poorest provinces. The flagship antipoverty program to come out of the presidential commission was the Social Reform Agenda (SRA), a complex, multisector program that included both altogether new initiatives, such as a credit-based livelihood program, and the reallocation of the budgets of the line ministries around flagship initiatives aimed at different vulnerable groups (called basic sectors).[23] The conceptual core of the SRA was a minimum basic needs approach based on geographical targeting (poor provinces, municipalities, and *barangays*) and the collection of new data on unmet needs by trained volunteers. These staff members would, in effect, act as policy entrepreneurs in mobilizing public and private support for targeted interventions, from day-care centers and nutrition and health interventions to livelihood programs and improved access to clean water and sanitary toilets.[24]

The administration undertook only marginal reforms of the core social security institutions—the Social Security System (SSS) and the Government Services Insurance System (GSIS)—but it did launch a major expansion of public health insurance.[25] The crisis of 1990–91 and administrative inefficiencies in the SSS and GSIS, which managed Medicare funds, provided incentives for a reform of Medicare. An expansion of the system could shift financing of health care from the cash-strapped national and local governments, which continued to provide a substantial share of all care through public hospitals and clinics, to employers and employees. The final law made coverage universal and mandatory, albeit with a permissive fifteen-year timetable for doing so, and required the national and subnational governments to fully subsidize the contributions of the indigent, which as ultimately defined accounted for no less than 25 percent of the entire population.

During the Asian financial crisis, the Philippines did not experience the degree of economic distress of the most seriously affected countries. Nonetheless, the crisis

---

23. The *basic sectors* were defined quite broadly to include farmers-peasants, artisan workers, fisherfolks, workers in the formal sector and migrant workers, workers in the informal sector, indigenous peoples and cultural communities, women, the differently abled, senior citizens, victims of calamities and disasters, youth and students, children, and the urban poor.

24. For evaluations, see Bautista (1999).

25. A major goal of the reform was to shift the management of these funds out of the top-heavy SSS and GSIS bureaucracies and into a new entity, the Philippine Health Insurance Corporation.

marked another swing in the policy cycle because the government was forced to make large cuts in appropriations. A World Bank review of the social sectors argued strongly that the crisis was an opportunity to rationalize the management of social spending; the priorities of the World Bank included "inefficient procurement, poor deployment of teachers, severe underfunding of textbooks and school maintenance, public health programs, and welfare institutions, creeping renationalization of devolved hospitals, [and] proliferation of low quality universities and colleges" (1998b, i).

However, electoral and deeper political pressures pushed in a quite different direction. The 1998 elections came in the midst of the Asian financial crisis, and movie actor Joseph "Erap" Estrada ran on an openly populist platform, carrying a lavish pro-poor agenda (Balisacan 2001). His Caring for the Poor (Lingap Para sa Mahirap, or simply Lingap) program marked a sharp departure from the Ramos administration. Rather than the wider targeting of disadvantaged regions, municipalities, and groups, the Lingap sought to identify the poorest one hundred families in each province and city and to focus welfare efforts on them; by one estimate, this approach would reach only 16,000 families, or 0.4 percent of all poor families (Balisacan 2001). Moreover, although the total funds devoted to the Lingap program was less than those devoted to the SRA, a higher share of those funds was under the direct control of the president or delegated to legislators, implying an even higher-than-normal diversion of social spending into pork-barrel activities. But these issues were only emblematic of much deeper management problems that plagued the social policy efforts of the Estrada administration: the organizational disarray in the policymaking process (Doronila 2001; Laquian and Laquian 2002); the weakening of various social policy institutions, including the use of SSS funds for personal gain and the corruption of the national housing program through the involvement of business associates and cronies; the weakening of already deficient program-evaluation mechanisms; and the steady deterioration of public finances. In the end, these problems were eclipsed by a sustained impeachment crisis and mass demonstrations that ultimately resulted in Estrada's ousting.

In sum, the transition to democracy forced greater attention to social issues than had been the case under the Marcos dictatorship, and through the core mechanisms we identify: electoral competition, including at the subnational level, and the reemergence of independent interest groups and pro-poor NGOs. The change in regime produced initiatives on basic health and health insurance, secondary education, housing, and rural poverty alleviation. However, the distinctive feature of the posttransition Philippine social policy story is the recurrence of severe fiscal constraints at the outset of the Aquino administration, at the end of her administration in 1990–91, during the Asian financial crisis in 1997–98, and yet again during and following the political crisis of 2000–2001.

Conclusion

This chapter has argued that the effects of the Asian financial crisis on the course of social policy were a function of a distinctive welfare legacy and the timing of democratic transitions. Some authoritarian governments in East Asia, most notably in Korea and Taiwan, had invested heavily in education. In general, however, governments did not support social insurance schemes. The transition to democratic rule therefore created strong incentives to expand social entitlements.

However, the overall economic and fiscal circumstances in which such transitions took place were also consequential. In Korea, Taiwan, and Thailand, politicians had not only the incentives to expand social policy commitments but the resources to do so. The consequences of democratization were also visible in the Philippines, although in the context of fiscal constraints that limited government capacity. The administrations of Aquino, Ramos, and Estrada all signaled a strong commitment to social policy reforms, but the ability to carry through on those promises was adversely affected by macroeconomic shocks, compounded in 1990–92, and in 2000–2001, and again in 2005 by political crises as well.

The regionwide crisis of 1997–98 posed both long-term and short-term fiscal challenges to governments in the region. There is some evidence of the rationalizing politics visible in Latin America and central Europe during their crises in the 1980s and 1990s, respectively; crises generated pressures for retrenchment of social policy commitments. But with the exception of the Philippines, governments in the region did not enter the crisis facing long-standing structural deficits or weak revenue bases. Nor did any of them inherit expansive social programs that were themselves a major source of fiscal imbalances. In contrast to Latin America and central Europe, recovery from the crisis was relatively rapid as well. As a result, we do not see strong evidence of a retrenchment of newly won social protections.

These findings suggest a very important conclusion regarding the debate about globalization and social protection. Despite having relatively open economies, and economies that were made more open by the crisis and subsequent reform efforts, the democracies of the region have experienced an expansion of social entitlements. This fact would seem to counter more pessimistic assessments that globalization and social policy stand in necessary contradiction.

But we do see developments in labor market policies in the more advanced countries in the region that support a somewhat more pessimistic conclusion. In the wake of the crisis, governments developed new and, in some cases, more permanent social safety nets. In addition to short-term reforms that had implications for labor, including the privatization of state-owned enterprises and corporate restructuring, we also see evidence of deregulation that increased the legal scope for temporary, part-time, contract, and other forms of informal employment.

Research on these developments remains preliminary, but it could well have a corrosive effect on the apparent trend toward wider social insurance coverage, as it has in the United States and elsewhere. First, despite legal mandates, small and medium-size enterprises that are more likely to draw on such workers are less likely to make necessary contributions or to enforce them on their workers. Similarly, in countries such as the Philippines and Thailand, where the rural sector remains an important social safety net, crises and reform have bred informalization. As urban workers migrate back to the countryside during downturns, they can fall outside the urban social safety net, which in any case is less generous than in Korea and Taiwan.

Without government incentives, such as matching or subsidized contributions, it is quite possible that workers outside the formal sector will in fact fall between the cracks of the new social insurance systems or only be reached by other forms of social policy delivered through different means (Deyo 1989). One such option is tougher regulation of the workplace and mandating of corporate safeguards, yet this solution suffers from the same disability as wider social insurance coverage and is vulnerable to the informalization that we have noted. A second option is the sort of focus visible in Thailand, where displaced workers are effectively managed through geographically based schemes, such as microfinance administered at the village level. A final alternative (visible in the political fights in both Taiwan and Korea) is pressure to slow the labor market reform process so that insiders who enjoy employment protections continue to do so. Critics of employment protections have argued that this approach could have the perverse effect of simply protecting insiders at the expense of those in the informal sector.

But the growth of the informal sector in the more advanced countries in the region suggests a deeper social problem of growing inequality that is already becoming politically salient. In the absence of stronger labor movements or labor-based parties, the expansion of the social contract in East Asia is likely to take a very distinctive form, with reasonably generous social insurance in the upper-income countries, but with continuing pressures across the region to maintain flexibility in labor markets. Such a model would counter the most pessimistic views of the effects of globalization, but would nonetheless vindicate at least some fears of the constraints associated with an open, export-oriented economy in the absence of strong labor organization or left parties.

PART II

Regional Responses

CHAPTER 6

Regional Financial Cooperation in East Asia since the Asian Financial Crisis

Jennifer Amyx

In 1997, regional intergovernmental collaboration on financial issues was virtually absent in Asia. All economies, with the exception of Taiwan, maintained membership in the International Monetary Fund (IMF). However, Asia lacked regionally based mechanisms for self-help in times of liquidity or balance-of-payments crises.[1] The Association of Southeast Asian Nations (ASEAN) maintained a foreign exchange swap network at the subregional level, but this arrangement involved tiny amounts and was not linked to a system of independent surveillance. The supraregional Asia-Pacific Economic Cooperation (APEC) Forum held annual finance ministers' meetings, but was not an output-oriented forum and not active in developing informal networks of communication among regional finance ministers. A regional central bankers' forum, the Executives' Meeting of East Asia-Pacific Central Banks

I thank Jerry Cohen, Peter Drysdale, Stephan Haggard, and John Ravenhill for helpful comments and feedback. I also acknowledge, with gratitude, the financial support provided by the Council on Foreign Relations and Hitachi Corporation in 2005–6, when I was an International Affairs Fellow based at the Institute for International Monetary Affairs in Tokyo and at the U.S. Department of the Treasury in Washington, D.C. The views presented herein are the sole responsibility of the author. The chapter draws on material gathered in interviews carried out in 1999–2007 with current and former finance ministry and central bank officials in the ASEAN+3. Interview locations and identities of interviewees are omitted in particular instances to preserve anonymity requested by those interviewed.

1. The absence of such regional mechanisms was not surprising. Where subregional or regional funds have emerged around the globe (examples include the Latin American Reserve Fund and the Arab Monetary Fund), they have involved very small amounts of money, never sufficient to motivate member countries to exit the IMF in favor of regional funds.

(EMEAP), met regularly from 1991, but focused on fostering greater familiarity at the most informal levels rather than on tangible regional projects.[2]

Much changed in the decade following the crisis. Finance ministers of the ASEAN+3 nations began meeting on a regular basis and launched a number of initiatives. They established a network of bilateral currency swaps to assist in the case of a short-term liquidity crisis. They also created an institutionalized program of policy dialog and information exchange that came to surpass in frequency and depth that found in any other forum. The previously mentioned central bankers' forum also launched a set of regional bond funds; the ASEAN+3 finance ministers advanced a set of initiatives aimed at strengthening regional bond market infrastructure and promoting the development of local currency bond markets. The ASEAN+3 finance ministers agreed, moreover, to study the potential utility of regional currency units.

The contrast between the precrisis state of weak and shallow linkages among financial and monetary authorities in the region and the strong ties in place a decade later was stark. How much of this change can we attribute to the financial crisis experience? And do these regional collaborations make Asia less vulnerable to crisis in 2007 than it was in 1997?

I argue in this chapter that the Asian financial crisis served as an important catalyst for regional financial cooperation in East Asia in the decade after crisis. However, the crisis experience alone cannot explain the acceleration in momentum for regional initiatives from 2003. To understand the pace and pattern of regional financial cooperation in Asia during this decade, we must also focus attention on other factors that significantly impacted incentives for individual national governments to cooperate on a regional basis. Two are particularly prominent: the rising Chinese economic and diplomatic presence in the region and the growing strategic role that the perceived Asian solidarity plays in international politics.

I further argue here that those looking for significant substantive outcomes from Asian regional initiatives will be disappointed. When we highlight the discrepancies between the objectives articulated and objectives realized, the evidence suggests that actors strongly share the desire to advance perceptions of regional solidarity in Asia and have, arguably, succeeded here. Shared general sentiments, however, have not translated into agreement on the details necessary to back up this perception in credible ways. Greatest progress has come in the areas of enhanced policy dialog and information exchange, as well as in using regionwide projects to strengthen individual domestic financial markets. Advances have been much less robust in areas such as shifting financing away from bank lending and to the capital markets or in establishing a substantive lending facility to serve as a supplement or complement to the IMF. This suggests that financial systems in the region retain some of the vulnerability that precipitated the earlier crises. However, those who place great

---

2. The precrisis activities of the EMEAP resembled those of the Bank for International Settlements (BIS) in its first decades, when the international forum for central bankers was clublike.

relative significance on the value of increased communication, enhanced transparency, and similar dimensions will find much to encourage them in the regional financial cooperation efforts since the crisis.

The chapter proceeds as follows. The first section examines the Chiang Mai Initiative (CMI), announced in 2000 and depicted by many as a major step toward establishment of a regional monetary fund. The analysis here of the evolution of the network of bilateral swap agreements under CMI suggests that this project primarily furthers strategic rather than functional objectives for regional actors. Nevertheless, CMI provides a rationale for heightened policy dialog and information exchange in the region and greater familiarity among regional actors—positive spillover effects that are clearly stability enhancing. The second section of the chapter examines cooperative efforts to better develop the regional capital markets, and the bond markets, in particular. The Asian Bond Fund (ABF) and Asian Bond Markets Initiatives (ABMI), launched in 2003–4, are the focus here. These initiatives are much less strategic in their orientation; both are aimed less at extra-regional actors and more at using region-level projects as leverage to move forward the domestic market reforms of individual economies. The third section examines the recent rising interest by regional actors in discussing and considering exchange rate arrangements, including those that might involve regional currency cooperation, by examining the emergence of ideas for an Asian currency unit (ACU).

The Chiang Mai Initiative: A Mechanism
for Short-Term Liquidity Support

The most immediate and obvious problem faced by countries in the region hit by the financial crisis in 1997–98 was a sudden surge in the need for foreign exchange to support the pegs of currencies to the U.S. dollar. Despite repeated interventions in foreign exchange markets, the economies hit by the crisis were unable to stem the demand for foreign exchange. And in the process of trying to defend their currency pegs, each saw its foreign exchange reserves evaporate.

Thailand was the first to experience a drain of its foreign exchange reserves when the baht collapsed in July 1997. Although the amount Thailand could draw on from the IMF was inadequate to stem the Thai crisis, an ad hoc effort organized by the Japanese to assemble bilateral aid proved surprisingly successful. Australia, Brunei, China, Hong Kong, Indonesia, Japan, Korea, Malaysia, and Singapore all committed funds in support of Thailand. The organization of bilateral aid packages for countries in crisis and in need of aid in excess of their allotted IMF quota was not in itself unique to the Thai crisis. For example, the United States helped engineer the rescue of the Mexican economy in 1994 by supplying large amounts of bilateral aid to supplement IMF support. However, the collective effort to aid Thailand was notable for a number of reasons. First, the countries pledging aid were all from the Asia-Pacific. Second, the United States did not participate. And third, within the coalition aiding Thailand, only Japan and Australia had previous extensive experience as bilateral aid donors. Most other economies in the region were more accustomed to being aid recipients.

The rally in support of Thailand suggested new possibilities for regional cooperation and served as encouragement to Japanese officials to raise the idea of creating a more permanent mechanism of regional support. Although there were significant amounts of foreign exchange reserves across the region as a whole at this time, no mechanism was in place to mobilize these reserves quickly to help regional neighbors. The failure of the United States to participate in the bilateral efforts to aid Thailand also encouraged the pursuit of a more regionally based ongoing support mechanism.

When Japanese Vice Minister of Finance for International Affairs Eisuke Sakakibara proposed the creation of an Asian Monetary Fund (AMF) in late 1997, the idea was opposed by the United States and IMF. Support from China and some countries within Asia was also lacking.[3] Notably, the crisis had not yet spread beyond Thailand to other countries in the region.

Once the crisis took on a contagious quality, many of the same economies that had pledged aid to Thailand were themselves beset by crisis. Accordingly, the ad hoc regional efforts to provide liquidity were also unsustainable. Crisis management in 1997–98 was thus carried out in the context of IMF negotiations with individual crisis-hit countries. This was done through bilateral aid packages provided by Japan to regional neighbors under financial duress and through policy dialog forums that included the United States and other extra-regional actors.

Ideas for a Regional Self-Help Mechanism Reemerge

By 1999, however, tensions surrounding policy conditions attached to the IMF rescue packages and the launch of monetary integration in Europe led many East Asian countries to think more seriously about the prospects for regional financial cooperation. In this year, the heads of state of the ASEAN member nations, China, Japan, and Korea (collectively known by this time as the ASEAN+3) decided to launch an annual meeting of finance ministers. Notably, the decision followed a proposal by Chinese officials, whose motivations were clearly not antipathetic toward the IMF (although an IMF member, China had never been a recipient of an IMF bailout). Instead, Chinese officials were motivated primarily by a desire to tame the growing worries of ASEAN members about the competitive threat posed by the rapidly growing Chinese economy (which was then growing at 10 percent).

In May 2000, at a meeting in Chiang Mai, Thailand, the finance ministers announced the CMI. The CMI was a plan to construct a network of bilateral currency swaps that would permit a country beset by a speculative attack or a short-term liquidity crisis to draw on the reserves of other nations. The arrangement was to

---

3. For details on the politics behind the Japanese AMF proposal and the diplomatic gaffes that occurred at this time, as well as the responses of China and other countries, see Amyx (2002, 2004a, 2005).

supplement existing international financial arrangements.[4] The initiative reflected a mixture of concerns regarding the IMF response to the Asian financial crisis (both in terms of the slowness of response and the nature of the conditions attached to the aid) and a desire to build on the success of the earlier ad hoc regional rescue effort for Thailand in 1997.

China lent its support to the CMI, but was not a major proponent of the initiative. Although expressing shared sentiments in favor of a cooperative arrangement, China adopted the most cautious position of any key actor in the negotiations over the basic modalities of the arrangement that ensued. Specifically, the Chinese proposed a 100 percent linkage of CMI funds to IMF programs. Malaysian officials, in contrast, argued for no linkage at all. When beset by the financial crisis, Malaysia had chosen not to seek IMF assistance, although the country did benefit both from Japanese financial assistance (part of the Japanese New Miyazawa Initiative of bilateral support to the crisis-hit economies) and from the confidence-supporting measure of a currency swap line established between the Japanese and Malaysian central banks. As the ASEAN+3 countries worked out the general terms of the swap arrangements, Japanese officials played the role of arbitrator. In May 2001, the ASEAN+3 finance ministers announced the general guidelines for the currency swaps, which would entail a linkage of 90 percent of the funds to negotiation of an IMF program (see Amyx 2004a). Bilateral negotiations of individual swap contracts commenced thereafter.

The CMI involved no up-front costs to participating governments, and the explicitly stated purpose of the CMI was to supplement existing IMF arrangements.[5] Many swaps were initially unidirectional rather than bidirectional. This reflected the starting point of some countries being clear creditors and others playing the singular role of potential borrowers.

From 2000, the ASEAN+3 Finance Ministers Process was the key forum working on the CMI. The ASEAN+3 maintained no official secretariat or physical institution. Information about its activities was disseminated via the ASEAN Secretariat and individual finance ministries and central banks. Two cochairs led the ASEAN+3 Finance Ministers Process each year—one country from ASEAN and one from the "plus three."[6]

A few characteristics of the CMI arrangement are important to note. First, by 2007, the CMI did not involve any formal pooling of funds; however, participants emphasized the potential for the simultaneous disbursement of funds by multiple

4. See joint statements issued by the ASEAN+3 finance ministers after their annual meetings from 2000–6, which explicitly reiterate these two core objectives, first mentioned in the 2000 statement.

5. ASEAN+3 Joint Statements in May 2005 and May 2006 explicitly included "CMI's two core objectives, namely, (1) to address short-term liquidity difficulties in the region and (2) to supplement the existing international financial arrangements" (Finance Ministers of ASEAN, China, Japan and the Republic of Korea (ASEAN+3) 2005).

6. The origins of ASEAN+3 lie in the ASEAN invitation for the "plus 3" to join them as guests after the annual ASEAN meeting. It has since evolved into a forum where the "plus 3" are clearly not simply guests. The ASEAN+3 first met formally in 1999.

countries. Second, if activated, the swap lines were to be drawn down proportionally. In other words, if a country ran into trouble, it would need to simultaneously borrow money from all other countries with which it maintained swap agreements; it could not selectively activate swap contracts. Swaps were essentially short-term loans, and this stipulation was intended to differentiate the CMI from purely bilateral efforts by ensuring the collective delivery of aid.

But such aspirations were distorted by two other characteristics of the arrangements. First, participating countries could opt out of swaps at any time. And some ASEAN+3 members effectively opted out from the start by negotiating swap contracts only with select countries. Thus, the CMI network was always incomplete. Second, although the degree of linkage to IMF programs and the length of the borrowing periods were decided as a result of negotiation among the ASEAN+3 and were consistent across the network, important details varied for individual swap contracts. Most notably, the premium charged above market interest rates—a key factor determining the cost of using any swap—varied from contract to contract.[7] The amounts involved also varied widely. This fact complicates enormously the cost-benefit calculations of any country considering request for aid via the CMI.

This variation in terms suggests that common depictions of the CMI as a very large regional pooling facility are mistaken. Virtually every press release or update issued on the CMI by the governments in the region highlights total amounts involved in CMI, implying that such amounts represent additional resources available to individual participating countries. The reality is very different.

In the next section, I examine more closely the evolution of the bilateral swap arrangements (BSAs) during the decade since the crisis. This analysis provides evidence that the self-help aspect of the CMI was less important to participants than were the symbolic or geostrategic benefits of maintaining the momentum of this regional project.

Evolution of Bilateral Swap Arrangements

The ASEAN+3 refer to two stages of the CMI: (1) the period through 2004 and (2) 2005–6. The negotiation of individual BSAs under the CMI rubric in the first stage proved very time-consuming for participating countries. For example, despite the announcement of CMI general modalities in 2001, China and Indonesia successfully negotiated their initial swap arrangement only in December 2003. Because initial swap contracts were put in place at very different times, the swaps within the network expired and were considered for renewal at a variety of times.

7. Although the premium charged by individual governments on CMI swaps were not made public, it was no secret that some governments such as China charged more for funds committed via the CMI than did other governments. In fact, this factor was widely considered to be the reason for the failure of China to come to agreement with Malaysia or Thailand on the renewal of its swaps with these governments after the expiration of initial swap contracts in 2005 (author interviews with government officials in the region, 2003–6).

Singapore also never agreed to a swap with Korea or China in the first stage, and it put its swap in place with Japan only in November 2003. Thailand, a key early supporter of the CMI (for obvious reasons) initially refused to renew its swap with Japan in 2004. And two of the Chinese swaps (with Thailand and Malaysia) expired in 2005 and, as of August 2007, had not been renewed.[8]

In the second stage of CMI (spanning 2005–6), the ASEAN+3 announced their intention to increase significantly the size of swaps. A few factors seem to be important in explaining this move and the willingness of the ASEAN+3 nations to consider the expansion of the arrangements at this time. These factors included deepened policy dialog among the countries in the region and greater familiarity and confidence with one another through work on regional bond market initiatives. The massive growth in foreign exchange reserves in the region also probably contributed to the cooperative dynamics (although this factor would also help reduce the sense of urgency for strengthening self-help arrangements). Finally, the symbolic or strategic dimension of cooperation was arguably very important in this period, given discussions in the global arena about reform of the IMF and demands by Asian countries for more equitable representation there. By appearing to strengthen regional solidarity, Asian governments could exercise greater leverage as a region in such discussions.

The ASEAN+3 finance ministers intended to enlarge the CMI in three ways: through an increase in the amounts of existing commitments, through the conclusion of new agreements, and through the transformation of one-way swaps into two-way swaps. Between 2005 and 2006, some of this seemingly came to fruition; the total envelope involved in the BSAs under the CMI rose from $39.5 billion to $75 billion, according to press releases, and some government dyads transformed their one-way swaps into two-way swaps. Moreover, the ASEAN+3 finance ministers raised the proportion of swap amounts that could be withdrawn without an IMF-supported program being in place from 10 to 20 percent. However, no new BSAs (aside from those emerging from the expansion of one-way into two-way swaps) were concluded in the 2005–6 period. For example, swaps between Singapore and China and between Singapore and Korea failed to materialize.

A closer examination of what the $75 billion total envelope in the CMI comprised at the beginning of 2007 also reveals grounds for suspicion about the degree to which the second stage of CMI furthered the self-help liquidity-support goals of the arrangement. Although $75 billion was touted by governments in the region as the total envelope of funds in the CMI, this amount includes the previously

8. These swaps were said to be in negotiation throughout this time. Thailand and Malaysia may no longer feel the urgency for CMI support and therefore feel more confident in negotiations and less willing to beg for a swap arrangement. Related to this, China is said to be charging a high premium on swap money, despite significant improvement in the credit ratings and economic conditions of many ASEAN countries. Many actors in the region stress that the Chinese government is very supportive of the CMI rubric in general because such support provides Chinese leaders with important political capital in the region. However, China is said to be highly risk-averse when it comes down to individual swap negotiations.

Table 6.1 Potential amounts available to individual countries under the CMI, January 2007 (billions of dollars)[a]

	Indonesia	Malaysia	Philippines	Singapore	Thailand
China	4	0 (expired)	1	0	0 (expired)
Japan	6	1	6	3	3
Korea	1	1.5	1.5	0	1
Sum	11	2.5	8.5	3	4
Amount not IMF-linked	2.2	0.5	1.7	0.6	0.8

Source: Ministry of Finance, Japan, http://www.mof.go.jp/english/if/pcmie.htm; government press releases (various countries) and author's calculations.
[a] Tiny amounts available via ASEAN Swap Agreement not included (total 'envelope' in this arrangement: $2 billion split among ten two-way bilateral swap agreements). In addition to the CMI, Japan has a swap line with Malaysia of $2.5 billion, put in place under the New Miyazawa Initiative (and not linked to an IMF program). ASEAN, Association of Southeast Asian Nations; CMI, Chiang Mai Initiative; IMF, International Monetary Fund.

mentioned expired swaps between China and Thailand and between China and Malaysia. Moreover, this often-cited amount did not represent the total amount potentially available to any single actor. Table 6.1 shows the maximum amounts potentially available to individual countries requesting assistance via the CMI at the beginning of 2007. As shown, the amounts available were highest for Indonesia (a total of $11 billion was potentially available, assuming no opt-outs by China, Korea, or Japan and assuming simultaneous disbursement). Of this amount, $2.2 billion could be disbursed without an IMF program in place. The Philippines ranked second among ASEAN countries in its access to resources, with a total of $8.5 billion potentially available ($1.7 billion in the absence of an IMF program). The amounts available to Thailand under the CMI at this time were notably less than the funding provided to Thailand through ad hoc support arrangements in 1997 in the wake of that country's crisis.[9]

The composition of the increased total envelope amounts in 2005–6 is also important to note. Most of this addition came from an increase in swap amounts between Japan and Korea. In July 2001, Japan and Korea concluded a U.S. dollar–won swap agreement to provide Korea with $2 billion in the case of crisis. In May 2005, the governments added a two-way yen–won swap in the amount of $3 billion. Finally, in February 2006, Japan and Korea increased the amount of their U.S. dollar–won swap to $10 billion and the amount of their yen–won swap to $5 billion. It was no coincidence that the expansion in the scale of the swaps between the two countries

9. In July 2007, Japan and Thailand negotiated a third bilateral swap agreement that doubled the total amount available to Thailand from Japan, thereby enabling Thailand to swap up to $6 billion. Although this means that total amounts available through the CMI virtually doubled (the Thai swap with China expired long ago, and Korea maintains only a $1 billion swap line with Thailand), it also suggests that the expansion of the CMI at this point had very little to do with strengthened *regional* solidarity. Rather, it suggests that the CMI basic modalities were increasingly being used as a basis for deepening *bilateral* relationships.

came while Japan served as cochair of the ASEAN+3, when the second stage of the CMI expansion promise was made in 2005, and while Korea served as cochair in 2006. Both governments reportedly felt pressure to show results (interviews with government officials involved in CMI negotiations, Tokyo, 2006). Although such increases in swap amounts enabled the ASEAN+3 finance ministers to announce a more impressive total envelope amount in 2006, few observers could imagine Japan or Korea actually making use of the CMI. And such increases were irrelevant to countries for which liquidity-support facilities could be imagined to be potentially relevant—countries such as the Philippines and Indonesia.

Positive By-products of the Chiang Mai Initiative

As the previous section shows, CMI provides small swap amounts relative to widely held perceptions. Yet the CMI negotiation and cooperation process argu-ably gives countries in the region a greater stake in one another's financial stability, and therefore a rationale for deepened policy dialog/surveillance activities in the region. Deepened information exchange, policy dialog, and familiarity among fi-nance ministries and central banks in the region are arguably stability-enhancing developments.

The deepening of surveillance and policy dialog related to CMI activities since 2000 is indisputable. In 2000 (the year in which the CMI was proposed), the ASEAN+3 finance ministers agreed to establish a network of contact people. In 2001, the forum also agreed to voluntarily exchange data on short-term capital flows and establish a study group to examine the use of the already-existing Economic Review and Policy Dialogue Framework.

In 2002, the ASEAN+3 initiated a regular policy dialog process. Seven of the economies agreed, as well, to a monthly bilateral exchange of short-term capital flow data (the exchange of data on short-term capital flows overseen by the IMF is done on an annual basis). The frequency of policy dialog by this time was greater and more substantive than that being carried out in APEC or in any other regional group. In 2003–4, actors reported a significant deepening of the quality of policy dialog within ASEAN+3 meetings. In 2005, an agreement to integrate and enhance ASEAN+3 economic surveillance into the CMI framework was also put forward. And, in 2006, the ASEAN+3 finance ministers agreed to set up a group of experts to supplement the ASEAN+3 policy dialog, suggesting the introduction of a two-tiered surveillance process.

In these ways, actors used the CMI rubric to deepen policy dialog and infor-mation exchange related to surveillance across the region. However, no delegated surveillance authority that also served as a delegated disbursement authority was established. Ironically, my interviews with actors across the region suggested that most viewed such surveillance activities were less useful for their role in reducing moral hazard than they were for providing opportunities for countries in the region to discuss concerns about developments in China (clearly a creditor in any CMI ac-tivation). This irony does not cancel out the good that such policy dialog processes promote. But it does suggest, again, that regional initiatives often prove most valuable for the unspoken benefits or by-products they produce.

Multilateralization?

In the absence of a delegated decision-making structure for fund disbursement and in the presence of opt-out clauses, the CMI provided no guaranteed resource pooling capacity for the participating countries in 2007; nevertheless, regional rhetoric about the CMI remained positive. In fact, at the annual meeting of the ASEAN+3 finance ministers, the Joint Ministerial Statement announced unanimous agreement, in principle, that a "self-managed reserve pooling arrangement governed by a single contractual agreement" was an "appropriate form of multilateralization" (2007). Some observers interpreted this statement as evidence that the region had taken a major step forward toward establishing an arrangement akin to an AMF. But the analysis here and a review of the joint ministerial statements by the ASEAN+3 finance ministers since 2001 suggest a much more cautious interpretation. Although all ASEAN+3 members agreed in the past in principle to the basic modalities of the CMI, individual countries refrained from participation. And "appropriate form of multilateralization" should not be equated with consensus on a "desirable form of multilateralization." Rather, joint ministerial statements about the CMI can arguably be read as statements intended to assure the international community that regional cooperation on this issue remains alive, even though evidence for concrete progress remains sparse.

On the surface, multilateralization might portend benefits for a range of actors in the region. For example, multilateralization might be expected to bring more certainty about the amounts of funds available through a simultaneous release of funds. Potential creditors also might be expected to desire access to the same information from all borrowers. It could also save time and resources and circumvent domestic politics if multilateralization resulted in a more automatic disbursement mechanism. For those frustrated at the uneven participation in the CMI by some ASEAN+3 members to date, multilateralization might also be seen as a way to induce the countries not currently participating fully to become more involved in the regional arrangement.

Yet hurdles to multilateralization were formidable in 2007, and it was far from clear that a multilateralization arrangement involving the central pooling of resources and a single contractual arrangement was a realistic possibility. Central pooling generally means the introduction of a borrowing quota for participating countries. Such quotas typically are determined relative to amounts that countries contribute. For countries such as Indonesia and the Philippines, the CMI was primarily a borrowing facility that entailed no up-front costs. Their swap commitments with other ASEAN countries were miniscule in size, and the perceived likelihood of one of the "plus three" activating a swap was near zero. Thus, for these actors, the costs of CMI participation might be expected to rise with multilateralization, assuming they could be called on to graduate from a pure borrower role to a dual creditor-borrower role. These same countries might also be expected to contribute to the costs of creating a secretariat (the ASEAN Secretariat costs are equally shared among member countries, and this is already a financial burden for some of them).

China and Singapore are also reported to have strongly opposed the development of an independent surveillance mechanism in the ASEAN+3 (interviews with regional actors, 2004–6). Such resistance works against concrete moves toward multilateralization or the evolution of the CMI into an arrangement more independent from the IMF.

In short, multilateralization appears to require a total paradigm shift. In 2007, that appeared highly unlikely, particularly given the seeming decline in demand in the region for an AMF-like facility for liquidity support. Indonesia, Korea, the Philippines, and Thailand shifted to floating exchange rate systems in the wake of the crisis. China and Malaysia also announced the adoption, in July 2005, of more flexible exchange rate regimes, although actual movements since this policy shift have been small (see Benjamin Cohen, chap. 2 in this volume). A dramatic accumulation of foreign exchange reserves by governments in the region in recent years (table 6.2), and since 2004, in particular, also reduces the likelihood of a repeated need for liquidity support of the magnitude seen in 1997–98.

The East Asian network of bilateral currency swaps carries more symbolic than substantive meaning for most actors. For a few actors in the region, such as Indonesia and the Philippines, this project represents, foremost, a borrowing facility, allowing these countries to potentially draw on more foreign exchange reserves than each alone possesses. For the "plus three," which have abundant foreign exchange reserves, it, foremost, provides an opportunity to build political capital with Southeast Asia, as well as some leverage for pressuring international financial institutions such as the IMF to address more seriously their underrepresentation of Asia. For other ASEAN economies, such as Singapore, Thailand, and Malaysia, this project is most useful for the opportunities that its accompanying policy dialog process provides to exert peer pressure on China. It also offers them insights into developments in

Table 6.2 Foreign exchange reserve holdings in key ASEAN+3 countries, 1990, 2000, and 2005 (millions of U.S. dollars)[a]

	1990	2000	2005
China	29.5	168.2	821.5
Hong Kong	24.5	107.5	124.2
Indonesia	7.4	28.5	32.9
Japan	78.5	354.9	834.2
Korea	14.7	96.1	210.3
Malaysia	9.7	29.5	70.1
Philippines	0.9	13.0	15.9
Singapore	27.7	80.1	115.7
Thailand	13.3	32.0	50.6

Source: Nakamura and Shinohara (2007), drawing on BOJ and IMF statistics and excluding gold reserves.
[a] ASEAN, Association of Southeast Asian Nations; IMF, International Monetary Fund.

China at a time when changes in the Chinese financial system and foreign exchange regime could have huge effects on the operations of its neighbors.

Bilateral swap arrangements were a convenient starting point for regional financial initiatives, but it is unclear where the ASEAN+3 will take them from here. Multilateralization would require a consensus on a uniform formula for each country—and working this out would involve a great deal of cooperation and discussion. Multilateralization would also require some ASEAN countries to move for the first time beyond viewing the CMI merely as a borrowing facility.

Regional Bond Market Development: The Asian Bond Fund and Asian Bond Markets Initiatives

Regional bond market development is the second major area of regional cooperation since the financial crisis. Regional collaboration initiatives began in the APEC Finance Ministers Forum in 1996 and focused on a discussion of how Asia might more effectively mobilize its savings. Approximately 40 percent of the world foreign exchange reserves belonged to economies in the Asian region at this time and were invested primarily in assets of OECD countries. Interest among the broader APEC membership (including the United States) in the development of bond markets in the region was weak prior to the Asian financial crisis, however.

The regional crisis highlighted the need to reduce reliance by corporate actors on short-term foreign currency loans to finance long-term local investments. When foreign creditors were bullish on growth prospects in the region and regional currencies seemed credibly pegged to the dollar, little attention was paid to the mismatch between the time horizons of the borrowers and lenders (because lenders were likely to continue to extend new financing) or to the possibility of local currency depreciation suddenly raising the costs of borrowing to local actors. With the crisis, the hazards of this double mismatch became evident; banks refused to extend new credit and existing loan values surged in local-currency terms with the depreciation of the local currencies.

The greater use of longer-term debt instruments such as bonds—particularly bonds denominated in local currencies—could clearly help reduce the vulnerabilities of excessive reliance on foreign bank financing. Because the development of local bond markets required deregulation and harmonization across a number of areas, however, formal collaboration on a regional project to develop local bond markets was slow to develop. In fact, some actors, such as Malaysia, Thailand, Indonesia and Korea, moved to *tighten* regulations in the aftermath of crisis. Deregulation and regulatory harmonization were more politically palatable topics by 2002, once the economies had recovered. Perceptions among the ASEAN+3 of successful collaboration on the CMI also generated optimism concerning prospects for cooperation on bond market development.

Additional factors provided momentum for regional bond market initiatives. The rapid accumulation of foreign exchange reserves by the governments stimulated greater discussion about the desirability for some diversification of foreign reserve investment. Underdeveloped capital markets also served as binding constraints on productive public investment programs in the region. Moreover, some multinational corporations (MNCs) operating in the region (Japanese MNCs, in particular) sought to finance their business operations in local currencies to avoid exchange risks. The introduction of new pension systems or pension-system reforms in the region also provided further impetus by stimulating considerable growth in the size of funds (pension funds tend to involve large bond allocations).

Two regional forums began discussing region-level collaboration on bond market issues in 2002–3 and announced two related initiatives soon thereafter. The regional central bankers' forum, the EMEAP,[10] launched the ABF initiative to create regional bond funds. Meanwhile, the ASEAN+3 finance ministers launched the ABMI to focus on strengthening the infrastructure for bond market development in the region. Notably, the focus of both initiatives was on development of *local* bond markets in the region and on promoting the greater integration of financial markets in the region. Together, the projects represented a linkage of financial stability and capital market development objectives. The ABF provided some demand for bond issues, and the ABMI focused on putting the necessary infrastructure in place to increase the range of issuers and amounts issued. Hong Kong and Japan were the earliest visible proponents of regional bond market development in the region and worked to place these projects on the regional agenda. However, governments throughout the region lent generally strong support to the efforts.

Establishing the Asian Bond Funds

The first phase of the ABF (ABF1), launched in 2003, focused on stimulating trading in government securities (table 6.3). EMEAP central banks invested $1 billion in a basket of U.S. dollar–denominated bonds issued by sovereign and quasi-sovereign issuers in EMEAP economies (excluding EMEAP members Australia, Japan, and New Zealand). Investment in regional sovereign bonds via the ABF was seen as a first step toward the development of private-debt markets because government bonds typically serve as benchmarks for private-sector bonds. The second phase of the ABF (ABF2) moved forward in 2005 and involved the establishment of a new kind of investment trust, holding a portfolio of sovereign and government-agency bonds of eight Asian economies (China, Hong Kong, Indonesia, Korea, Malaysia, the Philippines, Singapore, and Thailand) and central bank purchases (table 6.3).

ABF2 was most important for the way in which the project focused attention on the breaking down of regulations on investment by foreign investors (rather than on amassing massive amounts of funds from the region for investment). A prerequisite to making the ABF2 a pan-regional investment trust was the deregulation of nonresident investment in many of the participating countries. The creation of this

---

10. Membership in the EMEAP differs from the ASEAN+3 in that it includes Australia, New Zealand, and Hong Kong but not the less-developed ASEAN countries.

Table 6.3 ABF initiatives[a]

	ABF1	ABF2
Launch date	June 2003	June 2005
Amount of seed money (US$)	$1 billion	$2 billion
Constituent bonds	U.S. dollar-denominated sovereign & quasi-sovereign bonds in eight Asian markets	Local-currency-denominated sovereign & quasi-sovereign bonds in eight Asian markets[b]
Management style	Passively managed bond index fund	Passively managed bond index funds
Investors	EMEAP membership	Open to the public

Source: Hong Kong Monetary Authority/Julia Leung (2006). Presentation to FLAR-CEPAL Conference. Lima. July 18, 2006 and Executives' Meeting of East Asia-Pacific Central Banks (2006) Review of ABF2.
[a] ABF, Asia Bond Fund; ABF1, first phase of the ABF; ABF2, second phase of the ABF; EMEAP, Executives' Meeting of the East Asia-Pacific Central Banks.
[b] China, Hong Kong, Indonesia, Korea, Malaysia, Philippines, Singapore, and Thailand.

trust also required the central bankers themselves to walk through the process of listing a fund. That task proved difficult and time-consuming to accomplish across the region, but it raised awareness of the concrete hurdles to the establishment of bond fund products (and thereby shone a spotlight on the regulatory authorities of those countries and the areas of needed reform) (Leung 2006). In this way, the regionwide cooperative effort served as leverage for domestic actors by working to combat entrenched domestic interests against reform. And, because the fund listings were done in the context of a regional project rather than a national project, discussions could focus more on technocratic aspects and less on politics (Ma and Remolona 2005; interviews with actors in the region).[11]

Some concrete examples of where cooperation on ABF2 produced market reforms may be helpful. In China, the Pan-Asian Bond Index Fund (PAIF), part of ABF2, became the first foreign institutional investor granted access to the Chinese interbank bond market. Regulatory loosening was thus a prerequisite to Chinese participation in ABF2. The listing of the Malaysian single market fund of the ABF2 also required the liberalization of the Malaysian foreign exchange administration rules, the opening up of its domestic market to issuances by multilateral development banks and multilateral financial institutions, and the exemption of nonresident investors from withholding tax in Malaysia on interest income received from investments in ringgit-denominated debt securities. In Thailand, cooperation on ABF2 led that government to grant nonresident investors withholding-tax exemption for all income derived from investing in Thai government bonds and government agency bonds (EMEAP press releases; Executives' Meeting of East Asia-Pacific Central Banks (EMEAP) Working Group on Financial Markets 2006).

A number of additional regulatory changes were required before the EMEAP countries could list the bond funds or fixed-income exchange-traded funds in their

11. As of this writing, three of the eight countries (China, Indonesia, and Korea) were not yet listed, although their listing was thought to be imminent (Leung 2006).

markets. According to the actors involved, the regional project provided some leverage to accelerate these changes (interviews, 2005–6).[12] Governments were not uniformly willing to make changes, however; Korean officials, for example, were more reluctant to introduce regulatory changes to accommodate the ABF than were officials in Malaysia and Thailand. This variation in enthusiasm on details highlights again the very different political hurdles to agreeing on general regional cooperation objectives and implementing such projects.

In Korea, some domestic backlash against foreign investment emerged from 2003 on, which made the political climate less amenable to deregulation for nonresident investment. The Korean tax authorities, notoriously stubborn and politically powerful, also proved more difficult to convince about the importance of lowering the relevant taxes on nonresident investment. The weak political leadership on these issues under the Roh Moo Hyun administration contrasted with relatively strong political leadership in Thailand (until the coup in 2006) and Malaysia. In the latter countries, top leaders publicly endorsed the ABF project and repeatedly affirmed their support for development of regional bond markets.

The Thai and Malaysian governments also faced strong encouragement from Japanese MNCs with established operations in these countries and from Japan's Bank for International Cooperation (JBIC). The MNCs welcomed the development of local currency bonds as a means to expand the limited financing options to meet their manufacturing needs in these places. Innovative arrangements proposed by the JBIC under the umbrella of the ABMI also served as a catalyst for the introduction of various local-currency bond market development schemes in these two countries.

Additional positive spillover effects of ABF2 include the promotion of new investment products and improvement of market infrastructure. The PAIF and the eight single-market funds launched in the second phase of the ABF initiative represent a new asset class in Asia. All this is against the backdrop of the wide recognition that the countries in the region lack suitable debt instruments to make up the complete risk-and-return spectrum that investors need. It is anticipated that providing innovative, low-cost products in the form of passively managed bond funds will help raise investor awareness and interest in bonds in the region. For example, as a listed passive bond fund, the PAIF acts as a convenient and reportedly cost-effective investment fund for regional and international investors who desire diversified exposure to bond markets in the eight EMEAP markets. In setting up the ABF2 funds, EMEAP member countries also sought to improve market infrastructure in several aspects. For example, the introduction of the iBoxx ABF indices, which are reportedly designed to be transparent, replicable, and credible, is considered to be an important piece of market infrastructure for the region. The indices were launched by UK-based International Index Company and compiled

---

12. This role of the ABF project in accelerating regulatory changes is also documented in Ma and Remolona (2005).

based on prices provided by a number of active market makers.[13] Accordingly, the index should accurately reflect the prevailing market conditions of the underlying bonds (Leung 2006).

Regional central bankers also intentionally kept ABF investments tiny to avoid market distortion. As noted publicly by central bankers in the region, the shifting of all foreign reserve investment into the region could be harmful, working against the principle of decreasing risk through portfolio diversification. And numerous studies show there has been no wholesale shift out of U.S. Treasury bonds and into sovereign bonds in the region.

The Asian Bond Markets Initiative

ABMI efforts supported by the Asian Development Bank (ADB) center on regular dialog with academics and private-sector market participants. The four main areas of focus are (1) creating new securitized debt instruments and increasing the supply of local currency bonds, (2) studying new credit guarantee and investment mechanisms, (3) addressing foreign exchange transaction and settlement issues impeding cross-border bond investment and issuance in the region, and (4) enhancing the capacity of local credit-rating agencies. In 2005, various international and foreign institutions issued local currency-denominated bonds in a number of countries across the region.

Under the rubric of the ABMI, in 2006 the ASEAN+3 launched a research project on the possible future issuance of asset-backed Asian currency–basket bonds. A multicurrency bond project was seen as a potential tool for moving forward the development of a regional settlement system. A network of securities clearing depositories that would allow the settlement of Asian and international bonds in Asian time zones, was, in turn, anticipated to reduce the transaction costs and risks involved in investment in Asian bonds and to offer easier access to bond markets in Asia. The ADB also developed a proposal for a regional guarantee mechanism with a fixed term of operation.

Nevertheless, the focus remains on national bond market development. Action on the development of a regional settlement or guarantee mechanism is likely to move forward slowly. Technical complexities surrounding the development of a regionwide infrastructure are high, and it is widely recognized that much time is needed before the concept can move forward. More rigorous examination of feasibility and business viability, as well as more thorough discussions among authorities over respective jurisdictions, is necessary. Current efforts thus remain focused around leveraging and improving existing national bond market infrastructure, with a second step being the creation of a network of bilateral links between economies (in the area of settlement systems, for example).

13. The selection process involved open bidding among firms headquartered both inside and outside the region.

Assessment

Both the ABF and ABMI have clearly made progress in pushing forward market reforms and encouraging the strengthening of local currency bond markets in the region. The ABF has accelerated tax and regulatory reforms in directions consistent with international rules. Along with the ABMI, it has also helped to improve market infrastructure and introduce new asset classes into *national markets*. This not only facilitates the development of local currency bond markets but also promotes cross-border investment in Asia.

The EMEAP strategy of breaking down regulatory barriers resulted in significant financial-sector opening. But, by 2007, its ABF2 project had not yet spurred private-sector emulation of its experiences or the development of similar privately run funds.[14] Countries in the region also continue to have bank-dominated financial sectors and a limited range of regional savings and investment vehicles. Levels of bank assets relative to GDP have grown significantly over the past decade ("East Asia Needs Financial System Reform," *Oxford Analytica Daily Brief,* October 26, 2006).[15] Bond market capitalization to GDP also remains small in the region, and governments, rather than the corporate sector, continue to dominate bond issuance. As Andrew Sheng notes, it also remains easier for Asian companies to buy many asset diversification tools from private banks in New York than to buy them locally (Sheng 2005).[16] Thus, it seems that the region has a long way to go to eliminate structural weaknesses in intermediating savings into investment in the region.

Currency Cooperation

The third major area of regional cooperation, currency cooperation, has not yet yielded a concrete regional initiative. In 2001, the Japanese government proposed a project within the Asia-Europe Meeting (ASEM) of finance ministers, which became known as the Kobe Research Project. This involved the sponsorship of research by private institutes on possible lessons from the European experience for regional monetary cooperation in Asia. But it was only at the 2006 ASEAN+3 finance ministers' meeting that the issue of monetary collaboration was adopted as one of the ASEAN+3 annual Research Group projects. As of 2007, there is no consensus in the region—or prospect of reaching a consensus in the near term—on the issue of currency cooperation. The political dynamics underlying developments

14. The reasons, according to Julia Leung of the Hong Kong Monetary Authority, have largely to do with the cost and pricing structure of this type of fund.

15. The growth is China 125 to 163 percent, Indonesia 31 to 50 percent, South Korea 38 to 94 percent, Malaysia 101 to 159 percent, the Philippines 56 to 63 percent, Thailand 80 to 104 percent, and Singapore 122 to 185 percent.

16. As one example, Sheng points to exchange-traded funds, a common asset-diversification tool. Asian exchange-traded funds remain easier to buy in New York than through local exchanges in Asia (*Financial Times*, December 1, 2005).

in 2005–6 on this issue, nonetheless, reveal much about the complex challenges to regional financial cooperation and the challenges of understanding individual national motives on this issue.

The ADB, staffed at the top since its inception by former Japanese Ministry of Finance officials, played the key role in raising the profile of currency cooperation discussions in the region in 2005–6. It did so when its president, Haruhiko Kuroda, and other staff began to talk about an initiative brewing in the Asian Development Bank, referred to as the ACU Initiative.[17] This initiative was to involve the creation of a regional monetary index that would measure deviations in intraregional exchange rate stability and serve as a basis for possible policy coordination.

In 2005–6, Japanese officials inside and outside the ADB were prominently featured in the media, advancing arguments that countries in the region needed to prepare for an anticipated dollar depreciation by removing their implicit or explicit pegs to the dollar. They noted that coordination failures inhibited governments from shifting to a more optimal currency basket system. Japanese proponents of exchange rate coordination argued that it would minimize the transmission of shocks induced by changes in relative currency values within the region. In this way, some argued for increased policy dialog over currency movements as a small step toward stabilizing price competitiveness, trade balances, and capital flows.

As of 2007, the official launch of the ADB ACU Initiative has been delayed repeatedly because other countries are concerned about the details—the various weightings of the currencies and the methodology used to determine them. The question of whether to include Hong Kong and Taiwan in the index is another stumbling block, with obvious political overtones. In 2006, the Chinese sensed that the Japanese were taking off and running on a matter on which there was neither consensus nor shared interest. China (as well as other nations in the region) was very unwilling to agree to support, in principle, an initiative that had implications heavily contingent on the details. There was no consensus on the composition of a meaningful currency basket or baskets; therefore, the political and economic utility of a regional currency unit or units would vary dramatically, depending on the details.

A decline in the international use of the yen, despite active efforts by the Japanese government toward the internationalization of the yen, helped foster suspicion that Japan might use the composition and weighting of any index to promote the yen.[18] Opinions in the region (and outside the region) also varied considerably on the issue of whether an ACU as an index should include not only trade but also

17. Other suggestions regarding the potential for currency or monetary cooperation in the region appeared earlier, for example, in 2002, when a report by the ADB Regional Economic Monitoring Unit (REMU) suggested that the scope for potential cooperation in the region could even encompass eventual monetary union in the region (Asian Development Bank Regional Economic Monitoring Unit [ADB REMU] 2002). They received little attention, however, until changes in the currency arrangements of China and Malaysia in 2005 and pressure on the Chinese government to allow for greater flexibility in the yuan provided an atmosphere more receptive to discussions on this issue in 2005–6.

18. Such suspicions were apparently held particularly strongly by the Chinese.

investment data. Incorporation of the latter dimension was limited, however, due to the unavailability of relevant capital flow statistics across the region. Some felt that financial market size should be incorporated into the index—an idea that appealed more to the Koreans, for example, because they ranked number two after the Japanese on that dimension in 2006. But, even an index focused purely on trade weights would be complex. It would make a huge difference whether trade weights were calculated according to purchasing power parity (PPP), in which China looms very large but Korea is very small, or in real or nominal measures, in which Japan carries greater weight. Actors were also thinking not merely about *current* relative economic/financial weights in the region but also about likely *future* weights. These predictions affected their preferences on the desired timing of any potential initiative. In the lead-up to the 2006 ASEAN+3 finance ministers' meeting, the Chinese made it clear that they wished to study the issue further before any resolution was adopted.[19]

In addition to raising issues of appropriate weighting (depending on the formula, different currencies will dominate) and component currencies (whether to include Taiwan, in particular), currency cooperation raises numerous other issues. These include the issue of how the creation of such an index would be linked to enhanced surveillance of economic and financial variables of the countries. It was unclear in 2005–6 how an ACU index or various ACU indices would be used in a concrete way to aid regional cooperation. Various studies revealed that the reactions of real exchange rates in the region to external shocks would probably vary according to the type of shock. Quantitative analysis of exchange rate movements might arguably help enhance the understanding of exchange rate issues in the region; however, such index tracking was already taking place by nongovernment actors (see Ogawa and Shimizu 2005).

The ADB focus on currency or monetary cooperation issues did resonate in a more general way with actors in the region, however. Many ASEAN member countries and Korea were becoming increasingly concerned about the possible implications of rapid dollar depreciation and accompanying appreciation of their own currencies in light of Chinese currency arrangements that continued to artificially devalue the yuan. In such a context, the Chinese essentially fixed exchange rate system could mean an effective competitive devaluation of the yuan at a time when these countries were increasingly competing head to head with China in the manufacturing sector. The Japanese focus on the perils of intraregional exchange rate instability and the Japanese ACU proposals provided a welcome opening for more frank discussion about exchange rate issues for these countries—and a means to exert some indirect pressure on China to reform its currency arrangements. After all, for an ACU to be viable as a unit of value or for currency intervention, the component currencies

---

19. Notably, the Chinese did not participate in the ASEAN+3 Research Group in 2005–6, and it was in this forum that the Japanese presented a Japanese Ministry of Finance–supported proposal for the creation of an ACU (called an Asian monetary unit, AMU, in the study) as the first step in a longer process of currency cooperation.

of the ACU would need to be convertible. The liquidity of money markets of the component currencies and the need for market infrastructure development were therefore increasingly emphasized by the Japanese in 2005–6, a backdoor way of pressuring the Chinese to move toward convertibility of their currency.

Thus, even though the ADB ACU Initiative was a thoroughly Japanese-driven initiative and had very little (virtually no) support from other Asian countries, it did come at a time of growing concern about uneven currency movements in the region. The 2006 resolution by the ASEAN+3 finance ministers to study "the potential utility of regional currency units" acknowledged the relevance of exchange rate issues to future discussions (Finance Ministers of ASEAN, China, Japan and the Republic of Korea (ASEAN+3) 2006). But, significantly, this statement did so in a vague and noncommittal way; the resolution did not acknowledge a need for a regional response to such developments, and it certainly did not endorse a specific approach to dealing with developments. According to some of the actors involved, the resolution was, in fact, motivated less by a collective desire to move forward with currency-related dialog and more by a collective desire to rein in ADB efforts to take the lead on issues of regional currency cooperation.[20]

Interestingly, the resolution was misrepresented widely in the popular media as an agreement to study forming an ACU.[21] Indeed, a survey of media reports in the wake of the 2006 ADB and ASEAN+3 finance minister annual meetings would have left any observer confused. Although there was clearly a lack of consensus within the region on the potential utility of an ACU index, the United States was scapegoated in the popular press for allegedly obstructing movement in this direction.[22] This focus on alleged United States opposition and interference provided greater weight to perceptions of Asian solidarity because it suggested that the potential for an Asian monetary union was perceived to be real enough as to concern an actor such as the United States.

Conclusion

Regional forums advancing concrete collaborative initiatives or systematized programs of policy dialog were virtually absent in Asia prior to the regional financial crisis. Today, the ASEAN+3 finance ministers and EMEAP central bankers play

---

20. According to those involved in the negotiations, the Chinese and Malaysians were absolutely insistent that the resolution focus on the "potential utility of regional currency units" (in the plural rather than the singular); moreover, sources attest that there was no consensus on the need to create a single regional monetary unit or to take steps toward a common currency (interviews, 2006).

21. See *Nikkei Net Interactive,* May 5, 2006. See also articles in the *Financial Times* at this time. Korean government officials, in addition, commented to local Korean newspapers that the resolution might be seen as the first step toward the creation of a regional monetary union.

22. Confusion and misunderstanding here prompted U.S. Undersecretary for International Affairs Timothy Adams to clarify in June 2006 at the World Economic Forum in Tokyo the U.S. government view on efforts toward the creation an ACU; see U.S. Department of the Treasury (2006).

an active role in generating and advancing regional initiatives and in maintaining close communication across regional financial authorities. The regional crisis was an important catalyst spurring a shift to greater regional financial cooperation in the decade thereafter but other factors also provided critical momentum to projects. These factors include, most notably, the rise of China and a new shared sense of benefit to the regional actors of exploiting strengthened perceptions of regional solidarity in international affairs.

It is worth noting that, despite the arguably small measurable substantive gains made by regional financial initiatives to date, these efforts have drawn significant attention from outside as well as from within East Asia. In 2006, for example, the Latin American Reserve Fund held a conference to examine East Asian financial initiatives and consider possible lessons for Latin America. Both the ADB and the Bank for International Settlements also reacted to growing regional efforts by proposing their own new mechanisms of institutionalized support for Asian regional initiatives.

How much have the regional initiatives reduced the vulnerability of the financial systems to another crisis or equipped them to respond better to crisis? A multilateralized regional monetary fund for short-term liquidity support would represent the most direct connection between regional financial cooperation and the 1997–98 crisis, in the minds of most. As I have detailed, developments through 2007 on the CMI suggest that multilateralization in a meaningful sense is unlikely. Nevertheless, the CMI remains alive because it serves strategic purposes, as a symbol of Asian solidarity, and helps rationalize policy dialog and information exchange processes. The CMI represents a depth of collaboration that would have been unfathomable among these countries a decade ago. The mere existence of the CMI and what the arrangement suggests about the *potential* for cooperation in the region advances strategic objectives that are shared at the highest level across the region. It was the fear of the collapse of cooperation if the CMI were to stagnate and a year go by without some type of progress announced, rather than the prospects of realized gains from proceeding to a next step, that seemed to motivate actors to shift their attention to multilateralization in 2007. Keeping the CMI project alive encourages international perceptions of strengthening regional solidarity in Asia—perceptions that provide helpful leverage to regional actors on issues such as IMF governance reform (interviews with regional actors, 2006–7).

The absence of a published official review of the CMI is notable, particularly given the thorough review of ABF2 published by the EMEAP in 2006.[23] Ambiguity surrounding the CMI contrasts starkly with the relative clarity of the ABF and ABMI projects and reflects the very different motivations behind regional cooperation prevailing across initiatives.

Related to this difference, the ABF outcomes appear more substantive than strategic, moving participating economies in the direction of stronger financial systems.

---

23. This survey details both the successes and challenges faced by ABF2.

Nevertheless, progress here is more notable in the by-products of cooperation than on initially articulated objectives. The ABF was intended to aid in supplying funds to regional bond markets and was also touted as a means for diversifying the foreign exchange holdings of regional central banks. Yet the latter objective is constrained by the desires of central banks to also foster market development—too much investment distorts rather than jump-starts markets. A further constraint relates to foreign exchange reserve management. Foreign exchange reserves are not only a potential tool for financial statecraft but also an important tool for dealing with domestic problems in many states (such as the nonperforming loan problem in the banking sector in China).

The ABF Initiative, thus, is most important for how it was used as a tool by the EMEAP central banks to help induce regulatory changes across the region, particularly in areas of nonresident investment and in reducing tax impediments. On regional efforts to develop its bond markets, the internal drivers behind regional financial cooperation are key. These internal drivers include desires to reap the benefits of competition from more effective financial intermediation, deregulation, and the removal of cross-border impediments to investment. Region-level discussions enabled domestic leaders to bring new angles to domestic debates about regulatory reforms. These new angles were not necessarily decisive in explaining reform patterns, but they helped override some interests entrenched against market reform.

In spite of the ABF and ABMI, however, Asian financial markets remain fragmented and much more integrated with extra-regional financial markets than with their own.[24] Most governments in the region are also in agreement that their individual financial systems remain excessively bank-centered. Secondary markets continue to suffer from low liquidity, and the region lacks suitable debt instruments to make up the complete risk and return spectrum investors need. But, because of the less strategic nature of bond market development initiatives, the long-term sustainability and impact of such regional projects may be more promising than initiatives more directly linked to the crisis, such as the CMI. In contrast to the CMI, regional projects on bond market development can be used as bases for independent bilateral, trilateral, subregional, or supraregional cooperation in the future.

Concerns about the rapid appreciation of many currencies in the region in 2007 contrasted sharply with concerns by many regional governments about rapidly declining currency values in 1997–98. Currency cooperation appears to be the area of regional collaboration in which the least progress has advanced on a regional basis since the Asian financial crisis. It is also the area least likely to take off a decade after crisis. Nevertheless, the strategic dimensions of currency union discussions could prove intensely interesting in the coming decade, particularly if the Chinese currency attains full convertibility.

---

24. See Belaisch and Zanello (2006) for an excellent analysis of the status of Asian financial integration as of 2006, using a variety of metrics. The authors note that data limitations constrain the development of truly accurate measurements of regional (as opposed to extra-regional) financial integration.

Objective assessments of regional vulnerability are exceedingly difficult to make, especially given that the next crisis is unlikely to mimic the last. And regional actors do not share a single vision about how regional financial projects should be used to alleviate vulnerabilities. Yet the history of financial crisis resolution across the globe clearly suggests that networks of personal interconnections play a critical role, even in apparently impersonal markets (MacKenzie 2006). In this respect, Asia is clearly better poised than it was a decade ago. Its financial authorities and political leaders are not only better connected to one another as a result of regional financial collaboration, but they are also better connected to other global actors.

CHAPTER 7

Trading Out of Crisis

John Ravenhill

A chapter on trade might seem a curious contribution to a book that examines the medium-term responses to the Asian crises of 1997–98; these, of course, were *financial* crises. In discussions of the causes and consequences of the crises, commentators frequently portray trade as, at most, an epiphenomenon, the crises being driven by the inexorable logic of exchange rate misalignments. Scholarly discussion of the crises seems to lend support to Susan Strange's frequent observation that finance is the master subfield of international political economy.

Even though developments in the trade sphere may not have been the trigger of the crisis, they nonetheless did play an important role. They generated the underlying problems that made the economies vulnerable to crisis. They were also a significant factor in the contagion that followed the initial crisis in Thailand and, consequently, in the severity of the regional economic downturn in the immediate postcrisis period. Although a study of trade relations can often ultimately be reduced to a consideration of other underlying causes—factor endowments, rent-seeking and the other activities of political coalitions, the investment decisions of firms, or exchange rate alignments—the international dimension that trade represents warrants separate treatment.

Moreover, in contrast to the field of exchange rates, where, as Benjamin Cohen (chap. 2 in this volume) indicates, (unexpectedly) little change has been observed since the financial crises, significant developments have occurred in the last decade

I am grateful to André Broome and Jikon Lai for research assistance on this chapter. Funding for the research on which it is based was provided by the Australian Research Council under Discovery Project DP0453077.

in the trade of the East Asian countries. The most important of these are in intraregional trade, driven by a redirection of the production networks that span the region, the related rise in importance of China as a partner/rival for other East Asian states, the increased dependence of East Asian economies on exports, and the proliferation of discriminatory trade agreements that involve East Asian countries.

This chapter addresses four principal questions: What was the role of trade in the 1997–98 crises? To what extent have these trade factors changed in the decade since then? If change has occurred, was this a consequence of conscious policy choices made by states in response to the crises? And have changes in trade had any impact on the vulnerability East Asian economies to future crises?

Trade and the 1997–98 Financial Crises

Prema-chandra Athukorala and Peter Warr distinguish two dimensions of the currency crises that swept parts of East Asia in 1997–98: (1) the underlying vulnerability of the economies to crisis and (2) the trigger that transformed a situation of vulnerability into one of financial collapse and more general economic crisis (Athukorala and Warr 2002; Warr 2002). They equate the trigger with factors that caused a loss of confidence on the part of market participants in the future value of the currency, including, for example, contagion effects. They list three sources of vulnerability, all related to the financial situation of the country: the adequacy of reserves relative to the stock of volatile capital, financial-sector fragility, and real exchange rate misalignment.

Their analysis is not unusual in the vast literature spawned by the crisis in that it privileges financial factors over other sources of vulnerability. But trade may contribute both to underlying structural vulnerability (the symptoms of which may be most readily visible in financial-sector indicators) and to contagion, if the latter is considered to include more than just the expectations of holders of assets denominated in local currencies. When the financial crises began in Thailand in 1997, the trigger for the speculative attack on the baht was fears over the exhaustion of Thai foreign exchange reserves. But, in turn, these fears had been generated, as Warr (1998, 55) himself notes, by developments in Thai trade relations, specifically the collapse of export growth that had occurred over the previous two years—an early warning sign to investors, who became increasingly nervous about the overall economic performance of Thailand.

Trade and financial issues inevitably were closely interlinked. Exchange rate misalignment when the Thai currency, linked to the U.S. dollar, appreciated against the yen, was an important factor in the loss of competitiveness of Thai exports. But an inappropriate exchange rate was not the only source of vulnerability or the only reason for investors' loss of confidence; as Warr indicates, the Thai economy was suffering from underlying structural problems, including shortages of skilled workers (the consequence of inadequate government provision of education and technical training) and from infrastructural bottlenecks.

Korea provides a second example in which trade played a significant role in creating vulnerabilities in the run-up to the 1997 crisis. Korean exports were heavily concentrated in a limited number of sectors; electronics, textiles and clothing, motor vehicles, and shipbuilding combined accounted for 55 percent of Korean exports at the time of the crisis. All these sectors in the mid-1990s were characterized by global overcapacity and declining prices. As they became significant global players, Korean companies had themselves contributed to this surplus capacity. By the mid-1990s, for instance, Korean firms had captured one-third of the global dynamic random access memory (DRAM) market and were thus a sufficiently sizable force that their own production decisions affected their export prices. The Korean concentration on the export of goods where worldwide surplus capacity was growing was the major reason why its terms of trade turned negative in 1996, a substantial factor in the slowing of Korean export growth.

Export composition and the direction of Korean trade were part of the explanation for (but not, of course, the only reasons) why Korea fared much more poorly in the financial crises than did Taiwan, an economy similar in many other respects to that of Korea. In electronics, almost 60 percent of Korean exports were directed toward markets where demand was declining or stagnant (Japan, East Asia, other Asian countries, Latin America, and Eastern Europe); in contrast, about 55 percent of Taiwanese electronics exports went to the United States and the European Union. The growing Korean dependence on developing-country markets in the 1990s and the rapidly declining share of the United States in its total exports were evidence of the inability of Korean companies at this time to sell in markets where sophisticated consumers demanded products at the technological edge (Noble and Ravenhill 2000).

Developments in trade among East Asian economies also played a role in triggering the crises and in the subsequent contagion. Over one-half of the export growth that the booming East Asian economies enjoyed in the decade after 1985 was attributable to sales to other parts of the East Asian region. Growth in intraregional trade halted in 1995. Consequently, in Ross Garnaut's words, "decline in intra-regional trade growth preceded and helped to precipitate the crisis" (2000, 19). Trade problems were an early warning signal to outside observers that all might not be well in some Southeast Asian economies. Garnaut (1998, 16) had previously identified intraregional trade as one of three possible sources of contagion that ensured a rapid spread of the crises from Thailand to other parts of the region. Once the crisis began, the high levels of dependence of East Asian economies on one another exacerbated the impact of the economic downturn, a characteristic that distinguished the East Asian crises from those in Latin America that had preceded them.[1]

---

1. Although this is a superficially persuasive argument, the correlation between contagion (the severity of the crises in a country) and intraregional trade dependence is far from perfect. For instance, the Korean dependence on trade with Thailand, in particular, or with Southeast Asia, more generally, was very limited, especially in comparison with that of other Southeast Asian countries that were not as severely damaged by the crisis as was Korea. For further discussion of the role of contagion in the crisis, see Goldstein (1998).

A further trade dimension to the 1997–98 financial crises was the increased competition among East Asian economies for export markets. In particular, several commentators identified rapid Chinese export growth as a factor in the slowdown in exports from Southeast Asia in the mid-1990s (Goldstein 1998, 16; Warr 1998, 56). The Chinese contribution to the financial crises of 1997–98 remains a contentious issue. For critics, its devaluation of the yuan in 1994 was an important factor in the loss of export competitiveness in the next two years of other countries in the region, particularly those of Southeast Asia. For others, its decision to maintain the value of its currency rather than follow the depreciation of its neighbors in 1997–98 was a hallmark of responsible regional leadership and a factor contributing to the relatively quick recovery of most economies from the severe downturn they experienced. It may well be that both views contain some elements of truth.

East Asian Trade since the Financial Crises

To what extent have developments in the trade patterns of East Asian economies since the 1997–98 crises made them more vulnerable to economic crisis or to trade-linked contagion across the region?

Share of Trade in Gross Domestic Product: Economic Openness

The remarkable recovery of most East Asian economies from the financial crises of 1997–98 rested in large part on foreign (primarily extra-regional) sales, not surprising given the crisis-induced decline in the domestic (and regional) markets. Their success in restoring export competitiveness resulted in an intensification of their already high levels of dependence on international trade.

Data on the growth of East Asian exports are provided in table 7.1. The impact of the financial crisis is seen in the decline in exports in 1998. For the fifteen major economies of East Asia (ASEAN+3 plus Hong Kong and Taiwan), overall exports fell by 6.8 percent in 1998. Exports to other East Asian economies declined by close to 18 percent in that year, pointing to one element of the contagion effects of the crisis. To put this loss of revenue in context, in 2001, a particularly bad year in the electronics cycle, East Asian total exports dropped by 9.4 percent. Aside from 2001, East Asian exports grew rapidly in the postcrisis decade, averaging close to double-digit growth over the period. Overall exports from East Asia doubled in value in the first six years after the crisis, laying the foundations for economic recovery. Some of the most impressive performances were recorded by the lower-income ASEAN economies, especially Cambodia and Vietnam.

With the growth in exports substantially exceeding overall economic growth in the decade since the crises, East Asian economies have become even more open (using the conventional measure of the share of exports in GDP; table 7.2).[2] Again,

2. If the more comprehensive measure of openness—exports plus imports as a share of GDP—is used, the conclusion is unchanged. Imports have also grown rapidly in all East Asian economies, with the exception of Japan, in the decade since the crises. They have failed to keep pace with export growth, reflected in the growing trade surpluses in the region.

Table 7.1 Annual growth rates of East Asian exports, 1995–2006 (%)

	1995	1996	1997	1998	1999	2000	2001	2002	2003	2004	2005	2006
Cambodia	46.7	−18.0	113.6	49.2	11.4	7.9	15.4	14.9	18.9	24.1	12.4	26.8
China	23.2	1.5	21.0	0.5	6.1	27.9	7.0	22.4	34.6	35.4	28.5	27.2
Indonesia	13.4	9.8	7.1	−8.6	−0.4	27.6	−9.3	1.5	9.4	11.5	22.9	17.5
Japan	12.1	−7.2	2.4	−7.9	8.1	14.0	−15.7	3.3	13.2	19.9	5.1	
Korea, Republic of	29.6	4.8	4.7	−7.9	8.4	19.7	−12.7	7.9	19.4	30.9	12.1	14.4
Malaysia	25.5	6.1	0.9	−6.9	15.1	16.1	−10.1	5.9	11.3	21.0	10.9	10.3
Myanmar	27.5	−1.2	−4.3	0.6	22.4	42.1	33.1	16.5	−29.2	18.3	23.7	—
Philippines	29.3	18.3	22.7	16.9	20.3	8.7	−15.9	9.5	2.9	9.5	4.0	13.9
Singapore	13.7	5.9	0.2	−12.4	4.4	22.4	−11.8	2.7	24.4	20.5	14.0	12.8
Taiwan	19.4	3.8	5.3	−9.4	10.0	22.0	−17.2	9.8	10.8	17.9	4.5	14.2
Thailand	27.2	−3.8	3.5	−5.2	5.6	25.2	−5.6	1.4	13.7	16.5	14.6	11.4
Vietnam	38.7	32.8	27.1	−1.9	24.0	25.5	3.7	11.2	20.6	31.4	22.5	22.7

Sources: Asian Development Bank, Asia Regional Integration Center, Integration Indicators Database, http://aric.adb.org; Asian Development Bank (2007). Original data from IMF Direction of Trade database; CEIC database (for Taiwan).

Table 7.2 Share of exports of goods and services in East Asian economies GDP, 1995–2005 (%)[a]

	1995	1996	1997	1998	1999	2000	2001	2002	2003	2004	2005
Cambodia	31.1	25.4	33.7	31.2	40.5	49.8	52.7	55.5	57.4	64.5	65.1
China	23.1	20.1	21.8	20.3	20.4	23.3	22.6	25.1	29.6	34.0	37.5
Indonesia	26.3	25.8	27.9	53.0	35.5	40.9	38.2	32.0	30.1	32.1	33.5
Japan	9.2	9.9	11.0	11.0	10.3	11.0	10.6	11.4	12.0	13.4	na
Korea, Republic of	28.8	27.9	32.4	46.2	39.1	40.8	37.8	35.3	38.0	44.0	42.5
Lao PDR	23.2	22.7	23.9	36.5	35.9	30.1	28.4	28.4	25.9	24.8	27.2
Malaysia	94.1	91.6	93.3	115.7	121.3	124.4	116.4	114.8	113.3	121.1	124.9
Myanmar	1.2	1.0	0.8	0.5	0.4	—	—	—	—	—	na
Philippines	36.4	40.5	49.0	52.2	51.5	55.4	49.2	50.2	49.6	50.8	47.3
Singapore	na	140.2	na	na	na	na	191.6	192.4	213.5	230.4	243.0
Taiwan	46.4	45.8	46.6	46.3	46.4	52.4	48.9	51.6	55.7	61.9	na
Thailand	41.8	39.3	48.0	58.9	58.3	66.8	65.9	64.2	65.6	70.6	73.6
Vietnam	32.8	40.9	43.1	44.9	50.0	55.0	54.6	56.0	59.2	67.5	70.1

Sources: World Bank (n.d.); National Statistics Office online database, http://61.60.106.82/pxweb/Dialog/statfile1L.asp (for Taiwan); http://www.singstat.gov.sg/keystats/hist/gdp2.html (for Singapore).

[a] PDR, *People's Democratic Republic.*

some of the less-developed economies in the region have experienced some of the most substantial increases in the ratio of exports to GDP. But economies that were already relatively open by international standards (such as Thailand and Taiwan) have also seen large jumps in their ratios of exports to GDP.

Greater openness might be perceived to increase the vulnerability of economies to externally induced crisis. The experience in 1997–98, however, was that no correlation existed between economic openness and severity of crisis. Singapore suffered far less than its neighbor Malaysia, despite being substantially more open. Similarly, Taiwan fared better than Korea despite exports' contributing a one-third larger share of its GDP than was the case in Korea. Since China began opening to the world in 1978, only Myanmar and North Korea among the East Asian economies appear to prefer the relative security brought about by autarky to the vulnerabilities derived from integrating into the global economy (and in the case of Myanmar, the policy of isolation may be as much a matter of external imposition as of domestic choice).

To what extent has the further opening of East Asian economies increased their openness to contagion from within the region? Intraregional exports fell sharply when the financial crises simultaneously affected most economies in East Asia (figure 7.1). By 1999, the share of East Asian exports consumed by other countries within the region began to pick up, and by the following year it was close to its precrisis peak of 40 percent of total exports.[3] Subsequently, with the exception of 2001, the share has continued to rise, albeit at a slow pace; in principle, this increases (but only marginally) the risk of contagion across the East Asian region in any future crisis. These aggregate figures, however, conceal dramatic changes in the direction of trade both within the region and with external partners (discussed in more detail later in this chapter).

Export Concentration and Vulnerability

The concentration of East Asian exports in a limited number of sectors, particularly electronics, was one source of vulnerability to economic downturn that was identified at the time of the financial crises. To what extent has this vulnerability changed over the succeeding decade? To examine changes in export concentration, I calculated Herfindahl-Hirschman indexes for the crisis economies. These are presented in table 7.3. The results are mixed; export concentration has increased somewhat in Korea, Malaysia, and the Philippines, but it has decreased in Indonesia and Thailand.

---

3. How to calculate intraregional trade is contentious, not least because of the emotional attachment to East Asian integration that was fostered by the crisis. Much depends on how trade between Hong Kong and China is treated, a particularly problematic issue given the role of Hong Kong as an entrepôt. Approximately 45 percent of Hong Kong total exports go to the mainland; the mainland has accounted for more than three-quarters of the growth in Hong Kong exports in recent years. If trade between Hong Kong and China is included, the share of intraregional exports in all exports of East Asian economies increases by about 7 percentage points. On Hong Kong exports, see Hong Kong Trade Development Council (2003).

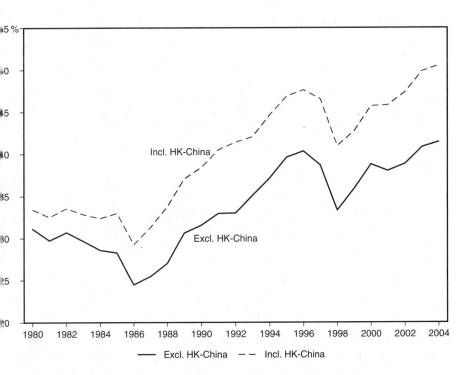

Figure 7.1 Share of intraregional exports in total exports, 1980–2004 (%).
Source: Calculated from data from IMF Direction of Trade Statistics; Taiwan National Statistics Office online database.

Table 7.3 Herfindahl-Hirschman Indices for export concentration of crisis economies[a]

	1989	1996	2005
Indonesia	0.088	0.035	0.031
Malaysia[b]	0.048	0.037	0.046
Philippines	N/A	0.085	0.091
South Korea	0.015	0.028	0.034
Thailand	0.023	0.018	0.017

Source: From UN Commodity Trade Statistics Database (COMTRADE) data.
[a] N/A, not available.
[b] Most recent data are for 2004.

Southeast Asian economies that have significant commodity exports have benefited from the rise in raw materials prices that occurred in the middle of the first decade of the twenty-first century (changes in the price of petroleum have been particularly important, affecting not only Indonesia but also Malaysia and Singapore). The consequence is that for all the Southeast Asian economies, with the

Table 7.4 Share of manufactures in total exports, 1985–2005 (%)[a]

	1985	1986	1995	2004	2005
Indonesia	9.68	15.60	46.40	48.13	40.68
Malaysia	25.74	34.74	71.04	68.36	na[b]
Philippines	22.51	25.18	38.60	52.89	87.53
Singapore	44.67	52.09	77.11	71.25	68.60
Thailand	35.82	41.24	68.48	67.01	67.00

Source: From UN Commodity Trade Statistics Database (COMTRADE) data.
[a] Manufactures are defined as SITC Rev.3 categories 6, 7, and 8, less categories 67 and 68. SITC, Standard International Trade Classification.
[b] Data for Malaysia are not available for 2005.

exception of the Philippines, the share of manufactures in overall exports has fallen marginally in the decade since the financial crises (table 7.4). This increase in export earnings from commodities has helped to reduce the export-concentration index for Southeast Asian economies.

A further concentration has occurred within manufacturing-sector exports, however. All the East Asian economies in table 7.5, with the exception of Korea, depend more heavily on exports of electronics and electrical machinery than they did in the period leading up to the crisis. The risks of such export concentration were evident in 2001 when the electronics industry entered one of its cyclical downturns. The impact on exports from the East Asian economies was actually more severe than that of the financial crises of 1997–98 (table 7.1), in itself a pointer to the ongoing dependence on extra-regional markets.

The share of electronics in total export earnings ranges from 5 percent in Indonesia to 46 percent in the Philippines. For the Philippines, the dependence on electronics is now extreme even in comparison with other countries in the region (and, indeed, in other parts of the world—it is ranked fourth in the world in its revealed comparative advantage in the export of electronic components; United Nations Conference on Trade and Development/World Trade Organization [UNCTAD/WTO] 2004).[4] Its exports of electrical circuits have expanded rapidly in the first years of this century. Of all the crisis economies, the Philippines now has the most concentrated pattern of exports and appears most vulnerable to economic downturn in one of the regular cycles that afflict the electronics industry.

Trade structure was identified as a factor contributing to the economic crisis in Korea. As reflected in the data in table 7.1, the Korean economy has become substantially more dependent on exports in the decade since the financial crisis. Again, this dependence poses risks of vulnerability to future downturns in foreign

---

4. The Balassa index of revealed comparative advantage compares the share of a sector in the total exports of a country with the share of that sector in total world exports. When the ratio is more than 1, the country is said to enjoy a comparative advantage in the exports from that sector. For the Philippines, the ratio for electronic components is 5.17; in other words, exports from this sector are more than five times more important for the Philippines than for the world as a whole.

Table 7.5 Share of electrical machinery, apparatus, and appliances in total value of exports (%)

	1995	2005
China	6.4	10.2
Indonesia	1.8	4.7
Malaysia	22.1	24.4
Philippines	13.3	46.5
Korea, Republic of	22.8	15.1
Singapore	21.6	28.8
Thailand	11.3	13.3

Source: UN Commodity Trade Statistics Database (COMTRADE), Standard International Trade Classification (SITC) Rev 2.

markets. Nowhere is this more apparent than in automobiles, arguably the principal success story of the Korean recovery since the financial crises (although, of course, continuing success in consumer electronics has also contributed significantly to the ongoing growth of Korea). The share of exports in the output of the Korean auto industry has increased dramatically since the turn of the century, a reflection both of slow domestic growth and of increased foreign enthusiasm for Korean brands. Despite Korean companies increasing their offshore production, especially in China and the United States, close to 70 percent of the domestic production of cars now goes to foreign markets. Although this unusually heavy dependence on external markets might be considered a source of vulnerability, markets for Korean automobiles are now much more diversified than in the mid-1990s; the earlier dependence on low-income markets has disappeared. Similarly, the Korean electronics industry is less dependent than it was at the time of the crisis on exports of a single product, DRAMs.

A Turn Inwards?: The Growth of Intraregional Trade in East Asia

The financial crises sparked at least a superficial sense of regional identity in East Asia. It was superficial for a couple of reasons. First, to the extent that it existed, regional identity was constructed primarily on a negative foundation, an anti-Western and, particularly, anti-U.S. backlash against the perceived indifference and/or predatory response of Western countries to the crises. There was little sense of what the positive foundations for an East Asian identity might be. Linked to this is a second factor—the very significant divisions within East Asia (Rozman 2004). When the initial momentum generated by the negative response of the West to the financial crises slowed (and the fate of the Japanese proposal for an East Asian Monetary Fund demonstrated how limited this momentum was; see Jennifer Amyx, chap. 6, and T. J. Pempel, chap. 8 in this volume), long-standing sources of division resurfaced, most obviously in tensions in Northeast Asia between Japan and its neighbors.

Nonetheless, the financial crises did generate a new enthusiasm for things regional; an increase in intraregional trade was widely seen as a stepping stone toward a more integrated East Asian economy that would be less vulnerable to the types of shock that triggered the 1997–98 crises. Masahiro Kawai, former chief economist at the World Bank for the East Asia region, asserts, for instance, that "the crisis prompted the regional economies to realize the importance of closer economic cooperation among themselves which were increasingly interdependent and to undertake various initiatives for the institutionalization of such interdependence." He notes in this context the proliferation of negotiations of trade agreements among countries in the region (Kawai 2004, 1).

Several points are pertinent in examining aspirations for greater regional collaboration on trade in East Asia. First, the direction of trade is primarily determined by market forces, including the responses of private-sector actors and movements in relative prices, rather than by government dictates. Second, to the extent that governments do play a role, this comes primarily through the negotiation of trade agreements. As the discussion in the final section of this chapter demonstrates, no consistent pro-East Asian regional bias has occurred in the pursuit by East Asian governments of preferential trade agreements over the decade since the crises. Third, as reflected in figure 7.1, although intraregional trade as a share of the total trade of East Asian economies has recovered from the postcrisis trough, the current figure is only marginally above that of the precrisis peak.[5] Intraregional exports in East Asia have grown far less rapidly than those within the North America Free Trade Agreement (NAFTA) countries. What has occurred has been primarily a reorientation of trade patterns in response to the rapid emergence of China as the assembly plant to the world. To the extent that intraregional trade has increased in East Asia, it is largely because economies in the region have grown more rapidly than those elsewhere, not because of any reorientation of trade; a World Bank study estimates that the relatively rapid growth of East Asian economies accounts for two-thirds of the increase in intraregional trade (Gill, Kharas, and Bhattasali 2007, 89).

The trade triangles that developed following the 1985 Plaza Accord (in which components manufactured in Northeast Asia were processed and/or assembled in Southeast Asia for ultimate export to the U.S. market) to a considerable extent have been supplemented, if not altogether replaced, by China-centric networks. Final products for the U.S. market are now being assembled in China from components sourced from elsewhere in East Asia—predominantly from Japan, Korea, and Taiwan but also, as the next section illustrates, from the ASEAN economies. Estimates suggest that processed (imported) components contribute between 60 and 80 percent of the value of all Chinese exports. These components, moreover, constitute more than 50 percent of the total value of Chinese imports (Gaulier, Lemoine, and Ünal-Kesenci 2004, 13).

---

5. Note that the data here are for exports only, arguably the more politically significant component of trade. The share of intraregional trade in total East Asian imports is higher than for exports—the smaller share of intraregional trade in overall exports being a reflection of the trade surplus that the region enjoys with other parts of the world.

Table 7.6 Changing direction of east Asian trade (%)[a]

(1)	(2)	(3) ASEAN	(4) China	(5) Hong Kong	(6) Japan	(7) European Union	(8) United States	(9) ASEAN+3+1
Japan	1990	11.6	2.1	4.6	—	20.7	31.7	24.4
	1996	17.9	5.3	6.2	—	15.6	27.5	36.5
	2000	14.3	6.4	5.7	—	16.8	30.1	32.8
	2005	12.8	13.5	6.1	—	14.6	22.9	40.2
China	1990	6.7	—	43.3	14.7	10.2	8.6	63.4
	1996	6.8	—	21.8	20.4	13.9	17.7	53.4
	2000	6.9	—	17.8	16.6	16.5	21.2	45.7
	2005	7.3	—	16.3	11.0	18.9	21.5	39.2
Hong Kong	1990	7.4	24.7	—	5.7	18.8	24.1	40.1
	1996	6.9	34.3	—	6.6	15.2	21.2	49.4
	2000	6.1	34.5	—	5.5	15.6	23.3	48.6
	2005	5.9	45.6	—	5.3	14.5	16.1	58.8
ASEAN	1990	18.9	1.9	4.7	18.3	16.2	19.6	46.9
	1996	24.5	3.0	6.2	14.2	14.5	18.1	51.5
	2000	23.0	3.9	5.3	13.2	15.0	19.0	49.3
	2005	26.2	8.3	6.6	11.6	13.1	14.8	56.7

Source: From IMF Direction of Trade database http://www.imfstatistics.org/DOT/.
[a] Percentage share of total exports of each country in column 1 going to markets in columns 3 to 9. ASEAN, Association of Southeast Asian Nations; ASEAN+3+1, the ten member states of ASEAN plus China, Japan, Korea, and Hong Kong; IMF, International Monetary Fund.

Two dimensions of the emergence of China as an important intermediary in trade are apparent from data on the direction of East Asian exports (table 7.6). The first is the rapid growth in the significance of China as a market for the exports of other East Asian economies. China has replaced the United States as the single most important export market for Korea. The Chinese share of the exports of Japan and of ASEAN has more than doubled since the financial crises. The increasing role of China in providing a market for the exports of other East Asian economies should go some way to allaying the fears in other parts of the region regarding competition from China (an issue discussed in the next section).

The other side of the rise of China has been the relative decline in the significance of extra-regional markets for other East Asian economies. Particularly important here is the decline in the share of the exports of other East Asian economies destined for the United States, down by one-fifth in the decade since the crisis. But does this mean that East Asian economies have become more closely integrated and regionally self-reliant? The answer is, at most, only partially so. As figure 7.1 illustrates, the overall dependence of East Asia on extra-regional markets has diminished only marginally since the period immediately preceding the financial crisis. The rise in the share of the exports of other East Asian economies going to China has been accompanied by a substantial increase in the extra-regional orientation of Chinese exports. The share of Chinese exports destined for EU and U.S. markets rose from 31 percent in 1996 to close to 40 percent in 2005. Its dependence on East Asian markets accordingly shrank in the same period from 55 percent of its exports to less than 40 percent (table 7.6).

Although the rapid growth of China has generated a reorientation of production networks in East Asia and arguably has led to a further fragmentation of the production process, it has not substantially increased regional trade self-sufficiency. China does not itself currently provide the engine for regional economic growth (Gaulier, Lemoine, and Ünal-Kesenci, 2006). East Asia remains more heavily dependent on and, thus, more vulnerable to developments in extra-regional markets than either European or North American economies do. On the other hand, this pattern renders East Asian economies less vulnerable than might otherwise be the case to within-region contagion.

The Chinese Threat

Some commentators saw increased competition from China as contributing to the slowdown in the growth in export earnings of Southeast Asian economies in the mid-1990s and thus as paving the way for the economic crises that followed. As the tortuous process of negotiating the details of the accession of China to the WTO came close to completion, so concern regarding the economic impact of China on Southeast Asia grew. Not surprisingly, this was expressed by some politicians and academics in terms reminiscent of Ross Perot's comments on the potential loss of U.S. jobs and investment to Mexico at the time of the NAFTA negotiations. Such populist expressions of potentially zero-sum competition between China and ASEAN for markets and foreign investment would not normally be expected to find resonance in the views of mainstream economics. A series of studies by the World Bank concluded, however, that lower-income ASEAN economies were the ones most likely to be adversely affected by the accession of China to the WTO, particularly after the country quotas associated with the Multifibre Arrangement were removed at the beginning of 2005. Several other studies reached similar conclusions.[6]

China now receives a substantial majority of the foreign investment that is recorded as flowing into East Asia as a whole, a fact that some commentators perceive as evidence that China is capturing a disproportionate share of such flows. The fears that underlie such statements are entirely understandable and appear to be substantiated by a casual look at the foreign direct investment (FDI) data, but they reflect a number

---

6. The most recent calculations by World Bank staff are included in Ianchovichina, Suthiwart-Narueput and Zhao (2004); Ianchovichina and Walmsley (2003). Earlier work is reported in Martin and Ianchovichina (2001). For similar conclusions drawn from a market-share analysis rather than a computable general equilibrium approach, see Weiss and Shanwen (2003); Weiss (2004). Lall and Albaladejo (2004) present a less alarmist scenario. Eichengreen, Rhee, and Tong (2004), using a gravity model, reach conclusions broadly similar to those of the World Bank, namely that Chinese growth will have a negative impact on low-income countries that export consumer goods but a positive impact on higher-income Asian exporters of capital goods.

of logical fallacies. These include mistaking correlation for causation, a misrepresentation of FDI as constituting a fixed sum and a consequent fallacy that competition for FDI is inevitably a zero-sum game, and implicit unwarranted assumptions about what an appropriate level of FDI for China might be. Moreover, any discussion of flows of FDI into China is complicated by the fact that a substantial portion of these flows takes the form of round-tripping capital, that is, a flow that originates in China itself (i.e., funds are sent out of and then brought back into the country to take advantage of the better treatment authorities afford foreign investment).

Space precludes a detailed examination of these issues in this chapter.[7] Here it is sufficient to note that although the overall record of ASEAN economies in attracting new flows of FDI in the aftermath of the financial crises was poor—both relative to their past performance and relative to that of many other developing countries in the last decade—little evidence points to any significant diversion of investment flows to China. Moreover, in 2004–5 (the most recent years for which data are available), FDI inflows to ASEAN substantially picked up. In 2005, they exceeded $36 billion, considerably in excess of the precrisis peak. Moreover, if we examine the data on FDI stocks rather than flows, which many specialists on the international operations of companies consider to be the superior measure of the significance of foreign investment, no evidence exists of China's outperforming ASEAN economies; in ASEAN, stocks of FDI more than doubled between 1995 and 2005.

The competition between China and ASEAN economies for export markets is more immediately relevant to the concerns of this chapter. Earlier conclusions about the likely negative impact of China on ASEAN export competitiveness were drawn from projections, primarily derived from computable general equilibrium (CGE) models. Data are now available (from the UN Commodity Trade Statistics [COMTRADE] database) that cover the first four years following the entry of China into the WTO; it is possible for the first time to observe the impact that this entry has had on ASEAN trade. To examine this in detail, I traced the evolution of the positions of ASEAN and China in the markets of Japan and the United States for five major categories of exports (aggregated at the two-digit level of Standard International Trade Classification [SITC] rev. 3): office machinery, electrical machinery, telecommunications and sound equipment, clothing, and footwear. The last two of these sectors feature relatively unsophisticated, labor-intensive manufactures. In both of these, the Chinese share of the U.S. and Japanese markets already exceeded that of ASEAN by 1995. The other three product sectors comprise relatively sophisticated manufactures. In all three of these in 1995, exports from ASEAN had a substantially larger share of the U.S. and Japanese markets than did those from China. In 2003, these five commodity groups combined accounted for 71 percent of all ASEAN manufactured exports to the world (81 percent of all manufactured exports from ASEAN to the United States and 62 percent of the total of manufactured exports to Japan).[8]

7. I examine these issues at greater length in Ravenhill (2006a, 2007).

8. To save space, only the summary results are presented in this chapter. A complete set of data is available from the author.

Table 7.7 Summary table of changes in ASEAN shares of the Japanese and U.S. markets[a]

Value up, market share up	Value up, market share down
Electrical machinery (Japan)	Telecommunications (Japan, United States)
	Apparel and clothing (United States)
Value down, market share up	**Value down, market share down**
	Office machinery (United States, Japan)
	Footwear (United States, Japan)
	Apparel and clothing (Japan)
	Electrical machinery (United States)

[a] Value down is when the value of imports from ASEAN in the final year in the period, 2005, was more than 10 percent below that of the peak year in the period 1995–2005. ASEAN, Association of Southeast Asian Nations.

The results make for grim reading from the ASEAN perspective. In only one sector-country combination (electrical machinery in Japan) did both the value of imports and the share of ASEAN countries in total imports increase during the ten-year period 1995–2005 (table 7.7). In only one other sector (telecommunications) did the value of imports from ASEAN increase in the Japanese market, even though ASEAN *lost* market share while that of China increased. For clothing, during these years still governed in the United States by the country quotas of the Multifibre Arrangement, the value of ASEAN imports increased, but their market share decreased. For all the other sector-country combinations, including the higher value-added sectors of office machinery in both the Japanese and U.S. markets and electrical machinery in the U.S. market, ASEAN economies suffered not only an erosion of their share of the import market but an absolute decline in the value of their exports.[9]

The aggregated earnings for ASEAN exports in the Japanese market for the products included in this study is largely unchanged, with losses in market shares in office machinery and telecommunications/sound equipment offset by gains in the market share for electrical machinery. In the U.S. market, however, if ASEAN had maintained at their peak its shares of imports of the three categories of advanced manufactures included in this study—electrical machinery, office machinery, and telecommunications/sound equipment—its total exports of these products would have been worth approximately an additional $21 billions in 2005 (a loss of about $7 billion in each of the product categories).

9. Care must be exercised in drawing any inferences from the descriptive data presented here. They are highly aggregated as to sector (SITC, two-digit level) and across all the major ASEAN economies, obscuring variance in performance across products and across countries. And, at best, they present a correlation between the ASEAN loss of market share and simultaneous gains in that of China. The underlying factor behind such a correlation might not necessarily be the competitiveness of Chinese exports, however. Supply-side disruptions in the crisis-hit ASEAN economies in the period from 1997 onward, for instance, may have been a major factor underlying the loss of market share in the ASEAN economies. The data, however, do support the conclusions of econometric work (e.g., Holst and Weiss 2004) that analyzed changing market shares in earlier periods and attributed ASEAN market-share losses to increased competition from China.

These results appear to substantiate fears commonly expressed in Southeast Asia that China and the lower-income ASEAN economies are in competition with one another and that the structural similarity of the economies precludes mutual gain.

> the lack of complementarity between the Chinese and ASEAN economies limits the capacity that each can absorb of the other's products. This obstructs to a certain degree the economic integration and interdependence of China and the ASEAN countries.... Mutually competitive, rather than complementary, structures of China and ASEAN prevented significant growth in trade, with the possible exception of China and Singapore.... In the area of traditional labor-intensive industries like textiles, clothing, and footwear, China's gains have come at the expense of ASEAN's.... China's emergence as a global manufacturing base has apparently also resulted in most ASEAN economies experiencing a severe hollowing out of their industries. (Wong and Chan 2003, 508n. 4, 517, 519, 525)

Such arguments, however, ignore the dramatic transformation that has occurred in the composition of trade between ASEAN and China over the last decade. Over the course of the 1990s, the value of ASEAN exports to China increased fourfold; their share in Chinese total imports increased by one-half, from 6 to 9 percent (Ianchovichina, Suthiwart-Narueput, and Zhao 2004, 58). Meanwhile, in the decade since the financial crises, the share of ASEAN exports going to China more than doubled to 8 percent of the total (table 7.6). Some ASEAN economies have benefited significantly from the Chinese need for raw materials imports to fuel its industrialization. But it is not just a matter of the ASEAN economies increasing their exports of raw materials; with the notable exception of Indonesia, whose exports continue to be dominated by energy products, a dramatic transformation in the composition of ASEAN exports to China occurred in the second half of the 1990s. The share of manufactures grew rapidly, so that by 1999 they constituted more than half of the value of total exports (table 7.8).

A more detailed breakdown of exchanges between ASEAN and China finds significant growth in intra-industry trade. The share of parts and components in

Table 7.8 Share of manufactures in Chinese imports from ASEAN (%)[a]

	1990	1995	1996	1997	1998	1999	2000	2001	2002	2003	2004
Indonesia	54.4	29.2	22.5	23.5	34.1	29.0	25.3	27.0	25.0	22.4	22.3
Malaysia	11.9	41.0	48.3	40.9	41.9	49.4	54.5	62.1	54.5	50.8	50.2
Philippines	1.8	6.5	18.6	24.1	45.6	58.4	59.9	69.2	79.3	81.0	92.5
Singapore	28.6	48.5	48.2	50.9	60.5	68.1	66.5	67.1	66.0	66.6	68.4
Thailand	10.4	14.5	21.5	31.7	47.7	45.2	44.5	45.9	53.3	46.7	59.7
ASEAN (weighted) average	31.1	34.9	36.5	39.1	49.2	52.2	51.7	56.0	56.1	54.1	55.5

Source: UN Commodity Trade Statistics Database (COMTRADE), http://unstats.un.org/unsd/comtrade/.

[a] Manufactures are defined as Standard International Trade Classification (SITC) 6, 7, and 8, less categories 67 and 68.

Table 7.9 Chinese imports of office machinery, telecommunications equipment, and electrical machinery from ASEAN (millions of current dollars)[a]

	1997	1998	1999	2000	2001	2002	2003	2004	2005
Office machinery	1,356	2,113	1,921	2,866	3,092	3,990	6,935	8,283	10,692
Telecommunications, sound equipment	305	369	411	692	735	815	1,184	2,127	2,799
Electrical machinery	934	1,309	2,384	4,498	5,509	9,086	15,365	21,765	28,489

Source: UN Commodity Trade Statistics Database (COMTRADE) data.
[a] ASEAN, Association of Southeast Asian Nations.

Malaysian exports of manufactures to China, for instance, rose from 6.4 percent in 1992 to 16.1 percent in 1996 to 50.6 percent in 2000; for Singapore, the figures were 23.1 percent, 41.9 percent, and 50.3 percent; for Thailand, they were 6.8 percent, 29.2 percent, and 54.0 percent (Athukorala 2003). Rapid industrialization in China *is* fostering a new division of labor in East Asia, including the ASEAN economies, and a significant expansion of intra-industry trade.

To a considerable extent, the increase of ASEAN exports to China has offset the losses that ASEAN economies have suffered because of Chinese competition in third-country markets. Consider the products examined in the study of ASEAN and Chinese competition in the Japanese and U.S. markets. ASEAN countries have increased their sales of these products in the Chinese market by approximately $34 billion since 2000, more than compensating for the losses suffered in the U.S. market (table 7.9). The principal gains have come in electrical machinery, for which exports increased more than sixfold from 2000 to 2005, primarily imports from Malaysia and the Philippines. Substantial increases also occurred in office machinery, with the value of exports up more than 300 percent; the single most important supplier for this product was Thailand. Again, various caveats must be taken into account in considering these data—the level of aggregation disguises the problem that the gains in one product sector and/or market do not necessarily offset the losses in another for individual countries, let alone individual companies. Significant adjustment costs may have been incurred. But they do point to an emerging regional division of labor that is incorporating ASEAN states to a greater extent than some anticipated, to growing dynamic complementarities, and to the stimulus that the growth of China has provided to some manufacturing sectors in ASEAN.

Regional Collaboration on Trade

Most observers agree that the financial crises were a significant stimulus to enhanced regional economic collaboration, both on finance (see Amyx, chap. 6, and Pempel, chap. 8 in this volume) and on trade. In trade, the crises added to concerns already being expressed in some East Asian foreign and trade ministries regarding the likely difficulties that a new round of multilateral trade negotiations would encounter and the potentially deleterious impact on East Asia of a proliferation and deepening of regional integration arrangements in Europe and the Americas.[10] The new interest in discriminatory arrangements was primarily a defensive move.

From being a latecomer to discriminatory trade, East Asia has emerged as the most active site in the world for the negotiation of bilateral and minilateral trade agreements in the first decade of the twenty-first century. In late 2006, more than eighty such agreements involving East Asian countries were either being implemented, under negotiation, or the subject of study groups (table 7.10). What are the likely impacts of these agreements on the trade of East Asian economies and their vulnerability to economic crises?

The novelty of the new bilateralism—with relatively few negotiations having been concluded to date and only a handful of treaties currently in force and, of these, several having extended timetables before all their provisions will be implemented—renders any effort to speculate on their likely consequences somewhat hazardous. Nonetheless, the content of the agreements and the circumstances in which they were negotiated allow several conclusions to be drawn.

A starting point in any assessment of these arrangements must be to emphasize that, like regionalism elsewhere, they have been driven by a variety of interests and actors. The furthering of trade relations is but one motive for the negotiation of trade agreements—and, in a number of instances, has been subordinate to other concerns. Consider Singapore, the most active East Asian player in the new discriminatory arrangements. The Singapore government chose New Zealand as its first non-ASEAN partner for a preferential trading agreement (PTA)—clearly not because of the significance of the New Zealand economy for Singapore but because it wanted to gain experience in negotiating a PTA with an industrialized economy sympathetic to trade liberalization. It has subsequently targeted those countries it regards as its most important *strategic* partners—the United States, China, Japan, India, and Australia—and has sought to use PTAs as a means of locking in these relationships. Economic interests, of course, are not absent from these arrangements, but the Singapore government has been willing to accept decidedly incomplete (with India) or arguably uneven (with Japan and the United States) economic agreements for the sake of securing noneconomic objectives (interviews with officials of the Singapore government, February 2006).

Noneconomic motives were also to the fore in the choice of partners made by other governments. Korea decided on Chile as its first PTA partner, ostensibly for the same reason that Singapore chose New Zealand—it allowed an opportunity to learn the ropes of PTA negotiations with an economy that was not a significant trading partner. This proved to be an unwise choice given domestic political sensitivities about potential Chilean exports of agricultural products. Political motivations have also dominated the Taiwanese PTA strategy, which has added another dimension

---

10. See, for instance, the analysis by the Japanese Ministry of International Trade and Industry ([MITI] 1999).

Table 7.10 Bilateral/minilateral PTAs involving east Asian countries, December 2006[a]

Country	Implementing/signed	Negotiating	Study group
ASEAN	AFTA, China, Korea	Australia–New Zealand, India, Japan	European Union, United States
Brunei	AFTA, Chile–New Zealand–Singapore[b]	Japan	United States
Cambodia	AFTA		
China	ASEAN, Chile, Hong Kong, Macau, Pakistan, Thailand	Australia, Gulf Cooperation Council, Iceland, New Zealand, SACU, Singapore	India, Japan-Korea, Korea, Peru, South Africa
Hong Kong	China	New Zealand	
Indonesia	AFTA	Japan, Pakistan	EFTA, India, United States
Japan	Malaysia, Mexico, Philippines, Singapore, Thailand	Australia, ASEAN, Brunei, Chile, Gulf Cooperation Council, Indonesia, Korea, Vietnam	Canada, India, South Africa, Switzerland
Korea	ASEAN,[c] Chile, EFTA, Singapore, United States	Canada, India, Japan	Australia, China, European Union, India, China-Japan, Malaysia, MERCOSUR, Mexico,[d] New Zealand, South Africa, Thailand
Lao PDR	AFTA	Thailand	
Malaysia	AFTA, Japan	Australia, New Zealand, Pakistan, United States	Chile, India, Korea
Myanmar	AFTA, BIMSTEC[e]		
Philippines	AFTA, Japan		Pakistan, United States
Singapore	AFTA, Australia, EFTA, India, Japan, Jordan, Korea, New Zealand, United States, Brunei–Chile–New Zealand[b]	Bahrain, Canada, China, Egypt, Kuwait, Mexico, Panama, Peru, Qatar	Pakistan, Sri Lanka, UAE
Taiwan	Guatemala, Nicaragua, Panama	Dominican Republic, El Salvador, Honduras, Paraguay	
Thailand	AFTA, Australia, China, India, New Zealand, BIMSTEC[e]	Bahrain, EFTA, India, Peru, United States	MERCOSUR

[a] AFTA, ASEAN Free Trade Agreement; ASEAN, Association of Southeast Asian Nations; BIMSTEC, Bay of Bengal Initiative for MultiSectoral Technical and Economic Cooperation; EFTA, European Free Trade Agreement; FTA, free trade agreement; MERCOSUR, Mercado Común del Sur; PDR, People's Democoratic Republic; PTA, preferential trading agreement; SACU, Southern African Customs Union; UAE, United Arab Emirates.
[b] After the Clinton administration proposal for an FTA among the United States, Australia, Chile, New Zealand, and Singapore lapsed, Chile, New Zealand, and Singapore signed the Pacific-Three FTA in October 2002. On June 3, 2005, with the accession of Brunei to the agreement, it was renamed the Trans-Pacific Strategic Economic Partnership.
[c] Excludes Thailand, which refused to sign after Korea excluded rice and two hundred other agricultural products from the agreement.
[d] After failing to reach agreement in their negotiation of an FTA, Korea and Mexico agreed in September 2005 to negotiate a more limited economic cooperation agreement.
[e] Bangladesh, Bhutan, India, Myanmar, Nepal, Sri Lanka, and Thailand.

to government efforts to secure diplomatic recognition. To date, only Guatemala, Nicaragua, and Panama have signed up for an agreement with Taipei.[11]

In many other instances, government strategies appear to have been dominated by the desire to minimize the domestic political cost of such agreements rather than to maximize domestic economic benefits. I have termed this a strategy of pursuing "liberalization without political pain" (Ravenhill 2003). Governments have been able to achieve this objective because of the lack of specificity of the WTO rules on PTAs. Article XXIV.8 allows for closer integration of economies that choose to implement free trade areas or customs unions, provided that the customs duties under the new agreement are not higher or more restrictive than the individual countries had previously imposed and that the new preferential agreement eliminates duties and other restrictions on "substantially all the trade" between the participants.

The wording in this article has generated enormous controversy over the years because members have failed to reach agreement on how to define and operationalize the clause "substantially all the trade." The WTO itself has noted that "there exists neither an agreed definition of the percentage of trade to be covered by a WTO-consistent agreement nor common criteria against which the exclusion of a particular sector from the agreement could be assessed" (World Trade Organization [WTO] 1998).

Member states have exploited the lack of specificity of Article XXIV.8 to negotiate agreements that are only partial in their coverage. Here the European Union has led from the front. It set a precedent for excluding sensitive sectors from bilateral agreements by excluding most agricultural products from its free trade agreements (FTAs) with Mexico and South Africa. These precedents were seized on by Keidanren in its lobbying in favor of Japanese negotiation of FTAs. Whereas, the Federation argued (Keidanren 2000), it was desirable "to liberalize as much trade as possible" in the agreements, the WTO requirement that they should cover "substantially all trade" among the participants provided an opening to omit "sensitive" items from the liberalization schedule, thereby minimizing the domestic political costs of the new regionalism; "as is evident looking at other FTAs, some items of the industry in question which simply cannot be liberalized because of the serious impact by the free trade agreement may result in being removed from the list." The paper then cites the example of products exempted from tariff liberalization in the EU-Mexican FTA, noting that "such examples should prove a useful reference in Japan's considering FTAs."

And this is precisely what the Japanese government did in its negotiation of the Japan-Singapore Economic Partnership Agreement (JSEPA); the few products in the ultra-sensitive agricultural sector that Singapore exported to Japan, principally cut flowers and goldfish, were excluded from the liberalization provisions. Zero tariffs apply to less than 10 percent of the volume of exports of agricultural products

---

11. Even after Taiwanese exports to Panama doubled in 2004, they constituted less than two-tenths of 1 percent of the total value of the exports of Taiwan. Two-way trade between Taiwan and Nicaragua totaled US$46.27 million in 2005 (Bilaterals.org 2006).

from Singapore to Japan; the JSEPA created no new preferences in the agricultural sector and excluded 90 percent of the (very modest) value of Singapore exports of agricultural products to Japan. In a similar manner, Japan made very few concessions in its bilateral trade agreement with Mexico, even to the extent that less than 90 percent of the total exports of Mexico to Japan are included in the agreement.[12]

Other East Asian countries quickly signaled that they intended to follow the Japanese precedent. The Korean government indicated that it would not expose its agricultural sector to additional competition from Mexico and Chile by lowering barriers as part of preferential agreements. And its refusal to include rice and two hundred other agricultural products in its FTA negotiated with ASEAN caused the Thai government to refuse to sign the agreement.[13] Other East Asian countries have made little pretense that their preferential trade agreements are WTO-compliant; they have happily negotiated agreements that are substantially incomplete in their coverage even of merchandise trade (and very few address trade in services), for instance, the Chinese and Korean FTAs and the agreement between Singapore and India. Indeed, rather than being WTO plus, one of the original justifications for using PTAs as a supplement to multilateralism, they are frequently WTO *minus* in their provisions. Here it is also important to recall that WTO Article XXIV applies only to PTAs that involve at least one industrialized economy. Preferential agreements among countries that classify themselves at the WTO as developing (all the East Asian countries, apart from Japan) are covered by the Enabling Clause, whose requirements on regionalism are even less stringent than those of Article XXIV.

The ambiguities of Article XXIV.8 provide a means by which the circle can be squared, a means of creating at least a nominally pro-liberalization agreement that avoids imposing adjustment costs on the least-efficient domestic sectors. But, of course, it is precisely these sensitive sectors where current levels of protection are highest and where trade liberalization in principle would bring the greatest benefits. When East Asian countries jumped on board the discriminatory trade bandwagon, some government officials expressed the hope that the new agreements would be an effective vehicle for promoting domestic reform (Munakata 2002, 2006a). The manner in which the negotiation of these agreements has unfolded has largely dashed such expectations. Pro-protection elements, particularly ministries of agriculture and their domestic constituencies, have triumphed over pro-liberalization foreign and trade ministries. Rather than weakening domestic protectionist forces, the new bilateralism arguably has strengthened them. In Japan, for instance, the move to preferential trade has yet to overcome what Pempel (2006a) has termed the country's "embedded mercantilism."[14]

---

12. For further discussion, see Solis (2003); Pempel and Urata (2006).

13. Of course, it is not just the EU and East Asian countries that exploit these loopholes in the WTO provisions on regional trade agreements. Witness the exclusion by the United States of competitive agricultural exports from Australia in the Australian-U.S. FTA.

14. Also relevant here is the low level of involvement of private-sector actors in these agreements. Like previous regional arrangements in the Asia-Pacific, the new bilateralism is overwhelmingly government-led. A rare exception is the agreement between Japan and Mexico, in which Keidanren

The behavior of governments in focusing their recent efforts in trade negotiations on these discriminatory arrangements is a type of forum-shopping, in which the lack of discipline of the minilateral arrangements (thereby maximizing national autonomy) is preferred to the rigors of the WTO (Pekkanen, Solís, and Katada 2006). Moreover, the outcome of some of the recent negotiations involving East Asian countries underlines the importance of power asymmetries that come to the fore in bilateral relationships and the advantages that the new bilateralism affords the more powerful economies of the region.

What, then, will be the likely impact of the new discriminatory trading arrangements on East Asian economies and on their vulnerability to future crisis? The conclusion must be that their aggregate economic, if not political, impact will be minimal.[15] Several factors are at work here. The overall levels of tariffs, even in the developing economies of the region, are now generally low, and where they are not, there are good political economy reasons why this is so—these sectors are the very ones likely to be exempted from the new agreements because of domestic political resistance. The problem of partial coverage is in many instances exacerbated by the lengthy time periods that countries have given themselves to phase in the new arrangements. And many of the agreements have been concluded by countries that are minor trading partners for one another. Despite the often-heroic assumptions made in some CGE models, their estimates show relatively small gains to GDP from the agreements, especially in comparison with what might be achieved through negotiations at the global level (Scollay and Gilbert 2001).

The significant exceptions to this argument are the agreements involving the United States—still the single most important trading partner for many East Asian countries and one with a template for FTAs that imposes WTO-plus discipline on its partners, especially on issues such as intellectual property rights and government procurement (although one whose trade-negotiating activities in the region are likely to be severely curtailed after the George W. Bush administration failed to gain renewal of its Trade Promotion Authority).

Reference to the United States raises another significant issue about the new FTAs—a large number of them have been negotiated with extra-regional partners. The move to discriminatory trade by East Asian governments has most definitely not been toward the construction of an exclusively East Asian preferential agreement. Quite the contrary, in fact. This is an evolution that is hardly surprising given that extra-regional states remain the most significant strategic and/or economic partners for most East Asian countries. The chances of securing an East Asia–wide PTA within the next decade are very slim indeed. Political antagonisms between Japan and its Northeast Asian neighbors remain an important barrier. But so, too, do the lack of confidence of Japan that the Chinese government would/could enforce

---

played a significant role (Manger 2005; Yoshimatsu 2005). Elsewhere, domestic interests that might have been expected to be pro-free trade (e.g., the *chaebol* in Korea), have largely failed to mobilize to counter domestic protectionist forces.

15. For further discussion see Ravenhill (2006b).

any commitments it made in a bilateral agreement and its own unwillingness to make concessions on agriculture (made even less likely with the loss of control of the Liberal Democratic Party (LDP) over the upper house in the July 2007 election). To the extent that the recent move to preferential trade has any effects on the overall patterns of trade, it might be expected to encourage a diversification of trade away from the region itself and toward previously neglected trade partners, such as India, which have increasingly become the focus of preferential trade negotiations (albeit of agreements with partial coverage) and thus could possibly serve to reduce (probably only minimally) the vulnerability of East Asian countries to trade-induced contagion in the event of further crises within the region.

Conclusion

Very significant changes in East Asian trade relations have occurred in the decade since the financial crises. By far the most important factor underlying these has been the sustained economic growth of China and its emergence as the location of choice for the assembly of manufactures for world markets. Production networks have been reoriented to take advantage of relatively low-cost labor, high levels of engineering skills, and good infrastructure in China. The voracious appetite of China for components produced elsewhere in the region has been the main factor behind its growing importance as a market for other East Asian economies. To be sure, the rapidly rising Chinese GDP has also created a demand for imports to supply its domestic market, but the main source of its growing importance in intraregional trade comes through its role in the processing of products destined primarily for extra-regional markets.

The vulnerability of the East Asian economies to trade-induced contagion from within the region, therefore, is little changed from the context in which the 1997–98 crises developed. Extra-regional links are still a more significant source of vulnerability, especially the ongoing dependence on the U.S. market. Because the increase in the Chinese dependence on exports to the United States has largely offset the decline in the U.S. share of the exports of other East Asian economies, the *overall* dependence of East Asia on the United States has declined only slightly from the levels in the mid-1990s. Moreover, East Asian economies are now substantially more integrated into the global economy than they were in the 1990s, with exports accounting for a much higher share of GDP than at any time previously.

Not just the increasing share of China in intraregional trade but also the changing composition of this trade should reassure those who viewed the rapid growth of China as a threat to the low-income economies in the region. Of course, the phenomenal growth of China presents a challenge to other economies in the region and has certainly displaced their exports in the U.S. and Japanese markets (less so in the European Markets; Gill, Kharas, and Bhattasali 2007, 103). But the old cliché that the other side of a challenge is an opportunity seems to be borne out by the success of the ASEAN economies in increasing their manufactured exports to China in the decade since the financial crises. Neither should we see the increasing importance of China as a market for other East Asian economies as necessarily providing it with greater political influence in the region. It is a matter of mutual dependence; the rapid economic growth of China rests to a considerable extent on the increase in its exports to extra-regional markets. This export growth—averaging more than 25 percent annually since 2000—in turn depends very substantially on imported technology and components and on the production networks not just of U.S. and European multinationals but of Japanese and Taiwanese multinationals as well.

Arguably a more significant source of potential vulnerability than competition from China is the increasing dependence of the region on exports from one sector—electrical and electronic products. Although the data for commodity composition of exports for individual years have to be treated cautiously given the significance of petroleum products for some countries in the region (not just for producers such as Indonesia but also for refiners such as Singapore), the data indicate a substantial increase in dependence on exports of electrical and electronic products, a sector particularly subject to cyclical fluctuations.

The major developments that have occurred in East Asian trade relations in the decade since the financial crises, as in the past, have been driven by private-sector actors, which have proved adept at circumventing barriers that governments have placed in their way. It has been new FDI in China that has been the principal driver behind the reorientation of production networks to make China the assembly plant of the world. The decisions by these private-sector actors have been little affected by the responses of the governments in the region to the financial crises.

Yet the postcrisis decade has also been one in which governments have been unprecedented in their trade policy activism, undoubtedly driven in part by the financial crises of 1997–98. To a considerable extent, a disjunction remains between the underlying pattern of private-sector activities and the actions of governments. As with previous trade policy activism, such as that pursued by the Asia-Pacific Economic Cooperation (APEC) grouping, the private sector, with few exceptions, has shown little interest in or enthusiasm for many of the new PTAs that governments have been busily negotiating. Most agreements are far from comprehensive and are driven as much by political cum strategic as economic logics. The limitations of these agreements suggest that they are unlikely to have any significant effect on the vulnerability of the region to future crises. And whatever rhetorical enthusiasm the crises may have sparked for East Asian regionalism, the new networks of PTAs that governments have constructed in the last decade do not indicate any move toward an East Asian regional trading bloc.

CHAPTER 8

Restructuring Regional Ties

T. J. Pempel

East Asian regionalism today is more complex, more institutionalized, and more Asian than it was when the crisis struck. Three contrasts are particularly striking. When the crisis hit, the overwhelming majority of links connecting East Asia were economic in nature. By selectively riding the broad wave of globalization, East Asia became more deeply integrated economically through the development of bottom-up, largely corporate- and market-driven networks (Hamilton 1996; Katzenstein and Shiraishi 1997; Pempel 2005b; Katzenstein 2006). Increasing amounts of foreign direct investment (FDI)—substantial portions of it East Asian in origin—created a criss-crossing web of transnational production networks, investment corridors, export processing zones, and growth triangles across the region. These, in turn, generated substantial increases in intraregional trade and an escalation of regional economic interdependence. Markets, investments, and corporations served as the key drivers of regional ties, leaving formal institutionalization quite thin and top-down governmental commands rather few (Grieco 1997). Several formally institutionalized bodies including the Association of Southeast Asian Nations (ASEAN), the Asia-Pacific Economic Cooperation (APEC) forum, and the ASEAN Regional Forum (ARF) did operate in precrisis East Asia, but all were minimally legalized, thinly staffed, and consequently constrained from exerting the kinds of binding control that could resolve disputes involving member states (Kahler 2000).

A second major characteristic of precrisis Asia was the preeminence of Japan. A mixture of foreign aid, bank lending, technological prowess, FDI, and dominance within the Asian Development Bank (ADB), along with the pervasive belief throughout much of Asia that the Japanese economic model provided a replicable alternative to laissez faire Anglo-American capitalism, combined to position Japan at the unquestioned top of the regional hierarchy (MacIntyre and Naughton 2005). Without question, Taiwan, Hong Kong, and South Korea were gaining a role as important exporters of capital across the region, contributing to the density of regional production networks. But their linkages were geographically limited, subordinating them to at best a subsidiary role to Japan. Economic growth in China had been phenomenal, jetting it to a position as the second largest economy in Asia, but the Japanese GNP remained still ten times larger and its per capita income was roughly ninety times greater than that of China (Pempel 1999b, 72). Asian regional ties reflected this Japanese primacy.

A third precrisis attribute was the Asia-Pacific nature of most regional bodies involving East Asia. The two most emblematic examples of open regionalism were APEC and the ARF. APEC had twenty-one member economies, including two nonstates, Hong Kong and Taiwan, as well as several states geographically outside East Asia, including the United States, Canada, Mexico, and Russia. The security-oriented ARF, meanwhile, had twenty-four members, most of them also in APEC. Unlike APEC, however, ARF includes the otherwise rarely regionalized Democratic People's Republic of Korea (DPRK) and the geographically distant European Union, while excluding unmistakably East Asian Taiwan. Finally and in contrast, the ASEAN with ten Southeast Asian member states was the earliest Asian regional body (formed in 1967), but in today's context it is best viewed as subregional because none of its member countries was from Northeast Asia. Equally salient, these different regional institutions had porous and nonoverlapping memberships. The outer boundaries of many of the East Asian regional institutions were thus heavily trans-Pacific, and different institutional agendas resulted in quite distinctive and nonoverlapping memberships.

The contemporary regional architecture provides striking contrasts on all three fronts. Economic linkages across Asia continue to deepen and expand. But although the Japanese financial and manufacturing presence anchored the expanding production networks before the crisis, its decade-plus of economic slowdown combined with the continued Chinese trajectory of high growth and vigorous regional engagement have combined to erode the once unchallenged regional preeminence of Japan. Equally, Southeast Asia became less attractive as a destination for investment capital, whereas China quickly came to occupy pride of regional economic place in many global production chains. Intra-East Asian trade continues to swell, rising from about 43 percent in 1996 to 55.3 percent in 2005. But as John Ravenhill (chap. 7 in this volume) makes clear, much of this trade represents a redirection of production networks to engage the rapidly expanding Chinese economy. Since the crisis, China has become even more attractive than it once was as a destination for incoming regional investment; China is now the most active East Asian processing center, taking imports from many parts of the region, processing them further, and then exporting the end products to the richer countries of the region as well as abroad. Furthermore, the once trade-dominated regional economic linkages have begun to expand beyond trade and into finance and other areas.

Formal institutions and overt governmental actions designed to shape them have also become more characteristic of the region. No longer are Asian regional ties preponderantly the by-products simply of bottom-up market connections. Instead, since the crisis, numerous Asian governments have more actively moved to enhance and integrate the regional architecture. Thus, bilateral and minilateral free trade agreements (FTAs), virtually nonexistent in Asia at the time of the crisis, have become a favored state instrument aimed at enhancing political control over trade and improving intraregional trade ties. Other governmental actions have spawned a diversity of regional bodies, including the ASEAN+3 (APT) process, the Chiang Mai Initiative (CMI), the Asian Bond Market Initiative (ABMI), the Asian Bond Fund (ABF), the Shanghai Cooperation Organization (SCO), the East Asian Summit (EAS) and the Six Party Talks (SPT), to cite only some of the most immediate institutional manifestations.

Finally, the new dynamism in East Asian regionalism has shifted from preponderantly open and Asia-Pacific ties to links that are more closed. Membership in the more recently formed organizations is now typically restricted to Asians only, whereas the earlier pan-Pacific bodies have been shunted to the sidelines. Pan-Pacific APEC, for example, became rather moribund following the crisis, and ARF has been incapable of creating anything approaching a regional security community; its actions have been concentrated on minimally restrictive confidence-building measures. In contrast, since the crisis, the APT process, and the thirteen countries that are part of it, have been at the core of regional activities. APT was the driver behind the CMI and the EAS; the CMI was also the mechanism that triggered the track-two Network of East Asian Think Tanks (NEAT), forged in the wake of the financial crisis. In addition, the eleven countries in Executives' Meeting of East Asia-Pacific Central Banks (EMEAP) that drove the ABMI exclude any on the eastern shores of the Pacific (e.g., the United States, Canada, and other APEC members). The most noteworthy exception to this model of Asian exclusivity has been the FTAs; many of these have been exclusively East Asian, but almost as many involve ties between East Asian and non–East Asian states. In addition, although clearly unrelated to the crisis per se, the SPT dealing with the nuclear program of the DPRK represents one new regional process that does include the United States.

This chapter begins by outlining what I refer to as the Asian governmental push-back. After the crisis, a host of state-led actions sought to assert a more active political role so as to filter the impacts of globalization. In large part, these aimed at counterbalancing the extra-regional forces that many Asian policymakers and business leaders concluded had been the main culprits in the economic crisis. I then examine the ways in which such steps toward Asian regionalism continue to fall far short of creating a cohesive or comprehensive project. I show that the major governmental actors critical to any regional bodies still lack a common vision concerning what an East Asian region should look like, what problem areas regional bodies should address, and, most important, how much national sovereignty they are willing to concede to any regional bodies. In addition, there is a sharp division over how any Asian regional bodies should best intersect with non-Asian powers. Should regionalism be restricted to the thirteen APT countries or expanded to other countries? Should expansion be based on geography (including Australia, New Zealand, India, and perhaps Russia, as is the case with the EAS)? Or should Asian regional bodies acknowledge the inevitability of U.S. influence across Asia, particularly in security and financial matters (as is the case with the APEC or ARF model)? And to what extent should different regional bodies have overlapping memberships regardless of focus, as opposed to allowing different memberships for a diversity of bodies, each addressing different issues?

Hence, the situation in East Asia following the crisis continues to reflect a tension between two competing forces: the centripetal drive toward closer regional ties and the centrifugal residue of nationally specific agendas. But, on balance, the regional architecture of East Asia has become unmistakably more comprehensive, denser, and more state-dominated than it was before the crisis struck.

The Asian Governmental Push-Back

The Asian crisis magnified a number of structural realities that had previously been lurking in the shadow of preexisting regional ties. In hindsight, at least four became unmistakable. First, although the crisis exerted differential impacts on specific economies, its effect was unmistakably regional, underscoring the interdependence of most economies across East Asia (e.g., Pempel 1999b). Second, few governments in East Asia had structured their economies along the lines of laissez faire Anglo-American capitalism. Nevertheless, the rapidity and devastation of the crisis brought home the heightened vulnerability of small individualized Asian economies confronting unfettered markets and highly mobile and exceptionally volatile capital flows—through what Winters (1999) aptly characterizes as plugging into a global economy without adequate governmental surge protectors. Third, existing minimalist and Asia-Pacific regional bodies demonstrated neither the willingness nor the ability to stem the spread of the crisis. Fourth, and finally, the crisis revealed how, with the end of the Cold War, the world had become unipolar and the United States no longer showed any predisposition to tolerate East Asian models of development when these conflicted with broader U.S. economic or security concerns. Indeed, U.S. actions during the crisis underscored a new willingness to use its influential position within global institutions such as the International Monetary Fund (IMF) to advance its own national economic interests and its own vision of global capitalism, even at the expense of friends and allies in East Asia. Nowhere was this clearer than in the livid opposition of Secretary of the Treasury Robert Rubin and his deputy Larry Summers to the Japanese proposal for an Asian Monetary Fund (AMF) and Summers's gleeful triumphalism over the IMF conditional aid packages to Korea, Thailand, and Indonesia. "The IMF," Summers crowed, "has done more to promote America's trade and investment agenda in East Asia than thirty years of bilateral trade negotiations" (quoted in Hale 1998, 25).

The countries of East Asia have responded with a combination of increased governmental actions aimed at taking greater control of their own and regional foreign economic policies. These represent assertive governmental push-backs against the forces of unbridled globalization. Among the most powerful of these efforts have been measures to enhance the regional architecture, particularly within the areas of finance and trade. Most specifically, the governments of Asia have made major efforts to mobilize underlying regional financial strengths in an effort to ward off any possible repeat of the crushing impact of the global forces that devastated the region in 1997–98.

Existing regional institutions, such as APEC and ASEAN, had shown themselves completely feckless in warding off the crisis or in coping with its aftereffects. APEC became further marginalized because the United States, with its singular focus on treating it solely as a vehicle for trade liberalization (at the expense of its other two goals of economic cooperation and economic development), had lost confidence in that institution when the Early Voluntary Sector Liberalization (EVSL) process failed to open Japanese primary markets (Krauss 2004; Tay 2006, 4). Further contributing to its marginalization in economic matters, APEC was pressed—as part of what Richard Higgott (2004) has called U.S. efforts to "securitize" economic globalization—to compromise its original economic focus in favor of taking a collective stand in support of the so-called Global War on Terror.

Asian governments responded by forging new institutions designed to afford them greater control over the conditions within which their economies functioned. In addition, given U.S. actions during and after the crisis, a preponderant bias emerged for a response that was Asian rather than Asian-Pacific.

With a few noteworthy exceptions, the APT process became the predominant model for much of the subsequent regional architecture and regional efforts. The APT format began in mid-1995 when ASEAN joined with China, Japan, and South Korea, offering an Asian counterpart to meet with the European Union. The result was the Asia-Europe Meeting (ASEM). Starting in 1997 at the height of the crisis, the ASEAN governments pressed for a more independent role for APT, shifting it from being simply a series of meetings among senior officials to becoming a meeting of finance and economic ministers and eventually to forming a more institutionalized set of links with their major northern neighbors that culminated eventually in an annual meeting of heads of state. This thirteen-nation summit became the major engine fostering regional cooperation on a variety of regional problems.

At the second APT Summit in Hanoi on December 16, 1998, Korean President Kim Dae Jung became one of the first Asian political leaders to press for a strengthening of East Asia's collective capacity to offset or deal with future crises. He proposed the formation of an East Asian Vision Group (EAVG) to pursue closer regional ties. The EAVG was institutionalized by APT as a body of twenty-six regionwide experts who reported to an East Asian Study Group of senior officials chaired by former Korean Foreign Minister Han Song Joo. The EAVG presented its final report at the fifth APT meeting in Kuala Lumpur in December 2001. This report suggested regional cooperation in a sweeping array of six sectors: economics; finance; politics and security; environment and energy; society, culture, and education; and institutions. It also called quite explicitly for "the evolution of the annual summit meetings of the ASEAN+3 into the East Asian Summit" (East Asia Vision Group [EAVG] 2001, recommendation #60). That summit met for the first time in December 2005 and then in Manila in January 2007 and Singapore in November of that year. It was the EAVG report that provided the major template for much of the regionalization that eventually occurred.

Among the first tangible regional moves were those in finance. Hindsight made it clear that Asian collective foreign reserves, had they been mobilized during 1997–98, could have alleviated the short-term problems in the affected countries, obviating the eventual IMF actions. In 1998, for example, the collective foreign reserves of the ten richest countries in Asia totaled $742 billion—well beyond the total of the three main IMF packages. By the end of 2006, the reserves of the APT countries had ballooned to nearly $2.5 trillion, roughly two-thirds of the world total and up from about $1 trillion in 2001. The People's Bank of China and the Hong Kong Monetary Authority lead the way with $1.33 trillion as of June 2006, with Japan a close second at nearly $900 billion; Taiwan (not a member of APT) held an additional $265 billion (*Economist*, December 23, 2006; International Monetary Fund [IMF] 2007). Even a small portion of these resources, if mobilized collectively, would have been more than many Asian countries could have received through multilateral financial institutions (Henning 2002, 13).

Japan, at the instigation of Sakakibara Eisuke, then vice minister of finance for international affairs, had initially attempted to take the lead in generating such a regional mobilization of financial resources through an Asian Monetary Fund (AMF). But U.S., Chinese, and IMF opposition to Japan's proposal quickly derailed that effort (Amyx 2004a). Once the dust had cleared, many participants remained interested in actualizing the potential benefits of deeper financial ties across Asia but in ways that would avoid any direct challenges to existing global monetary arrangements, such as that posed by the AMF.

The first collective response to this mix of incentives came with the CMI of May 6, 2000, an initiative generated in conjunction with the annual APT meeting. The CMI expanded existing ASEAN currency swap arrangements (ASA) and added a network of bilateral swap arrangements (BSA) among the ASEAN countries, China, Japan and the Republic of Korea (ROK). These were to provide emergency liquidity in the event of any future crisis (Grimes 2006; Jennifer Amyx, chap. 6 in this volume).

When the CMI originally went into effect, considerable stress was placed on the limited amounts of money involved in the swaps, as well as on the underlying requirement that most swaps be congruent with IMF regulations. Yet, by early 2005, some sixteen bilateral swap agreements had been organized under the CMI totaling $39 billion. At the eighth meeting of finance ministers of the APT in Kuala Lumpur on May 5, 2005, the APT agreed to double the amounts in the existing swap arrangements, raising the total to $80 billion. Further, the finance ministers meeting on May 5, 2007, went much further when they agreed, in principle, to multi-lateralize the CMI through a reserve pool and a single contractual agreement for the drawing of funds. Such an arrangement would move from a series of bilateral swaps to a more comprehensive reserve pool with a single contractual agreement, centralizing and multilateralizing the entire arrangement.

Current arrangements still fall well short of providing a comprehensive regional financial system. Nor do they constitute an explicit challenge to the IMF. All the same, they demonstrate a growing desire and ability by Asian countries to move collectively toward creating what elsewhere I have called a firebreak (Pempel 2005a) against future monetary crises and a partial alternative to unbridled dependence on the IMF and its policy prescriptions. Of at least equal if not greater importance, they have become a shell within which further regional monetary and financial co-operation can be nurtured.

The more-advanced economies in Asia have also moved to develop an enriched Asian Bond Fund (ABF) through the regional central banks, whereas the CMI has pushed a somewhat different Asian Bond Market Initiative (ABMI). These, in combination, will provide an additional mechanism of regional financial collaboration and will reduce Asian dependence on the U.S. dollar for financial reserves, currency baskets, and international transactions. On June 2, 2003, the EMEAP announced the establishment of a $1 billion ABF. This first ABF involved a group of eleven Asian central banks and a second ABF was begun a year later. The APT finance ministers' meeting subsequently opted to develop a local-currency bond market, including a regional clearing and settlement system, a bond-rating agency, a trading system, and so forth (for details, see Pempel 2005a, 2006b; Grimes 2006).

Driving these bond market endeavors is an effort to mobilize regional savings for intra-Asian investment, thereby reducing the dependency of the region on the U.S. dollar. A bond market denominated in local currencies also allows Asian borrowers to avoid the double mismatch problem that arose in 1997–98—that is, borrowing short in foreign currency (mostly dollars) and lending long in domestic currencies. If effective, Asian bonds also promise to free many Asian borrowers from their long-standing dependence on bank borrowing.

The ADB currently estimates that for each year between 2005 and 2010, East Asia will require $200 billion in gross investment for physical infrastructure alone. That means a total of $1 trillion, or 6–7 percent of regional GDP (ADB estimates in Greenwood 2006, 7). Using Asian capital directly to meet such expenditures makes considerable intraregional sense and could become a major source of enhanced regional financial cohesion.

Both the currency swaps and the bond markets have deepened and institutionalized regional financial integration, but many impediments still prevent them from functioning as powerful shapers of the regional political economy. Thus, when Indonesian currency was in trouble in late 2005, the currency swaps were not mobilized. And the bond markets continue to be quite illiquid, with most purchases coming from long-term investors such as governments, the Singaporean Provident Fund, the ADB, and so forth. Nevertheless, member governments are meeting, are attempting to standardize relevant domestic rules and regulations, and are committed to the principle of greater utilization of collective Asian savings for regionally agreed-on targets. This certainly represents much deeper financial cooperation than existed before the crisis. The current efforts, if enhanced, may also lead to a rise in Asian financial influence in both global markets and within the IMF. One small manifestation came in the 2006 reallocation of IMF voting rights; among the most notable changes was the increased voting power of China.

Also indicative of greater East Asian regional financial cohesion—although in an area only minimally subject to government oversight and control—have been changes in the location for initial public offerings (IPOs) of company stock. Prior to the crisis, the New York Stock Exchange (NYSE) was by far the most favored location for companies from around the globe to issue IPOs of their stock. Since the late 1990s, the U.S. share (measured by proceeds) has all but collapsed. In 2001, the NYSE dwarfed London and Hong Kong; by 2006, it was being beaten by both. For East Asia, the striking fact is that IPOs in Hong Kong (largely from companies in greater China) have jumped from virtually nonexistent in 1999 to about 17 percent of the world total today (*Economist,* December 23, 2006). Clearly, a vastly increased portion of Asian capital is being retained within postcrisis Asia.

Government actions bolstering formal state roles have not all taken the form of explicitly institutionalized regional bodies. Thus in the area of trade, there has been enhanced governmental action, but East Asian approaches to trade in the wake of the crisis have been far less exclusively East Asian. Some regional efforts have been undertaken. For example, in the wake of the financial crisis of 1997–98, ASEAN reaffirmed its commitment to the ASEAN Free Trade Agreement (AFTA), with the original six AFTA signatories promising to accelerate many planned tariff cuts by one year, to 2002 from 2003 (US-ASEAN Business Council 2003). But by far the more conspicuous moves on East Asian trade have been seen in the explosion in bilateral or minilateral FTAs.

In October 1, 2002, of the thirty top economies in the world, only five were not members of any such FTAs: Japan, China, South Korea, Taiwan, and Hong Kong (Pempel and Urata 2006). Since then, an explosion of bilateral, regional, and other preferential FTAs involving East Asian nations have been concluded or explored. Before the crisis, the AFTA was the only government-led initiative in the region; by 2006, according to C. Lawrence Greenwood (2006, 6) of the World Bank, some ninety-five bilateral and subregional FTAs involving East Asian countries were either in place or under negotiation; the number continues to rise rapidly. As Aggarwal (2006, 12) argues, many East Asian free traders had become frustrated by the combination of the slow progress in World Trade Organization (WTO) meetings in Seattle and Cancun, a possible reduction in access to U.S. markets, and the desire to develop enhanced regional trade outlets that might reduce their dependence on the U.S. market. For others, FTAs represented defensive or catch-up actions against what were perceived to be anti-Asian trade barriers erected by the North American Free Trade Agreement (NAFTA) and the European Union. Particularly in the cases of Korea and Japan, FTAs were also the favored instruments of domestic liberalizers seeking to overcome home-grown resistance to greater economic openness. The result has been an explosion in FTAs involving East Asian countries.

FTAs are weaving an increasingly dense spider web of bilateral and multilateral trade links across the region but also from Asia to other parts of the world, particularly Oceania, North America, Chile, and Mexico. Often, as John Ravenhill (chap. 7 in this volume) makes clear, these fall short of the levels of liberalization required by the WTO. But, in this regard, they are even more important in registering a broad-scale series of governmental preferences against the power of unmediated market forces. The existing bilateral pacts have attained nowhere near regional comprehensiveness in their coverage of East Asia. Indeed, the three largest markets in Asia—Japan, China, and the ROK—have been particularly slow in advancing FTAs with one another. Nevertheless, the recent FTAs are potential building blocs for a deeper regionwide free trade area.

These multiple activities demonstrate a series of moves toward a deeper and more politically shaped East Asian economic architecture since the crisis. Viewed collectively, they suggest a fundamental reorientation in the nature of East Asian regionalism over the past decade. At the same time, they remain embryonic and tentative, falling far short of any comprehensive and deeply legalized regional institutionalization.

Impediments to Deeper Regionalism

Competing Regional Visions and Security Tensions

The regional East Asian bed has become more accommodative since the crisis, but many of its current inhabitants continue to dream quite different dreams. As a result of the crisis, many actors in East Asia rethought their prior positions on regionalism; others became more deeply committed to preexisting positions. Today, however, at least three big differences of intra-Asian opinion continue to divide the major players. First, should regional bodies focus exclusively on creating economic and financial cooperation, which has certainly been an enhanced concern since the crisis? Or should the regional agenda be defined more broadly, seeking to include security cooperation as well? Second, which country or countries should exert the leadership role in any regional bodies—the bigger countries such as China and Japan or the smaller ASEAN group or, perhaps, Korea? Third, and finally, what should be the membership of any regional body; should participation be exclusively Asian (and if so, which countries are Asian?), or should it be Asia-Pacific in character?

There has been a tentative postcrisis embrace of regionalism in East Asian economics, but moves toward institutionalized regional cooperation in defense and security have been far less vigorous. In stark contrast to Western Europe facing the Soviet Union and its allies for the first forty-five years after World War II or to many Arab countries in the Middle East confronting Israel, East Asia faces no commonly perceived external threat. Rather, as Michael Yahuda points out, "the defenses of most East Asian countries are directed against one another" (2004, 229).

Moreover, many countries such as the Philippines, Indonesia, Thailand, and even China have legitimate concerns about internal, territorially rooted separatist movements driven by ethnic or religious differences and potentially underwritten from abroad. Regional approaches to security have thus been far less appealing across East Asia than they have been in trade and finance. This is particularly true in Northeast Asia. As Peter Katzenstein has argued, "for the foreseeable future, states will remain the main guarantors of national security and the basic building blocks of international order.... For good or ill, states remain the ultimate repository of power" (2005, 105).

Although hardly a complete security community (Acharya 2001), Southeast Asia since well before the crisis had, nevertheless, moved far closer to regional security cooperation than its neighbors to the north. The ASEAN countries had achieved some measure of internal security accord through the 1976 Treaty of Amity and Cooperation (TAC). The ARF was also created at the initiative of ASEAN to overcome regional security problems, even though, to date, ARF has restricted its activities primarily to informal confidence-building measures (CBMs).

Not surprisingly, the members of ASEAN, drawing on a legacy of up to thirty years together, came out of the crisis with a more comprehensive vision for regional activity. In addition to cooperation on trade and finance, regional security cooperation continues to be an important goal of most ASEAN member states. The ASEAN TAC calls for the peaceful resolution of intraregional disputes, and ASEAN succeeded in making support for the TAC a precondition for membership in the East Asian Summit, for the first time in postcrisis Asia weaving regional security into a relatively comprehensive mixture with trade and finance.

The ASEAN governments also share broad agreement that any East Asian region should mirror the ASEAN model, which is based on a combination of cross-national cooperation, thin institutions, and respect for national sovereignty. Following the crisis, there was renewed commitment across Southeast Asia that ASEAN should be the *primus inter pares* of any regional organization; potential domination by China or Japan was no less appealing to ASEAN members than was dominance by the United States and the IMF. To date, the Northeast Asian participants, particularly Japan and China, wary as they are of ceding leadership to one another, have been mutually deferential to this ASEAN leadership. Consequently, all current and any probable future Asian regional bodies demonstrate at best a thin bureaucratic infrastructure, few formal rules, and limited enforcement capabilities. Instead, they remain driven by informality and rolling consensus building.

The crisis did little to create any common consensus among the ASEAN states on an ideal regional membership. An overall goal of ASEAN remains weaving in and socializing its powerful Northeast Asian neighbors, particularly Japan and China, in hopes of reducing their independence of action, turning the ASEAN way into a more comprehensive Asian way (Acharya 1997). However, reflecting their particular security considerations more than their interpretations of the economic crisis, some such as Singapore, the Philippines, and Thailand are anxious to foster trans-Pacific regionalism. Meanwhile, Malaysia, Indonesia, and the four newest members of ASEAN, have favored a more narrowly Asian framework, roughly analogous to the East Asian Economic Caucus first proposed by Prime Minister Mahathir Mohamad in 1990.

The crisis had a particularly strong impact on Chinese leaders. As Edward Steinfeld (chap. 9 in this volume) shows, one of the major conclusions they drew was the need to speed up the movement away from state socialism and toward closer integration with global economic processes. Equally important, they were quick to show a new enthusiasm for regionalism in the wake of the crisis. For most of the postwar period, China had been skeptical of any approaches to the region as a collectivity, favoring instead the advancement of Chinese interests through bilateral ties and global institutions. With the economic crisis and the accession of China to the WTO in 2002, however, the country began to recognize explicitly how much regional strength could enhance Chinese influence. Edward Friedman offers an important observation on this Chinese embrace of regionalism: "Seeing the US block Japan's effort to create an Asian financial mechanism to cushion such crises, the CCP found that regional financial cooperation could stop American democracy. It therefore promoted regional financial cooperation" (2006, 126). Since then, China has been an active proponent of the CMI, Asian bond markets, and the East Asia Summit. It has also been exceptionally active in a variety of track II diplomatic ventures such as the Council for Security Cooperation in the Asia Pacific (CSCAP) and the Northeast Asia Cooperation Dialogue (NEACD), typically lobbying hard behind the scenes to shape agendas and major conclusions. It has also been the primary organizer of the Network of East Asian Think Tanks (NEAT), begun as a result of the EAVG report.

The enhanced economic muscularity of China has allowed it to play a heightened role in shaping regional economic institutions (Shambaugh 2005). More than half of total Chinese trade volume is within the East Asian region. The country is well positioned as a principal export platform of final-demand goods to North American and European markets. Of late, it has been the sole locomotive of intraregional trade and the major recipient of intraregional FDI. As well, most of the incoming Chinese FDI originates in East Asia and China is also increasingly becoming an exporter of FDI to the rest of the region.

One of the most important Chinese successes in combining its economic power with its regional strategy came with its proposal at the 2000 ASEAN Summit for an ASEAN-China FTA. This proposal helped convince ASEAN members that the rise of China might generate win-win economic cooperation in what would potentially be a market of some 1.7 billion people. Quite significantly, Chinese negotiators offered an "early harvest" of lower tariffs for agricultural goods from Southeast Asia coming into China. Because agricultural exports are so critical to the growth strategies of most countries in Southeast Asia, particularly to its newer members, the Chinese move proved particularly deft politically. In addition, it also underscored the extent to which democracies such as Japan, the United States, and Korea, although much richer, were constrained from making similarly generous gestures due to the power of their domestic farm lobbies.

Outside Southeast Asia, one of the biggest successes of China has come in forging intraregional ties with the ROK. Despite the long-standing friendship of China with the DPRK, it normalized relations with the south in 1992, announcing a "comprehensive cooperative partnership" in 2003 (Chung 2005, 164). Since then, and with accelerating speed since the crisis, the two countries have cooperated on trade, investment, tourism, educational and cultural exchanges, and other areas. In 2003, China surpassed the United States as the largest ROK export market and was the number one destination for outgoing Korean FDI.

Equally important has been the growth of linkages between Taiwan and China. Today, China buys about 40 percent of Taiwanese exports; and since 2002 more than one-half of Taiwanese FDI has been sunk into China (Ross 2006, 143). Roughly 1 million Taiwanese now live on the mainland, and the two economies are becoming increasingly interwoven. Nevertheless, these remain largely bilateral, rather than regional ties, although products from Taiwanese-owned factories in the People's Republic of China frequently make their way into other Asian markets. But the policies of both governments have been at least as critical to deepening this integration as have generic market forces.

Such enthusiastic Chinese support for economic and financial regionalism has been largely in the context of Asians only, aimed at least indirectly at limiting U.S. influence in the region. China has thus favored APT and EAS over pan-Pacific bodies such as the APEC. Furthermore, Chinese regional efforts have included central Asia and not just East Asia, as is reflected in the Chinese initiative to create the Shanghai Cooperation Organization (SCO), which includes China, Russia, and four central Asian republics.

But equally important, China has held back from supporting any regional bodies that might do either of two things: challenge its sovereignty on defense and security or, relatedly, allow Taiwan to join.

China has favored only CBMs within ARF and has resisted moves by Southeast Asian countries to expand ARF activities to include preventive diplomacy or conflict resolution. At the same time, the ready agreement of China to a Code of Conduct in the South China Seas and a generally more forthcoming engagement in the ASEAN Regional Forum and other frameworks have lessened the tensions that once marked security relations between China and Southeast Asia (Tay 2006, 7).

In addition, China has been adamant about preventing Taiwanese governmental or nongovernmental organizations from participating in regional (and global) bodies, a distinctively antiregional position. With even greater vigor since the crisis and the electoral success of the Democratic Progressive Party in Taiwan, China has sought to isolate Taiwan from any and all international and regional fora, even those that do not require statehood for membership, in addition to opposing Taiwanese regional assistance on matters of public health and disaster relief (Friedman 2006, 129–30).

In contrast to ASEAN but somewhat similar to China, the Japanese regional vision has been largely economic. But unlike both of them, its visions have been consistently trans-Pacific. Any regional bodies that Japan supports should, it believes, include the United States, or at least not be opposed by the United States.

The previously unchallenged Japanese economic leadership across East Asia was first undercut by its domestic economic slowdown and then by the simultaneous economic vigor of other Asian countries, most significantly, China. The failure of Japanese efforts to alleviate the pandemic Asian economic crisis of 1997–98 with its AMF proposal further undercut both its own national confidence and that of many of its neighbors in the Japanese ability to use its economic muscle to shape regional events. Although Japan remained absolutely the most economically sophisticated and industrially advanced country in Asia, its position at the unchallenged center of regional economic developments no longer seemed foreordained (MacIntyre and Naughton 2005).

The Japanese regional visions, from the Pacific Economic Cooperation Council and Pacific Basin Economic Council to APEC, have continually emphasized the economic and financial dimensions of regional deepening. The Japanese government has persistently sought to improve overseas investment conditions for its firms and to aid them in generating regional production hubs in conjunction with their overall global marketing strategies (Hatch 2000). Since the crisis, Japan has thus been active as a promoter and supporter of a number of new or recent regional institutions, particularly the APT process and the currency swap arrangements set out in the CMI of May 2000 and its subsequent revisions. The Japanese Ministry of Finance has also been particularly active in support the ABF and the ABMI. And although it has been more tentative in its efforts than many other Asian countries, including China and the ROK, Japan has been active in pursuit of various bilateral FTAs (usually called economic partnership agreements or EPAs by Japanese officials). At the same time, hemmed in by the domestic political power of its agricultural lobby, it has been far slower than authoritarian China to open its markets to Southeast Asian agricultural goods. "Japan places great importance on liberalization of services, protection for investors and intellectual property rights, and similar issues. However, Japan has not reached a consensus on the liberalization of agricultural trade, and the political will for a clean FTA has not manifested itself. In contrast . . . China has a clear political will for FTAs," including a willingness to open Chinese markets to Southeast Asian agricultural products (Fukagawa 2005, 24).

All these regionalizing endeavors, however, remain circumscribed by Japanese bilateral security arrangements with the United States. These arrangements have been the keystone of Japanese foreign policies throughout the post–World War II period, even as relations with the Asian region were always valuable supplements, particularly in economics. And with the singularity of U.S. unilateralism and military focus in its foreign policy since the onset of the George W. Bush administration, Japan has embraced the United States even more tightly, becoming increasingly conservative and nationalistic in its security policies. This was particularly true under Prime Minister Koizumi Junichiro, but the trend continued under the Abe Shinzo administration.

The ROK has still a different regional vision from all the rest. For the ROK, the sine qua non in building an Asian region is the unification of the Korean peninsula; presumably that unification would take place under eventual dominance by

Seoul. This unified Korea would ideally come about through the gradual deepening of economic, transportation, and communication links across the thirty-eighth parallel, rather than by any form of regime collapse within the DPRK. One of the more visible efforts made by the south toward weaving the north into closer economic links involves tourist visits from South Koreans to Mt. Kumgang. Between 1998 and August 2006, the ROK sent 13.3 million southern visitors to the DPRK, putting $452 million into DPRK coffers (*Nikkei Weekly*, October 23, 2006). Equally important, the Kaesong industrial zone in the southern portion of the DPRK became host to fourteen ROK companies anxious to take advantage of cheap DPRK labor, along with helping to build intra-peninsula economic ties that, it was hoped, would work toward creating closer bilateral and eventually regional connections.

Following any unification of the peninsula, Seoul would then be poised to serve as a hub for economic dynamism and peace building throughout the region. Moreover, for Korea the starting point in Asian regionalism would be in Northeast Asia, with Japanese and Chinese differences being balanced by the unified Korea; Southeast Asia and ASEAN remain rather marginal in official Korean thinking. To this end, the president's office maintained an ongoing Presidential Committee on Northeast Asian Cooperation Initiatives.

Complicating things still further, Taiwan, facing increasing diplomatic isolation as the result of Chinese pressures, would almost certainly join any regional body that would have it, although surely it would prefer that any such bodies included, rather than excluded, the United States. In contrast, the DPRK, with its self-reliance and military-first policies, remains by far the strongest resister of the general regional impetus—particularly as this focuses on enhanced regional trade and investment. Still, it is worth noting that Pyongyang is a member of ARF and the SPT and generally participates in CSCAP and NEACD at the track II level. But the DPRK has hardly been active in the sweep of production networks and regional trade that characterize the regional economy as a whole. And it has demonstrated little interest in APT, CMI, ABMI, ABF, or any bilateral trade pacts.

This is by no means the place to analyze the U.S. role in Asian regionalism in any depth. But at least three points need to be underscored because they affect the Asian regional architecture since the crisis. First, the Bush administration's overall anti-institutionalism has been reflected in its approach to East Asian regionalism and regional institutions. The APT process, by definition, has excluded the United States. But the United States under Bush has been largely dismissive of ARF; indeed, in 2005 and 2007, Secretary of State Condoleezza Rice was conspicuous in skipping the meetings, one of the few times this had happened since the foundation of the ARF in 1994. The Bush administration also downplayed APEC with its economic orientation, pressing continually for statements concerning opposition to terrorism. And the December 2005 East Asia Summit gave rise to explicit statements of opposition by former Deputy Secretary of State Richard Armitage: "My view is this is a thinly veiled way to make the point that the United States is not totally welcomed in Asia. I think that's a real mistake" (*Asahi Shimbun*, May 2, 2005). If governments in East

Asia have increasingly defined regionalism in terms that exclude the United States, there has been ample dismissive reciprocity from Washington.

A second point concerns the DPRK and its nuclear weapons program. When, in October 2002, the United States charged that the DPRK was attempting to develop a highly enriched uranium program to produce nuclear materials, it insisted, successfully, but in stark contrast to its unilateralism concerning most other issues, on a multilateral process to deal with the issue. China took the lead in what has become the SPT, still another—if ad hoc—regional body. China convened the SPT in 2003, which have gone through fitful starts and stops since their start. Throughout the negotiating process, China and the ROK have been relatively close in advocating measures designed to tease the DPRK into trading off its nuclear program for economic assistance and a greater integration into the regional agenda. In contrast, Japan and the United States have taken much harsher positions toward the DPRK nuclear program and focused more on military sticks and economic sanctions than on regional and economic carrots. But with the shutdown of the DPRK plutonium facilities and the welcoming of International Atomic Energy Agency inspectors in 2007, there were some grounds for optimism that the SPT would in fact move (albeit fitfully) toward a resolution of the crisis and, as a consequence, could evolve into some form of Northeast Asian security institution.

Finally, one additional area in which U.S. actions have been exerting an important impact on the Asian region and which for the most part, has been continuing long-established ties across the Pacific is economic. The United States continues to be a major market for many Asian exports, despite the rise in intra-Asian trade. Of increasing importance, however, have been financial and monetary ties. As part of its effort to enhance U.S. global influence through economic prowess and to create an Asia-Pacific regionalism, the Bill Clinton administration devoted considerable attention to internal U.S. fiscal balances, as well as to the strength of the U.S. currency and improved bond markets. When the Bush administration came to power, it inherited a budget surplus of $236 billion with a forecasted ten-year surplus of $5.6 trillion. The new administration, however, quickly reversed the earlier Clinton economic and financial policies.

A series of massive tax cuts generated a budget deficit that as of fiscal year (FY) 2005 had ballooned to $423 billion. The result was an expansion of the U.S. governmental debt to $8.4 trillion, half of this held by foreign entities, with Japan and China as the two largest holders.

The Bush policies have relied on importing deflation from both China and Japan, thus containing domestic inflationary growth. But, at the same time, U.S. Treasury officials and congressional leaders have periodically pressed the Chinese government to increase the value of the yuan, a move that would presumably make Chinese exports to the United States more costly, purportedly to protect American jobs and diminish the relative burden of paying back the monies borrowed. Of course, any such revaluation would also be hugely costly to U.S. consumers of global goods while in addition creating a tempting financial incentive for Chinese and Japanese holders of U.S. debt to reduce their holdings of U.S. Treasuries, thus driving up U.S. interest rates.

In that these U.S. policies create a greater dependency between the United States, on the one hand, and Japan and China, on the other, they are a plus for pan-Pacific ties and an offset to a closed Asian regionalism. At the same time, regardless of how the relationship eventually plays out, current U.S. financial and tax policies have meant a clear shift away from prior U.S. efforts to use its economic muscle to advance its interests in Northeast Asia thereby reducing the role of the U.S. government in shaping the economic agenda of the pan-Pacific region. These policies also diminish the U.S. role in affecting the growth of Asian regional financial ties. In the shorter run, as Ferguson has put it, "foreigners are accumulating large claims on the future output of the United States. However the borrowed money is used, whether productively or not, a proportion of the future returns on U.S. investments will end up flowing abroad as dividends or interest payments" ("Reasons to Worry," *New York Times Magazine* June 11, 2006, 48).

In sum, quite different visions and interests remain across East Asia and the Asia-Pacific. As such, they continue to shape the evolving regional architecture. Questions involving membership, scope of activity, and depth of institutionalization, to cite only the most striking issues, still divide the major players. Regional ties have deepened, particularly in trade and finance, and a number of new regional bodies and processes have begun. Yet, although these have become important milestones in regionalism, in other areas such as security East Asia continues to lack a commonly accepted regional vision.

Conclusion

In this chapter, I have examined the changing regional architecture in East Asia since the crisis of 1997–98. I have stressed the important moves toward regional institutionalization in economics and finance while showing the counterbalancing national differences in regional policies as well as the reluctance of important players in East Asia to move toward regional security cooperation. Following the crisis, and largely in response to what were perceived to have been excessive IMF interventions, the governments of Asia took a series of steps designed to prevent any recurrence. Many of these moves were at least as important for their regional symbolism as they were for actual market reshaping: the CMI, the ABF, and the ABMI, for example. In addition, a series of bilateral and minilateral trade arrangements have occurred; many of these are exerting significant market impacts. And, at least as important, Asian governments have begun to meet regularly in these and other new fora, such as the EAS, to explore ways to cooperate on financial and other matters. All of this suggests considerable potential for future regional institutionalization. For the most part, these new regional initiatives have excluded participation by the United States (although this is not true for some of the FTAs or for some regional organizations such as ARF, SPT and APEC).

The process of creating regional institutions remains rather primitive in East Asia. Informality remains the guiding principle. There is little likelihood that a trove of formal rule-bound institutions will appear soon. At the same time, although informality has the drawback of fuzzy ambiguity, it offers the flexibility that encourages wider participation and flexible adjustment to changing conditions. And, if East Asian regionalism is to advance, the first requirement is that the countries of the region show up for organizational activities.

To date, there has been far greater regional cohesion in Southeast Asia than in Northeast Asia. And Southeast Asian countries remain less than confident about the security intentions of their Northeast Asian neighbors. Meanwhile, throughout Northeast Asia cooperative relations have been impeded by serious security differences on a variety of unresolved territorial disputes, as well as uncertainties about the future intentions of their neighbors. Despite some recent moves to counter these trends and to weave new regional webs of cooperation, East Asia remains the site of powerful forces of divergence. In the short run at least, we are likely to see a continued struggle between these centrifugal and centripetal forces.

PART III

National Responses

CHAPTER 9

The Capitalist Embrace

China Ten Years after the Asian Financial Crisis

Edward Steinfeld

The Chinese Postcrisis Emergence on the Global Stage

The ten years since the Asian financial crisis have for China constituted a monumental coming of age, an extraordinary new emergence on to the global stage. The nation over the course of a decade has in many respects achieved, or very nearly approached, that which had previously eluded it for some 150 years—full integration into the global political and economic order. As Andrew MacIntyre, T. J. Pempel, and John Ravenhill (chap. 1 in this volume) note, the Asian financial crisis did not involve China directly, and nor did China suffer the same interlinked problems across currency liberalization, financial intermediation, and the real economy that apply to much of the rest of crisis-era East Asia. China's economic problems of the time were profound and, indeed, linked to connections between financial intermediation and industry, but given the nation's deferral of capital-account liberalization and its relative insulation from currency attacks, China faced problems that resided almost exclusively in the domestic realm.

Nonetheless, the crisis pushed China toward a radical and purposively induced break from the past, one directly motivated by lessons that Chinese policy architects drew from their neighbors' sudden and unexpected fall from economic grace. At one level, this departure from the past pertained to elite politics in that certain policymakers prevailed over others and newer ideas began to outstrip older ones. At a more profound level, however, the shift is best understood in societal terms. The very framing of policy issues in the public arena and the very nature of popular discourse surrounding the Chinese developmental mission and place in the world shifted, thus making possible in broad societal terms transformations that only a decade earlier would have been unimaginable. China was spared the direct economic effects of the East Asian financial crisis. Yet the crisis engendered within China a fundamental reframing of how elites and ordinary citizens alike understood the political, social, and economic challenges facing their nation. What resulted from this ideational shift was both the determination on the part of elites to push radical and socially dislocating change and a willingness on the part of broad portions of the populace—including those portions most adversely affected by the changes—to comply. Indeed, even those expressing resistance at the grassroots— rural peasants and urban workers—frequently did so by adopting the rhetoric and goals of the most forward-leaning central policies and then turning those against ostensibly regressive local political stalwarts (Gallagher 2005; O'Brien and Li 2006).

The point is that the basic spectrum of political and social discourse shifted, thus permitting fundamental change in the institutional underpinnings of the Chinese political economy. The effects, still unfolding today, extend across the status of the nation globally, the role of the state domestically, and the basic expectations and life chances of the ordinary Chinese citizen. MacIntyre, Pempel, and Ravenhill (chap. 1 in this volume) argue that, across East Asian nations, the most important legacy of the financial crisis lies less in the realm of pure economics than in the lasting political, institutional, and social changes that the economic shock left in its wake. Perhaps nowhere is this truer than in China, ironically enough, the one major East Asian economy almost entirely buffered from the currency attacks so central to the Asian financial crisis.

That said, the economic ramifications of the Chinese postcrisis response have been dramatic, to say the least. During the first two decades of reform in the 1980s and 1990s, China was primarily a self-contained story, an important case of postsocialist transition but one operating more on the fringes of the global economic order than in the center. Today, however, China is viewed as a linchpin of the global economy, a key driver of global economic, social, and environmental change. The fragmentation of global supply chains and the shift to China of so many manufacturing activities associated with those chains have indeed induced far-reaching change—change that, although interpreted differently in different parts of the world, is universally understood to be profound. Americans, for example, witness the massive trade surplus that China runs with their home economy and link that surplus to the job losses, downward wage pressures, and benefit cuts that they perceive in their immediate domestic environment. At the same time, those citizens enjoy the more beneficial flipside of the Chinese presence in the global economy: access to consumer goods made extraordinarily inexpensive through China-based production and access to low-cost consumer credit made possible by vast inflows of Chinese investment funds.

For observers within the East Asian region, the emphasis is somewhat different. China in recent years has increasingly been running trade deficits—substantial ones in many cases—with virtually every country in the region (table 9.1), an outcome suggesting a complementary division of labor within the supply chain between Chinese- and other East Asian–based producers (Gaulier, Lemoine, and Ünal-Kesenci 2005). Even though outsourcing many manufacturing activities to

Table 9.1 Top ten economies with which China runs a bilateral trade surplus or deficit, 2005[a]

Economies recording surplus	Trade surplus (billions of US$)	YOY growth (%)	Economies recording deficit	Trade deficit (billions of US$)	YOY growth (%)
1. United States	114.2	42.3	1. Taiwan province	58.1	13.5
2. Hong Kong SAR	112.3	26.0	2. Korea	41.7	21.1
3. Netherlands	23.0	47.6	3. Japan	16.5	−21.0
4. United Kingdom	13.5	31.5	4. Malaysia	9.5	−5.9
5. United Arab Emirates	6.7	20.7	5. Saudi Arabia	8.4	77.4
6. Spain	6.4	70.3	6. Philippines	8.2	70.9
7. Italy	4.8	71.9	7. Angola	6.2	37.2
8. Canada	4.1	410.6	8. Thailand	6.2	7.5
9. Belgium	3.7	59.6	9. Australia	5.2	3.3
10. Turkey	3.6	62.8	10. Brazil	5.1	88.5

Source: Ministry of Commerce of the People's Republic of China.
[a] SAR, Special Administrative Region; YOY, year-on-year.

Table 9.2 Global industrial output share by value of the top ten economies (%)

1990		2002	
Country	Share in world output	Country	Share in world output
Japan	22.5	United States	23.3
United States	20.7	Japan	18.1
Germany	10.2	German	7.9
France	4.7	China	6.6
United Kingdom	4.1	France	4.7
Italy	4.0	Italy	3.5
Russian Federation	3.2	Korea, Republic of	3.3
Brazil	2.5	United Kingdom	3.2
China	2.2	Brazil	2.2
Spain	2.0	Canada	1.9

Source: United Nations Industrial Development Organization (UNIDO) Scoreboard database.

China, and in the process moving the trade surpluses they once ran with the United States and Europe over to the Chinese ledger, the neighbors of China have been able to retain a firm grasp on the most proprietary, high-value activities associated with production (Steinfeld 2004). Assessments of national shares of global production value seem to confirm this for many of the neighbors of China and, indeed, for the United States as well (table 9.2). The point is that China has not just grown in recent years but has also evolved into a central driver of East Asian regional prosperity, a central component of global growth and production, and a primary consumer of global resources (with a host of complex ramifications for global resource producers, other large consumers, and the global environmental commons).

It is important to note, however, that within the context of breathtaking growth, China domestically since the Asian crisis has experienced a substantial socioeconomic

transformation, much of it purposively induced and much of it extraordinarily dislocating. Certainly with respect to deepening social inequality and declining public
welfare provision, China has exhibited outcomes similar to ones described for all
of postcrisis East Asia (MacIntyre, Pempel, and Ravenhill, chap. 1 in this volume).
For Chinese urban citizens, joblessness during the past decade, particularly in the
manufacturing sector, has outstripped anything experienced since the founding of
the People's Republic. Moreover, unemployment spiked at precisely the same time
that the traditional urban social safety net was torn down, whether through outright
elimination or reorientation to a fee-for-service basis. China, not unlike its neighbors (Stephan Haggard, chap. 5 in this volume), has shifted toward far more flexible
labor relations: increasing numbers of temporary and contract employees, fewer
managerial strictures on lay-offs, and little if any collective representation for workers. Particularly in relation to its democratically governed and far-wealthier neighbors, however, China has proven far less effective in coupling these changes with
expanded social welfare programs.

For Chinese rural citizens, the situation has been persistently more serious and,
by some estimates, even dire. Income disparities nationally have widened both substantially and rapidly during the past ten years, primarily to the detriment of the rural
population (figures 9.1 and 9.2). At the same time, public goods provision, already
limited in rural areas at the start of the postcrisis decade, lagged even further by the

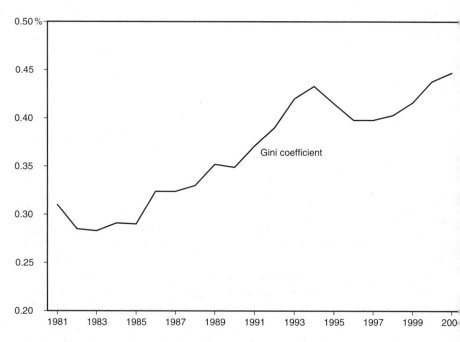

Figure 9.1 The problem of growing income disparity in China: changes in the Gini coefficient,
1981–2001.
Source: United Nations Development Programme and China Development Research Foundation (2005).

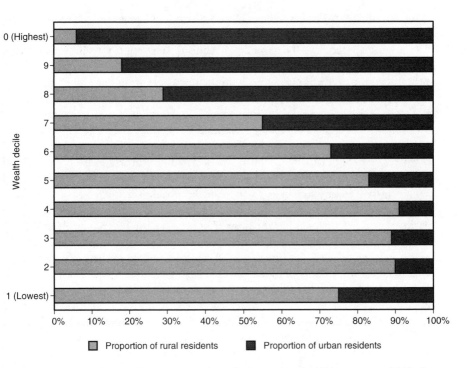

Figure 9.2 Chinese income disparity: proportions of urban and rural residents across wealth deciles in 2002.
Source: United Nations Development Programme and China Development Research Foundation (2005).

end, often significantly. It is quite clear that the emergence of China onto the global economic stage, so frequently interpreted by outsiders as exerting a detrimental impact on social welfare provision in their own countries (by inducing so much competitive pressure on domestic industry), has actually moved hand in hand with sweeping reductions in such provisioning within China itself. Again, China represents on this front but a more extreme form of that which has taken place across much of East Asia in the last decade (MacIntyre, Pempel, and Ravenhill, chap. 1 in this volume).

How and why has this transformation happened in China? What changes occurred in the aftermath of the Asian financial crisis, and why did those changes take the form they did? Why did growth and global integration accelerate at the same time public goods provisioning lagged? How has the nature of authority in Chinese society, and the social contract more broadly, changed in the process?

The Asian Financial Crisis and the Internal Reassessment by China

For so many of those in the region who endured the volatility of the late 1990s, the East Asian financial crisis served, and still serves today, as a cautionary reminder

of the fragility of markets and the ease with which they can go awry. For some, the
crisis underscored the risks of unfettered markets, the risks of encouraging liberalization to proceed in the absence of requisite state regulatory provision. For
others, the crisis was understood differently, as a story of excessive state involvement, albeit involvement not so much on the regulatory front but, rather, through
direct participation in commercial affairs—crony capitalism of the sort described
by Peter Gourevitch (chap. 4 in this volume). Different as they may be, however,
both interpretations, as they coalesced around a new emphasis on governance, law,
and transparency, were fundamentally about resetting capitalism.

So, it is striking that within China, a nation that in many respects both escaped
the immediate impact of the 1998 regional collapse and experienced the greatest
transformation of any East Asian nation in the decade since, the Asian financial
crisis was understood in an almost opposite fashion. The cautionary note—indeed,
alarm—heard in China was not about the risks of capitalism but, rather, about those
of socialism. Like its neighbors, China governmentally and societally began expressing the new rhetoric of governance, law, and transparency, but the new terms masked
what in China was a far more monumental shift. A twenty-year-old reform agenda,
one that since the late 1970s had tentatively and instrumentally employed market
mechanisms to sustain socialism, was in the aftermath of the Asian financial crisis
peremptorily and unceremoniously ditched. In its place, sweeping marketization—
capitalism, in effect—was embraced at considerable political and social risk. In the
past, reform had been largely about saving socialism or, at least, the vestiges of
socialism residing at the core of the Chinese political economy. With the Asian financial crisis, the agenda was flipped on its head. The mission now urgently became
to dismantle socialism to save reform or, more precisely, the economic growth and
concomitant systemic legitimacy that reform engendered. Reform as the salvation
of socialism, so to speak, became replaced by markets as the salvation of growth and
legitimacy. In the process, socialist institutions now came to be seen as key obstacles
standing in the way of progress. For China, a paradigm shift had occurred. Several
points should be noted about this shift. First, it began in tentative fashion some
five years before the Asian financial crisis, but the 1998 regional collapse dramatically accelerated and expanded the shift within China. Soon after the 1998 crisis,
wholesale institutionalized marketization became not a matter of policy debate but
an accepted fact. Although such changes require leadership (discussed later), so too
can they happen only if broad swathes of the populace are willing to go along. That
the Asian financial crisis was such a public event, such a publicly aired lesson, in no
small part contributed to the broader public acceptance of change.

Second, the urgency of this shift in the immediate aftermath of the Asian crisis
is underscored by the extent to which Chinese policy architects chose not to engage
in indigenous institutional design but, instead, outsourced institution-building to
overseas actors using overseas models. External reliance related to a broader strategy on the part of political elites, most notably then-premier Zhu Rongji. Rather
than slowly preparing the ground internally for wholesale marketization, in terms of
achieving a political settlement to mollify all the potential stakeholders or building

the administrative capacity needed to govern a modern market (as had been done with so many Chinese reforms previously), Chinese policy architects induced change by performing an end run around the system. They did so by, at once, tying China (and many Chinese economic actors) to external institutional strictures and disenfranchising key stakeholders in the old system, most notably the industrial line ministries and urban labor.

Third, the capitalist embrace—rapid marketization and the internalization of foreign modes of market governance—was understood to be urgent enough that it was pursued prior to the preparation of a social safety net to catch those who would suffer the costs of socialist dismantling. As a result, the embrace brought about substantial economic gains for the country, but also induced major social costs, costs that themselves, as a sort of engineered social crisis, became a significant motivator for a new policy agenda and a new overall mission for government. Hence, we find ourselves with a China today under Hu Jintao emphasizing as never before the need for broader public goods provisioning, sustainable development, and social equity. A dynamic has developed in which the government, having induced sweeping economic changes, now seeks preemptively to define a new social contract while the citizenry absorbs those efforts but then recasts them in its own understanding of an appropriate social contract. The upshot is that for all the economic change in China over the past decade, it is probably the underlying social and political transformation that will prove most profound, a situation that describes much of postcrisis East Asia (MacIntyre, Pempel, and Ravenhill, chap. 1 in this volume).

Pulling the Plug on Socialism: The End of the Equilibrium

By the mid-1990s, despite two decades of reform and policy experimentation, China—particularly in its urban industrial core—was stuck in a problematic socialist equilibrium. For all the competition introduced on the peripheries of the economy, state-owned enterprises (SOEs) still dominated production across most core industrial sectors and, equally important, accounted for the bulk of urban employment (Steinfeld 1998; Lardy 1998; Yusuf, Nabeshima, and Perkins 2005). Through their provision of lifetime employment, free housing, free health care, and a variety of other nonwage benefits, these firms also constituted virtually the entirety of the state social safety net for urban citizens. In part because of this social function, SOEs were at once indispensable and also incapable of competing commercially against new entrants from the nonstate sector. The policy solution entailed subsidization via the state-owned banking system. High household saving rates ensured liquidity for state banks, and state banks in turn—serving as a quasi-fiscal system for the state—ensured liquidity for SOE borrowers (Lardy 1998). That the pattern persisted for well over a decade is understandable given the range of traditional stakeholders that were mollified in the process. The persistence of unadulterated state ownership in both finance and industry reassured political conservatives that China, for all its reforms, remained intrinsically socialist.

In addition, the predominance of SOEs in key heavy industrial sectors satisfied bureaucratic interests in a large, important, and well-populated subset of the state apparatus, the industrial line ministries. Finally, and perhaps most important, support for SOEs and the employee entitlements associated with them pacified labor and, at least in the minds of government officials, preserved social stability. That this political economic equilibrium was racking up substantial financial liabilities in the state banking system was recognized by some policymakers but was generally ignored by most (Steinfeld 1998). The performance of SOEs continued to deteriorate, reform experiments continued to be applied one after another, subsidies (for reasons of political and social expediency) continued to flow in, and the circle was completed with further performance declines. To the extent that banks remained liquid, which they did, the equilibrium appeared sustainable, to the frustration of the more radical reformers within the system. In other words, the social and political risks of breaking the reform stalemate appeared very real and very substantial, but the economic costs of the stalemate—capital misallocation and perhaps some future impact on growth—remained distant and abstract. Hence, few observers at the time, including this author, believed that the Chinese government would or could pull the plug on socialism.

Yet with the Asian financial crisis and the contemporaneous rise of Zhu Rongji to the Chinese premiership, an extraordinary change occurred, one that began as a rhetorical recasting of the issues but soon spread to the heart of the policy agenda. Whether the Asian financial crisis directly motivated Zhu's radical reforms or simply provided a justification for them, the two were undoubtedly related. Moreover, within China at the time, observers could sense palpable change in the tenor of debate. It was as if, with the unexpected crashing of the neighboring regional economies, a light of recognition suddenly flipped on within China, not so much about what was taking place beyond the borders of China but, instead, about what had been taking place within China for so long. Of course, informed domestic observers, within the policy community and beyond, understood that the circumstances in places such as Thailand and South Korea differed from China. The absence in the Chinese system of full capital convertibility and the low levels of foreign-denominated debt insulated the country to a large degree from hot money flows, sudden capital flight, and currency collapse. At the same time, however, many observers began to acknowledge deeper similarities between China and its collapsing neighbors: economies dominated by politically connected industrial behemoths, bank-dominated and heavily state-influenced financial systems devoted to funding such behemoths, and high levels of household savings providing much of the liquidity. Terms such as moral hazard, nonperforming assets, and unfunded liabilities—all suddenly in vogue for describing long-hidden but long-accruing economic pathologies among the regional neighbors of China—seemed to apply just as equally, in the minds of many Chinese, to China itself. In essence, it was not capitalism that suddenly fell into doubt, something Chinese could have treated as a foreign problem, but, rather, the East Asian developmental model, something that Chinese unmistakably identified their own country as being part of.

Indeed, it was precisely during this period at the end of 1997 that the Chinese premier, after initially resisting, tacitly acknowledged the accuracy of what his central bankers were starting to point out—the technical insolvency of the Chinese state banking system. The insolvency of the system was not a new condition; its acknowledgement by the central government, however, was something novel. The admission provided a new framework for understanding the issues at hand and a new context for pushing change. Whereas previously the costs of maintaining the socialist equilibrium seemed abstract and the risks of disrupting it acutely real, now the opposite seemed true. The costs of inaction, politically as well as economically, became troublingly tangible, whereas the risks of pushing change somehow became more tolerable.

In some sense, the Asian financial crisis fostered an important complementarity within China between a broad societal reframing of the developmental agenda and a more specific process of intergenerational—and ideational—change among Chinese policy elites. In other words, new social norms regarding reform emerged as part and parcel of a new type of Chinese official. Technocrats (some of whom had overseas education, and virtually all of whom took for granted markets as the underpinning of best practice) were in, and socialists were out. Yesterday's debates about whether to marketize at all gave way to today's debates about technically how best to do it. Technocrats on the economic side—in the central bank, the Ministry of Finance, and the various government think-tanks—often disagreed with Zhu Rongji's approach, but generally, the criticisms were directed less at Zhu's radicalism than his perceived conservatism and proclivity in certain areas to govern through administrative coercion rather than market incentives. In short, the policy debate and the composition of policy elites had shifted enough so that people such as Zhu Rongji—people who would have appeared to be radicals only years earlier—by the late 1990s were labeled in certain arenas conservatives or traditional planners. Policy debates, therefore, continued with vigor, but because the spectrum of discourse, both within government and across society, had moved so substantially toward the pro-market side, truly traditional conservatives (particularly within state-owned industry) were left devoid of political footing, leverage, and voice.

Outsourcing Institutions

Whether it is termed conservative or liberal, the Chinese government—and, most specifically, its premier, Zhu Rongji—responded to the Asian crisis with measures that were at once wide-ranging and linked by a shared quality. They all tended to reach beyond Chinese borders for existing institutional strictures that could then be imposed more or less "as is" on Chinese domestic actors. In other words, existing foreign institutions—ones in which Chinese policymakers had played no part in designing, modifying, or otherwise legitimizing—were grasped as a means of urgently recasting the system. Such efforts stretched across a variety of domains, several of which are noted here.

World Trade Organization Accession

First, and perhaps most obvious, China in 1999 signed an agreement to join the World Trade Organization (WTO). After thirteen years of what had always appeared to be fruitless negotiation, with Chinese delegations repeatedly insisting on highly preferential accession terms and representatives of the advanced industrial nations insisting on the opposite, a breakthrough was finally reached a year after the height of the financial crisis. Moreover, the breakthrough involved across-the-board concessions by the premier's negotiators (Lardy 2002), a surrender that surprised audiences within China as much as it surprised those in Washington, Tokyo, and virtually everywhere else in the developed world.

The accession agreement tied the Chinese government to a series of external commitments to market deepening: reduction of tariffs, elimination of restrictions on foreign ownership and competition in key industrial sectors, modification of domestic laws so as to provide equal treatment for foreign and domestic competitors, and protection of intellectual property rights. Given the institutional status of the Chinese system in 1999, these commitments, if they were to be met, required radical domestic transformation. Yet that fact underscores the nature of Zhu's strategy. The effort was as aspirational (Clarke 2003a, 2003b) as it was ruthlessly tactical. The aspirational element involved making commitments (particularly in areas such as intellectual property rights) that could not possibly be met at the time they were made, so that the very act of committing would serve as an internal signal throughout the system that change was underway. The tactical aspect involved striking an external agreement without first consulting internal governmental constituencies and then using that fait accompli to shift responsibility on to outsiders or "objective" market pressures for the painful internal restructuring measures that would ensue.

Those measures indeed proved both substantial and painful. In the immediate aftermath of the accession agreement, Zhu Rongji summarily eliminated the government industrial line ministries, thus removing the major organizational vehicle representing traditional industrial interests; the governmental voice for traditional state ownership was effectively silenced. As noted previously, however, such a strike from above was possible because public discourse and intragovernmental debate had already shifted fairly substantially toward the pro-market side.

In the process, organized labor was also effectively disenfranchised. Lay-offs that had begun in the mid-1990s accelerated dramatically after the Asian financial crisis. With WTO accession and its implications for the ramping up of domestic competition, however, culpability could be shifted off to, and diffused among, a variety of external forces. Most notably, the government portrayed WTO accession as a key element of the Chinese modernization process, a key step toward joining the global standard associated with advanced industrial nations. The phrases "getting on the international track" and "adopting the international standard" cropped up repeatedly in policy statements, media reports, and the everyday conversations of economic actors themselves—enterprise managers, workers, and ordinary consumers.

If China was going to be modern (an ambition that has resonated within China for at least the past 150 years, and across myriad definitions of what exactly modernity entails), then it had to integrate with the global market standard. Integrating with the market standard, in turn, required huge societal change. In order to compete, domestic firms would have to shed workers and, for the downsized labor force that remained, shed the extensive benefits associated with the traditional socialist work unit (*danwei*). The elimination of the *danwei* (tantamount to the elimination of the traditional socialist welfare net), then, would necessitate the marketization of housing, health care, and education. Meanwhile, the cascading dislocations—beneficial for some citizens, painful for others, and earth-shaking for everybody—could all be attributed to the market, a force that was understood as at once unassailable and objective (or at least more nearly objective than the political preferences that previously had governed allocation). That so many of even the hardest hit populations in the hardest hit regions internalized this logic in part explains why resistance and upheaval was relatively light (Blecher 2002).

Citizens would be paying an onerous price, but to the extent their own identity was linked to the developmental success of their country—China's achievement, in effect, of world-class status—they appeared willing to comply. Here, again, we witness the complementarities between forward-leaning policymaking and broader societal consensus. Zhu Rongji's policy initiatives targeted precisely those in the bureaucracy who seemed to have fallen off the spectrum of socially acceptable reform discourse—the representatives not of liberalism or conservatism today but of stale, outmoded notions from yesterday. Similarly, the new government reform initiatives induced pain but simultaneously tapped into a widely shared commitment to a national modernization effort, one more often than not defined by the extent to which the nation appeared to converge to standards set by the most developed nations.

Overseas Listing: Exposing State-Owned Enterprises to Foreign Corporate Governance Mechanisms

WTO accession involved exposing the Chinese system broadly to foreign commitments and foreign definitions of fair competition. At the more micro-level, Zhu Rongji pushed an equally bold effort to expose the largest, most important, and often most-prized Chinese SOEs to foreign governance strictures. The mechanisms here were twofold: public listing on overseas stock exchanges, most notably in New York and Hong Kong, and incorporation into the SOE boardroom of world-class executives, namely Chinese nationals who had received advanced degrees abroad and spent substantial periods of time working in multinational firms.

Overseas listing involved a complicated series of compromises to bring in new rules while preserving a semblance of state ownership. In preparation for listing, the commercial assets of the SOE in question were segregated into what would become the listed arm while ancillary operations were carved out to form a parent enterprise that would hold majority ownership over (and would often share the same name as) the listed arm. In this respect, because the holding company remained traditionally state-owned, so too did, at least nominally, the subordinate listed firm (Yusuf, Nabeshima, and Perkins 2005). The government, then, by claiming it was not selling off prized national assets, could avoid comparisons to Russian privatization, widely viewed by Chinese citizens as an inherently corrupt sell-off to privileged, politically connected insiders. Indeed, if anything, many observers, including this author, felt at the time that overseas listing would have little impact on traditional state ownership (and the corporate behavior associated with it), particularly given the small portion of shares actually put up for offer.

Overseas listing, however, although not ceding overt ownership control, did bring in a new array of foreign rules, ones that (as discussed later) changed corporate behavior. Chinese companies listed abroad now were required to meet international accounting standards, abide by rules regarding related party transactions (an important issue given the tight relationships with parent companies), appoint independent nonexecutive directors to their corporate boards, and meet the transparency requirements of their market supervisory agencies (such as the U.S. Securities and Exchange Commission [SEC]) when undertaking major acquisitions or other important strategic endeavors. In short, they became accountable not just to the rules of their own government but, in very substantial ways, to those of another government.

Personnel of various kinds had to be brought in who could understand and operate within these new strictures. At one level, we have witnessed with increasing frequency the incorporation into the upper managerial ranks of Chinese nationals whose education and careers (and, by extension, outlooks) have been shaped abroad. Plus, whether or not such individuals could be brought in, overseas listing forced Chinese firms to engage and deeply rely on foreign advisory services, most notably global investment banks and international law firms. For better or worse, and whether by default or design, the purveyors of global best practice capitalism were catapulted into vital advisory positions in the Chinese SOE boardroom.

These advisors, however, had to be able to connect with corporate insiders, an imperative that drove personnel shifts within the listed firms. In spring 1999, Zhu Rongji, at a series of public venues including a speech delivered at MIT, highlighted the need for Chinese domestic firms to attract Chinese managerial talent that had migrated overseas. While imploring Western business schools to participate in a massive training up of Chinese MBAs, he also committed the state sector to rewarding talent with world-class wages. The message was clear—best-practice, world-class management was needed in the Chinese corporate boardroom and it would be compensated accordingly. The implicit message, one that became clearer as worker lay-offs proceeded in the state sector, was that the traditional socialist constituencies of old-style labor and old-style bureaucratic management had lost their seat at the table. Now, a new style of management, a new class of Chinese "insider outsiders" was about to gain its own. Within the next five years, overseas-listed SOEs in a variety of strategic sectors, including energy and banking, started to incorporate this new talent in the senior management ranks, particularly in chief financial officer (CFO) and corporate counsel positions, due to their degree of interaction with overseas rules and standards. In many cases, as the firms themselves became more involved in global business, these "insider outsiders," in large part because of their previous experience in dealing with global matters from within the multinational firm, took the lead in engaging boardroom advisors, negotiating overseas transactions, and managing global media relations. At the same time, in some cases at the urging of the "insider outsiders," foreigners were brought directly into the boardroom as independent nonexecutive directors.

Finally, in line with these changes, the premier himself began to appoint "insider outsiders" to key positions in the Chinese commercial regulatory apparatus. Chinese citizens with overseas economics doctorates and Hong Kong citizens with extensive global expertise were brought into senior positions in the Shanghai and Shenzhen stock exchanges, the China Securities Regulatory Commission, the central bank (People's Bank of China) and a variety of other high-level governmental policy bureaus. They served, in effect, to translate the newly established Chinese external institutional commitments into domestic legal and regulatory practice.

Labor Law

Throughout much of the 1990s, foreign business interests—particularly those from advanced industrial societies dealing in the more capital- and technology-intensive sectors in China—had been pushing for greater managerial autonomy and greater workforce control within their China-based operations. Because they were partnering generally with SOEs, and thus bumping up against the socialist equilibrium noted earlier, their desires generally went unmet. Workforces in the aggregate could not easily be trimmed, nor could individual worker tenure be easily tied to performance. Similarly, mid-level indigenous management could not be held accountable, in part because such managers (correctly) viewed as paramount their state-dictated mandate to maintain employment and social stability.

The early indicators of change had begun to appear in the mid-1990s, but the environment transformed dramatically after the Asian financial crisis, in no small part because of the factors already noted: WTO accession and the integration of foreign practice into the SOE boardroom. Accession into the WTO ramped up a societywide effort on the part of government to emphasize rule of law and global standards. The rule-of-law framing crept into many aspects of daily life, but it was perhaps most profoundly evident—and not just rhetorically but in everyday practice—in labor matters. What began to happen was that China replaced its traditional labor practices (practices that, although not necessarily empowering to workers, fostered lifetime employment) with new Western-style labor law, particularly labor law circa late twentieth century (Gallagher 2005). The new labor laws pushed the use of formal labor contracting between management and labor. Moreover, by vesting individual workers with contract rights (while simultaneously not granting them the right to bargain collectively), the law, by default or by design, put workers in the position of having to bargain individually with management. The phenomenon parallels what Stephan Haggard (chap. 5 in this volume) observes across much of East Asia, a shift in labor relations from the collective to the individual. The net result, again in a fashion not so different from what was taking place throughout the advanced industrial world in this era, was that the tables were being turned against organized labor. Labor had been given legal rights, but the rights, in effect, undercut the ability of labor to make collectivist claims. In the Chinese case, autonomous unions did not exist, and, in the context of Zhu Rongji's push to put China on the global track, the Communist Party labor organization receded into the background. By reaching out to and incorporating Western-style (most notably U.S.- or UK-style) labor law, the Chinese state effectively facilitated not just massive downsizing but also substantial reductions of benefits for remaining workers, much of which happened at the discretion of newly empowered corporate management.

The overall point of these examples is that, although in certain areas such as currency liberalization China may have slowed (but by no means stopped) its efforts at liberalization, in a variety of other areas, including those at the absolute core of traditional state socialism, China in the wake of the Asian financial crisis pursued an unprecedented, revolutionary, and socially far-reaching embrace of the institutions of global capitalism. The impacts would be profound, far-ranging, and, in some cases, unexpected.

The Impact of Institutional Outsourcing: Structural Change

China's postcrisis global embrace played out in a number of ways, illustrated by the contours of subsequent Chinese economic development. Growth surged, and with the run-up and ultimate accession to the WTO, levels of foreign direct investment (FDI) ballooned. Concomitantly, exports surged, most notably to the United States, the market on which not just Chinese growth but global growth came increasingly to rely. Within the Chinese export sectors, foreign ownership and investment continued to rise, with 57 percent of Chinese exports in 2004 booked by foreign-invested firms and 85 percent of the nation's high-tech exports (as defined by the Chinese Ministry of Commerce) in 2003 booked by such firms. China became increasingly integrated into global supply chains, and global ownership increasingly became integrated into the China-based industrial base feeding these chains.

A series of additional moves on the domestic policy front fostered a more general blurring of traditional ownership boundaries within China. In large part due to new fears about nonperforming loans and politically influenced lending in the banking system, Zhu Rongji aggressively backed a series of postcrisis measures to hold individual bank officers accountable for lending decisions and local government officials accountable for the financial liabilities of locally owned collectives. The move created substantial incentives for banks to rein in loans to collectives and for local governments to formally divest from such firms, thus pushing large-scale local privatization.

At the same time, and probably not coincidentally, Jiang Zemin, then head of state and party chairman, began a series of moves in 1999 to formally legitimize private entrepreneurship, a push that started with wording changes in the constitution and culminated in 2001 with a public declaration welcoming private entrepreneurs into the ranks of the Chinese Communist Party. Combined with the divestment pressures imposed on local governments, these moves on the economic front, by providing incentives for entrepreneurship, generated new outlets for job creation, albeit jobs that did not generally provide the benefits packages and social welfare provisions previously associated with state-sector employment. In a manner comparable to what Stephan Haggard (chap. 5 in this volume) observes for East Asian nations as varied as South Korea, Taiwan, Thailand, and the Philippines, the informal sector in China has boomed.

On the political front, these moves suggested a realignment of party interests toward a new constituency, the private entrepreneurs who were now running not the bicycle-repair stands and noodle shops of yore but, rather, some of the fastest growing, highest-tech, and most advanced firms in China. In the postcrisis environment, the Communist Party appeared to be less and less the bastion of labor and traditional SOE managerial interests and more the vanguard, so to speak, of globally focused restructuring advocates within the SOEs, of private entrepreneurs, and of foreign corporate interests. That U.S. Treasury Secretary Henry Paulson, in his former capacity as chairman of Goldman Sachs, in the postcrisis decade made by his own estimate seventy trips to China, many of which involved meetings with the most senior Chinese leaders, provides a sense of the kind of access that particular kinds of outsiders now had.

Taken together, many of the moves of the central government were linked by a common logic. Through institutional outsourcing, external pressures were induced to push domestic economic restructuring. At the same time, ties to external institutions facilitated increases in the number and influence of new and frequently externally connected players within Chinese domestic producers. New players, in turn, armed with new domestic regulations, even in core areas such as labor relations, acquired substantial control and autonomy in their efforts to achieve commercial success and, by extension, make China globally competitive.

From Reforming State-Owned Enterprises to Building National Champions

For two decades preceding the Asian financial crisis, the Chinese government described state enterprise reform (*guoyou qiye gaige*) as a central rung of its policy agenda. The very term itself, by identifying a particular target of reform and by identifying that target in terms of an ownership classification, substantially narrowed the terms of the debate. Policy success would be signified by the revitalization (*gao huo*) of an existing set of firms, incumbent SOEs (most of which predated the reform era), and an existing set of stakeholders, SOE employees and traditional managers. Reforms that brought commercial success to these firms were deemed effective, whereas those that did not were replaced by new reform measures and new financial bailouts.

With the changes initiated in the late 1990s, however, the overall governmental mission seemed to shift. Now, the ultimate objective, and the ultimate measure by which the government was implying that its efficacy should be judged by the public, became the creation of national champion firms (Steinfeld 1999; Nolan 2001; Gallagher 2005; Thun 2006). Such firms would ostensibly not just operate on global standards but also would raise the status of China in the world.

By emphasizing the building of national champions and by frequently juxtapositioning that objective with what government officials termed their comparative advantage (*bijiao youshi*) strategy of development (in other words, development through liberalized markets), policy architects were effectively opening the door to all sorts of new players while shutting the door on others. Policymakers were also establishing the basis for a shift in corporate governance from fairly traditional crony capitalism to something more akin to what Peter Gourevitch (chap. 4 in this volume) describes as a market-demanded or investor-led push for modern shareholder rights and transparency. Now, state industrial policy need not foster traditional SOEs and, according to some interpretations, should expressly not foster such organizations. Instead, publicly listed and foreign-invested SOE spin-offs, domestically owned private firms, ambiguously owned public (*minying*) enterprises (such as a variety of high-tech firms owned by public universities) could all now be understood as legitimate vehicles for state industrial policy, legitimate vessels of the national interest, and legitimate indicators of governmental policy efficacy. As such, their interests could be viewed as equaling, or even trumping, the interests of traditional stakeholders.

Indeed, this is precisely the message that has been conveyed by the Chinese government to its citizenry over the past ten years. China must grow and become modern; to do so, it must jump on the global market track; to do that, it must foster globally competitive national champions; and to do that, major social change has to take place. Moreover, this is change that is at once modern and initiated by an objective (and by extension, fair) force—the market.

Interestingly, as part of this shift, the Chinese government changed the name of some of its key branches. For example, the State Planning Commission became the National Reform and Development Commission; the State Statistical Bureau became the National Bureau of Statistics. "State" was out, and "national" was in. Similarly, far less frequently than in the past did policy architects refer to "state enterprise reform" or ownership of enterprises more generally. Instead, the discussion turned to less historically laden (and arguably less restrictive) phrases such as national competitiveness, national champions, and world-class enterprises. The phrasing opened the door to new stakeholders and new organizations while shutting out key stakeholders in the old system.

Business Reenters the Political Sphere: The National Champions Go Global

By pushing the most important SOEs in China to list on foreign exchanges, Chinese policymakers undoubtedly hoped to introduce new voices and new stakeholders into the senior managerial ranks and, in so doing, build globally competitive firms. At the same time, they probably assumed that the government could ultimately maintain control over such firms through its majority ownership position, one exercised tangibly by a state-owned holding company. That the objective of introducing new stakeholders has been achieved is indisputable; that the state has maintained control is far less certain. In other words, the state has consciously shifted its industrial policy objectives to a new set of corporate organizations. At the same time, those corporate organizations have been substantially empowered and internally transformed through a variety of institutional mechanisms, mechanisms that in many cases are far beyond the control of the Chinese governmental apparatus.

Here we witness a divergence from Singapore, the other case of East Asian, top-down, authoritarian governance reform (Gourevitch, chap. 5 in this volume). The Chinese system is obviously far larger and far messier than its Singaporean counterpart, yet the most important difference arguably resides in China's even more extreme ceding of corporate control from the traditional authoritarian party-state to internationally networked business professionals, Chinese and foreign alike. The result is that the national champion firms themselves, despite their centrality to Chinese governmental policy objectives, have developed an unprecedented ability to chart their own courses and to do so in international environments involving complex diplomatic, security, regulatory, and environmental externalities. Thus, although the state in abstract terms remains the majority owner of many important Chinese firms, observers find it more difficult in the Chinese case (especially in contrast to the Singapore) to speak meaningfully of top-down corporate governance or even more broadly of state-led development. The Chinese government has embraced global capitalism, but in so doing, it has fostered organizations that increasingly seem to be responding to the incentives of global capitalism and doing so in a fashion that places the central government in a highly reactive and even subordinate position. The result in China is not quite akin to what Gourevitch (chap. 4 in this volume) describes for Singapore, credible commitment (not to trample minority shareholder rights) by authoritarian choice. Instead, China ends up with credible commitment driven by the duet of institutional outsourcing, on the one hand, and sheer inability on the part of governmental overseers/owners to keep abreast of the complex, fast-paced, and increasingly internationalized activities of corporations, on the other.

One important example involves the 2005 effort by the China National Offshore Oil Corporation Ltd. (CNOOC) to acquire the U.S. oil and gas company Unocal, a move that provoked an uproar among the U.S. public and a hostile regulatory response by the U.S. Congress. The takeover bid was ultimately withdrawn, yielding the field to a competing bid by Chevron. From the perspective of most Americans, the nature of the CNOOC bid was transparently obvious. The geostrategically ambitious Chinese government, seeking to fuel the rapidly expanding energy needs of its economy, was determined to lock up global energy resources. It would do so in zero-sum terms, and it would do it through its commercial arms, its state energy companies.

The reality, however, is far more complex (Powell, 2005). The initial CNOOC bid was financed almost exclusively not by the Chinese state but by two major global investment banks, Goldman Sachs and JP Morgan. When the bid was upped in the context of a competing offer by Chevron, the additional increment of financing came from the CNOOC parent company, the nonlisted "CNOOC." What is far from clear is that the state had either the inclination or capacity to supervise in fine-grained fashion the strategies, financing, and day-to-day operations of the firm. This is all the more true given the central government's ambition in the postcrisis decade to have its national champion enterprises respond less to administrative fiat and more to market forces. Beyond having the power to appoint or fire senior managers in either CNOOC arm, the state appeared to send few detailed signals downward to these managers about what CNOOC specifically should be doing. Not unlike the U.S. government, the Chinese government frequently speaks about energy policy, but it speaks with many different voices and from many different perspectives. Although terms and objectives such as energy efficiency, energy autonomy, energy security, and overseas energy strategy are all bandied about, the real-world policy manifestations are unclear and often contradictory. Moreover, authority for energy policy within the Chinese central government is highly dispersed. There is no central Ministry of Energy, and the Energy Bureau of the National Development and Reform Commission, the senior-most government economic policy apparatus, has a staff of approximately thirty people. At most, this organization can approve vague directions in corporate strategy.

Whereas the central government's energy-related capacity is stretched desperately thin, corporate capacity, for many of the reasons discussed earlier, has grown rapidly. CNOOC CFOs in the years leading up to and during the Unocal bid were both MIT-trained MBAs. Moreover, since listing in New York and Hong Kong, CNOOC had brought influential non-Chinese on to its corporate board. At the time of the Unocal bid, those independent directors included a vice chairman of Goldman Sachs Asia and a former senior executive from Shell, people whose knowledge of global finance and global energy was undoubtedly broader than that of individuals within the state regulatory apparatus. Board meetings of CNOOC, it is worth noting, were (and still are) conducted in English. Interestingly, given that the bidder and target company were U.S.-listed firms, extensive filings were required by the U.S. Securities and Exchange Commission, filings that required the participation and consent of the CNOOC directors, both Chinese and non-Chinese. As part of their due diligence responsibilities, the board of CNOOC required the firm to perform an extensive valuation of Unocal, one that arguably prolonged the acquisition process enough for Chevron to put together a counterbid (Powell, 2005). All the while, according to SEC filings, multinational investment bankers and legal teams were performing extensive advisory services, as is typical for any global business acquisition.

The point is not that anything nefarious took place. Quite the contrary, the point is that the bid looked nothing like what we would expect of a strategic Chinese state acting coherently through a quasi-commercial arm. Indeed, we could plausibly argue that the investment banking and advisors, given their knowledge of global industry and their close ties to the board room, had an informational advantage over the distant policymakers in the central government. In that sense, we need not identify a central governmental directive to understand why CNOOC was seeking a major acquisition—the firm was flush with cash, and it was being showered with credit by the global investment banking community. By some accounts, the Chinese central government was as poorly informed and notified about the bid as was the U.S. Congress.

At the same time, we do have to bring in the complicated new corporate governance structures to understand the prolonged timing of the bid and, by extension, one of the reasons it failed. Regardless of whether the Chinese central state directed CNOOC to acquire Unocal, that acquisition had to be approved by the directors, both Chinese and non-Chinese, on regulatory terms set by the New York and Hong Kong stock exchanges (Powell, 2005). That process required time, particularly given that CNOOC was climbing a steep learning curve in the cross-border acquisitions game. The protracted process, then, impacted the strategy and competitive bidding environment in which CNOOC operated. Interestingly, the takeover bid could not be pursued by the fully state-owned parent because that firm, as part of the CNOOC terms for overseas listing, was forbidden by charter from engaging in the international upstream oil and gas exploration business. Outside rules were limiting the actions of inside players and of the Chinese government itself. That the rules were limiting is as interesting as the fact that the individuals being limited continued to abide by the rules.

Whether the Unocal bid made sense commercially, or geostrategically, is immaterial. Rather, the point is that that bid represented an intersection of extremely complicated interests, ones that straddled a variety of boundaries and transcended a simple "China versus the outside" categorization. Energy companies are by definition political players because their actions inevitably impact a variety of economic, diplomatic, military, and societal externalities. At the same time, observers generally do not view global energy majors such as Shell, BP, and Exxon-Mobil as arms of a central state. If anything, skeptics view these firms not as being unduly influenced by government but, rather, as unduly influencing governments. The interesting thing is that CNOOC, a substantially smaller player than any of the global majors, has increasingly come to resemble those majors with respect to the stakeholder relationships involved and the type of deals made (Herberg 2007, 10). Meanwhile, as companies like this pursue global deals, and do so under the guidance of global advisory firms (a situation made possible only by the Chinese government's post–Asian crisis efforts to internationalize corporate governance mechanisms), the Chinese government is forced to play catch-up, scrambling to respond to the diplomatic repercussions of Chinese-flagged corporate actors.

At least two additional points are worth noting with respect to this case. First, it suggests the possibility (one that still needs to be confirmed through further research over time) that overseas listing has had a greater impact on Chinese firms than on Korean, Japanese, or other East Asian firms that have undergone comparable overseas listing processes during the past decade. To the extent the observation proves true, we could, of course, argue that Chinese firms, starting from a socialist background, were far less advanced, in modern market terms, than their counterparts across the region; hence, Chinese firms, given their low starting point and given the vast distance they had to travel simply to become market players, could realize greater institutional returns from overseas listing than their more developed corporate brethren across East Asia. At the same time, however, we could argue that because Chinese developmental ambitions and national sense of self-worth have become so tied up with the adoption of externally defined institutional standards, Chinese firms may in fact prove more flexible and adaptable than their regional peers. It is undoubtedly true that the openness of China to FDI—an openness exceeding that of any other major player in the region—has permitted foreign interpenetration of China-based industry and China-based supply chains. It is equally (albeit less drastically) true that outsiders have increasingly been able to penetrate the corporate boardroom of Chinese firms, including even state-owned firms in strategic industries. It is difficult to imagine that any of that could have proceeded without a high degree of flexibility and adaptability among the various Chinese stakeholders involved.

That leads to the second point regarding the nature of the Chinese developmental model. Seeking to explain the Chinese economic emergence today, many observers reach back to ideas popular in the 1980s for understanding Japan. Twenty to thirty years ago, the success of Japan was viewed as a product of "Japan, Inc.," a national system characterized by state dominance over industry, strategic coherence across business and government, careful coordination of industrial competitiveness, and ruthless mercantilist ambition. Today, increasingly, China is being understood as "China, Inc." Whether the mercantilist lens was appropriate for understanding Japan in the 1980s is debatable; that it is deeply deficient for understanding China today, however, is indisputable.

The Old System Meets the New

Precisely because the Chinese political economy today does not operate as "China, Inc.," aspirational policymaking from the top—whether that of Zhu Rongji or his successor, Wen Jiabao—routinely butts up against a long-standing Chinese pattern of bottom-up local self-help. Since the earliest days of the reform era, and arguably even well before, China has been governed in part through locally initiated (or, at least, locally based) informal experimentation. Local governmental actors routinely engage in development-oriented policy experiments, ones that frequently diverge from, or even directly contravene, formal rules existing on the books. When those experiments prove successful, they are then often propagated regionally, and should success be sustained, they are often propagated nationally. Once they are operative at the national level, the experiments effectively set the de facto rules for economic behavior, although, again, the behavior remains proscribed by formal, de jure regulations. Only post hoc, once the behavior has become accepted as commonplace and the economic ramifications have proven positive, does the central government change the regulations, transforming the previously de facto into the currently de jure. A number of important policy initiatives have unfolded or are currently unfolding according to this pattern: agricultural decollectivization in the late 1970s and early 1980s, the rise of the private sector through the 1990s, and the development of energy infrastructure at present, just to name a few. In some sense, almost any manner of local experimentation becomes justifiable as long as local governmental actors are involved (in other words, as long as the activity is taking place under the purview of some part of the state) and economic growth results.

Of course, complicated outcomes arise. China often appears to insiders and outsiders alike as a nation composed of systems within systems. Different localities—provinces, municipalities, or even counties—operate according to their own rules, many of which do not seem to have been formalized at any level. Discerning the difference between acceptable local policy entrepreneurship (tolerated by higher-level authorities) and unacceptable local corruption or malfeasance (punishable by higher-level authorities) becomes a highly refined, highly uncertain art.

One of the main ramifications is that boundaries between business and government at the grassroots level remain highly ambiguous, regardless of the types of firms and forms of ownership involved. For example, if a private entrepreneur chooses to locate in a particular city because the municipal government is providing land for free (as frequently happens), the entrepreneur often knows that the land has been removed from previous agricultural uses illegally. Local governments, rather than following cumbersome national land regulations that protect rural citizens from eviction without proper compensation, simply ignore the rules, displace the rural constituents, and turn the land over to industry, all as part of local developmental efforts. The new user of the land benefits, but also needs the local government to provide protection should any claims arise based on formal national land-use rules. The local government, in turn, exercises a shadow equity position in the firm in compensation for the free-of-charge land grant and the protection required to guarantee the "property right." This was a rather common situation in the 1990s surrounding collective enterprises, and it is by no means infrequent today surrounding private firms. The general pattern, with regard to land use and other areas, is celebrated by some observers as developmentally oriented governmental flexibility (Oi 1992; Qian and Xu, 1993; Montinola, Qian, and Weingast 1995) and criticized by others as a driver of abusive behavior, particularly toward the rurally disenfranchised (Bernstein and Lu 2000; Chen and Wu 2006).

Regardless of whether local experimentation is viewed positively or negatively, it is worth noting at the present time how the local policy entrepreneurs of yore are linking up with the corporate interests newly empowered by institutional outsourcing. Again, the energy sector provides interesting examples. The Chinese electric power sector today has approximately 700 GW of generating capacity and is expanding by approximately 100 GW of power per year (France, for comparison, has a total national generating capacity of 77 GW). Officials in the central government, however, estimate that, of this 700 GW of installed capacity, 110 GW is illegal—it never received formal central approval and, by extension, probably does not meet central rules for environmental controls, fuel types, and engineering standards. Instead, this generating capacity, composed mostly of large coal-fired power plants, gets approved by local governmental actors, often working in coordination with national energy corporations, ones that are listed and often financed overseas.

Moreover, the local governments often invest as commercial players in these energy infrastructure projects. When Chinese energy majors seek to acquire overseas natural gas assets, for example, they often do so to fuel projects in which they have co-invested with regional governments in wealthy coastal provinces. In the case of natural gas, an entire energy infrastructure must be built: shipping trains for liquefied natural gas; harbor facilities and terminals in recipient Chinese ports; gasification facilities; local and regional pipelines; and then downstream commercial applications, power plants or other facilities. The energy companies, with all their various stakeholders, involve themselves across the supply chain, but so too do the regional governments, simultaneously as producers, consumers, and regulators. Meanwhile, much of the activity receives little if any clear central imprimatur, and indeed in some cases, the center resists late in the game (in the case of natural gas, by refusing to sign off on gas contracts, even after the infrastructure has been built). The companies and their regional governmental partners then have to lobby, push, and otherwise fight to ensure that their local experiments, some of which now involve billions of dollars and complex overseas deals, receive final approval to go into operation.

The point is that, even with so much structural change, so much reorientation of central governmental objectives, and so many new globalized players now involved, decision making in China still retains a high degree of informality, improvisation, uncertainty, and politicization. How such an environment manages consistently to encourage growth and entrepreneurship is as puzzling to explain for the small private and collective firms of the 1980s and 1990s as for the major multinational deals of the present decade. The system has been thrown on to the global track and tied to global institutional commitments, but in many ways it has retained a local and decidedly noninstitutionalized character.

Conclusion

In the aftermath of the Asian financial crisis, the most senior Chinese policy architects engaged in what effectively amounted to a form of shock therapy. By aggressively embracing the institutions of global capitalism, they broke down the last real vestiges of socialism in the country. In so doing, they unleashed changes that fostered further, and indeed accelerated, economic development. Their method, however, although purposive and decidedly top-down, empowered and unleashed a series of new societal actors. These actors became increasingly important contributors to the economic growth story, and as such, their sustenance became an important objective of state policy. Their emerging centrality in the Beijing policy agenda signified the ultimate vanquishment of the socialist equilibrium. At the same time, their decidedly boundary-crossing global character and their responsiveness to non-Chinese institutional strictures challenged—and are still challenging—traditional sociopolitical hierarchies in China. Put simply, forces have been unleashed that are no longer susceptible to traditional forms of control.

Perhaps most surprising, the rise of new interests and concomitant squashing of the old have proceeded relatively peacefully in China. Social dislocation has been substantial—even brutal, in many cases—yet the degree of political upheaval and social unrest has been fairly minimal.

Why have citizens been so compliant even in the context of the destruction of a long-standing social contract? The answer in part pertains to a common response to institutional outsourcing—institutional globalization, in effect—by citizens along virtually all points of the Chinese social spectrum. The most empowered citizens, those sitting atop the national champion firms on which the future of China is understood to turn, use their "insider outsider" status not only to carve out autonomy from governmental interference, but also to reach back in and shape policy to suit their own objectives. With impressive agility, they use the tools the government has granted them—access to outside institutional rules, access to external financing, and, most important, access to external business networks—to chart a new course for themselves as well as for the nation.

At the same time, and even more surprisingly, ordinary citizens (the urban working class, and even at times the rural poor) also grasp these new tools in ways that nobody in the near past could have anticipated. Many ordinary Chinese citizens have suffered substantial disruptions with the Chinese embrace of global capitalism, and many of the new rules of the game seem to have tilted the playing field not in the citizens' favor. Nonetheless, many citizens take the government's mission of modernization at its word. They accept the ostensible objectivity of markets and fairness of the outcomes of competitiveness: job losses, corporate downsizing, and benefits cuts. But they also take at its word the government claim that modern markets require modern laws and, more broadly, rule of law. So, with regard to labor law, property law, and even criminal law, citizens are increasingly displaying a rights consciousness, a belief that, even though the system may be stacked against them, the system has for the first time legitimized their claim to rights. With increasing frequency, they are employing those rights, doing what, in effect, the government has repeatedly informed them (perhaps disingenuously) they should do, "use the law as your weapon!" (Gallagher 2005, 98). The point is that the capitalist embrace has at once disrupted the social contract and legitimized it, but legitimized it in ways the government could never have anticipated. And that, perhaps, will ultimately constitute the greatest ramification of the Chinese response to the Asian financial crisis. Whether these sociopolitical changes are leading to constitutional democracy is unknown and perhaps unlikely. They are, however, clearly leading to a different kind of citizenship and a different kind of authoritarianism, one evolving along paths and through coalitions of actors that defy traditional governmental control.

CHAPTER 10

Politics of Economic Recovery in Thailand and the Philippines

Allen Hicken

One of the challenges of a volume such as this one is balancing the broad and the narrow. That is, we cannot focus so much on broad cross-national similarities that we lose sight of how domestic political environments shaped the nature of postcrisis recovery or ignore how the crisis helped reshape some of those domestic political environments. Thailand and Philippines are two interesting case studies in this respect. In Thailand—ground zero for the crisis—the collapse of the economy not only called into question the advisability and sustainability of the Thai economic strategy; it also served as the catalyst for significant political and institutional reform. In the Philippines, by contrast, the comparatively mild economic downturn was viewed in many quarters as a vindication of a set of economic reforms undertaken by the Fidel Ramos administration. The economic crisis did not generate a political crisis, nor did it lead, in any significant way, to major political and economic reforms. In short, the Thai experience is more like that of Indonesia, where a deep economic crisis quickly became a fundamental political crisis, eventually culminating in political/institutional reform. The Philippine experience, on the other hand, looks more like that of Malaysia, where the economic crisis did not generate major political reform and needed economic reforms were deferred.

This chapter compares the postcrisis economic and political trajectories of Thailand and the Philippines. I focus on the ways in which the political environment (and changes to that environment) shaped the nature of economic recovery in these two countries. In Thailand, the crisis brought to light a whole host of long-simmering economic vulnerabilities. After some delay, two successive Thai governments undertook a series of reforms to address many of these concerns. However, we cannot understand the timing and content of these reforms without taking the

Thai political environment into account. On the political front, the crisis served to rally public support around constitutional reforms that were already on the table but would otherwise have faced strong opposition from entrenched political interests. It also motivated Thai business interests to take a more active and direct role in politics than they had traditionally done in the past. In total, the crisis and subsequent political reforms combined to produce dramatic changes to the political economy of Thailand. These changes contributed to the robust recovery of Thailand from the depths of the crisis, but also left some precrisis vulnerabilities unaddressed and contributed to the emergence of a new set of concerns, which ultimately culminated in the September 2006 military coup and subsequent attempt to once again remake the Thai political environment.

In the Philippines, the relatively well-managed response of the government to the Asia financial crisis helped the country bounce back quickly from the initial economic setback. Observers hoped that this presaged an end to the perpetual status of the country as the "sick man of Asia." Indeed, the impressive reform program pushed through by the government of Fidel Ramos prior to the crisis provided grounds for optimism. Ironically, however, because the crisis did not engender the depth of political angst in the Philippines that it did in Thailand, the impetus for further reform, economic or political, was lacking. In the years since the crisis, the Philippines economy expanded at a modest pace but once again at a slower rate than most of its neighbors. At the same time, serious economic problems have largely gone unaddressed and threaten even the modest growth rate the Philippines has experienced during the last few years. The lack of reform since the crisis is also attributable to a breakdown in Philippine governance. Since mid-2000, when serious allegations of wrongdoing by President Joseph Estrada first began to emerge, the Philippine political environment has alternated between periods of political crisis and political malaise. Both have been equally inimical to any attempts at serious economic reform. The more time passes, the more the initially impressive response of the Philippines to the crisis looks like an anomaly rather than a sign of better times ahead.

Crisis and Recovery

Regardless of which indicator we focus, on it is clear the crisis took a much bigger toll on the Thai economy than on the Philippine economy. We should note, however, that the greater fall of Thailand came about in part because it had risen to greater heights than the Philippines. In 1985, Thailand still lagged behind its neighbor in terms of per capita income[1] (see table 10.1), but over the subsequent decade the Thai economy was among the fastest growing and best managed

---

1. This despite the collapse of the Philippine economy in the waning years of the Ferdinand Marcos dictatorship.

Table 10.1 Economic performance of Thailand and the Philippines[a]

	Thailand	Philippines
GDP per capita, 1985 (PPP, constant 2000 international dollars)	3,021	3,572
GDP per capita, 1996 (PPP, constant 2000 international dollars)	6,816	3,815
Average GDP growth rate, 1986–1996 (%)	7.6	1.3
Average inflation,[b] 1986–1996 (%)	4.8	8.9
Average gross capital formation, 1986–1996 (% of GDP)	37.2	21.2

Source: World Bank (n.d.).
[a] PPP, purchasing parity power.
[b] GDP deflator.

(in terms of the macroeconomy) in the world. The rapid rate of economic growth, lower rate of inflation, and higher level of capital formation in Thailand reflect the relative strength of the Thai economy vis-à-vis the Philippines during the latter part of the 1980s and first half of the 1990s (table 10.1). On the eve of the crisis, the Thai per capita income had not only caught up with Philippine GDP per capita, but had far surpassed it.

Despite its impressive performance, by mid-1990s the Thai economy was increasingly vulnerable. Like much of the rest of the region, a tidal wave of foreign capital inflows and weak financial-sector regulation combined to produce speculative booms in the real estate and stock markets (see Andrew MacIntyre, T. J. Pempel, and John Ravenhill, chap. 1 in this volume). At the same time, capital inflows undermined Thai competitiveness by pushing up inflation and the value of the baht, eventually leading to a decline in investment, a dramatic fall in exports, and an attack on the baht by currency speculators. By the time the Bank of Thailand was finally forced to let the baht float, investor confidence had been shaken and money began flowing out of Thailand, leading to a collapse of asset prices and of the rate of return on new capital investments.

Overall, the Thai economy contracted by nearly 14 percent in both the second and third quarters of 1998. But we are not interested here in rehashing the details of the crisis itself. Rather, our focus is on the pathways out of the crisis, and in this context, it is significant that economic growth returned fairly quickly in Thailand (figure 10.1). Growth began to pick back up in 1999, and for the year, Thailand posted a growth rate of 4.45. Growth has been at that level or above in every year since, save one. The sole exception is 2001, when a global slowdown reduced demand for Thai exports and slowed growth to 2.2 percent (figure 10.2). The Thai growth rate between 1999 and 2005 averaged 4.9 percent.

The crisis began in Thailand, and its effects quickly spread. The graph of the quarterly growth rates for the Philippines follows the general pattern for Thailand but with a much shallower slope (figure 10.1). Initially the Philippine government response was enough to keep investors happy during last half of 1997; for the year,

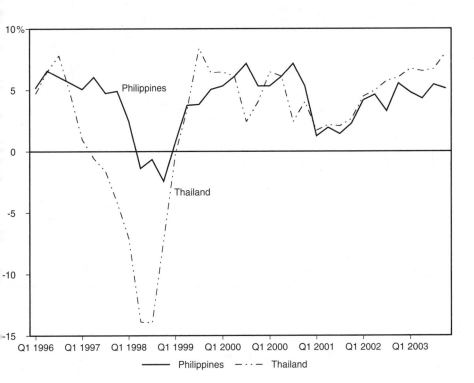

Figure 10.1 Quarterly growth rates in the Philippines and Thailand (constant prices), 1996–2000.
Source: Asian Development Bank, Asia Regional Information Center, http://aric.adb.org.

the Philippines posted a growth rate of 5.2 percent. Only in the midst of the Indonesian meltdown did economic growth dip below zero; it returned to positive territory in 1999. From 1999 to 2005 the Philippine economy grew at an average annual rate of 4.5 percent, with a temporary slowdown in 2001 (figure 10.2).

As instructive as the comparison of growth rates may be, it paints an incomplete picture of the postcrisis recovery trajectory in each country. Figure 10.3 charts the GDP per capita figures for Thailand and the Philippines. Growth in per capita income returned to both countries in 1999, although at a slower rate than prior to the crisis. The relative severity of the crisis in Thailand is reflected in the fact that it took Thailand six years of steady growth to regain the income level it had reached before the crisis. By contrast, per capita income barely dipped at all in the Philippines, and all the income losses were recovered by 2000.

Figure 10.3 also communicates another important fact about the postcrisis trajectories in Thailand and the Philippines. The strong performance of the Philippines in the midst and in the immediate aftermath of the crisis is largely offset by its lackluster performance since. Indeed, overall per capita income has barely budged from 1996 (or 1990) levels. Other economic indicators tell a similar story. There has

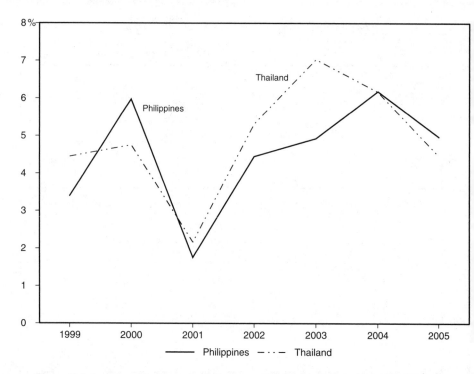

Figure 10.2 Annual growth rates in the Philippines and Thailand (constant prices), 1999–2005.
Source: Asian Development Bank, Asia Regional Information Center, http://aric.adb.org.

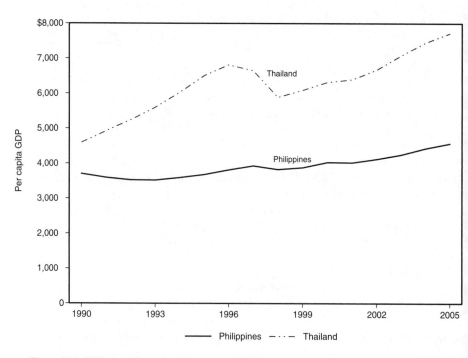

Figure 10.3 GDP per capita in the Philippines and Thailand (constant 2000 prices), 1990–2005 (PPP).
Source: World Bank (n.d.).

been a steady decline of gross capital formation (GCF) in the Philippines since the crisis. GCF was more than 24 percent of GDP in 1996, but fell to 18.8 percent by 1999. Since 1999, GCF has further declined to a low of 15.8 percent in 2005. By contrast, GCF in Thailand, although it also fell from a precrisis high of 42 percent to 20.5 in 1998 and 1999, has steadily increased to reach 31 percent of GDP in 2005 (World Bank n.d.). Likewise, although the peso initially retained more of its value than did the baht in the wake of the crisis, since June 2000 the peso has steadily lost ground to other currencies, including the baht. In the next two sections, I examine the recovery experience of each country in more detail.

Thailand: Institutional Reform and the Changing Political Economy of Policymaking

Thailand had the ignominy of being the first casualty of the Asian financial crisis. The coroner's report has been widely circulated, so there is little need for a detailed review of the causes of the crisis. It is only important to note that the crisis was as much evidence of a political failure as it was a failure of economic policy or strategy. Many had seen storm clouds on the horizon, but little was done to prevent the crisis from coming or to quickly contain it once it broke. Politics got in the way (Pasuk and Baker 1998; MacIntyre 2003). The crisis shone a spotlight both on the weaknesses and vulnerabilities inherent in the Thai growth strategy and on the shortcomings and failures of the Thai political system. The result was greater support for not only economic reforms but also political reforms in the form of a new constitution.

The crisis, then, generated greater support for constitutional reform than would have been the case otherwise; at the same time the crisis helped bring about a fundamental alteration of the political economy of Thailand. First, under severe stress from the crisis the Thai business elite abandoned their traditional behind-the-scenes involvement in politics and instead moved to play a more direct role in politics and policymaking. Second, the existing political elite (including the two largest Thai parties) were greatly weakened as a result of the crisis, leaving something of a political vacuum. Third, the crisis heightened the distrust among the Thai public toward globalization and foreign economic interests, and the initial decision to implement the austere International Monetary Fund (IMF) recovery plan only increased these feelings. In the end, Thaksin Shinawatra and the Thai Rak Thai (TRT) party were able to exploit these changes to cobble together a political party, secure a rare majority in the 2001 election, and then, most important, impose a level of party discipline and party cohesion previously unheard of in Thai democratic history.[2]

With a secure, disciplined majority in control of government, the Thai model of political economy was drastically revised. Gone were the short-lived, indecisive

---

2. For more details, see Hicken (2007).

multiparty governments that had been the distinguishing feature of Thai political economy since the 1970s. In their place was a majority party government that immediately demonstrated its ability to take decisive action on the policy front but that also set about bringing political and economic authority completely under the control of a single party, and more specifically, under the control of the prime minister.[3] In the remainder of this section, I discuss in more detail the role the crisis played in bringing about these changes in the Thai political economy and the consequences of those changes for policy.

The Crisis and Constitutional Reform

Thailand's prereform political system was criticized on many fronts, but a few aspects of the system received a large share of the blame. First, critics pointed to the highly unstable nature of Thai politics as a major weakness and a contributor to the crisis. The Thai political system prior to 1997 generated large multiparty governments that were notoriously short-lived. This undermined policy planning, continuity, and implementation while encouraging many actors to adopt a short-term and sometimes predatory outlook on government service.

Second, reformers, academics, and politicians themselves complained that Thai political parties were inadequate to the tasks at hand. Parties, as ephemeral alliances of electoral convenience, lacked any sort of coherent policy program. In addition, Thai politicians were chiefly concerned with directing government goods and services toward narrow groups of political supporters as part of an effort to build candidate-specific networks of support. The result of this state of affairs was a decided lack of any actor within the national government with strong incentives to provide national public goods (Hicken 2001).[4]

Finally, the Thai system came under criticism for not being sufficiently democratic. An appointed senate remained as a vestige of an earlier authoritarian era. Political and economic authority remained highly centralized within the Bangkok-based bureaucracy. In general, the system lacked a sufficient system of checks and balances that could rein in abuses by those in authority.

When the crisis struck, the process of amending the constitution had already begun. In 1996, the Thai parliament approved a bill that organized a Constitutional Drafting Assembly (CDA). The CDA convened in the early part of 1997 and by August had produced a draft that surprised many with the breadth and depth of its proposed reforms.

The crisis hit just as debate over the proposed new constitution was heating up. Despite parliament decision to convene the CDA, there was no guarantee that it would accept the CDA draft. In fact, the draft threatened the interests of many

---

3. It was this concentration of authority under Thaksin that alarmed Thaksin's critics, including, ultimately, the king and the military.

4. It is telling that the most ambitious Thai reforms during the early to mid-1990s came during the unelected government of Anand Panyarachun.

political and bureaucratic elite and was greeted with wariness and even outright opposition. The fact that most politicians ultimately voted to adopt the draft constitution, despite some very serious misgivings, is a direct consequence of the crisis. The crisis effectively raised the stakes connected with the draft by shining a spotlight on some of the shortcomings in the Thai political system. To a large number of voters and investors, the constitutional draft was a symbol of the government commitment to difficult but needed political and economic reforms. In fact, in the weeks before the final vote, expressions of opposition or support for the draft by leading officials generated corresponding moves down or up in the stock market and currency markets. In the end, the crisis raised the potential economic and political costs of a no vote and, as a result, the draft was adopted.

The new constitution addressed each of the three weaknesses in the old Thai system already described. First, in a bid to improve government stability and longevity, the constitution included provisions designed to reduce the number of political parties (and increase the chance of majority party governments) and increase the power of party leaders over their party members. This was particularly true of the prime minister, who received tools that gave him unprecedented leverage over members of the cabinet (Hicken 2007). Second, the constitution provided greater incentives for political parties to differentiate themselves on the basis of programmatic appeals through the creation of a national party list and the elimination of intraparty competition (members of the same party competing against one another in the same district). Finally, the constitution included a number of reforms designed to further democratize the Thai system. These included an elected senate in place of the appointed body and numerous semi-autonomous watchdog agencies or superintendent institutions. The constitution also called for an unprecedented level of political and economic decentralization, including elections for local offices.

The Political Economy of Economic Reform under a Multiparty Government

While the constitutional debate was raging, the government of Chavalit Yongchaiyudh was struggling to respond to the crisis. Wracked by party and factional divisions, the government was unable to muster a strong, coherent policy response—continuing a pattern established before the crisis in which the early efforts to head-off disaster by reformers within the cabinet were reversed or blocked (MacIntyre 2003). In this environment, the IMF proposed a US$17 billion stabilization package that came with a host of demands for reform and restructuring. Chavalit was quick to agree to the package, signing an agreement in August 1997, but his government was slow to move on most of the conditions set out in the agreement.

In the end, Chavalit was unable to survive the political damage inflicted by the inadequate response of his government to the crisis. Faced with imminent defections by some members of the coalition (including members of his own party), Chavalit resigned as prime minister in November 1997. A new coalition, led by the former opposition Democrat Party and its leader Chuan Leekpai, replaced him.

Chuan's government faced two sets of vulnerabilities in addition to the immediate task of stabilizing the economy. First, as was true of most of the region (see MacIntyre, Pempel, and Ravenhill, chap. 1 in this volume), Thailand needed to reform and restructure its financial system. This multifaceted task included establishing more stringent regulatory oversight, managing the restructuring or closing of insolvent financial institutions and the distribution of their assets, restoring liquidity and bank lending, and dealing with the massive number of nonperforming loans (NPLs) on the books of nearly all financial institutions.[5] The latter was a huge albatross on not only the financial sector but also the broader economy. Official government statistics placed the percentage of NPLs at nearly 50 percent of total outstanding loans, but some outside observers believed the number to be even higher (Asian Development Bank [ADB] 2000). The large number of NPLs made banks wary of additional lending and, as a result, credit was hard to come by for Thailand's many cash-strapped firms.

The second set of vulnerabilities concerned the decline of Thailand's competitive position in the world economy. By the time of the crisis, there were signs that the ability of Thailand to realize high rates of growth through accumulation and the export of labor-intensive goods was coming to an end (Jonsson 2001; Bosworth 2005, quoted in Richter 2006; Richter 2006). Competition for investment dollars combined with the crisis meant that Thai access to foreign investment capital was likely to decline relative to past levels. In addition, the Thai export-led growth strategy was becoming less sustainable given the changing international environment and increased competition from other low-wage countries—chiefly China (Doner n.d.).

Thailand was in many ways ill-prepared to compete in this new environment. During the boom years, it had "failed to develop the design and innovation capabilities necessary to move toward [a] more sophisticated production [profile]" (Felker 2001, 3). To continue to compete, Thailand needed to upgrade (Doner n.d.). This entailed taking steps to boost productivity and the rate of innovation and technological advancement, along with developing better linkages between the foreign-dominated export industry and potential local suppliers. There was also an acute need for new investment in upgrading Thai infrastructure to better use existing stocks of capital and labor and to attract new investment.

Upon assuming power, the Democrat-led coalition set out to stabilize the economy and address these vulnerabilities. Operating largely within a framework worked out by the IMF, reformers saw the crisis as an opportunity to push through much-needed and long-delayed economic and regulatory reforms.[6] Perhaps the most

---

5. See MacIntyre, Pempel, and Ravenhill (chap. 1) and Natasha Hamilton-Hart (chap. 3 in this volume) for a comparative view of financial reform throughout East Asia.

6. The framework called for restructuring the financial sector (including allowing more foreign participation), privatizing state-owned enterprises, reforming the civil service, allowing greater participation by the private sector in infrastructure projects, and introducing regulatory reforms in both the financial and corporate sectors.

controversial element of the IMF program, in retrospect, was its requirement of a severe tightening of fiscal and monetary policy. This prescription misunderstood the nature of the Thai crisis; government profligacy was not to blame for the economic problems. In addition, given the state of paralysis in Thai financial and business sectors, the government was the only reliable source of liquidity and economic stimulus. The fiscal monetary tightening ended up deepening and prolonging the economic recession. The Chuan government responded by finally abandoning this portion of the stabilization program and instead increasing government expenditures (mostly in the form of increased spending on the social safety net) in a bid to stimulate domestic demand.[7]

The implementation of the stabilization program won the government few supporters. Initial enthusiasm for the strong government commitment to economic reform (a marked change from the inept Chavalit regime) faded away as the economy continued to decline. Moreover, as the government continued to push its reform program, it began to encounter strong opposition from both business and political circles. Recall that, although the new constitution was adopted in October of 1997, many of its provisions where not fully in place until the first postreform election in 2001. As a result, Chuan's government operated under many of the constraints of the previous system. The exigencies of the crisis bought the government some time and political capital, but reforms were often blocked, delayed, or watered down by members of the government coalition or the senate. The government did move swiftly to completely close down the failed financial companies and got the Financial Sector Restructuring Agency (to organize the workout of the failed finance companies) and Asset Management Company (to purchase and dispose of nonperforming assets) up and running as part of the financial restructuring effort. It also significantly improved the supervisory and regulatory framework surrounding the financial sector (ADB 2000). However the government efforts to reduce NPLs, encourage corporate restructuring, and induce banks to restructure and resume lending moved much more slowly as a result of disagreements within the government about how to proceed (*Bangkok Post*, April 14, 1999). As the delay wore on, the number of NPLs continued to grow, with more and more firms succumbing to the deepening recession and liquidity crunch (figure 10.4). A government restructuring program was eventually adopted but was subsequently shunned by most banks. As a result the number of NPLs continued to grow for more than a year, peaking at nearly 48 percent of all bank loans before beginning a slow decline.

By the end of the Chuan administration, the economy had stabilized and economic growth had resumed. But only limited progress had been made in financial-sector restructuring—NPLs were still more than 20 percent of bank loans. In addition, almost nothing had been done to address the longer-term question of Thai competitiveness. Efforts to promote technological upgrading received some

---

7. This was done with the approval of the IMF (IMF, 3rd LoI, February 24, 1998; 4th LoI, May 26, 1998). See Stephan Haggard (chap. 5 in this volume) for more information about social safety net spending.

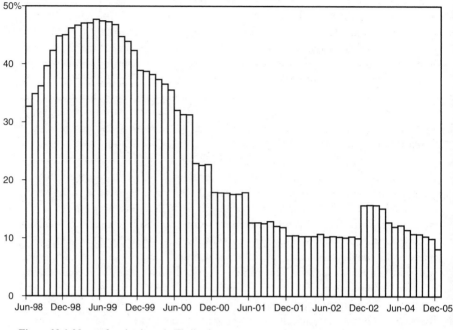

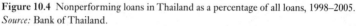

Figure 10.4 Nonperforming loans in Thailand as a percentage of all loans, 1998–2005.
Source: Bank of Thailand.

lip service but little else. The government had also steadily cut public investment in infrastructure development; efforts to promote more private participation in infrastructure projects had fallen flat (Richter 2006).

Meanwhile the dogged implementation of the IMF neoliberal reform program by the government, led to growing opposition across the political, economic, and social spectra. Consistent with the ideational shift that occurred in other East Asian states, hostility toward globalization and foreign capital began to grow (see MacIntyre, Pempel, and Ravenhill, chap. 1 in this volume). A loose alliance of nongovernmental organizations (NGOs), domestic businesses, intellectuals, politicians, workers, and even the Thai king came together to oppose what they saw as external interference in Thai sovereign affairs and a fire sale of local assets to foreign investors (Hewison 2006, 98). Domestic Thai businesses were especially concerned. The crisis had greatly weakened domestic businesses, and they struggled to survive in the face of greater foreign competition. The combination of lower barriers to foreign investment and good deals on distressed Thai assets led to a sharp increase in foreign direct investment. Businesses responded by appealing to the government for protection of their interests, but without success.

As Kevin Hewison (2004, 2005) describes it, this unprecedented threat to domestic business interests led Thai business groups to abandon their traditional behind-the-scenes support of a variety of political parties and politicians and enter politics directly in a bid to win protection for their interests. Their means of entering politics was the newly formed TRT party. TRT was organized by Thai business tycoon Thaksin Shinawatra in preparation for the 2001 house election, the first to be held under the new constitution. Thaksin actively recruited domestic capitalists to the party by promising them a seat at the policymaking table and a shift in government priorities toward protecting and promoting the interests of Thai companies.

Thaksin and the TRT party seized on the prevailing anti-IMF nationalist sentiment and harnessed it to the benefit of the TRT's electoral fortunes. In his rhetoric, Thaksin talked of protecting Thailand from foreigners out to swallow the country and its assets. Even the name of the party (Thais love Thailand) evoked this nationalist sentiment. However, Thaksin did more than campaign on a nationalist platform. He also struck an explicit bargain with Thai voters. In exchange for domestic business interests controlling the economy *and* politics (which he promised they were uniquely qualified to do), Thaksin promised to devote increased attention and resources to social welfare/social protection. In effect, he pledged that the government would take an active role in reducing poverty and raising rural incomes (see Hewison 2004). In line with this pledge, TRT campaigned on a platform that included a 1 million–baht grant for all Thai villages, a 30-baht health-care scheme, a debt moratorium for farmers, and a *tamboon* development plan dubbed OTOP (one *tamboon*, one product).[8]

When the election was held in January 2001, the TRT fell one seat short of a majority in parliament, a fact soon remedied when a smaller party merged with the TRT after the election. Thaksin thus became the first elected prime minister to enjoy the support of an absolute majority of house members. He later invited two other parties to partner with the TRT, further bolstering his majority. After serving a full term (a first for an elected prime minister), Thaksin and TRT were reelected in a landslide in 2005.

What explains the electoral success of TRT? Undoubtedly, Thaksin's personal assets (financial and otherwise) were important tools in attracting candidates and voters to the party. TRT also benefited from the crisis-induced weakness of the Democrat and New Aspiration parties. Finally, the constitutional reforms also played a role by establishing electoral rewards for national programmatic appeals, reducing the number of parties, and giving Thaksin added leverage over factions within his party (Hicken 2007).

The Political Economy of Economic Reform under Thaksin

The TRT electoral victory dramatically altered the Thai political economy in two ways. First, it represented a fundamental shift in business-government relations.

---

8. Thaksin also accelerated Thailand's repayment of its debt to the IMF and succeeded in paying off the loan in July 2003, two years ahead of schedule. The final Thai Standby Agreement with the IMF, with its attendant conditions, expired in June 2000.

Gone was the competitive clientelism described by Doner and Ramsey (2000); it was replaced by a ship of state directly helmed by business interests. Second, the election brought a majority party to power—something unprecedented in Thai democratic history. The advent of majority government meant that Thaksin and the TRT were able to act more decisively than any of their elected predecessors in implementing their preferred policies.

The various accounts of the evolution of the policymaking environment under Thaksin all tell a similar story. Thaksin, through a variety of reforms, worked to centralize power and authority within the TRT and specifically within the office of the prime minister. Measures such as bureaucratic restructuring, budgetary reform, reform of the armed forces, new duties for provincial governors, and the marginalization of semi-autonomous supervisory agencies reduced political fragmentation while strengthening the position of the TRT vis-à-vis bureaucratic and partisan rivals (Painter 2005; Hicken 2005).

There were both costs and benefits to this new state of affairs. To begin with, the Thaksin government was much more decisive than its elected predecessors. It was able to pursue its preferred initiatives, which included a multitude of programs targeting poor and rural areas. In addition, there were efficiency gains to be had from single-party control of the bureaucracy as the party coordinated the government's various programs. On the other hand, under Thaksin government policy and institutions became the instruments of the ruling party and its leader, existing to serve their interests and goals. In the past, bureaucratic and partisan rivalries combined to prevent any one party or faction from seizing control of the machinery and resources of government. This was no longer the case. The government under Thaksin was, in many respects, an extension of TRT and Thaksin (Hicken 2007).

The combination of new interests in power and new power for those interests had significant consequences for the Thai political economy and its recovery from the crisis. Upon taking power, Thaksin immediately put the brakes on privatization and liberalization. When the privatization effort was finally revived in 2003, shares were generally offered only to domestic shareholders, and where foreign investors were allowed to participate, their shares did not carry voting rights (Hewison 2005). In the area of telecommunications, the setting up of an independent regulatory agency, mandated by law, slowed to a crawl. At the same time, the government worked to keep the sector closed to foreign participation—all to the potential benefit of Thaksin's companies (Pasuk and Baker 2002).

The government also moved quickly to address the vulnerabilities in the financial sector. To tackle the dual problems of NPLs and an enduring shortage of domestic credit, Thaksin established a new agency, the Thailand Asset Management Corporation (TAMC). As the state banks transferred their bad loans to TAMC and then complied with the government direction to increase lending, the number of NPLs declined and the credit crunch began to ease in 2002 (Pasuk and Baker 2004).[9]

---

9. In total, state banks were responsible for 112 percent of the net increases in credit in 2002 and 96 percent in 2003 (Pasuk and Baker 2004).

Thaksin also began plans to improve Thailand's competitiveness and stimulate economic growth through a program of megaprojects designed to upgrade the infrastructure of the country. The government committed to raising public investment in infrastructure by 70 percent over a five-year period. The Asian Development Bank (ADB) estimated that megaproject investments could have contributed 0.5–0.7 percentage point of GDP growth per year beginning in 2007 (ADB 2006, 225).

Thaksin's government also broke from past practice by aggressively pursuing bilateral preferential trading agreements. Consistent with the trends outlined by MacIntyre, Pempel, and Ravenhill (chap. 1 in this volume), the government shifted its focus away from regional and multilateral trade arrangements and toward agreements with key economic allies.[10] Thaksin signed (controversial) preferential trading agreements (PTAs) with China, Australia, and Japan and was in the process of negotiating a PTA with the United States when he was ousted.

In short, the changes to the Thai political environment helped the country consolidate its recovery from the crisis and address some of the economy's chief vulnerabilities. But significant challenges remained. Beyond infrastructure investment, the government did little to upgrade Thai competitiveness. In fact, to the extent domestic business interests were shielded from competitive pressures, it did just the opposite. Observers were also concerned about the true status of the Thai financial system. After capturing the premiership, Thaksin replaced the head of the central bank with a political ally. Thaksin's government was not shy about using the state banks and the TAMC to reward its supporters, and there were concerns that political priorities had trumped prudence and economic efficiency (Crispin 2003; Pasuk and Baker 2004, 112).

The Fall of Thaksin and the New (Old) Political Environment

The power amassed by Thaksin, and his willingness to wield it in pursuit of his interests, left the government vulnerable to charges of manipulation, favoritism, and corruption. Exhibit A is the political crisis that engulfed Thaksin and the TRT in 2006, culminating in a military coup in September. The catalyst for this crisis was the sale of shares in Shin Corp, a telecommunications company built by Thaksin and still owned by his family, to Temasek Holdings in Singapore. The deal went ahead only after the government reversed its earlier restrictions on foreign ownership in the telecommunications sector. The sale brought a nearly US$2 billion tax-free profit for Thaksin's family, emboldening Thaksin's critics and at the same time undermining his support among some allies. After the January 2006 sale, the ongoing but previously low-level anti-Thaksin protests within Bangkok grew in both size and strength.

To try to diffuse the protests, Thaksin dissolved the parliament, called new elections, and stepped down as prime minister. The major opposition parties chose to

---

10. The government did, however, participate in regional efforts to reduce vulnerability to future shocks, such as the new currency swap arrangements and regional bond initiative.

boycott the elections and the elections results, which had the TRT winning handily, were later thrown out by the courts. Despite this setback, the TRT was poised to win the new election scheduled for October or November 2006. At the same time, the anti-Thaksin protests showed no signs of abating. The stalemate was finally resolved via a military coup in September 2006 that ousted Thaksin and his government.

Shortly after the coup, the new Thai leadership formed an interim government and announced that one of its top priorities was constitutional reform with the goal of correcting some of the perceived shortcomings (and unintended consequences) of the 1997 constitution. In August 2007 a new constitution was approved via a close-fought referendum. Elections were subsequently held at the end of 2007. The new constitution should once again bring about a significant shift in the Thai political economy, returning Thailand to a pre-Thaksin state of affairs. This is by design. Thaksin's popularity and his centralization of political power ultimately threatened the authority of the traditional centers of power in Thailand. These actors are using constitutional reform try to return Thailand to an era when parties were weak, governments were large and unstable, and prime ministers lacked the tools to bring other actors in the political system to heel (Hicken forthcoming).[11]

In the wake of the new constitution we expect future policymaking to look very much like pre-Thaksin Thailand. Weak, short-lived, multiparty governments tend to undermine policy planning, continuity, and implementation and encourage actors to adopt a short-term outlook. Needed national policies and reforms will be undersupplied, and politicians will spend their time and resources in pursuit of electorally rewarding pork and particularism.

While awaiting the new constitution and new elections, Thailand was in limbo, headed by a caretaker government whose top priority was not economic reform and economic growth. This is different from the military's last stint in power in 1991. Then, the military appointed a respected civilian businessman as interim prime minister, who then proceeded to push through a series of ambitious economic and regulatory reforms. This time around, the coup leaders appointed as prime minister a respected military figure who lacked economic credentials. Under the interim government, economic policy/reform took a back seat to political reform and dealing with unrest in the south. In fact, the government regularly misstepped in its handling of economy while domestic and international confidence in the Thai economy continued to erode (*Nation*, August 9, 2007).

To summarize, in the past dispersed political authority often made it difficult for Thai governments to act. This changed with the 1997 constitution and the election of the TRT. But this new concentration of political authority also carried with it new risks. When power is concentrated, as it was in Thailand, economic actors become highly sensitive to perceptions of the strength and competence of those who wield that power (MacIntyre 2003). Thailand is currently experiencing some

---

11. Changes include replacing the elected senate with a partially appointed body, readopting multi-seat districts, allowing party switching, banning party mergers, and reducing the power of the prime minister (Hicken forthcoming).

of the effects of that sensitivity. The recent uncertainty has delayed spending on the megaprojects; driven away foreign investors, who were already showing some reluctance to invest in Thaksin's Thailand; eroded consumer confidence (consumer spending was a major growth engine under Thaksin); and ultimately threatened to derail the economy. The centralization of power set in motion a political effort to undo some of the consequences of the 1997 constitution and restore a less effective, but for some less threatening, political environment.

The Philippines: The More Things Change...

After the Asian financial crisis broke, the Philippines emerged in comparatively good shape. Of the crisis economies, the Philippine economy took the smallest dip and quickly recovered its strength. The financial and corporate sectors in the Philippines also survived the crisis in much better condition than their counterparts in Thailand and Indonesia. How did the Philippines, with its reputation as a chronic underperformer, manage to fare better than its high-flying neighbors? Three factors played a role. First, the Philippine financial system was in much better shape than others in the region (Noland 2000). After an earlier financial crisis, the Fidel Ramos government undertook a series of reforms designed to strengthen the financial system. The level of NPLs and bank capitalization had improved prior to the crisis, and the financial sector was much less exposed in the real estate sector than financial institutions elsewhere in the region (Noland 2000). The greater health of the Philippines finance sector vis-à-vis Thailand can be seen in its much lower percentage of NPLs (figure 10.5). Second, because liberalization and economic rehabilitation were slow to arrive in the Philippines, due to the disaster of the Ferdinand Marcos era and the uncertainty surrounding the Corazon Aquino administration, the country was a belated participant in the speculative investment and private-debt booms (Hutchcroft 1999; Noland 2000; Hutchison 2006). Finally, the Philippines benefited from relatively consistent and coherent crisis management and a political system that enabled the government to respond in a timely, credible manner (MacIntyre 2001).

Ironically, the period of the crisis arguably represents the apex of economic and political performance in the Philippines over the last twenty years. Since the financial crisis, although maintaining a modest growth rate, the Philippine economy has once again descended into dangerous territory. In many respects, the economic situation is worse today than it was immediately after the crisis. The debt and budget-deficit levels are unsustainable, government spending in needed investments and services is declining, and there are new worries about the health of the financial system.

In part, this economic malaise can be traced back to the fact that the crisis was relatively mild and thus did not generate the momentum for economic and political reform that we saw elsewhere after the crisis. Once the Ramos administration stepped down in 1998, the progress toward needed reforms stalled. Successive Philippine governments have failed to address three related vulnerabilities since the crisis: debt, tax revenues, and money losing state-owned enterprises (called government-owned

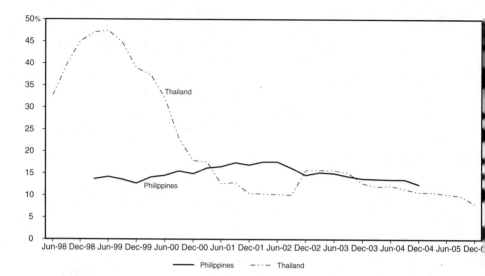

Figure 10.5 Nonperforming loans in Thailand and the Philippines as a percentage of all loans, 1998–2005.
Source: Bank of Thailand; Bangko Sentral ng Pilipinas.

and -controlled corporations [GOCCs] in the Philippines). To understand how and why this failure has occurred, we must first understand the political economy of policymaking in the Philippines—specifically, the crucial role of the president. I argue that the recent Philippine economic deterioration is, in large part, a function of a series of political crises that have paralyzed two successive presidents.

The Political Economy of Policymaking

As in prereform Thailand, the Philippine political system is one that discourages the development of strong programmatic political parties (Hicken 2002). Philippine parties are characterized by factionalism, frequent party switching (called "turncoatism" in the Philippines), and party labels that generally mean little to voters or candidates. As a result, the parties in the house and senate are not cohesive unitary actors pursuing unique policy agendas. Rather, they are temporary alliances of narrowly oriented politicians primarily concerned with distributing the spoils of government (pork) to themselves and their supporters (Cruz and Chua 2004a, 2004b).

Given the incentives of members of congress to raid the public purse in pursuit of narrow interests, what exists to prevent legislators from overgrazing on the budgetary commons to the detriment of fiscal health and the pursuit of needed national policies? One potential antidote is the presidency, with its national constituency. But in order for a president to successfully fulfill the role as national policy provider and check against legislative parochialism, at least two conditions must hold. First, the president must have some leverage over the other actors in the policy process to push through his or her policy agenda. Second, the president must have incentives to provide national public policies/goods.

Fortunately, Philippine presidents are equipped with a variety of formal and informal powers that gives them leverage over legislators, including large amounts of pork that they can distribute to congressional supporters or withhold from opponents. Philippine presidents can and do use the control over the pork barrel to build legislative coalitions in support of presidential initiatives.

The ability to push through national policies means little, however, without some incentive to pursue those policies in the first place. Typically, we assume that presidents have stronger incentives to pursue national public goods than do legislators (Shugart and Haggard 2001). This certainly tracks with the experience in the Philippines, where historically the provision of national public goods has been the domain of the president (Hicken 2002). Yet it is important to note that a great deal of variation can exist among presidents regarding their policy preferences and their incentives to forge legislative coalitions in favor of national policies. In part, these preferences reflect individual core beliefs—Ramos, for example, was deeply committed to economic reform, whereas his successor, Joseph Estrada, by most accounts was not. However, politicians also respond to incentives generated by the political environment. In the years since the crisis, the presidential incentives for policy reform have decreased dramatically along with the capacity for pushing those reforms through a recalcitrant congress.

President Fidel Ramos skillfully used the tools of his office to cobble together legislative coalitions in support of a package of liberalizing reforms during his six years in office. However, since the exit of Ramos in 1998, the Philippine political system, never the most efficient and effective to begin with, has broken down. The crisis played an indirect role in this. The comparative shallowness of the Philippine crisis meant that the pressure or support for political reform that occurred elsewhere in the region did not emerge.[12] In fact, attempts by Ramos supporters to pursue "cha-cha" (charter change) were quickly derailed by opponents who saw these as primarily a move to keep Ramos in power.[13]

Initially, attitudes toward Ramos's successor, Joseph Estrada, were cautiously optimistic. Even though Estrada had close ties to both former Marcos-era cronies and a group of cronies all his own, the administration appointed highly qualified and well-regarded individuals to its economic team and made no moves to reverse the liberalizing reforms enacted under Ramos. In addition, during his first two years in office the economy began to reap some of the rewards of the earlier reforms, rebounding quickly from the crisis-induced slump to grow at 3.4 percent in 1999 and 6 percent in 2000. By mid-2000, however, a growing wave of corruption

---

12. See Thomas Pepinsky (chap. 11 in this volume) for a similar argument about reform in Malaysia.

13. I am not suggesting that a severe crisis is sufficient to generate political reform, merely that such crises make political reform more likely.

scandals involving the president and his associates had begun to undermine this picture of policy continuity and economic health (de Dios and Hutchcroft 2003). The scandals eventually led to Estrada's removal from office, paving the way for the swearing in of Vice President Gloria Macapagal-Arroyo.

From the outset, President Macapagal-Arroyo's administration was plagued by instability. The manner under which Macapagal-Arroyo had come to power undermined the president's legitimacy, and from the outset she faced regular challenges to her authority. Throughout the remainder of her term, her first priority was building and solidifying a power base and preparing for an electoral mandate of her own in 2004.[14]

The 2004 election was a chance for Macapagal-Arroyo to put to rest questions about her legitimacy. After trailing in the polls, the president won the election by the narrow margin of 1 million votes over challenger Fernando Poe, Jr. But she enjoyed only a brief honeymoon. A year into her term, the president had to deal with new questions about her legitimacy that surfaced in the form of a tape of wiretapped conversations between the president and an official in the Commission on Elections. The tapes allegedly captured the president directing the election officer to rig the 2004 election to ensure she won by at least a million votes. This news triggered renewed political instability and a failed attempt to impeach the president. In response to the growing instability and out of fear of large-scale street protests, the president issued an executive order forbidding demonstrations without a permit, followed by an executive order forbidding executive branch officials from testifying in congressional inquiries without Macapagal-Arroyo's prior consent.[15] On February 24, 2006, the president declared a state of emergency after uncovering an alleged coup plot. The decree was lifted a week later, but in the interim the government used it as justification for dispersing antigovernment demonstrators, arresting government opponents, cracking down on leftist political leaders, and conducting raids on media outlets critical of the president.

In short, the years since the Asian financial crisis swept over the Philippines have been marked by instability and political turmoil, broken up by brief periods of political malaise. This kind of environment has not been conducive to difficult but needed economic reforms. The regular legitimacy crises deprived presidents of the political capital necessary to push through costly reform programs and raised the cost of building legislative coalitions. More fundamentally, the focus on economic reforms that have high short-term political and economic costs but long-term benefits has been eclipsed by the more immediate need to survive each successive political crisis. To successfully deal with the mounting economic problems would have "require[d] unprecedented cooperation and open-mindedness among the country's political elite as well as a great deal of forbearance and capacity for sacrifice among the people" (de Dios et. al. 2004, 22). Unfortunately, these qualities of cooperation,

---

14. In 2002, her popularity at an all-time low, Macapagal-Arroyo pledged not to run for election; she reversed her decision in 2003.

15. The supreme court eventually declared both orders unconstitutional.

forbearance, and sacrifice are likely to be in short supply during periods of political turmoil and uncertainty such as the Philippines has experienced since 2000.

It is possible that such cooperation for reform will not occur until the Philippines once again finds itself in the midst of an economic collapse. Such a collapse has become much more likely since the Asian financial crisis. In the remainder of this section, I focus on three interrelated vulnerabilities that have largely gone unaddressed: (1) the crippling debt burden, (2) inadequate government revenues, and (3) money-losing GOCCs.

Economic Vulnerabilities

In 1998, the year after the crisis, the national government debt was more than 56 percent of GDP. Since then, government debt has steadily grown, reaching a peak of 79 percent of GDP in 2004 before declining slightly in 2005. The total outstanding debt of the public sector as a whole was even larger and followed the same increasing trend, reaching levels as high as 118 percent of GDP (figure 10.6).[16]

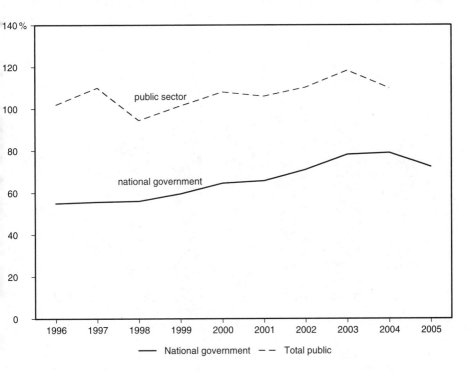

Figure 10.6 Total national-government and public-sector debt in the Philippines, 1996–2005 (percentage of current GDP).
Source: Bangko Sentral ng Pilipinas.

16. These figures are conservative estimates of the debt burden. Other estimates place the public-sector debt as high as 130 percent of GDP (de Dios et al. 2004).

The danger that this level of debt represents is obvious. Such exposure leaves the Philippines extremely vulnerable to external shocks such as a rise in global interest rates, a sustained increase in world oil prices, a sudden rise in imports, or a sharp drop in remittances from overseas workers.[17] In addition, debt service payments are an ever-growing burden on Philippine development and investment plans. Around 30 percent of government spending currently goes to service the debt (ADB 2005a). Once we add in nondiscretionary spending on things such as government salaries and operating expenditures, that leaves only around 10–20 percent of the government budget to cover all the investment and developmental needs of the country. Since 1998, this share of discretionary spending has fallen steadily (figure 10.7). This explains the regular cuts in infrastructure spending, gross domestic investment, and other spending programs since the crisis, as well as the yawning gap between the government promises and what it actually delivers by way of goods and services (ADB 2005a).

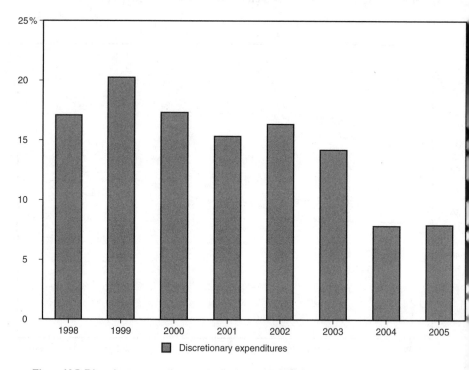

Figure 10.7 Discretionary expenditures in the Philippines, 1998–2005 (percentage of total expenditures). *Source:* Budgetary data from the Philippine Department of Budget and Management; Philippine Institute for Developmental Studies.

17. The foreign exchange from these remittances has been a key to avoiding some of the dire consequences of such a high level of debt to this point.

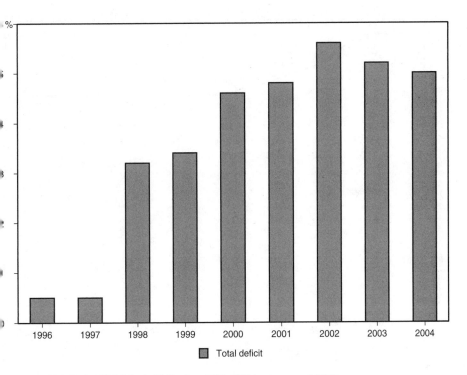

Figure 10.8 Budget deficit in the Philippines, 1996–2004 (percentage of GDP).
Source: Philippine Institute for Developmental Studies.

The two biggest causes of the growth in the Philippines debt burden since 1997 have been the chronic government budget deficits (which account for 43 percent of the increase) and government commitments to cover the liabilities of GOCCs (which account for 37 percent of the increase) (de Dios et al. 2004, 3). Let us look first at budget deficits; figure 10.8 shows that, after beginning the crisis with a nearly balanced budget, the budget deficit steadily grew from 1998 onward, surpassing 5 percent of GDP by 2002. Rising debt service payments are only partially to blame for the growing deficit.[18] Nor are the changes to the budget deficit due to large increases in government spending. Total spending has held steady since the crisis, and primary spending (net of debt service) has actually declined (de Dios et al. 2004, 4). Instead, the primary cause of the greater budget deficit is a declining tax and revenue effort. From their peak in 1997, both the taxes the government collects and the revenue it takes in have fallen by more than 20 percent

18. The primary surplus (excluding debt payments) also declined, going from a surplus of around 4 percent of GDP in 1996 to 0.6 percent of GDP by 2003 (de Dios et al. 2004).

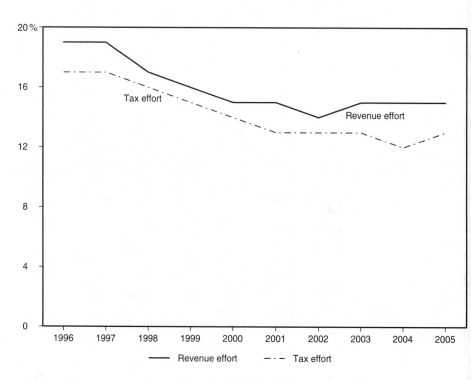

Figure 10.9 Revenue and taxes in the Philippines, 1995–2005 (percentage of GDP).
Source: World Bank (n.d.).

(figure 10.9).[19] Adding insult to injury is the fact that this has occurred in the midst of continuous moderate economic growth. The blame for this state of affairs, then, lies squarely with the government. For at least ten years policymakers have recognized the need to drastically overhaul the Philippine tax codes and tax administration to improve revenue collection. But tax increases and stricter collection have been anathema to already weak presidents and legislators worried about reelection. Only recently have significant steps been taken to increase tax revenue (Hedman 2006).

The other major cause of the ballooning debt is the debts and liabilities the government has assumed from or on behalf of public-sector corporations/GOCCs such as the National Power Company and the Public Estates Authority. In principle, these organizations are expected to sink or swim on their own without government subsidies or bailouts. In practice, the government has frequently stepped in and

19. *Revenue* measures the taxes a government collects plus receipts from social contributions (e.g., social security) and other revenues (such as fines, fees, rents, and income from property or sales; World Bank n.d.).

assumed the debts of these corporations when they have run into trouble or has acted to implicitly or explicitly guarantee further borrowing (de Dios et al. 2004). Although precise estimates are hard to come by, the government could ultimately end up responsible for as much as P4.13 trillion in assumed liabilities (approximately forty-eight times the annual GDP). The means to prevent future liabilities of this sort lie within the control of the government: namely, privatization and restraint.

Under presidents Aquino and Ramos, the government began to divest itself of corporations and assets, many of which had been accumulated under Marcos. But many of the big-ticket items—the National Power Corporation, for example—remained in government hands. Plans and commitments to sell or partially privatize many of these entities fell by the wayside as successive presidents struggled with more pressing political problems. Presidents have also been unwilling to exercise much restraint in assuming new liabilities. Philippine presidents have the unilateral power to decide whether and to what extent to assume the liabilities of GOCCs without the approval of congress. Every president in the last four decades has used this power, and Estrada and Macapagal-Arroyo are no exception (de Dios et al. 2004). Faced with a choice between (1) forcing a GOCC to become responsible for its own debts, which carries the real risk of price hikes or disruptions in services, or (2) assuming the debts knowing that most of the costs will fall to future administrations, presidents have invariably chosen the latter.

Conclusion

The case of the Philippines illustrates an irony of crisis and recovery. The countries that escaped the crisis in relatively good shape—the Philippines and Malaysia—also avoided launching costly reforms and may, as result, be more vulnerable in the long run, The momentum for reform is always difficult to sustain (as discussed in the Thai case), but the solid performance by the Philippines in response to the crisis had the perverse effect of undermining any sense urgency in addressing the rising debt level, inadequate revenues, and burdensome GOCCs in the country. The political instability since the crisis has prevented the two postcrisis Philippine presidents from acting as the champions and coalition-builders for needed reforms—a role no other actor is equipped to fulfill in the Philippine political system. Although economic growth has been steady since the crisis, these unaddressed vulnerabilities threaten to send the economy into another crisis that might prove more difficult to escape.

By contrast, the Asian financial crisis not only damaged the Thai economy but also shook Thai political foundations. The crisis became a catalyst for far-reaching political reforms that eventually brought about a shift from indecisive multiparty coalitions to a very powerful majority government and an accompanying shift in the political economy of economic reform. The government of Thaksin Shinawatra quickly implemented reforms that reduced NPLs and jump-started bank lending. However, Thaksin's government also used the power and resources of the state to further the interests of its members and supporters. The recent instability brought about by the excesses of the TRT government, subsequent military coup, and new constitution now threaten to undermine some of the gains that Thailand has made since the crisis while delaying the reforms and investments necessary for future growth.

CHAPTER 11

Institutions, Economic Recovery, and Macroeconomic Vulnerability in Indonesia and Malaysia

Thomas Pepinsky

In Indonesia and Malaysia, the Asian financial crisis was as much a political crisis as an economic one. Policies adopted by the two governments had fostered over a decade of strong economic growth, but this growth came with structural weaknesses that left each country vulnerable to the vagaries of investor confidence and cross-border capital movements. These weaknesses arose from the political economy of each country; in both, authoritarian governments used economic policy and political favoritism to reward their supporters with little regard for their potential costs. The Asian financial crisis led each country to take extraordinary adjustment measures and ignited distributional conflicts that ultimately drove Soeharto from power and severely tested the ruling coalition in Malaysia. Subsequently, the years since the crisis have seen political contests in each country over the implementation of reforms designed to foster economic recovery.

In this chapter, I show how politics has defined the course of economic recovery in Indonesia and Malaysia. The Malaysian economic recovery began earlier and remained more robust than in other countries in Southeast Asia, in some accounts as a result of the Malaysian adoption of selective capital controls and an exchange rate peg, together with expansionary macroeconomic policy. But the successful Malaysian stabilization package meant that the government escaped the tough economic reforms that could have promoted more healthy long-term growth. Just as the Malaysian model of growth with redistribution has survived the crisis, most of

I thank Jennifer Amyx, Chandra Athukorala, Harold Crouch, Don Emmerson, Natasha Hamilton-Hart, Yan Islam, Bill Liddle, Chris Manning, John Ravenhill, Garry Rodan, and, especially, Allen Hicken and Hal Hill for their insightful comments on earlier drafts.

the same structural weaknesses that made Malaysia vulnerable to the Asian financial crisis persist today, even after the retirement of former Prime Minister Mahathir Mohamad. These include extensive political intervention in the economy for interethnic redistribution and inefficiency in government-owned and politically favored firms, which impose barriers to the upgrading, retooling, and human capital investment needed to propel Malaysia toward becoming a fully developed nation. By contrast, the fall of Soeharto and the subsequent democratization of Indonesia, along with International Monetary Fund (IMF) mandated stabilization measures and institutional reforms, have not had the much anticipated effect of promoting rapid economic recovery. In particular, the Indonesian decentralization program has not yet led regions to create investment-promoting legal and institutional facilities, and the implementation of economic reforms has been hamstrung by political instability at the national level. Only under President Susilo Bambang Yudhoyono, elected in September 2004, have reform measures began to show fruit.

The experiences of Indonesia and Malaysia suggest several insights for the political economy of economic reform. Far-ranging political transitions, such as took place in Indonesia, can lead to delays in economic recovery due to the extensive transactions costs associated with institutional reequilibration, the process whereby economic and political actors adjust to new institutional rules. Democratic transitions, fiscal decentralization, and competition over the ability to define new institutional rules can yield new opportunities for rent-seeking. The product of these reforms in Indonesia has been a complex regulatory regime coupled with weak legal enforcement. Although normatively desirable, democratization and decentralization have not overcome the fundamental problem of weak institutions that hinder economic growth. Political continuity, as in Malaysia, minimizes the transactions costs associated with institutional reequilibration. The political trade-off is that economic recovery can mask the need for economic reform and obscures the same macroeconomic vulnerabilities that earlier led to a severe economic crisis.

The focus on institutions here does not deny the importance of other influences on the course of economic recovery in the two countries. The crisis in Indonesia was far worse than in Malaysia, in part due to the almost total breakdown of Indonesian economic and political institutions in 1998. Political changes in Indonesia also extended far beyond legal and institutional reform; in the provinces of East Timor, Aceh, and West Papua, secessionist movements have threatened the very integrity of the Indonesian state. Sectarian violence in Maluku and Kalimantan brought simmering social conflicts to light, and the Indonesian military has had to reevaluate its role in Indonesian politics. Malaysia has had none of these problems. Corruption, too, has always been more extensive in Indonesia than in Malaysia. Most important, any comparison between the post-crisis recovery of the two countries must take into account their vastly disparate levels of socioeconomic development and bureaucratic capacity. Yet there is still much to learn from a comparison of these two countries. Focusing on the (often informal) institutional bases of the economy of each country helps us to understand the mechanisms through which growth occurs and macroeconomic vulnerabilities develop. On this count, the comparison between institutional change and continuity in Indonesia and Malaysia reveals important themes in the East Asian recovery.

Economic Crisis and Recovery

The Malaysian economic contraction was shallower, and its subsequent growth more robust, than the Indonesian contraction. A common view is that the Malaysian crisis was less severe than Indonesian crisis because Indonesia was ex ante more vulnerable. The sources of financial vulnerability differed across countries—both faced property-sector overheating with heavy bank exposure, but Indonesia faced a more severe problem of imprudent bank lending than Malaysia, whereas Malaysia experienced a reckless stock market boom financed by foreign portfolio investment. Several indicators reflect these differences. Nonperforming loans (NPLs) in Indonesia, by some estimates, exceeded 40 percent of all loans by mid-1998 and were the result of a rapid buildup of short-term unhedged foreign debt (see, e.g., Hill 1999; Djiwandono 2001). In Malaysia, which has always enjoyed better financial regulation, short-term unhedged debt was low, and NPLs only reached around 20 percent of all loans.[1] But Malaysian development financing was concentrated in the stock market rather than in bank lending. Buoyed by rapid inflows of foreign portfolio capital (Jomo 2001), the Malaysian stock market capitalization exceeded 227 percent of GDP in 1995, compared to just 19 percent in Indonesia (Jomo and Hamilton-Hart 2001). Capital inflows preceding the crisis were a larger proportion of GDP in Malaysia in 1996 (9.6 percent) than in Indonesia (4.8 percent) (Jomo and Hamilton-Hart 2001), and the ratio of reserves to mobile capital in 1997 was substantially worse in Malaysia (0.559) than in Indonesia (0.705) (Athukorala 2001).

So, although superior bank regulation in Malaysia allowed the country to avoid the Indonesian problem of imprudent lending, Malaysian reliance on its stock market for financing big-ticket development projects and distributing patronage brought its own set of vulnerabilities that rapid capital inflows exacerbated.[2] Both countries sought desperately to find adjustment policy solutions to the crisis, and their final choices diverged substantially. Ultimately, the severity of the economic shock in each country depended on these adjustment policies to combat the crisis. Figure 11.1 compares the growth rates in the two countries, illustrating economic contraction and subsequent recovery.

The data show that economic contraction actually began earlier in Malaysia than in Indonesia, with negative growth rates first recorded in the first quarter of 1998. Political feuding between Mahathir and Deputy Prime Minister and Finance

---

1. J. P. Morgan estimated that between 30 and 35 percent of all loans in Indonesia were nonperforming at the height of the crisis. In Malaysia, the figure was 15–25 percent. Figures from Standard and Poor's are 40 percent for Indonesia and 20 percent for Malaysia (Berg 1999).

2. The Kuala Lumpur Stock Exchange (KLSE) Composite Index shrank 79.3 percent, from 1271.6 to 262.7, between February 21, 1997, and September 1, 1998.

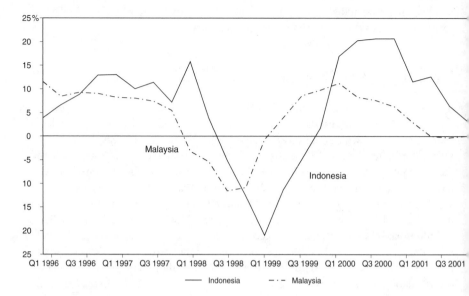

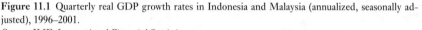

Figure 11.1 Quarterly real GDP growth rates in Indonesia and Malaysia (annualized, seasonally adjusted), 1996–2001.
Source: IMF, *International Financial Statistics.*

Minister Anwar Ibrahim contributed further to the Malaysian economic downturn. But in September 1998, Malaysia embarked on its controversial adjustment strategy of macroeconomic expansion, made feasible by capital controls with a fixed exchange rate—and Mahathir sacked Anwar. Despite this political shake-up, the Malaysian economy quickly stabilized and had turned around by mid-1999. In Indonesia, by contrast, although growth slowed abruptly in late 1997, it did not trend negative until the third quarter of 1998, following Soeharto's resignation on May 21, 1998. But in the wake of Soeharto's resignation, the Indonesia economy contracted severely, enough that Indonesia registered a stunning 14 percent economic contraction in 1998. After bottoming out in the first quarter of 1999, the Indonesian economy rebounded to register positive seasonal growth of just under 2 percent in the fourth quarter of that year.

The comparatively swift Malaysian economic recovery, despite its radical departure from IMF orthodoxy of financial openness and macroeconomic discipline, sparked some debate about the causal role of Malaysian adjustment policies in spurring economic recovery. Paul Krugman (1999), who saw some virtues in the Malaysian policies of temporary capital controls and monetary expansion, nevertheless was circumspect in attributing economic recovery to them rather than to a secular improvement in the investment climate. After all, after three quarters of GDP contraction, Malaysia may have simply bottomed out. Moreover, South Korea and Thailand began to recover about the time that Malaysia began to recover, and Malaysia might have recovered still faster had it not imposed capital controls. To assess the counterfactual that Malaysia would have recovered even without capital controls and a ringgit peg, Kaplan and Rodrik (2001) compare a number of economic indicators in Malaysia with other indicators in South Korea, Indonesia, and Thailand, taking into account that the other countries adopted IMF policies long before September 1998, whereas the Malaysian economy was still deteriorating at that time. They find strong support that capital controls in Malaysia were better associated with a smaller drop in GDP growth, industrial output, and real wages than the IMF programs in other crisis countries. The conclusion, then, is cautiously positive for the Malaysian heterodox adjustment strategy. Despite fears that exchange controls would suffer from abuse by low-level officials eager to exploit black-market exchange rate differentials or that they would inevitably frighten long-term investors, at the very least Mahathir's policies do not seem to have done much harm. And by facilitating macroeconomic expansion and eliminating stock and currency speculation, capital controls appear to have given Malaysian policymakers the breathing room to engineer economic recovery (see Athukorala 2007).

After 1999, the year in which the crisis in the two countries had finally abated, economic growth in both countries resumed, although at lower rates than before the crisis (figure 11.2).

In Indonesia, real GDP grew by an average of 7.83 percent between 1991 and 1996, but this slowed to 4.18 percent between 1999 and 2005. In Malaysia, the corresponding figures are 9.56 and 5.36 percent. The Malaysian GDP did contract in 2001 due to a slump in global demand for Malaysian electronics exports (see Martinez 2002). But the trends over time are clear; the economic crisis represents a break in each country between a period of rapid economic growth amidst relatively stable politics and a period of more modest economic growth.

Indonesia: Institutional Change and Macroeconomic Vulnerability

The Indonesian economic crisis drove Soeharto from power, spelling the end of the New Order regime over which he had ruled for thirty-two years. Soeharto's handpicked successor, B. J. Habibie, was singularly unable to contain the Indonesian *reformasi* movement. In 1999, following the first democratic Indonesian parliamentary election since 1955, he was replaced as president by the liberal Muslim politician Abdurrahman Wahid (Gus Dur) of the National Awakening Party. Gus Dur, however, served erratically, alienating pro-democracy activists and allied political parties alike while mismanaging the Indonesian economic recovery and using his position to amass financial resources through the state logistical monopoly Bulog (Liddle 2001; Malley 2002). He himself succumbed to a corruption scandal in 2001 and was succeeded by his vice president, Megawati Sukarnoputri of the Indonesian Democratic Party of Struggle (PDI-P). In contesting the first Indonesian direct presidential election in 2004, Megawati lost to her former coordinating minister

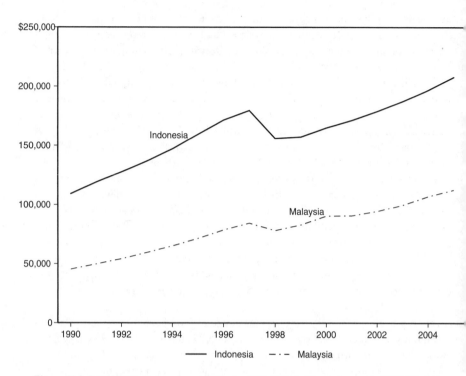

Figure 11.2 Real GDP in Indonesia and Malaysia, 1990–2005 (millions of constant 2000 U.S. dollars at market rates).
Source: World Bank (n.d.).

for politics and security, General Susilo Bambang Yudhoyono (usually known by his initials, SBY). This total of five presidents within the space of just eight years indicates the vast political changes ushered in by the Indonesian economic crisis.

The biggest change is, of course, the return to democracy. Democratization has meant competitive elections, leading to much broader electoral coalitions supporting the government than had been the case during the New Order, in which informal channels of influence were the dominant method of political influence. Gus Dur's legislative coalition was initially broad, with support from Islamists and secular reformists alike, but it fractured as the economy stagnated. SBY, unlike his predecessors, was elected directly, and built an electoral coalition based on popular dissatisfaction with Megawati's own economic management after she replaced Gus Dur.

Elections notwithstanding, informal bases of support remain vital for the leaders of democratic Indonesia. Rather than eliminating informal pressure groups, electoral pressure now competes with interest-group pressure for political influence. At the informal level, the country has seen the continued prominence of wealthy *pribumi* (indigenous, i.e., non-Chinese, Indonesian) business figures with ties to the government. SBY's vice president is Jusuf Kalla, formerly the head of the influential conglomerate NV Hadji Kalla, who rose in the ranks of the dominant party Golkar during the New Order. His brother Achmad Kalla currently heads PT Bukaka Teknik Utama, a multinational firm with diversified construction investments, of which Jusuf was a commissioner until 2001. Under SBY, Bukaka and Hadji Kalla have won a number of important concessions from federal and regional governments. In addition to Jusuf Kalla, other members of SBY's United Indonesia Cabinet have clear links with the Indonesian business community, including Coordinating Minister for People's Welfare and former Coordinating Minister of the Economy Aburizal Bakrie, whose family controls the influential Bakrie Group, and Minister for National Planning Paskah Suzetta, whose business interests have included property and investment. The Bakrie Group openly collaborates with the National Planning Board (Bappenas) to develop its land holdings, and Aburizal's wealth has grown substantially since he joined SBY's government (*Kompas*, May 24, 2006). Foreign economic observers agree that such business interests have hindered the course of Indonesian trade policy reform (interviews with officials at international development agencies in Jakarta, February to March 2006). Government trading monopolies and government-owned enterprises still exist in many sectors; these firms are reported to be rife with corruption, and privatization drives yield speculation of favoritism (*Bisnis Indonesia*, February 15, 2006; *Bisnis Indonesia*, March 31, 2006). More broadly, efforts to extricate the Indonesian military from the corporate world have been halting (*Kompas*, March 4, 2006).

In contrast to these influential business groups, many economic ministers in SBY's cabinet, notably current Coordinating Minister for the Economy Boediono, Minister of Finance Sri Mulyani Indrawati, and Minister of Trade Mari Elke Pangestu, have reputations as technocrats rather than business magnates. The technocrats have directed several contentious but much-needed policy reforms, including the fuel-subsidy cuts of October 2005 that were deeply unpopular with many Indonesians. Yet the bifurcation of SBY's cabinet between technocrats and well-connected entrepreneurs recalls the policy divide under Soeharto between the technocrats and the so-called "financial generals" and nationalists (see Crouch 1978; Liddle 1991; Mackie and MacIntyre 1994). Based on the presence of so many members of the New Order establishment in post–New Order governments, some have suggested that Indonesia has developed a ruling oligarchy that has weathered a difficult institutional transition without actually losing power (see, e.g., Robison and Hadiz 2004).

This is probably an exaggeration. The particular business interests backing the regime have changed, with a shift from a coalition of military-linked firms and ethnic-Chinese cronies under Soeharto to a *pribumi* business class. Moreover, even though many members of the New Order elite have survived the transition to democracy, the rules of the game have changed in important ways. Democratization on a national scale is only the beginning. In 2001, Indonesia embarked on a decentralization experiment that dismantled many of the institutions of centralized political rule under the New Order. Constitutional amendments in 2004 reinforced this move toward regional autonomy (*otonomi daerah*). Not only are national elections democratic, so are provincial and local elections. With decentralization has come a new phenomenon of regional splitting (*pemekaran daerah*), referring to the further subdivision of existing subnational political units. Since 1998, seven new provinces have been created, raising (with the loss of East Timor) the number of Indonesian provinces from twenty-seven in 1998 to thirty-three today. At the subprovincial level, over one hundred new regencies (*kabupaten*) and cities (*kota*) have been created.

The logic of political decentralization—in particular, fiscal decentralization—is to induce subnational political units to compete with one another, adopting good policies to attract investment (see, e.g., Tiebout 1956; Weingast 1995). For example, provinces that eliminate inefficient labor regulations will attract more investment, encouraging other provinces to emulate them. Combined with local-level democracy, this gives citizens a powerful tool for enhancing government responsiveness and spurring local economic development. Even if provincial administrations do not respond to the logic of interjurisdictional competition, and instead use their newly autonomous positions to generate personal profit or to protect vested interests, with democratic elections, their constituents will punish them by voting them out of office. In Indonesia, several studies have found that local-level corruption has decreased since decentralization in 2001 (Henderson and Kuncoro 2004, 2006). This is consistent with cross-national evidence that finds a negative relationship between decentralization and corruption at the national level (Fisman and Gatti 2002).

But many Indonesian political observers have found a perverse logic to decentralization and regional splitting. Instead of fostering interjurisdictional competition, decentralization and regional splitting have increased the opportunities for local corruption by expanding the number of independent veto points and government agencies across the country (interview with an official at an international development agency in Jakarta, March 2006). Without the heavy hand of Soeharto in the background, these agencies are now even more willing to extort bribes and levies. Local elites interested in securing regular funding from the central government can create what amount to personal fiefdoms in new subprovincial jurisdictions. The logic is similar to that of Shleifer and Vishny (1993), who suggest two different institutional equilibria that support corruption. In one, a strong central government has maximized its total take in bribes from an economy and punishes subordinates who extract excessive bribes that discourage growth and investment. New Order Indonesia matched this model well (see MacIntyre 2000). The alternative institutional structure has no central apparatus that can coordinate bribery and corruption among bureaucrats or government agencies. The implication for investment, growth, and development is that centralized corruption, although inefficient, is *more* efficient than decentralized corruption. There are now higher transactions costs to negotiating contracts and getting investment approval; without central coordination, it is less clear whom to bribe, how much to bribe, or whether each bribe paid will be the last. For this and related reasons, many observers consider the welfare-enhancing effects of regional splitting and decentralization to be ambiguous, if not negative (see e.g. *Jawa Pos*, November 21, 2005; *Kompas*, March 3, 2006; *Kompas*, March 20, 2006).

This perspective suggests a tantalizing hypothesis about the overall effect of decentralization on long-term economic growth. Could Indonesian decentralization actually be harmful to long-term growth by decoupling the many opportunities for political interference in the Indonesian economy from a strong, centralized leader? For one, corruption does not appear to have decreased under democracy. Indonesia has always been one of the most corrupt countries in the world, consistently registering at the bottom of cross-national indices of corruption. On a scale of 1 to 10, with 1 the most corrupt and 10 the least, Indonesia averages around 2 according to Transparency International (table 11.1).

By way of a regional comparison, the Philippines averages just under 3, Thailand just over 3, Singapore over 9, and Malaysia around 5. The figures in table 11.1 show that despite democratization and decentralization, according to the Transparency International scores, Indonesia is about as corrupt in 2005 as in 1996.

Indonesian investment receipts remain lower than prior to the crisis, although they have rebounded from their trough in 2002. Net foreign direct investment (FDI) flows were actually negative until 2003 (figure 11.3).

In an open, export-oriented economy, such as in Indonesia, this fall in investment is probably the single greatest cause of slower economic growth in the wake of the crisis. What explains the slow rebound in FDI in Indonesia? The rise of China, India, and Vietnam as low-cost competitors for FDI has probably played some role (see also John Ravenhill, chap. 7 in this volume). Civil strife has also probably given domestic and foreign investors pause. Since democratization, moreover, labor has been free to organize for better wages and working conditions, which may have driven away some investors who formerly enjoyed the Indonesian controlled labor force.[3] But anecdotes of specific political barriers to attracting investment abound. For example, the government revealed in March 2006 that of ninety crucial infrastructure projects for which the government has sought tenders, less than 20 percent had attracted any attention from investors—a fact largely blamed on weak institutional safeguards for foreign investors and an almost total halt to public infrastructural investment. Shortly thereafter, World Bank President and former U.S. Ambassador to Indonesia Paul Wolfowitz stated that corruption was the single

Table 11.1 Indonesia: corruption scores, 1995–2005

1995	1996	1997	1998	1999	2000	2001	2002	2003	2004	2005
1.9	2.7	2.7	2.0	1.7	1.7	1.9	1.9	1.9	2.0	2.2

Source: Transparency International (1995–2005), at www.transparency.org.

3. Survey evidence, however, suggests that labor activism and labor regulations have not harmed investment; see *Kompas*, March 20, 2006.

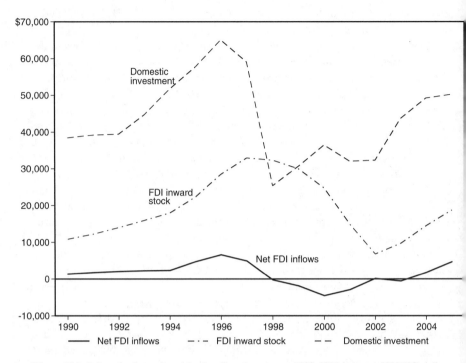

Figure 11.3 Indonesia: domestic and foreign direct investment, 1990–2005 (constant 2000 U.S. dollars at market rates).
Source: Data from UNCTAD, *Foreign Direct Investment Online.*

greatest hindrance to investment in Indonesia (*Bisnis Indonesia,* March 8, 2006; *Bisnis Indonesia,* April 11, 2006.).

Other characteristics of post-Soeharto Indonesian politics reinforce how decentralization has not been as successful as many hoped in attracting investment. Since his election, SBY's administration and Indonesian business groups have repeatedly exhorted provincial and subprovincial governments to adopt streamlined investment regulations (*Kompas,* April 6, 2006; *Bisnis Indonesia,* May 9, 2006).[4] In April 2006, the central government announced two new regulations to facilitate regional growth, permitting regions to designate special economic zones without central government approval and forbidding regions from imposing any new taxes; yet although regions can now issue investment permits, they must still seek approval from the central government (*Bisnis Indonesia,* April 18, 2006). In March 2007, the Dewan Perwakilan Rakyat (DPR, or house of representatives) passed a new investment law that revamped investment regulations dating from the late 1960s, offering new tax incentives and guarantees for foreign investors (*Asian Wall Street Journal,* March 30, 2007). The fact that SBY and his cabinet members

4. For more encouraging views, see *Kompas,* April 11, 2006.

continue to prevail on regional administrations to embark on such reforms, and that the central government continues to shoulder the responsibility for creating a good investment climate, indicates that decentralization itself is not yet having its desired impact (*Bisnis Indonesia,* February 17, 2006; interview with Aburizal Bakrie, coordinating minister for people's welfare, March 14, 2006).

There are, then, two seemingly opposing claims. According to several studies cited previously, at the provincial and subprovincial level decentralization seems to be associated with lower corruption. Yet, at the regional level, regulations still hamstring investment, and at the national level, corruption remains a serious issue. Perhaps the safest conclusion about the Indonesian transition to democracy and the move to decentralization and regional autonomy is that their beneficial effects, at least until now, have been small and delayed, with provinces and subprovincial administrations slow to adopt reforms that attract investment.

At the national level, several measures have addressed political barriers to investment and growth. Successive governments have empowered supervisory agencies such as the Capital Market Supervisory Agency, the Finance and Development Supervisory Agency, and the Office of Public Accounts to combat financial improprieties, and reform of the clumsy and corrupt tax collection agencies remains a high government priority. SBY's government has staked its reputation on eradicating corruption and has created two new investigatory bodies that build on the influential Corruption Eradication Commission, formed in 2002. But results have been slow, with overlapping responsibilities, limited protection for witnesses, and a lack of coordination among the several extant anticorruption agencies hindering successful prosecution of suspects (see Yuntho 2005b; *Kompas,* February 22, 2006; *Kompas,* March 17, 2006). There are also frequent criticisms that the most corrupt figures escape prosecution due to their political connections (*Kompas,* February 16, 2006). In the case of the Bank Indonesia Liquidity Support scandal—in which a massive amount of liquidity support was doled out to crony-controlled banks at the height of the crisis—some of the biggest corruptors simply vanished overseas and others arranged to have their repossessed assets overvalued by government auditors (Mintorahardjo 2001; Yuntho 2005a; *Kompas,* May 23, 2003; interview with Yosef Ardi, reporter for *Bisnis Indonesia,* March 6, 2006). In other areas, despite several high-profile convictions of corrupt politicians and businessmen, the deterrent effect of national anticorruption efforts seems minimal. Credible reports appear periodically that members of the Corruption Eradication Commission have accepted bribes and intimidated witnesses (*Kompas,* May 31, 2006). Those accused include Soeharto's half-brother, Probosutedjo, who confessed to bribing Chief Justice Bagir Manan, and Achmad Djunaidi, formerly of the state workers' insurance firm PT Jamsostek, who claimed to have bribed government lawyers to avoid jail time in his corruption trial (*Asian Wall Street Journal,* April 23, 2003; *Kompas,* February 10, 2006; *Kompas,* April 29, 2006).

A focus on policy failures and institutional shake-ups risks neglecting other changes and continuities in the Indonesian political economy since 1998. This would be a mistake. Interestingly, even as the business coalition backing the regime has changed, the ideological basis of economic policymaking has remained consistent. The expansion of meaningful franchise with the return of Indonesian democracy amid economic upheaval might have engendered a populist backlash against liberal economic principles. Yet successive governments have not retreated from a broad commitment to economic openness (see also Natasha Hamilton-Hart, chap. 3 in this volume), despite occasions of populist rhetoric, extensive popular frustration with the IMF in the wake of painful structural adjustment process, and the rise of independent labor activism.

Of course, economic policymaking in Indonesia can hardly be described as liberal or orthodox in any real sense, but this is no different than Indonesia was under the New Order, which combined capitalism with a heavy dose of statism. And the barriers to policy reform come from entrenched business interests close to the state rather than from a broad populist coalition demanding trade protection or industrial-sector employment. For instance, shortly after the DPR approved new investment regulations in March 2007, a presidential regulation expanded the so-called Negative Investment List of sectors wholly or partially closed to FDI (*Tempo,* July 6, 2007). The process by which regulators agreed on specific percentage limits on foreign ownership, or chose which sectors further to open (e.g., banking and insurance) and to restrict (e.g., telecommunications) remains unclear, but it does not appear to reflect distributional or populist concerns.

In sum, we can draw several conclusions about the post-Soeharto Indonesian political economy. Despite continued close relationships between the government and business interests, Indonesian political economy has changed dramatically since the Asian financial crisis. Along with the rise of *pribumi* business groups, the institutional context of government-business relations has changed dramatically with decentralization and democratization. The national government must now negotiate with provincial governments, few of which have made great strides in improving the local investment climate. Corruption is now decentralized and continues to plague the Indonesian economy. There is tentative evidence that local corruption has decreased with decentralization and local political competition, but this has not been accompanied by a rise in competitiveness or a race to adopt attractive investment policies. At the national level, even with the attempts by the SBY administration to adopt market-enhancing reforms and to foster political accountability, progress has been slow. Perhaps, ironically, these vulnerabilities are what will probably shield Indonesia from the same sort of meltdown that it experienced in 1997–98 in that foreign and domestic investors still appear more hesitant to invest in Indonesia than in the mid-1990s. Substantial foreign capital inflows, dominated by private borrowing inadequately hedged against foreign currency risk, do not appear to be a threat to the Indonesian economy.[5] The vulnerability of Indonesia

---

5. Even in nominal terms, foreign bank loans to Indonesia in 2006:Q3 (US$31,799 million) remained well below the totals for 1997:Q2 (US$59,818 million) (Bank for International Settlements [BIS], International Monetary Fund [IMF], Organisation for Economic Co-operation and Development [OECD], and World Bank, *Joint External Debt Hub* online database, http://www.jedh.org/).

is now of a different sort—that of a low-investment, low-growth equilibrium that undoes public support for democracy and regional autonomy (see Mujani 2006).

Malaysia: Institutional Continuity and Macroeconomic Vulnerability

Economic recovery in concert with political repression allowed Mahathir's regime to withstand a political challenge from his erstwhile Deputy Prime Minister and Finance Minister Anwar Ibrahim and a newly galvanized political opposition. The engine of this political opposition was Malaysia's *reformasi* movement, which championed the causes of reform and social justice and catalyzed the formation of the Barisan Alternatif (Alternative Front, BA), an electoral coalition among the Pan-Malaysian Islamic Party (PAS), the largely ethnic-Chinese Democratic Action Party (DAP), and the pan-ethnic National Justice Party (Keadilan) founded by Anwar's wife Wan Azizah Wan Ismail. In the 1999 general elections, PAS captured an additional state legislature, for a total of two out of thirteen, and expanded its small share of seats in the Malaysian lower house. Yet the ruling Barisan Nasional (National Front, BN) coalition, led by the United Malays National Organisation (UMNO) and Mahathir, easily retained the two-thirds majority in the lower house that it had enjoyed since the restoration of parliament in 1971. In the wake of the BN victory, Mahathir moved against many of his political opponents, reinforcing his firm grip over Malaysian politics and society. Mahathir ruled until 2003, when he handed power to Deputy Prime Minister Abdullah Ahmad Badawi. Abdullah led the BN to an overwhelming victory in the 2004 general elections, with PAS losing two-thirds of its seats, the DAP regaining its position as the main parliamentary opposition party, and UMNO and BN reaffirming their position at the apex of Malaysian politics.

This political continuity means two things. First, the coalitional basis of the Malaysian regime remains largely intact; the UMNO (and hence the BN) relies on the same cross-class Malay coalition that it always has, although some of the big players have changed. Second, at the institutional level, the Malaysian political economy has changed little. Data on investment show that, like Indonesia, Malaysian investment levels have yet to recover to precrisis levels, but this is the result of weak global technology markets in 2000–2 and (similar to Indonesia) the subsequent rise of China as a regional competitor for electronics assembly and production (Ernst 2004). This is apparent in the slump in inward FDI stocks, coinciding not with the Asian crisis but with the bursting of the tech bubble (figure 11.4).

But, in contrast to Indonesia, where democratization and decentralization have revamped political institutions, institutional continuity in Malaysia has ensured that little meaningful reform has occurred in the policy areas that contributed to the macroeconomic vulnerability of the country in the late 1990s. As measured by Transparency International, for example, Malaysia is almost precisely as corrupt in 2005 as it was in 1995.

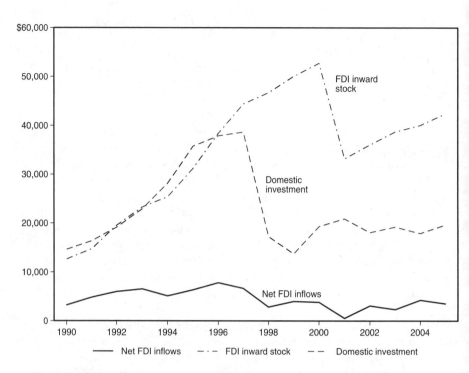

Figure 11.4 Malaysia: domestic and foreign direct investment, 1990–2005 (constant 2000 U.S. dollars at market rates).
Source: Calculated from UNCTAD, *Foreign Direct Investment Online*.

The Malaysian recovery strategy led to widespread accusations that capital controls and expansionary macroeconomic policy allowed the regime to rescue politically connected firms without the fear of punishment from foreign traders. To resolve outstanding issues of corporate debt and weak financial institutions, the government created two quasi-governmental bodies that were to acquire NPLs and inject capital into weak banks (Danaharta and Danamodal). A Corporate Debt Restructuring Committee facilitated these tasks (see Mahani 2002). But there was clear evidence of favoritism in the operations of these bodies, including government buyouts of crony-controlled firms such as Renong Bhd, one of the UMNO corporate arms (*Asian Wall Street Journal*, March 16, 2001; *Asian Wall Street Journal*, July 26, 2001). Simon Johnson and Todd Mitton (2003) find that the stock prices of publicly listed companies with links to Mahathir recovered faster than stock prices of unaffiliated firms and that both recovered faster than stock prices of firms associated with Anwar.

Yet, despite the Malaysian heterodox adjustment strategy, accompanied by triumphal rhetoric lambasting neoliberal economic policies and threats to force a consolidation of the domestic banking sector, Malaysia remains today a fundamentally open economy. This has continued to be the case under Abdullah's tenure in office. Abdullah's inauguration was indeed a moment of optimism for many observers of Malaysian politics and economics (Welsh 2005). Under his leadership, the final remnants of the Malaysian radical adjustment measures—bans on short-selling of stocks and the hard peg of the ringgit to the U.S. dollar—were lifted. Abdullah has a reputation of being personally incorruptible, and he immediately embarked on an ambitious program to streamline government-linked companies (GLCs) and root out public-sector inefficiency. On these counts, he can claim some modest success, having introduced procurement standards and efficiency guidelines and replaced ineffective executives in some GLCs (*New Straits Times*, February 20, 2004; *Berita Harian*, March 24, 2006). It appears, then, at a rhetorical level that Abdullah's regime is even more pro-market than Mahathir's regime, whose big push toward heavy industrialization in the 1980s and extensive pro-Malay redistributive efforts produced a mix of economic policies that were decidedly interventionist.

Closer examination of Malaysian politics and economic management shows that although the regime is avowedly capitalist, a tight relationship between business and politics persists. Several important promised reforms, such as the establishment of an open tender system for government procurement and a fair competition law, have yet to come to pass (*Economist Intelligence Unit—Risk Briefing*, May 23, 2006; interview in Kuala Lumpur with Lim Kit Siang, DAP MP, July 12, 2006; interview in Kuala Lumpur with Tan Sri Ramon Navaratnam, president of Transparency International (Malaysia), July 17, 2006). Although the late 1980s saw the official privatization of many companies, the government retains a large stake in conglomerates in key sectors. Some government-controlled firms, such as Telekom Malaysia (telecommunications) and Petronas (petroleum exploration and refining), are notably professional and have expanded beyond the borders of Malaysia, but others, such as Tenaga Nasional Berhad (power generation), have retained their influence through size rather than efficiency. Furthermore, the regime still protects clearly inefficient companies such as the national automobile company Proton, reflecting both the continued influence of Mahathir on daily politics (he is now Proton's special advisor) and Abdullah's inability to combat entrenched interests (*Berita Harian*, March 24, 2006; *New Straits Times*, March 25, 2006).

From the standpoint of the UMNO leadership, control over budgetary purse strings has reached paramount importance. As part of his strategy to sideline Anwar, Mahathir took temporary control of the Ministry of Finance and later gave the Finance Ministry portfolio to Daim Zainuddin. Daim served until 2001, when Mahathir assumed the position himself. Daim ostensibly resigned on his own accord, but political observers have noted that Daim's business interests had come into conflict with the business interests of Mahathir's son Mokhzani Mahathir (*Asian Wall Street Journal*, July 5, 2001). Since rising to the position of prime minister, Abdullah has continued Mahathir's practice of holding the Finance Ministry portfolio. Also of note is the continued existence of the National Economic Action Council, a super-constitutional organ that Mahathir created in late 1997 to find a solution to the Malaysian economic crisis. At the head of its Executive Committee sits the prime minister, the deputy prime minister, and an executive chair who also serves as minister in the Prime Minister's Department. Meanwhile, the Economic Planning Unit (also within the Prime Minister's Department) shoulders the responsibility for Malaysian development planning. If anything, this is evidence of more political centralization of economic policy formation than before the crisis.

In addition to maintaining Mahathir's centralized economic policy apparatus, Abdullah has retained a number of Mahathir's cronies who had under Mahathir served as members of his economic team, including Minister of International Trade and Industry Rafidah Aziz and Minister of Works S. Samy Vellu. Such continuity of Malaysian politics reveals that, despite Abdullah's reputation as a clean politician, entrenched interests in the UMNO and BN remain influential. Moreover, Abdullah's son-in-law Khairy Jamaluddin, viewed as having extraordinary personal influence over Abdullah, has seen his personal wealth grow extensively since 2004 through what many believe to be shady investment deals dependent on political favoritism (interview with anonymous Malaysian economist, July 2006). In addition, Abdullah's deputy Najib Abdul Razak has none of Abdullah's reputation for moderation and clean government. Instead, he is known as a staunch defender of Malay special rights and of the UMNO, and he is often identified with the politics of his father, Abdul Razak Hussein, who engineered the move toward overt UMNO dominance of Malaysian politics during the period of suspended democracy from 1969 to 1971 and later ushered in the New Economic Policy (NEP) that has defined Malaysian economic policy making since the early 1970s.

It is important not to underestimate the influence of interethnic redistributive concerns on modern Malaysian policymaking. Existing in an uneasy relationship with relatively free markets is the consistent advocacy by the regime of Malay dominance and favoritism in business and society. (In Malaysia, positive discrimination officially benefits all *bumiputras*—non-Chinese and non-Indians—but Malays are the main beneficiaries of this favoritism.) Political-business links in Malaysia accordingly extend far beyond the business interests of key political actors and corporate-sector players seeking political favoritism. The very stability of Malaysia depends on the ability of the regime to redress Malay grievances about interethnic inequality, grievances that originate in the colonial period. In fact, the continued emphasis by the regime on the NEP (despite the fact that it officially expired in 1990) provides ideological cover for much of its continuing involvement in the economy. A revealing document is the Ninth Malaysia Plan (Government of Malaysia 2006), the country's first five-year development plan issued under Abdullah, which the government released to great domestic fanfare in February 2006. The plan, like its predecessors, places heavy emphasis on the government role in coordinating the redistribution of wealth and equity in favor of *bumiputras*, largely at the expense of the large ethnic-Chinese minority (*The Star*, April 1, 2006).[6]

---

6. One interesting development is that, for the first time, Indian Malaysians have been identified as requiring government assistance (*New Straits Times*, May 23, 2006).

There are many ways in which the government intervenes in the economy to sponsor interethnic redistribution. For instance, in a continuation of policies long implemented under Mahathir and his predecessors, the government continues, through its investment arm Permodalan Nasional Berhad (PNB), to manage a number of *bumiputra*-only unit trusts with heavy involvement in the KLSE. These unit trusts increase the wealth flowing to Malays, and the government has launched new trusts in the wake of the crisis. In addition to the PNB capital market investments, the government maintains an active interest in areas such as power generation, shipping, and transportation through its strategic investment arm Khazanah Nasional Berhad. Perbadanan Nasional Berhad, formerly under the Ministry of Finance, before privatization in 1996, facilitates the growth of a *"bumiputra* commercial and industrial community"* by investing in *bumiputra*-controlled start-ups and distributing franchises to *bumiputras*. Perbadanan Usahawan Nasional Berhad (PUNB), a wholly owned subsidiary of Yayasan Pelaburan Bumiputra (of which PNB is another subsidiary), has since 1991 complemented Perbadanan Nasional Berhad in nurturing *bumiputra* entrepreneurs, and its responsibility for creating *bumiputra* franchisees and businesses owners expanded notably in the Ninth Malaysia Plan *(Berita Harian,* May 2, 2006). A wide array of government-linked coordinating bodies and policy development organizations support these efforts both at the federal level and among the Malaysian states *(Berita Harian,* May 24, 2006).

Through such institutions, economic policies—created with an eye toward improving the economic status of Malays—still reward political efficacy rather than economic efficiency. The NEP strictures hamstring firms eager to retool, streamline, and upgrade to better compete with firms in more advanced economies. At the same time, the Malaysian educational system, the key driver of human capital investment, languishes under political restrictions and ethnic quotas. Furthermore, as in the past, politicians may influence national investment companies to invest in uneconomical ventures connected to political allies. In addition, because the regime has such a direct stake in the performance of stocks owned by Malays, it has a strong incentive to protect dividends at all costs.

And while many governments across the world have quasi-corporate subsidiaries that facilitate strategic national investments, the danger in Malaysia comes from the vulnerability of supervisory agencies to political interference. Bank Negara Malaysia, the Malaysian Central Bank, is by no means independent from political influence—during the 1998 crisis political pressure led its governor and deputy governor to resign. The Anti-Corruption Agency has the statutory authority to investigate and prosecute a wide number of offenses among public servants, but in practice, it is successful against only low-level functionaries *(New Straits Times,* March 21, 2006). The Malaysian judiciary, stripped of independent authority by Mahathir in the late 1980s but tentatively reasserting its independence since 2004, still faces accusations of bowing to political pressure and bribery *(New Straits Times,* May 31, 2006). In the 1980s and 1990s, as the economy boomed, weak regulation fostered the growth of money politics and corporate scandals tied directly to UMNO and other BN component parties (see Gomez 1994; Gomez and

Jomo 1999; Milne and Mauzy 1999). During the crisis, Mahathir used these and other investment arms to protect the interests of favored groups, using, for example, funds from Khazanah and the publicly owned pension fund, the Employees' Provident Fund, to shore up the sagging KLSE (*Utusan Malaysia*, September 4, 1997). Indeed, Mahathir clearly explained the radical adjustment measures as having been vital not only for economic recovery in general but also more narrowly for protecting Malay welfare (Pepinsky 2007). Today, without meaningful reform, the same danger exists.

Of course, while interethnic redistribution justifies broadly pro-Malay policies, factional conflicts *within* the Malay corporate community persist, revealing that political protection remains valuable for well-connected corporate figures. Daim's falling out with Mahathir appears to have left him particularly vulnerable, as evinced through a Court of Appeals ruling on an old corporate scandal from his days as finance minister in 1990 that implicated him as well as his protégés Halim Saad and Annuar Othman (*New Straits Times*, January 13, 2006; *Star*, January 27, 2006). The case has yet to reach a conclusion, but it is revealing that the case against Daim moved forward only after he fell from political favor. Under Abdullah, additional political scandals reveal that UMNO politicians still often use their offices for corporate gain, leading most observers to question the true extent to which Abdullah is able to combat entrenched party interests.

So, in contrast to the case of Indonesia, in Malaysia political continuity has produced a stable institutional platform for economic recovery, at the cost of continued macroeconomic vulnerabilities. Malaysia is still a fundamentally open economy, but one in which the old model of ethnic politics and political favoritism persists. Keenly aware that interethnic grievances can undermine social stability, the regime continues to strike an uneasy balance between redistributive intervention and economic openness. The link between the Malaysian political system and macroeconomic vulnerability is easy to miss in relatively fat times, but it is important to recall that the Malaysian economic crisis in 1997–99 began following a similar period of seemingly healthy expansion. Risk consultancies continue to warn that the dark areas of the Malaysian political economy persist, and although foreign investment has steadily recovered in the past several years, investors remain well aware of the recent Malaysian history of interventionist economic policies.

Conclusion

The experiences of Indonesia and Malaysia after the Asian financial crisis reveal the difficulty of establishing institutions that can foster healthy economic growth. Indonesia since 1998 has experienced rapid and far-ranging institutional change toward institutions that scholarly consensus holds should be both welfare- and efficiency-enhancing. But its experience suggests that the benefits of democratization and decentralization can be delayed by the difficult task of adjusting to these new institutional arrangements. Malaysia reaffirms what many consider an uncomfortable common wisdom that, despite their high costs in terms of personal freedoms, repression and autocratic political stability can be a platform for economic recovery. In both countries, policy weaknesses stemming from government-business linkages remain the greatest source of macroeconomic vulnerability. But the institutional context of government-business linkages has changed in Indonesia from a highly centralized system of hierarchical exchange to a decentralized system of bribery and influence peddling. In Malaysia, the main players have changed with the resignation of Mahathir, the ouster of Anwar, the marginalization of Daim, and the rise of Abdullah and Khairy, but the system has proven remarkably resilient.

On the vulnerability of each country to another financial panic, records are mixed. Insofar as the currency of neither country appears overvalued, the risk of an externally generated financial crisis is lower a decade after the Asian financial crisis than it was in the mid-1990s. Furthermore, political developments in Indonesia have discouraged the inflow of volatile short-term capital through bank and corporate borrowing, which reduces the likelihood that another mass of NPLs will emerge in Indonesia the short to medium term. In Malaysia, a reasonably well-managed banking sector should forestall a similar buildup of imprudent foreign-denominated loans, as it did in the mid-1990s, but the regime continues to use the Malaysian stock markets as a tool for interethnic redistribution. The absence of fundamental reform, as evinced through corporate bailouts and political favoritism that persist in Malaysia even today, means that politician could promote risky stock market expansion in the future, even if such an expansion is at present unlikely. Political-business linkages in Malaysia are not themselves the causes of financial vulnerability,[7] but they enable particular vulnerabilities to emerge. In sum, the experiences of the two countries suggest that neither institutional change nor institutional continuity will necessarily produce the policies required to eliminate macroeconomic vulnerability, which persists in both countries for different reasons.

Institutional change signifies for Indonesia a break from the model of economic development that had proven so successful under the New Order. No longer does a relatively insulated decision maker sit atop a steep political hierarchy, capitalizing on eager international investors, abundant labor and natural resources, and a political apparatus that instantly transforms executive preferences into policy. The current challenge for Indonesia is to create good policies that attract investment and sponsor growth rather than relying on informal guarantees from the executive branch to reassure investors. The breakdown of the Indonesian model becomes more striking when compared to the Malaysian development model, which has changed little since 1997. Ethnic politics and redistribution still underlie almost all policy choices in Malaysia. This is the main legacy of heterodox adjustment measures that shielded Malaysia from the upheaval that Indonesia experienced.

Despite this pessimistic outlook, one sign of change shared by both countries is the rise of an active civil society, eager to monitor government excesses and agitate

---

7. For a similar view on the Asian financial crisis, see Chang (2000).

for reform. In Indonesia, decentralization and democratization have contributed to policy uncertainty, but an alternative pathway from political liberalization to economic growth may develop in which empowered citizens form new advocacy networks that demand good economic management from the democratically elected government. Indeed, hundreds of nongovernmental organizations (NGOs) have sprung up in Indonesia, such as the influential Indonesian Corruption Watch, which has taken the lead in tracking and publicizing cases of corruption (*Kompas,* May 15, 2006). Meanwhile, in Malaysia, draconian legislation that restricts civil society organizing remains in effect. Nonetheless, a lively opposition presses the government for further reform, and NGOs energized during the *reformasi* movement still vocally criticize the BN regime. Even the government-controlled print media have become bolder in covering political and economic scandals since Abdullah's rise to power. Evidence of social pressures producing clean governance remains scarce in both countries. Nonetheless, these pressures for responsible government may be the key to fostering macroeconomic stability and healthy long-term economic growth in the two countries.

CHAPTER 12

The Korean Economic System Ten Years after the Crisis

Jongryn Mo

The 1997 Asian financial crisis was a turning point in Korean economic history. Its economic impact was severe because it brought bankruptcy to many heavily indebted Korean corporations and banks and unemployment to hundreds of thousands of workers. The psychological impact of the crisis was equally important. People had lost faith in their old economic system and looked for an alternative model. The public pressure for reforming the old economic system continued even after the Korean economy officially returned to solvency in 2001 (i.e., when the IMF bailout loan was fully repaid).

But how much has the Korean economic system changed as a result of the crisis and subsequent reforms? In particular, how differently are Korean banks and companies behaving now compared with before? Answering this simple question goes a long way toward understanding the transformation of the Korean economic system since the economic crisis.

Opinions on this question vary. On the one hand, many analysts argue that Korea has gone furthest in transforming its economic system into a market economy, not only among the crisis-hit countries but also among East Asian countries in general. They point, in particular, to the penetration of foreign capital into Korean financial markets. On the other hand, there is still strong skepticism about the openness and regulatory consistency of the Korean government. Critics cite the dampening effects of government investigations of foreign investors on investor confidence, a prominent example of which is the investigation into Lone Star for its purchase of Korea Exchange Bank in 2003. On balance, however, Korea is generally recognized as a successful case of postcrisis reform.

An important question, then, is why economic restructuring and reform have been more successful in Korea than elsewhere. Because the reform process in any country is fundamentally political, we must ask what role politics played in shaping both the process of reform and its outcome. As the cases presented in this volume make clear, reform paths have differed across the crisis-hit countries. Although differences in the nature of the initial problems confronted by crisis-stricken countries may account for some difference in their reform approaches and priorities, technical imperatives cannot provide all the answers; we must look for the political factors that brought about the variations in the reform process and outcome.

In this chapter, I investigate the Korean case closely, with particular emphasis on the reforms in its corporate and financial sectors. My overall conclusion is that it is the interaction between the forces of financial globalization and domestic politics that holds the key to understanding the process and outcome of reform in Korea.

One caveat: this chapter focuses only on institutional change, that is, changes in the structure of the Korean economic system. Because the financial crisis of 1997 was an insolvency crisis, the first priority was to return Korean banks and companies to solvency through restructuring. By and large, the financial soundness of Korean banks and companies had been restored by 2000, and we must ask and explain why restructuring was successful in Korea. But I do not directly address this issue in this chapter. Although restructuring itself laid the foundation for subsequent competitive and financial successes of Korean banks and companies and the delineation between restructuring and institutional reform measures is difficult, I believe that institutional change represents a more enduring and important change from the perspective of comparative capitalism.

The Key Dimensions of the Korean Economic System: Financial and Corporate Governance

To appreciate the impact of postcrisis reforms on the structure of the Korean economic system, it is important to be clear about what kind of system was in place before the crisis occurred. The precrisis system in Korea is conventionally viewed as a developmental state, very similar to Japan, the prototypical developmental state. As the name indicates, the developmental state is fully committed to economic growth, with other government policy objectives such as social welfare or maximizing consumer choices considered to be secondary. The developmental state is also characterized by a set of favored policies: macroeconomic stability, high savings rates, and export/industry promotion based on close business-government relations (World Bank 1993).

In addition to policy objectives and choices, a particular system of financial and corporate governance is another defining characteristic of the developmental state. In Korea, like Japan, the government created a financial system in which banks, rather than stock markets, dominated. Banks channeled savings to corporate investors; consumer lending was purposely discouraged. Given the extensive intervention of government in the banking sector (and implicit government protection) it is not surprising that Korean banks were slow to develop market-based practices and were beset by problems of moral hazard such as excessive risks and special treatment for cronies.

The Korean developmental state was also associated with a system of corporate governance that represented stakeholder, as opposed to shareholder, capitalism. Korean corporations were neither organized nor governed to maximize shareholder value. Instead, they reflected a desire to balance the interests of shareholders with those of other stakeholders such as banks, workers, and government. The *chaebol* (large business conglomerates) are the most important organizational form of Korean stakeholder capitalism. As a corporate form, the *chaebol* are characterized by "three distinct *structural* elements: a *governance structure* of family dominance; an *organizational structure* of a holding company controlling legally independent firms (multi-subsidiaries rather than multi-divisions); and a diversified *business structure* encompassing a number of discrete products and services" (Haggard, Lim, and Kim 2003, 3).

After reaching a peak in the 1970s, however, the developmental state model had come under increasing economic and political pressures. Catalysts for change came from the twin forces of democratization and globalization, which became increasingly salient in the 1980s. The Korean transition to democracy began in 1987 after almost two decades of authoritarian rule. At the same time, Korean firms faced increased competition in international markets and needed more-open domestic markets to compete more effectively with their foreign rivals.

Given this environment, some change away from the developmental state model was inevitable; it simply could not provide the sufficient levels of transparency, accountability, openness, and competition that the new environment demanded. Indeed, the developmental state began to show increased signs of distress. Economic growth became uneven after the late 1980s, and economic fundamentals sharply deteriorated by the mid-1990s, even before the contagion hit from the Southeast Asian economic crises.

The 1997 Economic Crisis and Subsequent Reforms

When the economic crisis (finally) arrived in 1997, the Korean government turned to the International Monetary Fund (IMF) for help. Tough negotiations led to the agreement under which the South Korean government pledged to restructure the troubled banking sector and place many weak companies under bank-led restructuring programs. The government also promised to carry out extensive institutional reforms aimed at strengthening the long-term competitiveness of Korean banks and companies. The goal of the reforms was to replace the system of governed markets with a system that was more market-oriented. Good governance, liberalization, and deregulation became catch phrases in the postcrisis policy debates and pronouncements.

After the IMF bailout agreement, the task of implementation fell squarely on president-elect Kim Dae Jung, who won the election on December 18, 1997. At the time, it was not clear that Kim Dae Jung would be able to implement the reforms that had been promised to the IMF. Many doubted if he could command the necessary political support from key domestic actors such as the bureaucrats and the *chaebol*, which had long mistrusted him.

As soon as Kim Dae Jung took office in February 1990, he quickly moved to stabilize the devastated financial markets. This involved multiple tasks. First, the government had to close or merge insolvent financial institutions and strengthen the capital base of those that remained viable. This required the disposal of nonperforming loans (NPLs) and recapitalization of financial institutions either through public funds or foreign investment. Second, the regulatory system needed to be reformed to ensure transparency, accountability, and sound management in financial institutions. Third, deregulation and liberalization of financial markets were important to induce foreign investment as well as to show government commitment to financial reform. Last, the government had to develop the institutional capacity to carry out these reforms.

Fortunately for Kim Dae Jung, the institutional and legal foundations for financial reform had already been laid by the time he came to power. In December 1997, the National Assembly passed the thirteen financial reform bills that the preceding Kim Young Sam administration had wanted so desperately during the months preceding the IMF bailouts. They consolidated fragmented regulatory agencies into one with streamlined responsibilities (to become the Financial Supervisory Commission), reformed the deposit insurance system, and created the legal foundations for raising bank bailout funds and reorganizing troubled financial institutions. After several months of adjustment and preparation, the new institutional arrangement became fully operational in April 1998.

With the necessary institutions in place, the Kim Dae Jung government moved to force out insolvent financial institutions. In January 1998, the government effectively nationalized two commercial banks (Korea First Bank and Seoul Bank) by reducing existing shareholder equity by one-eighth and injecting 1.5 trillion won (US$1.5 billion at the exchange rate of 1000 won per dollar) of new equity into each. It then proceeded to sell the banks to foreign investors. In April, the government listed twelve banks that failed to meet the capital adequacy requirement of the Bank for International Settlements and asked them to submit restructuring plans for a further review of their status. Government actions against troubled nonbank financial institutions were also swift. By April, thirteen out of thirty merchant banks had had their licenses revoked, one merchant bank had been suspended, one trust company had been closed, and two securities firms had been suspended. At the same time, the government, through the Korea Asset Management Company, purchased nonperforming assets from financial institutions and sought to reduce their debt burden by purchasing the bonds that they had issued.

In the following months, the government committed additional public funds, totaling 50 trillion won, to support the purchase of nonperforming assets, recapitalization, and deposit protection. On June 29, 1998, the government finally decided the fate of the twelve banks without adequate capital provisions. Five of them (Donghwa, Dongnam, Daedong, Kyunggi, and Chungchung) were suspended and ordered to merge with stronger banks. The rest survived, but with strong restructuring conditions, such as change of management, reduction of workforce, and new equity financing. As a result of these measures, financial market stability returned; banks again began to lend with falling interest rates.

Financial reforms continued after 1998. Subsequent reforms have continued to emphasize the strengthening of central banking and financial supervision systems, financial-sector restructuring, prudential regulations, capital account liberalization, governance of financial institutions, and capital market reforms (Hahm and Lim 2004). Important reform measures included the introduction of financial holding companies (FHCs) (including the incorporation of Woori FHC and Shinhan FHC in 2001), a new set of prudential regulations limiting bank lending to one borrower and to large shareholders in 2002, and raising the bank ownership limit of domestic residents to 10 percent in 2002.

The Kim Dae Jung government also pursued corporate restructuring hand-in-hand with financial restructuring. Corporate and financial restructurings were inseparable because corporate-sector insolvency had driven Korean banks into their own insolvency. Since the 1980s, Korean companies had been seeing their profitability decline even as they increased their borrowings. By the time the crisis came, most large Korean firms were already having difficulty servicing their debts.

On January 13, 1998, Kim Dae Jung, then president-elect, reached an agreement with corporate leaders on five principles of corporate restructuring: enhancing transparency in accounting and management, resolving mutual payment guarantees among *chaebol* members, improving the financial structure of firms, streamlining business activities, and strengthening managers' accountability. By February, the government was ready to implement the principles after revising ten relevant laws.

The reliability of the accounting data of Korean firms became an issue because murky accounting practices allowed firms to bypass restrictions on investment and transfer pricing and discouraged foreign investment. In response, the Kim Dae Jung administration pushed the revision of the Outside Auditor Law to accelerate the adoption of consolidated financial statements and require listed firms to establish an outside auditor selection committee. The National Assembly passed these revisions on February 14, 1998. Consolidated financial statements provided more accurate information about the *chaebol* financial conditions by showing internal transactions among *chaebol* subsidiaries, including their cross-shareholdings and mutual payment guarantees. The government also strengthened the role of outside auditors by having them selected by a committee of shareholders and creditor banks rather than by controlling shareholders alone and by increasing the penalty that the outside auditors had to pay for any wrongdoings.

The government moved to resolve the issue of mutual payment guarantees by prohibiting the new issuance of such guarantees among the *chaebol* subsidiaries, beginning on April 1, 1998, and requiring the *chaebol* to phase out existing ones by March 2000. Such authority was granted to the government by the revision of the Fair Trade Law made on February 14, 1998.

To induce corporations to reduce their debts, the government directed banks to negotiate financial restructuring agreements with their debtor companies by April. A total of sixty-four conglomerates or debtor groups were directed to this program, and the five largest *chaebol,* in particular, were asked to reduce their debt ratios below 200 percent by the end of 1999. Officially, these agreements between the banks and *chaebol* were voluntary, but there was no doubt that the government was deeply involved. To discourage future corporate borrowings, the government revised the corporate tax law on February 14 to disallow tax deductions of interest payments on excessive borrowings beginning in 2000.

The government also relied on the banks to close insolvent firms and force the *chaebol* to streamline their business activities through liquidating and consolidating subsidiaries. This included exchanges of subsidiaries among the *chaebol* (called big deals) and other restructuring measures. On June 18, the banks announced a list of fifty-five insolvent firms, including twenty *chaebol* subsidiaries, which were to close. Other firms, judged to be troubled if not insolvent, were required to enter into work-out plans with their main creditor bank, under which the troubled firms would receive additional financial support in return for restructuring efforts. The work-out plan has been applied to the smaller *chaebol,* those ranked sixth or below in total sales.

The fifth and last principle of corporate restructuring aimed at holding owner-managers accountable for their decisions. Although the *chaebol* owner-managers had exercised effective control over their subsidiaries, they held positions with questionable legal status, such as group chairman. Thus, they were not legally liable for the damage their actions may have caused. To address this problem, the government changed the regulations to force *chaebol* to abolish the office of group chairman and appoint owner-managers to the board of at least one of the member firms. To enhance the monitoring of corporate decision making, the government required listed firms to appoint outside directors by revising the regulations on listing in the stock market in February 1999. The government further strengthened minority shareholder rights in May 1999 by lowering a minimum-share requirement (from 1 to 0.01 percent) for filing a derivative suit. Such a suit represents a personal liability suit against management for an illegal activity or a serious breach of due diligence. Efforts to enhance the rights of minority shareholders had begun with the Kim Young Sam administration, and subsequently a popular grassroots movement had developed led by the prominent citizen group People's Solidarity for Participatory Democracy (Jang 1999). These changes in corporate governance have allowed citizen groups, acting as representatives of minority shareholders, and sometimes foreign investors, to uncover questionable transactions in several prominent *chaebol* firms, including SK Telecom and Samsung Electronics. Many predicted that the new corporate governance system, more than any other reform, would bring about fundamental changes in the way companies are run in Korea because foreign shareholders, whose number increased rapidly as a result of financial liberalization, have started demanding accountability and board representation.

After 1998, the focus of corporate reform moved on to competition policy and corporate corruption. The shift in emphasis was made necessary by the *chaebol* postcrisis expansion. In August 1999, the government added three new principles of corporate reform: improved management structure of secondary financial institutions, a limit on *chaebol* equity investment, and prevention of irregular inheritance and gift giving. The government also restored the thirty-group-designation system under which the investment decisions of the thirty largest business conglomerates are closely monitored.

The Postcrisis Performance of the Korean Economic System

How did these institutional reforms change the structure of the Korean economic system? Describing reform measures is one thing, but measuring their actual impact objectively is another. We must also distinguish performance from the set of institutions necessary to achieve the level of desired performances. Note that the main criticism directed at the Korean developmental state was its lack of financial discipline. Korean banks and companies under the developmental state were opaque and unaccountable, thus vulnerable to excessive borrowing/investment and lending.

Are Korean banks and corporations more transparent and accountable now than before the crisis? Although it sounds like a simple question, answering it is actually quite complex. The main problem is the lack of data. Even indirect measures such as survey data are not adequate. Although the *Global Competitiveness Report* (World Economic Forum 2002, 2004, 2006) offers some relevant data,[1] none of the financial transparency data I report here covers the entire period of this study (table 12.1). The data on insider trading covers the period between 1996 and 2000, and as of 2000, the level of financial market transparency shows no real evidence of significant improvement (table 12.2). The scores on the quality of disclosure requirements

Table 12.1 Financial market transparency[a]

	1999	2000
Korea	4.73	4.60
Japan	5.25	5.30
China	3.71	4.30
Mean	5.16	5.10
Mean + SD	5.92	5.89

Sources: World Economic Forum (2002, 2004, 2006).
[a] SD, standard deviation.

1. The relevant survey questions in the *Global Competitiveness Report* are: (1) "Is the level of financial disclosure required extensive and detailed?" and (2) "Is insider trading not common in the domestic stock market?" (World Economic Forum 2002, 2004, 2006).

and the prevalence of insider trading for Korea also remained well below world averages until 2000, suggesting that financial market transparency continues to be a problem.

However, the survey data suggest that corporate governance is improving. Although progress was slow in the first seven years, the evaluation of the effectiveness of corporate boards began to show a marked improvement starting in 2003. In 2005, the Korean score on the effectiveness of corporate boards surpassed the world mean for the first time (table 12.3). The effectiveness of boards is, of course, only one of the many conditions for good corporate governance. Thus, instead of evaluating each component of good corporate governance, it may be more useful to evaluate the impact of corporate governance on share prices. Here the signs are not very encouraging. In spite of all the progress that has occurred in the area of institutional reform, there remains a significant "Korea discount" on share prices. The price/earnings ratio for Korean shares averaged 7.6 in 2003, well below 14.6 in Taiwan and 9.7 in Thailand.

Therefore, it is fair to conclude that, although there are clearly areas of progress, especially in enforcing corporate discipline, the overall assessment of institutional performance after ten years of reform cannot yet be considered to be unequivocally positive. In fact, the limited data indicate that the levels of transparency and accountability are still far from the global best practice.

Table 12.2 Insider trading, 1996–2000[a]

	1996	1997	1998	1999	2000
Korea	3.81	4.30	3.74	4.10	3.80
Japan	4.85	5.66	5.05	5.26	5.60
China	3.47	3.62	3.31	3.45	3.40
Mean	3.87	4.39	4.34	4.31	4.26
Mean + SD	4.66	5.33	5.19	5.24	5.14

Sources: World Economic Forum (2002, 2004, 2006).
[a] SD, standard deviation.

Table 12.3 Effectiveness of corporate boards in Korea and Japan, 1996–2005[a]

	1996	1997	1998	1999	2000	2001	2002	2003	2004	2005
Korea	3.67	3.30	2.88	3.63	3.90	3.50	3.8	4.40	4.20	4.90
Japan	3.85	3.93	3.62	4.14	4.10	2.90	2.2	4.40	4.80	4.60
Mean	3.90	4.21	4.13	4.53	4.44	4.14	3.97	4.46	4.53	4.56
Mean + SD	4.39	4.80	4.82	5.16	5.03	4.97	3.18	5.27	3.93	3.93
Mean − SD	3.41	3.62	3.44	3.90	3.85	3.31	4.76	3.82	5.13	5.18

Sources: World Economic Forum (2002, 2004, 2006).
[a] Where corporate governance by investors and boards of directors in each country is characterized on a scale in which 1 = management has little accountability and 7 = investors and boards exert strong supervision of management decisions. SD, standard deviation.

Table 12.4 Transparency International Corruption Perceptions Index for South Korea, Japan, and Taiwan, 1996–2005[a]

	South Korea		Japan		Taiwan	
Year	Rank	CPI score[b]	Rank	CPI score[b]	Rank	CPI score[b]
1996	27	5.0	17	7.1	29	5.0
1997	34	4.3	21	6.6	31	5.0
1998	43	4.2	25	5.8	29	5.3
1999	50	3.8	25	6.0	28	5.6
2000	48	4.0	23	6.4	28	5.5
2001	42	4.2	21	7.1	27	5.9
2002	40	4.5	20	7.1	29	5.6
2003	50	4.3	21	7.0	30	5.7
2004	47	4.5	24	6.9	35	5.6
2005	40	5.0	21	7.3	32	5.9

Source: Transparency International (2006).
[a] CPI, Corruption Perceptions Index.
[b] Maximum CPI score = 10.

General lack of progress in the quality of corporate governance is consistent with other governance indicators. Transparency International, for example, reports that the perceived level of corruption in Korean society has not improved at all. The Korean corruption perceptions index score in 2005 was the same as that in 1996, suggesting that ten years of reform simply brought Korea back to where it was before the crisis (table 12.4). In fact, from a comparative perspective, Korea's relative performance has significantly worsened. Whereas Japan and Taiwan have maintained their relative positions over the past ten years, the Korean transparency ranking fell to fortieth in 2005 from the precrisis rank of twenty-seventh (table 12.4).

The Structure of the Korean Economic System

The reason for the slow progress in institutional performance may be that change takes time. This possibility should be given serious consideration because Korea is still in a transition period. It may take time before the newly reformed economic system significantly improves the governance of Korean banks and companies.

If the lagged-effect story is true, we should redirect our attention to the structure of the economic system as the source of significant institutional change. In particular, I pay close attention to the structures of governance in the financial and corporate sectors. In the financial sector, the key to understanding structural change is the role of the government, that is, whether the structure of the financial system has changed in ways that give it a sufficient level of independence from the government.

Key indicators for a market-based financial sector are the ownership of financial institutions and the development of the capital market. We cannot talk about meaningful market reforms if the government owns commercial banks. Furthermore, allowing foreign ownership of Korean banks and companies is also important. Given the level of development of the Korean financial market, foreign participation is considered critical to ensuring the smooth operation of market principles in financial markets.

The growth of the capital market is another indicator in considering the transformation of the Korean developmental state. The bank-centered financial system was an integral part of the developmental state. If the financial system becomes more concentrated on the capital market, in effect moving away from reliance on bank lending, the government will find it more difficult to intervene in the financial sector but easier to promote market-based corporate discipline.

An analysis of the corporate sector should, on the other hand, focus on the structure of corporate governance, that is, whether family control of the *chaebol* has weakened. Many believe that a desire to maintain control through family ties is the main cause of poor corporate governance in Korea. The problem of family control is especially serious in Korea because the dominant family, despite holding only a very small equity stake, usually maintains effective control of its business group. Thus, it is important to investigate the effects of the crisis and subsequent reforms on family control of the *chaebol*.

Let me begin with a discussion of broader change in the governance structure of the Korean economic system. One important indicator of the general role of government in the economy is the level of economic freedom. Economic freedom data are collected from *Economic Freedom of the World: 2006 Annual Report* (Gwartney and Lawson 2006). It measures the degrees of economic freedom present in five major areas: (1) size of government (expenditures, taxes and enterprises), (2) legal structure and security of property rights, (3) access to sound money, (4) freedom to trade internationally, and (5) regulation of credit, labor, and business. Because the index in Gwartney and Lawson (2006) relies mostly on third-party data, it can be calculated back to as early as 1970.

The Korean economy as a whole has become freer since the economic crisis. The *Economic Freedom of the World* score increased to 7.07 in 2004 from 6.33 in 1990 (table 12.5). However, considering that the world mean also increased during the same period, we should add that the relative economic freedom of Korea does not seem to have changed much. Indeed, in 2004, it was ranked thirty-fifth, which was better than in 1995 (forty-eighth), worse than in 1990 (thirty-fourth), the same as in 1980, and worse than in 1970 (thirtieth).

Outside views of the change in the financial sector have been positive. The IMF, for example, reports that government influence over financial markets has been reduced significantly:

> Directed credit has been abolished, protectionist barriers largely eliminated, the exchange rate floated. The bulk of the banking system has been placed in private hands, while the *chaebol* have been restructured and their leverage reduced to US levels. As a result, Korea now has one of the more open and liberal economies in the emerging market universe. Foreign investors, for example, now hold 43 percent of equity market capitalization, the 4th highest share in the world. (International Monetary Fund [IMF] 2005b, 5)

Table 12.5 Economic Freedom Index for Korea, Japan, and China, 1970–2004[a]

	1970	1975	1980	1985	1990	1995	2000	2001	2002	2003	2004
Korea	5.36	5.36	5.65	5.70	6.33	6.75	6.63	6.97	6.91	6.93	7.07
Japan	6.22	5.88	6.38	6.45	7.10	6.95	7.33	7.04	6.95	7.42	7.48
China	N/A	N/A	3.84	4.81	4.25	4.91	5.82	5.88	5.81	5.86	5.66
Mean	5.75	5.17	5.14	5.18	5.46	5.91	6.39	6.41	6.41	6.41	6.47
Mean + SD	6.89	6.29	6.26	6.42	6.81	7.22	7.46	7.40	7.39	7.41	7.51

Source: Gwartney and Lawson (2006); data from http://www.freetheworld.com (accessed February 15, 2007).
[a] The index measures the degree to which the policies and institutions of countries are supportive of economic freedom. Thirty-eight components and subcomponents are used to construct a summary index and to measure the degree of economic freedom in five areas: (1) size of government, (2) legal structure and protection of property rights, (3) access to sound money, (4) international exchange, and (5) regulation. Scores range from 1 (lowest) to 10 (highest). N/A, not available; SD, standard deviation.

Table 12.6 Foreign ownership and control of commercial banks, December 2005

Banks	History	Foreign ownership	Foreign control
Kookmin	Kookmin + Housing (2001)	85.7	No
Korea Exchange Bank	To Lone Star (2003)	74.2	Yes (Lone Star Funds)
Hana	Hana + Seoul (2001)	72.3	No
Shinhan	Shinhan + Choheung (2003)	57.1	No
Woori	Hanil + Commerce (1998)	11.1	No
Citibank	Citibank + Hanmi (2004)	100.0	Yes
SC Cheil	Standard Chartered + Cheil (2005)	100.0	Yes

Source: Various newspaper articles.

The most striking change in the banking sector is the rise of foreign ownership and control in the banking sector. Among the seven nationwide commercial banks operating now, only Woori FHC is still owned by the government; almost all commercial banks were effectively nationalized in the wake of the financial crisis. Table 12.6 shows that foreign investors now have majority stakes in six out of the seven commercial banks and have gained control of three (Korea Exchange Bank [KEB], Citibank, and Standard Chartered Bank). It has been estimated that foreign-controlled banks account for 33.3–50.0 percent of bank assets in Korea.

The other three banks (Kookmin, Hana, and Shinhan), in which foreign investors have a majority shareholding but lack a controlling interest, have at least one foreign director on their boards, indicating that foreign investors have gained some influence over the direction of bank management in those banks (table 12.7). This suggests that since the crisis began, the ownership of Korean commercial banks has been effectively transferred from the government to foreign capital rather than to domestic capital.

Another important development is the growth of the capital market. From the initial stages of crisis management, the government undertook a series of reform

Table 12.7 Board directors at domestic banks

Non-foreign-controlled banks	Executive	Nonexecutive	Total
Kookmin	4 (0*)	9 (1)	13 (1)
Hana	4 (0)	9 (3)	13 (3)
Shinhan	3 (0)	12 (1)	15 (1)
Woori	2 (0)	7 (0)	9 (0)

Source: Bank websites: www.kbstar.com, www.hanabank.com, www.shinhan.com, and www.wooribank.com.
* Number of foreigners.

policies aimed at strengthening the capital market. Its adjustments focused on the deregulation and liberalization of capital and foreign exchange markets. At the same time, various reform measures were introduced to promote corporate governance and to upgrade accounting and disclosure standards to facilitate investment and to buttress the self-correcting function of capital markets. The qualitative nature of these reform measures was clearly geared toward shifting Korea from a bank-based to a market-based financial system (Lim and Hahm 2006).

Foreign investors have also been the main source of investment funds in the equity market. The share of equity-market capitalization by foreign investors has been rising steadily, reaching 43.3 percent in 2005. But they have not been active in other capital markets, such as corporate bonds.

Although the structural conditions favorable to a more market-based financial system seem to exist, it is still too early to conclude that a full-fledged market system has been established in Korea. For instance, Hahm and Lim (2004) computed the time series of the size, activity, and efficiency indices of Demirguc-Kunt and Levine (1999) to characterize the transitional pattern of the financial system in Korea. As figure 12.1 shows, the Korean system was evolving toward a more market-based system when the crisis struck. However, evidence based solely on this index suggests that Korea has in recent years gradually been returning to a bank-based system (Lim and Hahm 2006). This is also consistent with the trend in the size of the capital market. The size of the capital market, as measured by the ratio of the total capitalization of stocks and bonds to GDP, has remained relatively constant since 2000, suggesting no follow-through on the initial embrace of the capital market. The structure of corporate governance has also been slow to change, as the persistence of the family control of the *chaebol* shows. Although the proportion of shares that they directly own has declined, the owner families have been able to maintain control through extensive intersubsidiary shareholdings. Table 12.8 shows that the average in-group share for the top thirty *chaebol* owned by the families and by subsidiaries was 43.4 percent in 2000, which is almost equal to the 1995 and 1996 levels, even though the proportion of family-owned shares fell to 4.5 percent in 2000 from 10.5 percent in 1995 and 10.3 percent in 1996.

This growing gap between the shares directly owned and the shares actually controlled by the owner families shows that the *chaebol* are even more vulnerable to

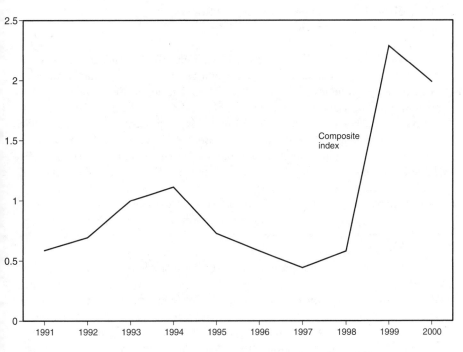

Figure 12.1 Composite index for market-based financial system for Korea, 1991–2000.
Source: Hahm (2004).

Table 12.8 In-group ownership share for the top *chaebol*

	1995	1996	1997	1998	1999	2000	2001	2002	2005
Top 30	43.3	44.1	43.0	44.5	49.6	43.4			
Family	10.5	10.3	8.5	7.9	5.4	4.5			
Subsidiaries	32.8	33.8	34.5	36.6	45.1	38.9			
Top 5			45.2	46.6	53.5				
Family									
Subsidiaries			36.6						
Samsung	49.3	49.0	46.7	44.6					31.13
Family									4.41
Subsidiaries									26.72

Sources: Korea Fair Trade Commission; Yoo (1999).

the threat of the expropriation of minority shareholders by controlling shareholders than before. Samsung is a typical case. In 2005, the founder's family controlled 31.13 percent of shares and their direct ownership share fell to 4.41 percent. Before the crisis, the founder's family had controlled close to 50 percent of shares (table 12.8).

The Political Economy of Reform: The Role
of Financial Globalization

Let me summarize the findings so far. First, Korean banks and companies have failed to reach transparency and accountability standards comparable to those of their competitors in advanced economies. Hard data supporting strong improvement over time are also lacking. Second, the movement of the financial system toward a market-based system has been progressing, albeit at an uneven pace. The role of government in the economy, as measured by the economic freedom index, has been reduced. Third, foreign investors have taken a dominant position in the Korean banking sector after the Korean government sold most of the restructured banks to foreign investors. Foreign investors also own substantial stakes in the bulk of Korean blue-chip companies, but do not yet control them.

Given these findings, the best story that we can tell at this point is that foreign capital has made inroads into Korean financial markets and even dominates the banking sector.[2] Now our task is to explain this outcome analytically.

Before doing so, let me emphasize that this outcome was by no means predetermined or obvious at the outset. The postcrisis policy environment was fluid and dynamic. It was not clear ex ante which policies or groups would be blamed for the crisis, who would frame the issues and offer solutions, and which issues would emerge as key reform issues. The difference in the response in Korea, compared to that of Thailand, Indonesia, Malaysia, and the Philippines, as shown by Thomas Pepinsky (chap. 11) and Allen Hicken (chap. 10 in this volume), makes clear how important domestic politics was to the specificity of national responses to the crisis.

It is also important to evaluate this outcome normatively. Can we consider this a success or failure? Although this exercise is necessarily subjective, it serves useful purposes. Factors to consider in evaluating reform outcomes include the gap between outcomes and the objectives originally stated by reformers, the gap between reality and the expectations of various stakeholders, and objective measures of change or distance to an ideal-type market economy model.[3] For now, I do not

---

2. For similar views on the postcrisis character of the Korean economic system, see Lee and Han (2006); Lim and Jang (2006).

3. Identifying meaningful patterns in the reform process is also crucial because they can serve as additional dependent variables. One way of conceptualizing the patterns of reform is the sequencing of reform measures. For example, the problems of corporate reform in Korea can be divided into several largely distinct subareas: restructuring of insolvent firms, corporate organization (i.e., *chaebol* organization), and corporate governance (transparency and accountability of management and the organization and role of board of directors). Among these areas, the government had to decide which area should receive priority. The problem did not end here. Each area, in turn, had its own set of alternatives. Three different policy instruments, for example, were available for improving corporate governance: external discipline (the market for corporate control and institutional investors), internal disciple (outside directors, cumulative voting, and small shareholder rights), and accounting transparency (which falls in between the areas of external and internal discipline). Because the government could not attack every problem area and choose every instrument at the same time, it had to sequence them according to their priorities, which was inherently a political process. An interesting issue in Korea is why there has been

hesitate to make sweeping value judgments on the outcome. If the postcrisis reform process has been a success, our findings indicate that it has succeeded primarily in freeing the banking sector from government control.

How do we explain this outcome? First, we should consider the initial conditions that prevailed before the buildup of reform pressure. At least four variables characterized the initial conditions: the nature and severity of economic crisis, the initial level and composition of foreign-capital penetration, the preferences and capabilities of the bureaucracy, and the character and strength of domestic reform coalitions.

These four independent variables shape the relative bargaining power of the three main drivers of reform: foreign investors, bureaucrats, and pro-reform groups. The severity of the economic crisis and the existing level of foreign investment can indicate how influential foreign investors could be in forcing their agendas. We may argue that the more serious the crisis and the smaller the existing level of investment, the stronger the foreign investors will be. Using similar logic, we can evaluate the bargaining power of the other reform groups. But the policy preferences of pro-reform groups cannot be deduced ex ante because they depend on the economic and political conditions of each country.

Among the factors contributing to institutional change, the role of financial globalization is particularly noteworthy. After all, the crisis of the late 1990s began as a financial crisis. More important, unprecedented amounts of foreign capital have flowed into Korea as a result of the crisis, making foreign investors dynamic players in domestic policy and economic activities.

There have been a vast number of studies on economic reforms and financial globalization since the economic crisis of the late 1990s but they remain largely separate issues in the literature. Thus, it is hard to get a complete understanding of the interaction between foreign capital and economic reform, especially in regards to the active role that foreign investors played in reforming economic institutions. Even if we narrow our analysis to the role of foreign capital as the main driver of reform, the question of where and how active foreign capital participates in the reform process still remains. The actual impact of its political action on reform outcomes is not a central concern here. Instead, this approach will help us better understand how financial globalization translates into specific political actions by agents of international capital.

Foreign investors, even though they may differ among themselves in their specific orientations, typically have policy agendas that are distinct from the old Korean model and from many domestic stakeholders. This is fairly clear in cases in which foreign investors or their representatives make explicit policy demands during trade or bailout negotiations. Although there are certain reform policies that all foreign investors favor, different individual investors may have varied preferences in other

---

so much emphasis on small shareholder rights as opposed to accounting transparency. That is, this particular pattern of sequencing has to be explained.

areas, so it may be necessary to disaggregate them into politically meaningful sub-groups such as financial intermediaries, short-term investors, and long-term investors. In addition, some investors may reflect the national biases of the countries in which they are situated.

Conceptually, there are three ways in which foreign investors can contribute to institutional reform: (1) by advocating policy changes by the government, (2) by exercising their existing investor and shareholder rights, and (3) by implementing international best practices in their own operations and thus setting examples (see table 12.9).

There is no reason to assume that foreign influence involves simply the views of foreign investors on government activity. Foreign investors can and do monitor actions by the private sector. It is possible that foreign investors are much more effective in forcing domestic economic actors to comply with new rules than in having new rules adopted in the first place. If this is true, foreign investors may contribute considerably in narrowing the gap between formal rules and actual practices.

Table 12.9 Role of foreign capital in reform process[a]

Methods for exercising influence (in order of increasing causality)	Methodological issues
Ideas/persuasion	Foreign ideas are not uniform.
	Ideas are a difficult variable to measure.
	The effects of ideas are indirect.
Example making/competitive pressure	Foreign examples may not diffuse widely to domestic firms.
	It takes too long for global standards to drive out local standards in market competition.
	Foreign firms tend to adapt to local environment instead of seeking to change it.
The electronic herd	Capital flows respond to economic fundamentals, not
Credit ratings	necessarily to institutional performance.
	Financial markets suffer from herd behavior.
	Threat of exit is less effective against capital surplus countries.
International rule making	Institutional rules on second-generation reform issues
BIS	such as transparency, accountability, and prudential
IMF	regulations are still at an early stage of development.
OECD guidelines/conventions	Formal subscription to international rules does not always indicate effective compliance.
Ownership activism	Ownership activism is rarely coordinated.
Shareholder rights	Foreign investors are reluctant to take political action in the
Organizing associations	host country.
International certification	Only those who are already good seek international
Foreign listings	certification.
Bilateral interstate negotiations	Opportunities for bilateral negotiations are rare.
IMF	Bilateral negotiations tend to focus on market opening.
WTO	
Section 301	

Source: Mo and Okimoto (2006).
[a] BIS, Bank for International Settlements; IMF, International Monetary Fund; OECD, Organisation for Economic Cooperation and Development; WTO, World Trade Organization.

Political economic theory helps explain the pattern of political participation by foreign investors. Even if the role of foreign capital is minimal, it is still interesting to ask why that is the case (Amyx 2004c). Several variables are expected to affect the level and type of participation in the process of domestic reform. First, there are the initial conditions, in which some home countries are capital importers whereas others (e.g., Japan) are capital exporters. Also, configurations of foreign-capital portfolios (direct investment versus portfolio investment) and the existence of an external debt crisis may also be important initial factors. Second, there are government policies. The basic point here is that the host government policies toward different types of capital largely shape the environment in which foreign capital participates in the domestic policy process. The last group of variables can be loosely called domestic political variables, that is, those that determine the political strength of foreign capital such as the strength of traditional policy networks, the presence of domestic allies (such as nongovernmental organizations [NGOs] and reform-oriented bureaucrats), and the quality of idea markets (such as the media, think tanks, and experts).

Why Has Foreign Capital Been Influential in Korea?

In thinking about the factors contributing to the influence of foreign capital in Korea, we should first point out the Korean dependence on foreign capital before, during, and after the crisis. In 1996, Korea was a large capital importer. Because of large current-account deficits, Korea had to borrow from abroad to finance its deficits. Most of these foreign liabilities were external borrowings by Korean banks. But the dependence of Korean companies on foreign capital was relatively small. Foreign investors owned only 13.0 percent of Korean shares in 1996 and Korean firms rarely borrowed directly from foreign banks.

The Korean precrisis dependence on foreign capital (i.e., bank loans) necessarily made foreign capital the main actor in crisis management and postcrisis economic reforms. Foreign capital exercised influence in all stages of the reform process. At the bailout stage, it was the IMF that imposed foreign-capital-friendly conditions as part of its bailout program. At the restructuring stage, foreign banks and investors provided a significant portion of restructuring funds; after all, almost all foreign bank creditors restructured their existing loans through debt-restructuring negotiations with the Korean government. Even after Korean financial institutions recovered their health, foreign investors have been a constant source of reform pressure as short-term portfolio investors and long-term direct or strategic investors. In 2002, foreign investors owned 36.0 percent of Korean shares; the foreign share of Korean stocks reached 44.0 percent in 2004, but fell back to 38 percent by 2006 (*Korean Times*, September 17, 2006).

However, the unusual level of foreign-capital dependence does not tell the whole story. First, the government has been a strong supporter of foreign investors when the interests of both have been aligned in favor of corporate and financial reforms.

Most of the reform measures that Korea agreed to as part of the IMF bailout agreement were ones that the Kim Young Sam government had pursued before the crisis, and some of them were actually placed on the agenda by the government during the negotiations.

In the subsequent restructuring and reform processes, too, we can say that foreign capital was allowed to have influence. In a country such as Korea, where the government still has extensive powers of intervention at its disposal, it is appropriate to assume that large inflows of foreign capital are largely consistent with the core interests of the government. Reform-oriented Korean policymakers, regardless of their ideological orientations, have long sought to keep the Korean *chaebol* under control. More specifically, they have tried hard to prevent the *chaebol* from owning commercial banks, a policy designed to separate financial and industrial capital. When the government could no longer control the banking sector due to the forces of globalization and democratization, it allowed or induced foreign capital to hold a dominant position in Korean financial markets.

Second, it is important to note that civil society has also been favorable toward foreign capital for the same reason. Anti-*chaebol* sentiments are strong among NGO activists, and like government bureaucrats, they also saw foreign capital as a check on *chaebol* powers. Thus, the expansion of foreign capital into the Korean banking sector has been possible not only because the demand for foreign capital was strong in a country short on foreign capital but also because such expansion was consistent with the political interests of the government and activist groups.

The role of anti-*chaebol* sentiment in South Korean reform politics is not limited to the financial sector. It has shaped all other areas of reform, including corporate governance and political institutions, a point explored in depth by Peter Gourevitch (chap. 4 in this volume). Although it is true that the concentration of economic power in the hands of a few *chaebol* hinders the emergence of a genuinely open market economy in Korea, it is equally important to recognize that ministries and NGOs have their own self-interests in regulating the *chaebol* and that some of these interests may not be conducive to the promotion of a market economy.

Whether the influence of foreign capital will endure in Korea is not yet clear. First, the foreign investor interest in the Korean financial market may already have peaked. Foreign investment declined in 2005 and 2006, with a $10 billion outflow of investment in 2006 alone. As a result, the foreign share of Korean Composite Stock Price Index (KOSPI) stocks has decreased from 42 to 37 percent and is projected to go down to 35 percent (Klingner 2006). According to Bruce Klingner, short-term portfolio investors have concerns about the following factors:

1. The economy not doing as well as expected.
2. The North Korean situation adding uncertainty.
3. The government not proceeding on deregulation and economic reform as quickly as foreign investors would like.
4. A negative public and government attitude toward foreign private-equity firms, which represents future money, as shown by the hostility toward Lone Star and Newbridge.

5. The South Korean dividend payout ratio and investment profit margin never being as good as in other countries.

These push factors have contributed to the outflow of foreign capital from Korea over the last two years, but a strong pull factor has also been at work in global markets. China and India have been magnets for foreign capital, and this investment rush has reduced capital flows into other emerging countries, including South Korea. This investment-polarization phenomenon has been particularly acute in the banking sector in that foreign investors have gobbled up tens of billions of dollars worth of the shares of Chinese banks.

Second, foreign investors have not been as active politically as their size indicates. Generally, foreign portfolio investors, the dominant type of foreign investors in Korea, tend to exit (i.e., cut their losses and leave) rather than exercising voice (i.e., staying to pressure the government). This has also been the case in Korea. One way to resolve the apparent gap between the appearance and reality of foreign capital influence in reform politics is to evaluate its influence at different stages of reform. Some scholars argue that foreign investors tend to be influential in the issue-emergence stage (i.e., recognizing and framing the issues) (Hahm and Lim 2004; Tiberghien 2004). But they have limited ability to influence the process at later stages of reform politics, when reform measures are contested, adopted, and enforced in the domestic political arena.

Conclusion

The Korean experience since the 1997 financial crisis shows that financial globalization has finally caught up with Korean capitalism. External financial pressures have forced the Korean government, companies, and banks to change at a pace they do not find comfortable.

Nevertheless, it would be too early to declare the triumph of financial globalization over the Korean national political economy. Both on performance and structural dimensions, the Korean financial and corporate systems are still far short of global standards. It is clear that the old model has been abandoned, but where relations are heading and whether governments, corporations, and the financial systems are behaving as they are expected to do in a market economy are less clear.

The Korean case also demonstrates the limits on financial globalization. Without powerful domestic partners, it would have been difficult for foreign capital to have been an effective force for reform in Korea. It was the overlapping and combined interests of the government and civil society, together with those of foreign capital, that produced a banking sector dominated by foreign capital.

The control of the domestic banking sector by foreign investors may create new uncertainties and vulnerabilities. Concerns have already been raised over the business practices of foreign-controlled banks. One criticism is that they do not lend enough to industrial companies and that, when they do, they tend to favor politically safe companies such as small and medium enterprises (SMEs). Short-term considerations also seem to dominate foreign-controlled bank lending policies. For instance, after plunging into the consumer credit card business at great cost, they now have the bulk of their assets tied up in unstable real estate markets. It will be interesting to see whether the Korean government will be able to achieve its industrial policy objectives with a foreign-controlled banking sector.

The Political Economy of East Asia

Directions for the Next Decade

Andrew MacIntyre, T. J. Pempel,
and John Ravenhill

In this concluding chapter, we present our effort to look forward rather than back. We reflect on what we see as key forces for change across several dimensions of the political economy of the region, most of them unleashed by the crisis of 1997–98. Although we draw on the themes and issues explored in the other chapters of this volume, we make no attempt in this chapter to synthesize all that has come before. We focus here on three key dimensions of the evolving political economy of East Asia: (1) the East Asian model and the changing patterns of business-government relations, (2) trends in regional integration and cohesion, and (3) the extent of the vulnerability of the region to future economic shocks.

The East Asian Model Today

The notion that a single East Asian model exists that is capable of capturing the essence of the political economy of all the high-growth economies of the region has always been more than a little problematic. Beyond the simple commonality of high rates of economic growth, important differences have long been present among the cases. This was something the literature on the region came increasingly to recognize as the pace of economic growth in Southeast Asia accelerated in the late 1980s (Mackie (1988) provides an early cogent argument). Reflect, for a moment, on the basic contrasts between the first wave of capital-intensive economies—Japan, South Korea, Taiwan, and Singapore—and the second wave of resource-rich economies in Southeast Asia. Moreover, the third wave—the formerly socialist economies, dominated by China—manifest very different characteristics. Even *within* these categories, enormous differences existed on key dimensions of political economy. Consider, for instance, the contrast in the treatment of foreign direct investment (FDI) between Singapore and South Korea or the differences in state capacity among Indonesia, Malaysia, and Thailand. Further complicating the discussion of any single East Asian model has been the fact that the pivotal episodes of sustained high growth took place at different times. Roughly speaking, in Japan the transformative decades (after World War II) were the 1950s, 1960s, and 1970s; for the newly industrialized countries (NICs) they were the 1960s, 1970s, and 1980s; for the resource-rich Southeast Asian nations they were the 1970s, 1980s, and 1990s, and for China and Vietnam they were the 1980s and 1990s to the present.

Nevertheless, there is a loose sense in which the scholarly literature and policy discourses employed the notion of a single East Asian model as a kind of shorthand for a mix of policy, political, and institutional arrangements that pertained in varying degrees across the high-growth economies of the region. More than anything else, what drew attention to East Asia as a region over the past three to four decades was its very rapid rate of economic growth. Enormous analytic energy was devoted to making sense of the spectacular economic transformation of countries across the region, much of which is summarized in a loose conventional wisdom, commonly referred to as the East Asian model. Most accounts highlighting policy aspects of the East Asian model have emphasized macroeconomic management, investment in public goods such as education, and opening to the international economy, with debate about the extent to which government intervention in particular sectors contributed to the result (Wade 1992; World Bank 1993; Asian Development Bank [ADB] 1997; Yusuf 2001).

Driving such policies were the political preferences of the coalitions in power, which were generally conservative in character and (for a range of reasons) strongly emphasized the pursuit of industrial development. These ruling coalitions worked within institutional frameworks that concentrated power heavily in the executive branch of government in ways ranging from straightforward authoritarian regimes to the former Japanese single-dominant-party model. The common result was that governments enjoyed substantial autonomy in coordinating and controlling policy and in limiting demands from societal groups that might force major diversions from a maximization of economic growth. A central element in the political economy of these countries was the close and cooperative ties between business and government, ranging from depersonalized institutional relationships to cozy crony ties (Deyo 1989; Haggard 1990; MacIntyre 1994; Root 1996).[1]

If this stylized combination of policy, politics, and institutions captures something essential in the political economy of East Asian countries during the various key decades of their respective industrial transformations, we argue it is much less

---

1. Some accounts went deeper still, focusing on systemic factors such as demographic and social make-up, international security conditions, and access to global markets (Woo 1991; Stubbs 1999; Doner, Ritchie, and Slater 2005).

useful today. Certainly, considerable continuity is evident postcrisis in the sound macroeconomic management pursued by countries in the region. Gross savings as a percentage of GDP are extraordinarily high across the region, averaging substantially more than 30 percent (with the notable exception of the Philippines). Inflation rates remain low. Governments continue to run budget deficits that are, at worst, only a small percentage of GDP. And, a continuing source of controversy with trading partners, they manage their exchange rates with an eye toward keeping their exports competitive, the consequence being that they enjoy substantial current-account surpluses.

Continuity may characterize what have been considered to be the core economic dimensions of the East Asian model; it is far less obvious in the political domain. This is clear from the changes in the institutional landscape, the political complexion of governments, the expansion of the media sector, and the heightened global economic engagement. Although by no means uniform, broad moves in these general directions enable us to talk of substantial changes in the underlying political economic patterns of the region. The East Asia of 2007 was not the East Asia of 1997, much less the East Asia of 1987 or 1977. Some elements in this story of change stem from the shocks and disruptions of 1997–98, but many others grow out of slower-moving but deeper-running processes of change unleashed by sustained high growth itself. And the international context within which East Asian governments have to develop their domestic and international strategies has changed dramatically. Four main aspects of change illustrate this: political and legal institutions, changing political preferences, the mass media and information flows, and global economic engagement.

Political and Legal Institutions

Perhaps the most fundamental changes bearing on the established conceptions about the East Asian political economy involve political and legal institutions. In essence, the domestic political frameworks of most of the countries are no longer characterized by such heavy concentrations of power as in the past. Not all of East Asia has moved quickly in this direction, and some countries have had partial ·countermovements. But the primary trend across most of the region has been toward a deconcentration of power. The executive branch of government is no longer so dominant relative to other branches of government and, significantly, there is a greater turnover among those in control of the executive branch. This has meant that political leaders are more constrained in their options and that, typically, the coordination of policy has involved an increasingly diverse set of actors, making it more difficult to pursue any single direction. No longer is policy as tightly controlled and as insulated from public pressures. Civil society actors have become much more significant. For the most part, these trends have been a function of democratization, democratic consolidation, and refinement of democratic institutions. Some cases have clearly stood apart, most conspicuously China, Vietnam, and Singapore, whereas Malaysia has seen at best minimal change in this direction.

However, in most cases—South Korea, Taiwan, Indonesia, Thailand (with a caveat for the military hiatus) and even the Philippines (when compared to the Marcos period)—changes have moved broadly in this direction. In the case of Japan, the last decade and a half has seen substantial refinement of democratic processes, with the bureaucracy becoming more responsive to elected politicians and the possibilities for a turnover in parliamentary control becoming much more real.

Closely related to changes in the national political architecture of the region have been shifts in legal institutions. Change on this front has been more gradual but apparent nonetheless. Throughout most of East Asia, the law had long functioned predominantly as a heavily subservient tool of executive governments. Today, this is less the case. In some cases—South Korea, Taiwan, Thailand, the Philippines, and Indonesia—there has been a marked shift since the height of their respective periods of rapid growth. Japan has had an independent judiciary throughout the postwar period, but it too has become more active. Interestingly, although the Chinese political executive remains all-powerful, we see the beginnings of judicial activity, at least in some civil and commercial matters.

Contrary to many liberal assertions, there is no necessary connection between independent and capable legal systems and levels of economic development, as the case of Singapore clearly illustrates (Jayasuriya 2003). But the significance of these changes for summary understandings of the political economy of the region is that, here again, we see further decentralization of power and greater contestation. More specifically, the increasing significance of the judicial sector has rendered close relationships between policymakers and large firms more susceptible to challenge. Local or foreign firms, aggrieved by collusive or other prejudicial policy conditions secured by their competitors or perhaps upstream suppliers, now have greater scope for seeking redress through the judicial system. Changes to judicial institutions, together with the weakening of executive control and increased political turnover, have made it much more difficult to sustain previous patterns of enduring and close relationships between government and business that are so often associated with the East Asian model.

Political Preferences

The second key dimension of change is the political complexion of governments across the region. Broadly speaking, East Asian governments have become less uniformly conservative in their political orientation. In particular, anticommunist national security preoccupations have receded; there is less emphasis on internal political controls and less common automatic presumption that large business interests are to be preferred over competing interests such as labor and the environment. Although causality runs in both directions here, institutional changes (broadly speaking, the repercussions of democratization) have opened the door to this development. With the marked exception of China, across much of East Asia today there is less of an all-consuming conviction that full-speed economic growth is of the utmost national importance. Less, that is, than was the case with Japan during its post–World War II reconstruction phase, than was the case for the NICs facing what they saw as severe external security threats during the cold war, and than was the case for the resource-rich Southeast Asian states facing what they saw as severe internal security threats, also during the cold war. Other substantive priorities are receiving more official attention than previously, particularly equity and distributional considerations but also environmental considerations. And, as shown by the data presented in MacIntyre, Pempel, and Ravenhill (chap. 1 in this volume), governments have given priority to reducing vulnerability to external shocks by accumulating massive reserves of foreign currency at the expense of higher rates of domestic investment and economic growth.

In varying degrees, we see this change in the complexion of politics in Japan, South Korea, Taiwan, Thailand, the Philippines, Indonesia, and even Malaysia. To be sure, there are still large conservative parties in all these countries, and they remain influential in setting the policy agenda. But, in most cases, they are either less conservative than before and/or face serious competition from nonconservative parties. For the most part, this shift in the center of political gravity has been gradual, but in some cases, it was quite stark and grew out of the financial crisis. Where governments with pro-reform agendas and constituencies were in power or came to power soon after, they introduced dramatic reforms in areas such as corporate governance and financial regulation. South Korea, Japan, and Indonesia provide the clearest illustrations of this.

The Mass Media and Information Flows

The development of increasingly sophisticated markets for information supplied by local and foreign media companies is frequently overlooked. Yet it is an important dimension of change in its own right, with significant implications for the political economy of the region. In the past, most East Asian countries were characterized by radical information asymmetries. To varying degrees, political leaders were able to maintain control of information and public debate, sharing policy-relevant information with allies in the corporate sector on a discretionary basis and limiting what was known by potential challengers to the dominant regime. This has changed very markedly over the past ten to twenty years due to democratization, the gradual strengthening of legal institutions, and the development of technologies that have combined to lower the cost of information dissemination. Furthermore, the growth of vibrant media companies throughout the region has expanded the competition to distribute information. The widespread penetration of the Internet, despite the efforts of many governments to constrict its availability, has further opened up vast new access to global information pools.

Around East Asia today, markets are much better informed, political oppositions are much better informed, and publics are much better informed. In terms of the classic East Asian model, the net effect has been to further reduce the dominance of the executive branch of government, to fuel challenges to close business-government relationships regarded as collusive and, more broadly, to open up public discussion about policy. All these diminish prior patterns of centralized governments that sought to, and were capable of, controlling and coordinating policy in partnership with sections of the corporate sector.

Global Engagement

The fourth broad trend across the region that shows evidence of radical shifts from past patterns is the increasingly global engagement of most East Asian economies. Before the crisis, almost all of the East Asian economies were active participants in global trade. Their involvement has become even more pronounced, so that the ratio of East Asian exports to the overall GDP of the region is now higher than in any other region in the world, surpassing even Europe (World Bank 2006, 4). Changes in investment have occurred more slowly, but foreign capital is increasingly present in much of the region, most strikingly, in China but also in places such as Korea and Japan, which for much of their developmental phases were effectively closed to FDI. Indeed, this is one area in which we see a measure of convergence across the region; unlike the past, today all of East Asia is actively seeking FDI.

Although inferring causality from increased global economic engagement has its own problems, continued export access and continued capital flows necessitate increased sensitivity to developments elsewhere; the combination brings with it enhanced potential for internal change. Moreover, the encroachment of multilateral regulatory regimes imposes new compliance obligations on Asian governments. There is increased evidence of substantial change in the area of corporate governance, for example, with, not surprisingly, Japan and South Korea being the most conspicuous instances. Interestingly, however, as Edward Steinfeld shows (chap. 9 in this volume), significant changes are evident in China as well, although more in terms of corporate behavior than in the regulatory environment. Greater global economic engagement brings new commercial players, greater contestability, and greater constraints imposed on policymakers by events elsewhere. And these all represent significant changes from precrisis patterns.

To summarize, we see important change in these four areas. In some cases, changes have gradually unfolded over several decades; in others, it has been a rapid response to the upheavals of 1997–98. Our concern here is to draw attention to such changes and to the fact that, cumulatively, they represent substantial departures from established conceptions of how East Asian political economies have functioned. We emphasize our caution in making these summary judgments because, just as the conventional wisdom about East Asia was never more than a loose ideal type, trying to capture the essence of the political economy of the region today is fraught with scholarly danger. This said, we nevertheless make a strong claim about the broad direction of change.

East Asia today is marked by less-strong executive governments, greater political pluralism and contestation, more frequent political turnover, stronger legal systems, less-close and -stable relationships between business and government, much easier access to information, and greater engagement with the global economy. In short, in important respects, the political economies of many parts of East Asia are now organized differently and operate differently. This makes it much more challenging to pursue the sorts of highly disciplined policy regimes that are generally believed to have underpinned the spectacular economic transformations of most of the countries in the region.

In addition to eroding the potential for highly disciplined policy regimes, these changes also erode the scope for continuing the various patterns of close relationship between firms and policymakers. Greater contestability, greater turnover in political leadership, somewhat stronger legal institutions, greater diversity in the political preferences of ruling parties, reduced information asymmetries, and greater market contestability through foreign investment—all these trends have the effect of diminishing the scope for close and stable relationships between political and corporate leaders. We can see this even in the extreme form of such relationships—the highly personalized crony capitalist relationships so conspicuous in much of Southeast Asia during the initial decades of rapid growth. Cronyism has certainly not disappeared in East Asia (anymore than it has in other economies), but it is generally no longer as prominent. It persists because the potential benefits to firms that are able to establish close ties to powerful political leaders are so great, but they are becoming less conspicuous as the political and legal environments become less conducive. Acquiring and sustaining such relationships for more than a few years have become much more difficult and risky than in the past. In place of the long-term close relationships of the past, many of which were a key component of a common commitment to long-term national growth, we see more short-term political exchange relationships, with both parties in pursuit of more immediate gratification of their particular needs.

Crisis and the East Asian Political Economy

The contagion from the collapse of the Thai baht did not discriminate among regime types in East Asia—it was equally devastating for what had always been regarded as one of the strongest states in the region (Korea) as for one of its weakest (Indonesia). State capacity apparently had no impact on the vulnerability to crisis. Of far greater significance were basic economic variables, particularly the volume of foreign exchange reserves that countries held and the ratio between these and short-term foreign debt.

What association was there between the crisis, state capacity, and changes in the political economy of the region? It is tempting to posit a straightforward relationship between the depth of the crisis and the subsequent magnitude of changes made in the domestic political economies—a correlation apparently borne out in our two Southeast Asian paired comparisons. In both comparisons, the more severely affected economies (Indonesia and Thailand) experienced much greater postcrisis change in their domestic political economies than did the less affected economies (Malaysia and the Philippines). In both cases, the crisis led directly to the fall of the incumbent political regimes—Chavalit in Thailand and Soeharto in

Indonesia—opening the way for reform-minded governments. In Korea, the onset of the crisis coincided with the presidential election of November 1997 and may have contributed to the narrow victory of Kim Dae Jung over the ruling party candidate Lee Hoi Chang. Certainly, the severity of the crisis made it easier for Kim to pursue an active reform agenda once in office.

Such a straightforward argument about the relationship between the depth of the crisis, change in regime, and subsequent policy change, however, removes agency from the equation and denies the saliency of ideas. It discounts the capacity of governments to learn, not least from the experience of other countries in the region that may be suffering far deeper crises than the one afflicting their own economy. Nowhere is this capacity for learning from the crisis elsewhere more evident than in China. As Steinfeld (chap. 9 in this volume) shows, the Chinese leadership adopted a radically different set of economic policies in direct response to its interpretation of the causes of the crises elsewhere in the region.

Before the crisis, Beijing had looked to Korea as a potential model for the modernization of the Chinese economy and particularly to the Korean *chaebol* as a potential prototype for reforming state-owned enterprises. This enthusiasm disappeared with the crisis. Indeed, the crisis effectively marked the death knell of the developmental state approach across the region. In an increasingly integrated global economy, in which participation in production networks is often the key to penetrating foreign markets, the old-style developmental state approach that attempted to exclude foreign participation in domestic production processes has outlived its usefulness. To some extent, then, we see greater uniformity in developmental models across the region in the postcrisis period than at any time in the previous half century; all states (with the exceptions of the pariah regimes of Myanmar and the Democratic Republic of Korea) now are open to foreign investment and have shown themselves keen to enter into free trade agreements (FTAs) with their major extraregional trading partners. When these agreements involve industrialized countries as trading partners (with many states keen to sign on to agreements with the United States and, more recently, with the European Union, given its new willingness to enter into preferential agreements with East Asian states), they will extend beyond the current World Trade Organization (WTO) provisions on issues such as intellectual property and trade in services, and will inevitably bring even more international discipline to domestic economic policies.

This is not to suggest that East Asian economies are necessarily converging toward an Anglo-American variety of capitalism nor that governments have abandoned a belief that state intervention can be beneficial in the acceleration of economic growth—witness the ongoing role of government-linked companies in Singapore and the determination of the Chinese government to promote national champions in key industrial sectors. And some countries, as part of a more general backlash against globalization, are witnessing a new populist reaction against the foreign presence that has increased dramatically following the postcrisis liberalization. This has occurred, for instance, in the policies of the post-Thaksin military government in Thailand (seemingly inspired in part by the king's ongoing call for greater self-sufficiency, first made in December 1997 at the height of the crisis), in new restrictive foreign investment laws introduced in Indonesia in July 2007, and in court judgments in Japan and Korea that have supported moves by local companies to mount poison-pill defenses against hostile takeovers by foreign corporations, especially equity capital companies.

Trends in Regional Integration and Cohesion

Before the onset of the crises, extra-national ties for most of the East Asian region generally fell into one of three types. First, and congruent with the broad export orientation of most successful Asian economies, there was considerable economic linkage in the form of cross-national investments spawning regional production networks and enhanced intraregional trade. For the most part, these were corporate-driven processes devoid of explicit government controls and oversights, although, as is widely acknowledged, corporations in most of East Asia (Taiwan being the obvious exception) rarely operated in direct opposition to national governmental goals and governments encouraged the production networks through duty-drawback arrangements and export-processing zones. Many of these economic links were indeed intra-Asian, but virtually all of the Asian exporting countries simultaneously maintained extensive market dependence outside the region, most notably on the United States.

The second type of extra-regional arrangement involved more explicitly governmental efforts and multilateral fora. But these were predominantly global rather than regional institutions: the United Nations, IMF, General Agreement on Tariffs and Trade (GATT)/WTO, World Bank, and so on. Subglobal multilateral bodies with East Asian memberships were few: the Association of Southeast Asian Nations (ASEAN), Asian Development Bank, and such pan-Pacific bodies as the Asia-Pacific Economic Cooperation (APEC) grouping and the ASEAN Regional Forum (ARF).

Finally, a third type of arrangement had Asians looking beyond their national borders. These were the various bilateral arrangements that were forged, primarily in the security arena. Of particular importance were formal U.S. treaties with Japan, South Korea, the Philippines, and Thailand. Also relevant were various bilateral fora set up to resolve border disputes between China and many of its neighbors. Of a similar nature were various military-to-military exchanges across the region.

Overall, therefore, the precrisis regional architecture of East Asia was closely tied to access to U.S. markets and dependent on the multilateral and bilateral fora developed and fostered by the United States as part of its overall global strategy. Aside from ASEAN and the series of bilateral security ties among various Asian countries, there were virtually no independently generated and specifically East Asian institutional bodies.

The crisis changed this. Like most such major traumatic events, the economic crisis delivered an exogenous shock that challenged political and business elites across Asia to reassess their earlier norms and operating assumptions. The crisis by no means determined their eventual choices, but it provoked fresh thinking and consideration of many previously ignored alternatives in the collective effort to prevent future disasters. One particularly striking trend since the crisis has been the move toward more governmentally initiated efforts to create new regional institutions.

Following the crisis, Asian elites embraced a bevy of new institutions and processes at the regional level. In effect, East Asians have since 1997–98 been creating a new layer for political and economic activities between that of markets and multilateral institutions. Such new institutions, it seemed clear, were essential, given that neither the markets that had woven the webs of corporate interconnection nor the limited political institutions already in place had been effective in warding off the crisis or in dealing with it once it had hit. At the same time, such new bodies were a supplement to, rather than a replacement for, both market forces and global engagements. East Asia continued to be responsive to global market pressures as well as to the classic workings of international politics. What was different was that the new regional institutionalism afforded Asia the potential to engage global markets and global power struggles from a position of greater collective strength.

An important impetus for the new regional thinking came from Korean President Kim Dae Jung. At the ASEAN+3 (APT) meeting in Hanoi in December 1998, Kim proposed forming an East Asia Vision Group (EAVG) to examine areas where the region could profitably pursue regional approaches to collective problems. Three years later, the EAVG presented a sweeping set of proposals for greater regional cooperation. Its report clearly stated the underlying motivations and goals: "the Asian financial crisis of the recent past provided a strong impetus to strengthen regional cooperation. It spurred the recognition that East Asia needs to institutionalize its cooperation to pre-empt or solve similar problems that may arise" (East Asia Vision Group [EAVG] 2001).

The goals of the EAVG were sweeping: to prevent conflict and promote peace; to develop closer economic cooperation through trade, investment, finance, and development; to increase human security through environmental improvements and good governance; to enhance cooperation in education and human resource development; and, most comprehensively, "fostering the identity of an East Asian Community" (EAVG 2001). The most tangible institutional outgrowth of the EAVG report was the creation of the East Asia Summit (EAS), which met for the first time in Kuala Lumpur in December 2005.

As Pempel (chap. 8 in this volume) notes, however, from its inception membership in the EAS went beyond the EAVG reference of APT to include Australia, India, and New Zealand. In many respects, the contest over membership in the EAS was a concretization of the growing struggles between China and Japan for regional leadership. China has long preferred regional institutions in which the influence of the United States is circumscribed, perceiving this as a means of enhancing its own role. Japan, in contrast, with its strong strategic ties to the United States and a growing reluctance to see the regional influence of China bolstered, has consistently sought to foster a much more inclusive, pan-Pacific region. It was clear that the United States was not going to join (or be invited to join) the EAS, and so Japan, along with Singapore, pressed successfully for the larger membership. The EAS quite explicitly described itself not as a replacement for the smaller APT but rather as a complement to all existing regional mechanisms.

One of the first areas in which new efforts were made to institutionalize regional collaboration was, naturally enough, in finance. Thus as Jennifer Amyx (chap. 6) and Pempel (chap. 8 in this volume) make clear, the Chiang Mai Initiative (CMI), the Asia Bond Fund (ABF), and the Asian Bond Markets Initiatives (ABMI) were all put into place as regional institutions charged with providing an additional buffer between global financial markets and the national Asian economies. The potential for regional solutions to the problems of financial vulnerability has been enhanced by the massive increase in East Asian holdings of foreign exchange. At the time of the crises, Asian reserves stood at $742 billion. In 2005, these had more than tripled to $2.5 trillion.

Amyx (chap. 6 in this volume) makes clear, however, that simply having these reserves available does not, in fact, mean that they can be instantly and collectively mobilized in the event of some future crisis. CMI remains a series of limited bilateral swap arrangements rather than a pooled body of readily available emergency money (although in 2007 an agreement was reached, in principle, to move toward a common pool). And as Pempel observes, the Asian bond markets remain illiquid and are mostly used by national governments or major regional or para-statal institutional investors such as the Asian Development Bank or the Singapore Central Provident Fund. Yet, looking to the future, the Asian bond markets are clearly poised to develop into more liquid and well-subscribed engines of capital investment that have the potential to be significant new instruments allowing Asian monies to be mobilized in support of the vast number of Asian development projects that are expected to occur in the next decade plus.

Beyond the creation of formal governmental institutions, the postcrisis period and, at least as important, the post-9/11 period, saw renewed diplomatic energy invested in the so-called track II process. Like the formal regional institutions already noted, track II processes remain state-centric and national in their conceptualization. Unlike track I negotiations, which involve direct government-to-government talks, track II processes bring together private experts and government officials in their private capacities to engage in focused discussion on such problems as maritime security, human trafficking, and countering weapons of mass destruction. One such track II body, the Council for Security Cooperation in the Asia Pacific, has representation drawn from some two dozen security centers in countries around the Asia-Pacific; one of its two cochairs is always from an ASEAN country. Another, the Northeast Asia Cooperation Dialogue, is narrower in scope, with members drawn from the countries that are currently part of the Six Party Talks concerning the nuclear program of the Democratic Republic of Korea (University of California Institute on Global Conflict and Cooperation 1996).

The crises heightened the perceived need for broader policy dialogues and information exchanges across the region. Track II dialogues fit that need well because the purpose of such bodies is to engage in enhanced mutual understanding, confidence, and cooperation among countries in Northeast Asia through dialogue. Their meetings serve as laboratories in which different ideas can be explored and tested, alternative agendas can be set, and possible policy options can be explored (Ball, Milner, and Taylor 2006; Job 2003). In addition, track II meetings have been highly valuable in creating an epistemic community of regional norm entrepreneurs across East Asia. Such individuals, by their regular participation in such meetings, are able to develop mutual trust and understanding, engage in collective socialization, and push forward collectively arrived-at norms (Tay 2005).

Both track I and track II meetings have expanded greatly, particularly since the attacks on the United States on September 11, 2001. National governments have not focused exclusively on tightening their ties to one another through formal regional institutions. As Pempel (chap. 8) and John Ravenhill (chap. 7 in this volume) point out, in the wake of the crisis, the region has also seen a proliferation of bilateral and minilateral FTAs. No longer satisfied to wait for agreements at the global level through the WTO and Doha, individual governments have begun to forge multiple overlapping trade bargains with one another. Some reflect the influence of domestic liberalizers anxious to use FTAs as a wedge to break up previously rigid protectionist forces at home; most enhance the regional liberalization of trade. But significantly, they all provide an important departure from precrisis economic patterns of institutional collaboration and economic interaction.

At the same time, the FTA process has hardly ignored issues of national competition and global strategic positioning. Thus, Japan and many of its allies in the United States, such as Fred Bergsten of the Institute of International Economics, have pressed for the creation of a Western Pacific free trade area that would supplement the recent wave of bilateral FTAs, ensuring, in Bergsten's words that Asia would avoid the tendency to "draw a line down the middle of the Pacific" (2006, 15). A push for a Pacific FTA is complementary to the Japanese approach to regional institutions more generally. China, in contrast, has laid great stress on enhancing its FTA with ASEAN.

The governments of East Asia have thus moved postcrisis toward more broadly enhanced intraregional cooperation with one another. Such formal cooperation in itself is, of course, only a first step to any institutionalization of the region. Sentiments favoring a deepening of regional cooperation continue to be offset by specific governmental perceptions of national interest. Moreover, market forces rarely line up perfectly with government preferences. They, too, continue to drive regional developments, both toward cooperation and competition. Regional cooperation within Asia, although expanding, does not detract from the continual interactions of the region with the broader international arena. As Munakata has poignantly noted, East Asian countries "obtained autonomy in designing their regional cooperation, but they could keep this autonomy only by gaining the confidence of the private sector in the effectiveness of their regional institutions, as well as earning the trust of extraregional governments in the positive contributions the region could make" (2006b, 13).

Today's region bears no resemblance to the elegant and structured metaphor afforded by the flying geese model, which pictured each national economy in the region moving methodically and systematically toward improved positions in the product life cycle, presumably following the lead goose, Japan, with the various newly industrializing economies close behind. Instead, a series of complex production networks and investment corridors criss-cross one another; the pattern of intraregional trade has become far more complex, reflecting the fragmentation of manufacturing engineered by production networks and the consequent growth of intraindustry trade. And, in particular, China has become by far the most favored site in the region for FDI, making that country the vortex of ever-increasing amounts of regional economic activity.

Within this greater economic complexity, however, another trend stands out. The export-oriented economies of East Asia have, for the most part, reduced their direct dependence on sales to the U.S. market. Ravenhill's data on this are clear. Between 1996 and 2004, the Japanese dependence on the U.S. market fell from 27.5 to 22.7 percent; ASEAN saw its dependence fall from 19.6 to 15.6 percent. In addition, the Korean trade profile shifted dramatically. The United States, which ranked as the number one export and import partner of Korea prior to the crisis, lost considerable ground. It fell, in the postcrisis years, to number three for Korean imports and number two for exports. China, meanwhile, jumped to be the number one Korean export market, with a 21.8 percent share (the United States, in the much weaker number two slot, had a 14.6 percent share). The major exception to this pattern has been the increasing dependence of China on sales to the United States, reflecting its growing significance as a source of U.S. imports. And it is emblematic of the much broader increase in the Chinese regional role. Rapid Chinese economic growth, combined with the kinds of increased openness to global and regional markets analyzed by Steinfeld, has catapulted China into becoming the number one trading partner for Japan, South Korea, and several ASEAN countries.

The reduction in the centrality of the U.S. market to East Asian exports has been mirrored by a diminished institutional presence by the United States, in large part a consequence of actions by the George W. Bush administration. When the administration took office in 2001, it was committed to weakening the prior U.S. commitments to multilateralism and, hence, to throwing off what it saw as the multilateral shackles on unilateral action. Soon after coming to power the United States broke with fifty years of U.S. multilateralism by explicitly renouncing a host of long-standing and relatively new global agreements, from the antiballistic missile (ABM) treaty to the Kyoto Accord to the Convention Against Small Arms, the Biological Weapons Convention, the Chemical Weapons Convention, the International Court of Justice, and many others (Ikenberry 2001; Daadler and Lindsey 2003, 13; Walt 2005, 97). In virtually all cases, the U.S. government had been a proponent of these regimes prior to Bush.

APEC and ARF, both bodies that provided the United States with regularized high-level interactions with East Asia, declined in stature after the crisis and even more so with the accession of the Bush administration. APEC was criticized by

U.S. officials as having failed to secure adequate liberalization of markets in Asia. Subsequently, it lost some of its focus as a result of U.S. efforts to use its meetings to advance statements of political support for the so-called global war on terror. ARF, as well, lost U.S. support in the face of much greater skepticism about multilateral approaches to security than the prior administration had. Indeed, in 2005 and 2007 Secretary of State Condoleezza Rice did not even show up for the ARF meetings.

The prior U.S. combination of economic plus security preeminence in Asia has been eroded, starting with the crises and Asian reactions to perceived U.S. high-handedness. But the erosion has accelerated since 9/11. The former U.S. centrality to the political economy and regional architecture of East Asia has been overshadowed by its obsessive attention to security generally and to the Middle East in particular. U.S. neglect has freed up policy space for Asians to explore opportunities for cooperation—and contestation—without the defining centrality of the United States. Many of the changes in the regional architecture reveal that shift.

All the same, many governments in Asia, particularly many of the ASEAN countries and Japan, remain concerned about the decline in U.S. attention to the region, dreading the prospect that a not-always-benevolent China may fill any consequent power vacuum. As a consequence, these governments have worked actively to retain U.S. interest and involvement in the region. Heavy ASEAN lobbying, for example, resulted in Secretary Rice's appearance at the ARF meetings in 2006 after she had skipped the 2005 meeting (although she was absent again in 2007). And the United States, along with a number of European and Australasian countries, has been a regular participant in the IISS Shangri-la Dialogue on security since its inauguration in 2002.

Thus, since the crisis, the governments of East Asia have shown an increased predisposition to come together in response to perceived threats from increased globalization or, at least, as a way to enhance Asian collective bargaining power within global institutions. The result has been an increasing array of regional institutions, most of them with exclusively Asian memberships. It is also clear that markets within Asia have become increasingly interwoven and complex, with China, rather than the United States (or Japan), sitting at the vortex of many of the new developments. Moreover, as Asians have looked for ways to deal more effectively with future crises, they have sought to take advantage of their collective resources and to build up regional strengths rather than relying so heavily (as in the past) on purely global institutions, these having increasingly been seen as unresponsive to specific Asian needs. This intra-Asian focus has been bolstered by a declining economic centrality for U.S. markets and actions by a U.S. administration that has been far less predisposed to bind itself through the multilateralism and Asian-Pacific regionalism that it previously accepted. Yet Asian cooperation in many matters of the purse has not been matched by similar cooperation in security. There the Asian picture is far less cohesive and exclusively Asian. The United States continues to play a large part in Asian security matters, in many cases at the welcome behest of Asian governments.

East Asian regionalism is currently characterized by organizations with both overlapping and contested memberships and functions. Which institutionalization of regionalism will prevail—ASEAN Plus Three or ASEAN Plus Three Plus Three (India and Oceania) or Asia-Pacific—remains to be determined. One important factor in this contestation over the definition of the region is whether successors to the Bush administration reverse the recent moves away from Asian economic engagement. But in the short to medium term, it is clear that, just as the East Asian model no longer provides an apt description of realities on the ground, so too prior conceptions of an Asian region held together simply by market forces or exclusively committed to pan-Pacific principles have also begun to change substantially.

East Asian Vulnerability to Future Crises

The key question that governments and publics in East Asia a decade after the crisis want answered is: Have the problems that rendered economies vulnerable to crisis in 1997–98 been resolved? In the contemporary global economy, no country is entirely immune from crisis, not least because of the possibility of contagion because any crisis can spread from the weakest links to the relatively healthier economies. And, as with wars, governments typically are fighting the symptoms of previous crises rather than successfully anticipating the sources of future vulnerability. The volume of short-term funds under private control in global financial markets can swamp even the largest national holdings of foreign reserves (those of China and Japan), whereas IMF resources can at best play but a token role in rallying support for besieged currencies. East Asian governments continue to worry about the effects of capital flows on their capacity to achieve core economic objectives, including control over inflation and exchange rates, and hence their capacity to maintain the competitiveness of their exports.

In the absence of perfect foresight, the best that governments might be expected to do is to address the factors that were widely identified as the principal sources of vulnerability to financial crisis in 1997–98. These include:

- Overly rigid exchange rates tied to an inappropriate peg (the U.S. dollar).
- Inadequate foreign exchange reserves measured against short-term foreign liabilities.
- Excessive dependence on bank lending for corporate financing.
- The mismatch between banks' long-term domestic lending in domestic currencies and their unhedged short-term borrowing in foreign currencies.
- Financially unsound banking systems burdened with high ratios of nonperforming loans (NPLs).
- State-owned and/or state-directed banking systems that relied heavily on relational banking.
- Weak systems of prudential regulation.

Changing the exchange rate regime would seem to be one of the easiest of the financial sector problems to fix. The choice of exchange rate regime, after all, is under government control; moreover, there are typically few domestic interests with strong preferences that will mobilize in support of one type of regime rather than another. Yet, as Benjamin Cohen (chap. 2 in this volume) shows, substantial continuity has occurred in exchange rate regimes in East Asia in the decade since the crisis. Not only have most governments retained a soft peg, rendering their currencies vulnerable to speculative attack, but the U.S. dollar is still the dominant referent even when governments have chosen a basket of currencies against which to peg. And a determination to maintain exchange rate stability has imposed other costs through, for instance, impeding attempts to develop derivatives markets.

As Cohen argues persuasively, for governments preoccupied with maintaining export-led growth (and when the United States remains an extremely important final destination for the exports of many countries), there is method in this madness. And some learning has occurred in the policies of the East Asian governments on exchange rate regimes in response to the disasters of 1997. Some governments—most notably Indonesia, Korea, and Thailand—have allowed their currencies to fluctuate substantially more than in the precrisis years (an average monthly change over the years 2000–6 of close to 3 percent for Indonesia, 1.5 percent for Korea, and 1.25 percent for Thailand; not radically different from the monthly average of 2 percent for freely floating Japan) (World Bank 2006, 9, exhibit 7). The won appreciated by more than 35 percent against the dollar between 2001 and early 2007; the Thai baht appreciated by more than 20 percent in eighteen months starting in the middle of 2005.

The key question is whether such additional flexibilities will render currencies less vulnerable to speculative attack. Here, another factor enters the equation—the huge increase in East Asian government holdings of foreign exchange reserves since the crisis (figure C.1). This accumulation, built up by the increased trade surpluses (an estimated $362 billion in 2006; World Bank 2007, 3), is perhaps the single most dramatic change in the financial realm over the last ten years. By the end of 2006, both China and Japan had close to $1 trillion in reserves, accounting for around 40 percent of the world total foreign reserves. The Korean holdings, in excess of $220 billion, were more than ten times those at the onset of the crises. Increases in other countries have been less spectacular, but most have doubled their foreign exchange holdings in the years since the crisis, in the Taiwanese case from an already substantial base. The volume of foreign reserves under national control continues to dwarf the limited amount of finance currently available under the regional bilateral swap arrangements of the CMI (see Amyx, chap. 6 in this volume). For most countries, the current value of foreign exchange holdings is substantially in excess of total debt, let alone short-term debt, so nonrenewal of short-term lending would not have the catastrophic effect it had in 1997 (Griffith-Jones and Gottschalk 2006, 21). Many commentators now suggest that East Asian economies may be holding excessive levels of reserves and, by continuing to absorb large inflows of capital by running balance of payments surpluses, may be generating problems for domestic economic management.

The increased flexibility in some exchange rates coupled with the enhanced capacity for intervention in foreign exchange markets that these increased foreign

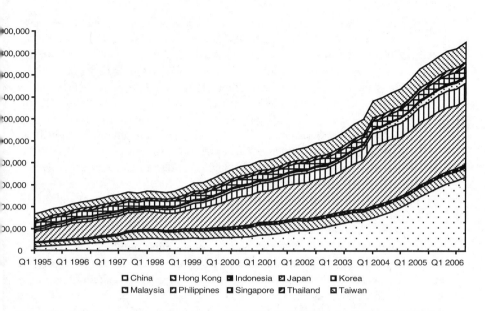

Figure C.1 East Asian foreign exchange reserves, 1995–2006 (SDR [millions]; 1 SDR = US$1.50 on February 15, 2007). SDRs, special drawing rights.

reserves afford may just tip the balance in any future battle between governments and speculators. For government intervention to be successful, it must be backed by sufficient reserves so that speculators will be uncertain as to the direction of the next move of the currency. Most observers believe that the foreign exchange holdings of East Asian governments are of a sufficient magnitude now that the central banks will be able to resist a speculative attack.

For many observers, the critical link between financial-system weaknesses and the real economy came through the excessive reliance in many East Asian economies on bank lending as the primary source of corporate finance. The problems arising from a mismatch between the banks' short-term borrowing internationally and their long-term lending domestically (a practice that was entirely rational from an individual corporate perspective) were compounded by the failure of banks to hedge against foreign exchange risk (again an understandable approach in an environment in which the government was believed to be providing a guarantee of exchange rate stability). The heavy dependence of the corporate sector on bank finance, critics argued, also facilitated state interference with lending policies and led ultimately to the moral hazard quandary of banks that were regarded to be too big to fail. To what extent have these two problems—the lack of hedging against foreign exchange risks and the excessive reliance on bank lending for corporate finance—been overcome since the crisis?

Obtaining data on the hedging practices of private banks is not at all easy. As a proxy for measuring the hedging problem, the Bank for International Settlements

(BIS) calculates what it terms a foreign–currency mismatch ratio, the foreign currency share of total debt divided by the ratio of exports to GDP. This ratio has fallen substantially since the crisis, in part because of the increased denomination of international bank lending in local currencies (Bank for International Settlements [BIS] 2006, 44–45). Aggregate international bank lending to East Asian countries has declined since the financial crisis, down from $691 billion in 1995 to $477 billion in 2004, although bank lending to China and to three of the crisis economies—Malaysia, the Philippines, and Korea—has increased (although only marginally in the case of Korea) (Ghosh 2006, 30). Another positive sign in terms of reducing dependence on volatile international lending is the decline since the crisis years of the share of short-term debt in overall debt (table C.1).

In the years since the crisis, Asian governments have actively promoted the development of bond markets to provide an alternative to bank-based financing for corporations. A vibrant bond market would also help fund the massive infrastructure investments that East Asia will require in the coming decades. Moreover, some believe that an efficient local bond market will also help overcome the costs of the current global system of capital flows, whereby Asian current account surpluses are invested in low-yielding assets offshore (typically in U.S. Treasury bills) and some of the money then re-lent to the region by foreigners (often banks and hedge funds) at substantially higher rates of interest.

Various factors historically have impeded the development of bond markets in East Asia. Among the most important are the relatively small size of many of the economies, the absence of public-sector funding needs (because most governments have historically not run significant budget deficits), relatively high and variable interest rates, a history of capital controls, and a poor regulatory environment (Eichengreen and Luengnaruemitchai 2006). Combined, these produced a context that made it risky for investors, especially foreigners, to make the long-term commitment to fixed-interest securities.

Following the financial crisis, many East Asian governments encouraged the development of domestic bond markets. In addition, as Amyx and Pempel (chaps. 6 and 8 in this volume) detail, the regional grouping of central banks, Executives' Meeting of East Asia-Pacific Central Banks, promoted the development of a regional bond market. To date, however, the volume of funds under this initiative (totaling only $3 billion) pales in comparison with developments at the national level—the importance of the regional initiatives lying not in the volume of funds

Table C.1 Share of short-term debt in total debt (%)

	1995	1996	1997	1998	1999	2000	2001	2002	2003	2004
Indonesia	21	25	24	13	13	16	16	17	17	17
Malaysia	21	28	32	20	14	11	15	17	18	22
Philippines	13	18	23	11	8	9	10	9	10	8
Thailand	44	42	34	28	24	19	20	20	21	22

Source: World Bank (n.d.).

involved but in exposing the governments in the region to the practical problems associated with establishing viable bond markets. It has been at the national level that the main growth of bond markets has taken place. As table C.2 shows, several East Asian countries in addition to Japan—most notably Korea, Malaysia, Hong Kong, and China—by the end of 2004 had sizable domestic markets for corporate bonds (in excess of $30 billion).

Also evident from table C.2, however, is the fact that despite an increase in the size of corporate bond markets in the postcrisis era, they remain relatively insignificant sources of financing compared with either bank lending (domestic credit) or equity (stock market capitalization, which is particularly important in Hong Kong and Singapore). (Columns 2–5 of table C.2 compare the value of corporate bonds and other financing sources expressed as a percentage of GDP.)

Clearly, East Asian bond markets still have a long way to go before they assume the same significance as a source of corporate financing that they enjoy in most industrialized economies. A number of factors underlie this constricted development, almost all related to government actions or omissions (largely, it seems, through the government's privileging of other economic and/or political objectives rather than because of the influence of nongovernmental actors; although some banks might have been expected to oppose the development of bond markets as an alternative to bank credit, the liberalization and internationalization of the East Asian banking systems after the crisis weakened the political influence of local banks). Several countries—most notably China, Indonesia, Malaysia, and the Philippines—maintain restrictions on access to bond markets by foreigners. Many also retain significant restrictions on issuers of debt. These restrictions are usually linked to limits on capital mobility, all driven by a concern to protect the local currency from speculation and to maintain export competitiveness. In many countries, these restrictions have

Table C.2 Corporate bond markets and other financing sources in east Asia, end of 2004

	Corporate bonds		Other financing sources (as % of GDP)		
	(1) Amount outstanding (billions of US$)	(2) Percentage of GDP	(3) Domestic credit	(4) Stock market capitalization	(5) Government bonds
China	195.9	10.6	154.4	33.4	18.0
Hong Kong	61.9	35.8	148.9	547.7	5.0
Indonesia	6.8	2.4	42.6	24.5	15.2
Japan	2,002.0	41.7	146.9	76.9	117.2
Korea	355.6	49.3	104.2	74.7	23.7
Malaysia	49.7	38.8	113.9	140.8	36.1
Philippines	0.2	0.2	49.8	37.5	21.8
Singapore	21.7	18.6	70.1	211.4	27.6
Thailand	31.9	18.3	84.9	67.1	18.5
United States	15,116.6	128.8	89.0	138.4	42.5

Source: Data from Gyntelberg, Ma, and Remolona (2006, 14, table 1).

produced thin markets, thereby constraining the available range of financial instruments, particularly derivatives (Hohensee and Lee 2006).

In most countries, the exceptions being Hong Kong and Singapore, regulation and prudential supervision of bond markets remain far from international best practice. As Eschweiler (2006) notes, the problem often is less one of inappropriate principles than lack of effective enforcement. Among the issues here are the lack of independence of supervisory/regulatory authorities from the government, the absence of sufficient qualified and experienced staff within these agencies, and a general absence of the technical capacity to monitor markets so as to identify manipulation and systemic risk.

Reference to these weaknesses returns us to issues directly relevant to the broader health of the East Asian financial systems. On one dimension, the ratio of NPLs, banking systems have returned to at least the position that they were in before the onset of the crisis. As table C.3 documents, government efforts to relieve banks of their NPLs, often at significant expense to the public coffers, had been largely successful by 2005.

As Natasha Hamilton-Hart (chap. 2 in this volume) documents, the role of the state in East Asian financial systems today is not necessarily smaller than in the precrisis period. The collapse of financial systems during the crises necessitated that the states took over bankrupt institutions. Some of these institutions have subsequently been reprivatized, in particular those in Indonesia, Korea, and Thailand, often leading to a substantial increase in foreign ownership compared with the precrisis period. Others remain in state hands. The trends toward privatization and internationalization may be expected to continue as markets improve, although, as Hamilton-Hart indicates is the case in Indonesia, there is no inevitability that governments will move to completely relinquish their ownership or control over the banking systems.

Greater foreign participation in East Asian financial systems can be expected, other things being equal, to increase competition and to bring these systems closer to international best practices. Ultimately, however, much will depend on the quality of the regimes of supervision and prudential regulation. Although most countries have made substantial progress in both areas, the lack of skilled personnel with the requisite experience in a particularly complex field limits the effectiveness of ongoing efforts at financial system reform.

Table C.3 Nonperforming loans in the commercial banking system of the crisis-affected countries, December 1997–2006 (% of total loans)

	1997	1998	1999	2000	2001	2002	2003	2004	2005	2006
Indonesia	7.2	48.6	32.9	18.8	12.1	7.5	6.8	4.5	7.6	6.1
Korea	6.0	7.3	13.6	8.8	3.3	2.4	2.2	2.0	1.3	0.9
Malaysia	na	10.6	11.0	9.7	11.5	10.2	9.0	7.5	5.8	4.8
Philippines	4.7	10.4	12.3	15.1	17.3	15.0	14.1	12.7	8.5	6.0
Thailand	na	45.0	39.9	19.5	11.5	18.1	13.9	11.6	8.3	8.1

Source: Data from World Bank (2007, appendix table 9).

In sum, the changes that have occurred in East Asian financial systems over the last decade have rendered these systems less vulnerable to crisis. By far the most dramatic change has come in national holdings of foreign exchange reserves, which are now of sufficient magnitude to give many countries an opportunity to, at least temporarily, resist speculative attacks on their currencies. Coupled with this is the increased flexibility—albeit not as substantial as many economists might advocate—of several of the exchange rates around the region (presumably, again other things being equal, having the effect of reducing the overall magnitude of foreign reserves required and making the work of speculators more difficult). The problem of currency mismatches, if not entirely resolved, appears to have been reduced, and according to BIS data is certainly less of an issue in East Asia than in other developing regions. Finally, progress has occurred in the development of nonbank sources of corporate finance and in improving supervision and prudential regulation of the financial system. Things may not be perfect, but substantial strides have been taken in the right direction, and East Asia as a whole has erected substantial barriers against possible future crises.

Conclusion

This volume has been concerned with the extent to which significant change has taken place in the political economy of East Asia since the financial crisis of 1997–98 and with the causes and consequences of such change. In concluding the volume, rather than seeking to synthesize all that has come before, we have tried to look forward and reflect on how the changes already underway are likely to evolve and how they have affected the vulnerability of East Asia to future crises. We have highlighted the major trends emerging across the region on three key dimensions: the evolving national political economies of East Asian countries, patterns of regional integration, and responses to perceptions of external vulnerability of East Asia.

In domestic political economy, a trend away from all-powerful executive government continues to gather momentum. East Asian political systems are characterized by increasing political pluralization and contestation, increasingly institutionalized leadership turnover, gradually strengthening legal systems, rapidly expanding public access to information, and intensifying engagement with the global economy. The financial crisis was by no means the sole (nor always the primary) cause of these developments, but it was an important contributing factor, sometimes reinforcing trends that were already underway as part of the wave of democratization that swept the region in the 1980s. The net effect of these changes is that tightly disciplined policy regimes, close and long-running relationships between political and corporate leaders, and a presumption that the state is the all-important key to development are likely to continue to gradually recede.

The financial crisis itself played a much more direct role in driving the other major developments we highlight in this chapter. A desire to strengthen regional cohesion flowed directly from the dissatisfaction of the East Asian governments with the response of the international community to the catastrophe that enveloped much of the region in 1997–98. The region has moved from a situation in which it was often characterized as underinstitutionalized to one in which it has become the most active global site for the negotiation of agreements on trade and financial cooperation. It may be premature to speak of an *East Asian* identity being institutionalized. Nonetheless, the years since the crisis have seen new East Asian regional institutions come into being despite the initial still-birth of the Asian Monetary Fund (which would have led countries in a different direction). In some official circles, a significant emotive attachment to East Asia has developed.

Concurrently, however, ongoing tensions among the major states of the region are leading some governments to hedge their bets by reinforcing their extra-regional linkages. These moves embrace security, diplomatic and economic linkages, including the reinforcement of alliance relations with the United States, the inclusion of non-East Asian actors such as India in regional institutions, the new Chinese–Russian–central Asian linkages under the Shanghai Cooperation Organization, and the negotiation of preferential trade agreements with the United States, the European Union, and countries in South America. Although the rapid economic growth of China has led to a major reorientation of production networks across East Asia and has been the major factor driving the increasing share of East Asian exports that are consumed within the region, nowhere currently is there any sentiment for constructing a closed region. The region is not turning inward on itself but, instead, the deepening of intraregional ties is part of a wider pattern of deepening global economic engagement. The porosity of the East Asian region that Katzenstein (2005) notes has been unchallenged by developments since the crisis.

The final theme we highlight is the progress made toward reducing the vulnerability of the East Asian countries, both individually and collectively. Although the possibility of a future financial crisis has certainly not been eliminated in East Asia (any more than elsewhere in the global economy), significant steps have been taken to reduce the risk of a reoccurrence of a crisis similar to that of 1997–98. National reserves of foreign exchange are now much more substantial, there is somewhat greater flexibility in the foreign exchange regimes of a number of countries, and progress has been made in strengthening banking-sector governance and corporate governance more broadly.

The financial crisis that shook East Asia in 1997–98 has proved to be a marked disjunction on several dimensions of the domestic political economies and international relations of the countries. Peering into the future is always a hazardous business, but our expectation is that the three trends identified here will be significant elements in what lies ahead.

References

Acharya, Amitav. 1997. "Ideas, Identity and Institution-Building: From the 'ASEAN Way' to the 'Asia-Pacific Way'." *Pacific Review* 10(3): 319–46.

———. 2001. *Constructing a Security Community in Southeast Asia: ASEAN and the Problem of Regional Order.* London: Routledge.

Adsera, Alicia, and Carles Boix. 2000. "Trade, Democracy, and the Size of the Public Sector: The Political Underpinnings of Openness." *International Organization* 56(2): 229–62.

Aggarwal, Vinod K. 2006. "Bilateral Trade Agreements in the Asia-Pacific." In *Bilateral Trade Agreements in the Asia-Pacific,* edited by Vinod K. Aggarwal and Shujiro Urata. London: Routledge.

Amsden, Alice H. 1989. *Asia's Next Giant: South Korea and Late Industrialization.* New York: Oxford University Press.

Amyx, Jennifer. 2002. "Moving beyond Bilateralism?: Japan and the Asian Monetary Fund." Pacific Economic Paper no. 331, Australia-Japan Research Centre, Australia National University, Canberra.

———. 2003a. "The Ministry of Finance and the Bank of Japan at the Crossroads." In *Japanese Governance: Beyond Japan Inc.,* edited by Jennifer Amyx and Peter Drysdale. London: RoutledgeCurzon.

———. 2003b. "A New Face for Japanese Finance?: Assessing the Impact of Recent Reforms." In *Challenges for Japan: Political Leadership, U.S.-China-Japan Triangle, Financial Reform, and Gender Issues,* edited by Gil Latz. Tokyo: Tokyo International House of Japan, for the Shibusawa Eiichi Memorial Foundation.

———. 2004a. "Japan and the Evolution of Regional Financial Arrangements in East Asia." In *Beyond Bilateralism: U.S.-Japan Relations in the New Asia-Pacific,* edited by Ellis S. Krauss and T. J. Pempel. Stanford: Stanford University Press.

———. 2004b. *Japan's Financial Crisis: Institutional Rigidity and Reluctant Change.* Princeton: Princeton University Press.

Amyx, Jennifer. 2004c. "The Politics of Reform in Japanese Finance: Assessing the Relative Influence of Foreign Investors." Unpublished manuscript, University of Pennsylvania.

———. 2005. "What Motivates Regional Financial Cooperation in East Asia Today?" Asia-Pacific Issues Paper no. 76. East-West Center, Honolulu.

Asian Development Bank (ADB). 1997. *Emerging Asia: Changes and Challenges.* Manila: Asian Development Bank.

———. 2000. *Asian Development Outlook 2000.* Manila: Asian Development Bank.

———. 2005a. *Asian Development Outlook 2005.* Manila: Asian Development Bank.

———. 2005b. *Bond Market Settlement and Emerging Linkages in Selected ASEAN+3 Countries.* Manila: Asian Development Bank.

———. 2006. *Asian Development Outlook 2006.* Manila: Asian Development Bank.

———. 2007. *Key Indicators: Inequality in Asia.* Manila: Asian Development Bank.

Asian Development Bank Regional Economic Monitoring Unit (ADB REMU). 2002. *Study on Monetary and Financial Cooperation in East Asia (Summary Report).* Manila: Asian Development Bank.

Aspalter, Christian. 2002. *Democratization and Welfare State Development in Taiwan.* Burlington, VT: Ashgate.

Association of Southeast Asian Nations (ASEAN). 1999. "Final Communiqué of the Meeting of ASEAN Heads of Government." Manila, Philippines.

Athukorala, Prema-chandra. 2001. *Crisis and Recovery in Malaysia: The Role of Capital Controls.* Cheltenham, UK: Edward Elgar.

———. 2003. "Product Fragmentation and Trade Patterns in East Asia." Working Paper in Trade and Development 2003/21, Division of Economics, Australian National University, Canberra.

———. 2007. "The Malaysian Capital Controls: A Success Story?" Working Paper in Trade and Development 2007/07, Division of Economics, Australian National University, Canberra.

Athukorala, Prema-chandra, and Peter G. Warr. 2002. "Vulnerability to a Currency Crisis: Lessons from the Asian Experience." *World Economy* 25(1): 33–57.

Balisacan, Arsenio. 1995. "Anatomy of Poverty during Adjustment: The Case of the Philippines." *Economic Development and Cultural Change* 44(1): 48–57.

———. 2001. "Did the Estrada Administration Benefit the Poor?" In *Between Fires: Fifteen Perspectives on the Estranda Crisis,* edited by Amando Doronila. Pasig City, Philippines: Anvil.

Ball, Desmond, Anthony Milner, and Brendon Taylor. 2006. "Track 2 Security Dialogue in the Asia-Pacific: Reflections and Future Directions." *Asian Security* 2(3): 174–88.

Bank for International Settlements (BIS). 2005. *75th Annual Report.* Basel: Bank for International Settlements.

———. 2006. *Annual Report.* Basel: Bank for International Settlements.

Bank Indonesia. n.d. "The Indonesian Banking Architecture." Available from: www.bi.go.id/web/en/Info+Penting/Arsitektur+Perbankan+BI/.

Bank Indonesia. 2006. "Financial Statistics." Available from: www.bi.go.id/web/en/Data+Statistik/.

Bank Negara Malaysia. 2005. "Operational Flexibilities to the Locally-Incorporated Foreign Banking Institutions Operating in Malaysia." Press release 12/05/09, December 28. Available from: http://www.bnm.gov.my.

———. 2006. *Annual Report 2005.* Kuala Lumpur: Bank Negara Malaysia.

Bank of Korea. 2004. "Recent Financial Restructuring." Available from: http://www.bok.or.kr.

Bank of Thailand. 2004. "Financial Sector Master Plan." Available from: www.bot.or.th/ bothomepage/BankAtWork/FinInstitute/FISystemDevPlan/ENGVer/pdffile/eng.pdf.

Barth, James, Gerard Caprio, and Ross Levine. 2006. *Rethinking Bank Regulation: Till Angels Govern.* Cambridge, UK: Cambridge University Press.

Baskaran, Manu. 2007. "The Asian Financial Crisis Ten Years Later—Lessons Learnt: The Private Sector Perspective." Paper presented at the Asia Financial Crisis Ten Years Later conference, Rajaratnam School of International Studies, Nanyang Technological University, Singapore, June 25–26.

Bautista, Victoria A. 1999. *Combating Poverty through Comprehensive and Integrated Delivery of Social Services (CIDSS).* Quezon City, Philippines: National College of Public Administration and Governance, University of the Philippines.

Belaisch, Agnès, and Alessandro Zanello. 2006. "Deepening Financial Ties." *Finance and Development* 43(2): 16–19.

Berg, Andrew. 1999. "The Asian Crisis: Causes, Policy Responses, and Outcomes." IMF Working Paper WP/99/138, International Monetary Fund, Washington, D.C.

Berglöf, Erik, and Stijn Claessens. 2004. "Corporate Governance and Enforcement." World Bank Research Working Paper 3409, Washington, D.C.

Bergsten, C. Fred. 2006. "A Free Trade Area of the Asia Pacific in the Wake of the Faltering Doha Round: Trade Policy Alternatives for APEC." In *An APEC Trade Agenda?: The Political Economy of a Free Trade Area of the Asia Pacific.* The Pacific and Economic Cooperation Council & The APEC Business Advisory Council, Singapore.

Berkowitz, Daniel, Katharina Pistor, and Jean-Francois Richard. 2003. "Economic Development, Legality, and the Transplant Effect." *European Economic Review* 47: 165–95.

Bernstein, Thomas, and Xiaobo Lu. 2000. "Taxation without Representation: Chinese State and Peasants in the New Reform Era." *China Quarterly* 163(September): 742–63.

Bilaterals.org. 2006. "Taiwan to Sign Free Trade Pact with Nicaragua June 16." June 15. Available from: http://bilaterals.org/article.php3?id_article=5002.

Blecher, Marc J. 2002. "Hegemony and Workers' Politics in China." *China Quarterly* 170: 283–303.

Blyth, Mark. 2003. "The Political Power of Financial Ideas: Transparency, Risk, and Distribution in Global Finance." In *Monetary Orders: Ambiguous Economics, Ubiquitous Politics,* edited by Jonathan Kirshner. Ithaca: Cornell University Press.

Booth, Anne. 1999. "Education and Economic Development in Southeast Asia: Myths and Realities." *ASEAN Economic Bulletin* 16(3): 290–306.

Brown, Andrew, and Kevin Hewison. 2005. " 'Economics Is the Deciding Factor': Labor Politics in Thaksin's Thailand." *Pacific Affairs* 78(3): 353–75.

Calvo, Guillermo A., and Carmen M. Reinhart. 2002. "Fear of Floating." *Quarterly Journal of Economics* 117: 379–408.

Caraway, Teri. 2002. "International Organizations, Labor Reform and Labor Rights in Asia." Unpublished manuscript, University of Minnesota.

Chandler and Thong-Ek Law Offices. 2006. "Global Banking & Financial Policy Review 2005–2006. Thailand: Developments in the Legal and Regulatory Framework." 27 June. Available from: www.ctlo.com/bank.htm.

Chang, Ha-Joon. 2000. "The Hazard of Moral Hazard: Untangling the Asian Crisis." *World Development* 28(4): 775–88.

Chang, Sea-Jin, and Jung-Ho Kim. 2000. "The Chaebol Reforms." Paper presented at Joint International Conference of the Weatherhead Center for International Affairs and Korea University, Cambridge, Mass., March.

Chen, Guidi, and Chuntao Wu. 2006. *Will the Boat Sink the Water?: The Life of China's Peasants.* New York: Public Affairs.

Chen, Hsiao-hung Nancy. 2004. "Universal Values vs. Political Ideology: Virtual Reform Experience of Taiwan's National Pension Plan (Draft)." Unpublished manuscript, National Chengchi University.

Chey, Hyoung-kyu. 2006. "Explaining Cosmetic Compliance with International Regulatory Regimes: The Implementation of the Basle Accord in Japan, 1998–2003." *New Political Economy* 11(2): 271–89.

Chin Kok Fay. 2004. "Malaysia's Post-Crisis Bank Restructuring." In *After the Storm: Crisis, Recovery and Sustaining Development in Four Asian Economies,* edited by Jomo Kwame Sundaram. Singapore: Singapore University Press.

Cho, Yoon Je. 2002. "Financial Repression, Liberalization, Crisis and Restructuring: Lessons of Korea's Financial Sector Policies." Tokyo: Asian Development Bank Institute.

Chow, Peter C. Y. 2001. *Social Expenditure in Taiwan (China).* Washington, D.C.: World Bank.

Chung, Jae Ho. 2005. "China's Ascendancy and the Korean Peninsula: From Interest Reevaluation to Strategic Realignment?" In *Power Shift: China and Asia's New Dynamics,* edited by David Shambaugh. Berkeley: University of California Press.

Cihak, Martin, and Richard Podpiera. 2006. "Is One Watchdog Better than Three?: International Experience with Integrated Financial Sector Supervision." IMF Working Paper WP/06/57, International Monetary Fund, Washington, D.C.

Claessens, Stijn, Simeon Djankov, and Larry H. P. Lang. 2002. "The Separation of Ownership and Control in East Asian Corporations." *Journal of Financial Economics* 58: 81–112.

Clarke, Donald. 2003a. "China's Legal System and the WTO: Prospects for Compliance." *Washington University Global Studies Law Review* 2: 97–118.

Clarke, Donald. 2003b. "Puzzling Observations in Chinese Law: When Is a Riddle Just a Mistake?" In *Understanding China's Legal System,* edited by C. Stephen Hsu. New York: New York University Press.

Clarke, George R. G., Robert Cull, and Mary M. Shirley. 2005. "Bank Privatization in Developing Countries: A Summary of Lessons and Findings." *Journal of Banking and Finance* 29(8–9): 1905–30.

Cohen, Benjamin J. 1977. *Organizing the World's Money: The Political Economy of International Monetary Relations.* New York: Basic Books.

———. 1993. "The Triad and the Unholy Trinity: Lessons for the Pacific Region." In *Pacific Economic Relations in the 1990s: Cooperation or Conflict?,* edited by Richard Higgott, Richard Leaver, and John Ravenhill. Boulder: Lynne Rienner.

———. 1998. *The Geography of Money.* Ithaca: Cornell University Press.

Committee on the Global Financial System (CGFS). 2005. "Foreign Direct Investment in the Financial Sector: Experiences in Asia, Central and Eastern Europe and Latin America." CGFS Papers no. 25. Basel: Bank for International Settlements.

Coordinating Ministry for Economic Affairs, Indonesia. 2006. "Trade and Investment News." 29 May. Available from: www.dprin.go.id/eng/publication/IndReview/2006/20062905.htm.

Corsetti, Giancarlo, Paolo Pesenti, and Nouriel Roubini. 1999. "What Caused the Asian Currency and Financial Crisis." *Japan and the World Economy* 11(3): 305–73.

Crispin, Shawn. 2003. "Banks Hold Up Full Recovery." *Far Eastern Economic Review* 166(37): 24–25.

Crouch, Harold. 1978. *The Army and Politics in Indonesia.* Ithaca: Cornell University Press.

Cruz, Yvonne T., and Booma B. Chua. 2004a. "Legislators Feed on Pork." September 6–7. Available from: http://www.pcij.org/stories/print/2004/pork2.html.

——. 2004b, 6–7 September. "Pork Is a Political, Not a Developmental, Tool." *Our Latest Report*. Available from: http://www.pcij.org/stories/2004/pork.html.

Daadler, Ivo, and James M. Lindsey. 2003. *America Unbound: The Bush Revolution in Foreign Policy*. Washington, D.C.: Brookings Institution.

de Dios, Emmanuel. n.d. "Philippine Economic Growth: Can It Last?" *School of Economics, University of the Philippines*.

de Dios, Emmanuel, Benjamin Diokno, Emmanuel Esguerra, Raul Fabella, Ma. Socorro Gochoco-Bautista, Felipe Medalla, Solita Monsod, Ernesto Pernia, Renato Reside, Jr., Gerardo Sicat, and Edita Tan. 2004. "The Deepening Crisis: The Real Score on Deficits and the Public Debt." School of Economics Discussion Paper no. 04–09, University of the Philippines.

de Dios, Emmanuel S., and Paul D. Hutchcroft. 2003. "Political Economy." In *The Philippine Economy: Development, Policies, and Challenges*, edited by Arsenio M. Balisacan and Hal Hill. New York: Oxford University Press.

De Nicolò, Gianni, Luc Laeven, and Kenichi Ueda. 2006. "Corporate Governance Quality: Trends and Real Effects." IMF Working Paper WP/06/293, International Monetary Fund, Washington, D.C.

Delhaise, Philippe F. 1998. *Asia in Crisis: The Implosion of the Banking and Finance Systems*. Singapore: John Wiley & Sons.

Demirguc-Kunt, Asli, and Ross Levine. 1999. "Bank-Based and Market-Based Financial Systems: Cross-Country Comparison." Unpublished manuscript, World Bank.

Department of State, U.S. 2006. "Investment Climate Statement—Indonesia." Available from: www.state.gov/e/eb/ifd/2006/62358.htm.

Detragiache, Enrica, Poonam Gupta, and Thierry Tressel. 2005. "Finance in Lower-Income Countries: An Empirical Exploration." IMF Working Paper WP/05/167, International Monetary Fund, Washington, D.C.

Detragiache, Enrica, Thierry Tressel, and Poonam Gupta. 2006. "Foreign Banks in Poor Countries: Theory and Evidence." IMF Working Paper WP/06/18, International Monetary Fund, Washington, D.C.

Deyo, Frederick C. 1989. *Beneath the Miracle: Labor Subordination in the New Asian Industrialism*. Berkeley: University of California Press.

Dixon, John, and Hyung Shik Kim, eds. 1985. *Social Welfare in Asia*. London: Croom Helm.

Djiwandono, J. Soedradjad. 2001. *Bergulat dengan Krisis dan Pemulihan Ekonomi Indonesia*. Jakarta: Pustaka Sinar Harapan.

Dodd, Philip. 1989. "'Time-honoured Disguise' and 'Borrowed Language': Some Recent Reflections on the Revolution in France." *Yearbook of English Studies* 19: 290–97.

Donaldson, Dayl, Supasit Pannarunothai, and Viroj Tangcharoensathien. 1999. "Health Financing in Thailand: Technical Report." Asian Development Bank no. 2997. Boston: Management Sciences for Health.

Doner, Richard F. n.d. "Growth Challenges: Institutions, Politics and Economic Change in Thailand." Unpublished manuscript, Emory University, Atlanta, GA.

Doner, Richard F., Gregory W. Noble, and John Ravenhill. 2004. "Production Networks in East Asia's Automotive Parts Industry." In *Global Production Networking and Technological Change in East Asia*, edited by Shahid Yusuf, M. Anjum Altaf, and Kaoru Nabeshima. Washington, D.C.: World Bank/Oxford University Press.

Doner, Richard F., and Ansil Ramsay. 2000. "Rent-Seeking and Economic Development in Thailand." In *Rents, Rent-Seeking, and Economic Development: Theory and Evidence in Asia*, edited by Mushtaq H. Khan and Jomo Kwame Sundaram. Cambridge, UK: Cambridge University Press.

Doner, Richard F., Bryan K. Ritchie, and Dan Slater. 2005. "Systemic Vulnerability and the Origins of Developmental States." *International Organization* 59: 327–61.

Dooley, Michael P., David Folkerts-Landau, and Peter Garber. 2003. "An Essay on the Revived Bretton Woods System." National Bureau of Economic Research Working Paper 9971, Cambridge, Mass.

Doronila, Amando. 2001. *The Fall of Joseph Estrada: The Inside Story.* Pasig City, Philippines: Anvil.

East Asia Vision Group (EAVG). 2001. "Toward an East Asian Community: Region of Peace, Prosperity, and Progress." Available from: http://www.mofa.go.jp/region/asia-paci/report2001.pdf.

Eichengreen, Barry. 1994. *International Monetary Arrangements for the 21st Century.* Washington, D.C.: Brookings Institution.

——. 1999. *Toward a New International Financial Architecture: A Practical Post-Asia Agenda.* Washington, D.C.: Institute for International Economics.

——. 2004. "The Case for Floating Exchange Rates in Asia." In *Monetary and Financial Integration in East Asia: The Way Ahead,* edited by Asian Development Bank. New York: Palgrave Macmillan.

——. 2005. "The Parallel-Currency Approach to Asian Monetary Integration." *American Economic Review* 96(2): 432–6.

——. 2006. "China, Asia, and the World Economy: The Implications of an Emerging Asian Core and Periphery." *China & World Economy* 14(3): 1–18.

——. 2007. *Global Imbalances and the Lessons of Bretton Woods.* Cambridge, Mass.: MIT Press.

Eichengreen, Barry, and Richardo Hausmann. 1999. "Exchange Rates and Financial Fragility." National Bureau of Economic Research Working Paper, Cambridge, Mass.

Eichengreen, Barry, and Pipat Luengnaruemitchai. 2006. "Why Doesn't Asia Have Bigger Bond Markets?" *BIS Papers* 30(5): 40–77.

Eichengreen, Barry, Yeongseop Rhee, and Hui Tong. 2004. "The Impact of China on the Exports of Other Asian Countries." Berkeley: University of California, Berkeley.

Ernst, Dieter. 2004. "Global Production Networks in East Asia's Electronics Industry and Upgrading Perspectives in Malaysia." In *Global Production Networking and Technological Change in East Asia,* edited by Shahid Yusuf, M. Anjum Altaf, and Kaoru Nabeshima. Washington, D.C.: World Bank.

Eschweiler, Bernhard. 2006. "Bond Market Regulation and Supervision in Asia." *BIS Papers* 30(28): 335–52.

Executives' Meeting of East Asia-Pacific Central Banks (EMEAP) Working Group on Financial Markets. 2006. "Review of the Asian Bond Fund 2 Initiative." June. Available from http://www.emeap.org/ABF/ABF2ReviewReport.pdf.

Felker, Greg. 2001. "Industrial Policy and Industrialization in Malaysia and Thailand." In *Southeast Asia's Industrialization: Industrial Policy, Capabilities and Sustainability,* edited by Jomo Kwame Sundaram. Houndsmills, UK: Palgrave Macmillan.

Fell, Dafydd. 2004. "Measuring and Explaining Party Change in Taiwan, 1991–2004." *Journal of East Asian Studies* 5(1): 105–33.

Finance Ministers of ASEAN, China, Japan, and the Republic of Korea (ASEAN+3). 2005. "The Joint Ministerial Statement of the 8th ASEAN+3 Finance Ministers' Meeting 4 May 2005, Istanbul, Turkey." Available from: http://www.mof.go.jp/english/if/as3_050504.htm.

Financial Stability Forum. 2000. *Report of the Working Group on Capital Flows.* Singapore: Financial Stability Forum.

Fisman, Raymond. 2001. "Estimating the Value of Political Connections." *American Economic Review* 91(4): 1095–102.

Fisman, Raymond, and Roberta Gatti. 2002. "Decentralization and Corruption: Evidence across Countries." *Journal of Public Economics* 83(3): 325–45.

Foley, Martin. 1998. "Accounting Adjustment." *China Business Review* 25: 22–24.

Frankel, Jeffrey A. 1999. *No Single Currency Regime Is Right for All Counties or at All Times.* Princeton: International Finance Section.

Freedom House. 2007. "Freedom in the World." Available from: http://www.freedomhouse. org/template.cfm?page=15&year=2007.

Friedman, Edward. 2006. "The Fragility of China's Regional Cooperation." In *Regional Cooperation and Its Enemies in Northeast Asia,* edited by Edward Friedman and Sung Chull Kim, 125–42. London: Routledge.

Fukagawa, Yukiko. 2005. "East Asia's New Economic Integration Strategy: Moving beyond the FTA." *Asia-Pacific Review* 12(2): 1–29.

Fukuda, Shin-ichi, and Sanae Ohno. 2005. "Post-Crisis Exchange Rate Regimes in ASEAN: A New Empirical Test Based on Intra-Daily Data." Discussion Paper. University of Tokyo, Center for International Research on the Japanese Economy.

Gallagher, Mary. 2005. *Contagious Capitalism.* Princeton: Princeton University Press.

Garnaut, Ross. 1998. "The East Asian Crisis." In *East Asia in Crisis: From Being a Miracle to Needing One?,* edited by Ross H. McLeod and Ross Garnaut. London: Routledge.

———. 2000. "East Asia after the Financial Crisis." In *Reform and Recovery in East Asia: The Role of the State and Economic Enterprise,* edited by Peter Drysdale. London: Routledge.

Gaulier, Guillaume, Françoise Lemoine, and Deniz Ünal-Kesenci. 2004. "China's Integration in Asian Production Networks and Its Implications." Paper presented at Resolving New Global and Regional Imbalances in an Era of Asian Integration conference, Tokyo, June 17–18.

———. 2006. "China's Emergence and the Reorganisation of Trade Flows in Asia." Paris: Centre d'Etudes Prospectives et d'Informations Internationales.

Genberg, Hans. 2006. "Exchange Rate Arrangements and Financial Integration in East Asia: On a Collision Course?" Working Paper 41, Bank of Greece, Athens.

Genberg, Hans, Robert McCauley, Yung Chul Park, and Avinash Persaud. 2005. *Official Reserves and Currency Management in Asia: Myth, Reality, and the Future.* Geneva: International Center for Monetary and Banking Studies.

Ghosh, Swati R. 2006. *East Asian Finance: The Road to Robust Markets.* Washington, D.C.: World Bank.

Gill, Indermit Singh, Homi J. Kharas, and Deepak Bhattasali. 2007. *An East Asian Renaissance: Ideas for Economic Growth.* Washington, D.C.: World Bank.

Goldstein, Morris. 1998. *The Asian Financial Crisis: Causes, Cures, and Systemic Implications.* Washington, D.C.: Institute for International Economics.

———. 2002. *Managed Floating Plus.* Washington, D.C.: Institute for International Economics.

Goldstein, Morris, and Philip Turner. 2004. *Controlling Currency Mismatches in Emerging Economies.* Washington, D.C.: Institute for International Economics.

Gomez, Edmund Terence. 1994. *Political Business: Corporate Involvement of Malaysian Political Parties.* Townsville, Australia: Centre for South-East Asian Studies, James Cook University of North Queensland.

Gomez, Edmund Terence, and Jomo Kwame Sundaram. 1999. *Malaysia's Political Economy: Politics, Patronage and Profits.* Cambridge, UK: Cambridge University Press.

Goodman, Roger, Gordon White, and Huck-ju Kwon. 1998. *The East Asian Welfare Model: Welfare Orientalism and the State.* London: Routledge.

Gough, Ian. 2001. "Globalization and Regional Welfare Regimes: The Asian Case." *Global Social Policy* 1(2): 163–89.

Gourevitch, Peter. 1978. "2nd Image Reversed: International Sources of Domestic Politics." *International Organization* 32(4): 881–911.

——. 1986. *Politics in Hard Times: Comparative Responses to International Economic Crises.* Ithaca: Cornell University Press.

Gourevitch, Peter, and James Shinn. 2005. *Political Power and Corporate Control: The New Global Politics of Corporate Governance.* Princeton: Princeton University Press.

Government of Malaysia. 2006. *Ninth Malaysia Plan 2006–2010.* Putrajaya: Economic Planning Unit, Prime Minister's Department.

Gowa, Joanne. 1994. *Allies, Adversaries, and International Trade.* Princeton: Princeton University Press.

Greenwood, C. Lawrence. 2006. "Thinking Regionally and Acting Nationally." Paper presented at East Asia's New Stage of Economic Integration Conference, Singapore, 26 June.

Grenville, Stephen. 2000. "Capital Flows and Crises." In *The Asian Financial Crises and the Global Financial Architecture,* edited by Greg Noble and John Ravenhill. Cambridge, UK: Cambridge University Press.

Grieco, Joseph M. 1997. "Systemic Sources of Variation in Regional Institutionalization in Western Europe, East Asia, and the Americas." In *The Political Economy of Regionalism,* edited by Edward D. Mansfield and Helen Milner. New York: Columbia University Press.

Griffith-Jones, Stephany, and Ricardo Gottschalk. 2006. "Financial Vulnerability in Asia." *IDS Bulletin* 37(3): 17–27.

Grimes, William W. 2006. "East Asian Financial Regionalism in Support of the Global Financial Architecture?: The Political Economy of Regional Nesting." *Journal of East Asian Studies* 6: 353–80.

Gwartney, James D., and Robert Lawson, with William Easterly. 2006. *Economic Freedom of the World: 2006 Annual Report.* Vancouver, Canada: The Fraser Institute.

Gyntelberg, Jacob, Guonan Ma, and Eli Remolona. 2006. "Developing Corporate Bond Markets in Asia." *BIS Papers* 26(4): 113–21.

Haggard, Stephan. 1990. *Pathways from the Periphery.* Ithaca: Cornell University Press.

——. 2000. *The Political Economy of the Asian Financial Crisis* Washington, D.C.: Institute for International Economics.

——. 2004. "The Evolution of Social Contracts in Asia." In *Asian States: Beyond the Developmental Perspective,* edited by Richard Boyd and Tak-Wing Ngo. London: Routledge.

——. 2005. "Globalization, Democracy and the Evolution of Social Contracts in East Asia." *Taiwan Journal of Democracy* 1(1): 21–47.

Haggard, Stephan, and Robert Kaufman. In press. *Development, Democracy and Welfare States: Latin America, East Asia and Central Europe.* Princeton: Princeton University Press.

Haggard, Stephan, Wonhyuk Lim, and Eusung Kim, eds. 2003. *Economic Crisis and Corporate Restructuring in Korea: Reforming the Chaebol.* Cambridge, UK: Cambridge University Press.

Hahm, Joon-Ho. 2004. "Financial Restructuring." In *The Korean Economy beyond the Crisis,* edited by Duck-Koo Chung and Barry Eichengreen. Cheltenham, UK: Edward Elgar.

——. 2005. "The Resurgence of Banking Institutions in Post-Crisis Korea." *Journal of Contemporary Asia* 35(3): 386–403.

Hahm, Joon-ho, and Wonhyuk Lim. 2004. "Financial Globalization and Korea's Post-Crisis Reform: A Political Economy Perspective." Unpublished manuscript, Yonsei University.

Hale, David D. 1998. "Dodging the Bullet—This Time." *Brookings Review* 16(3): 22–25.

———. 2007. "The East Asian Financial Crisis." Paper presented at A Decade Later: Asia's New Responsibilities in the International Monetary System conference, Seoul, May 29–30.

Hall, Peter A. 1993. "Policy Paradigm, Social Learning and the State: The Case of Economic Policy in Britain." *Comparative Politics* 25(3): 275–96.

Hall, Rodney Bruce. 2003. "The Discursive Demolition of the Asian Development Model." *International Studies Quarterly* 47(1): 71–99.

Hamilton, Gary, ed. 1996. *Asian Business Networks*. Berlin: Walter de Gruyter.

Hamilton-Hart, Natasha. 2002. *Asian States, Asian Bankers: Central Banking in Southeast Asia*. Ithaca: Cornell University Press.

———. 2003. "Asia's New Regionalism: Government Capacity and Cooperation in the Western Pacific." *Review of International Political Economy* 10: 222–45.

———. 2004. "Capital Flows and Financial Markets in Asia: National, Regional or Global?" In *Beyond Bilateralism: The US-Japan Relationship in the New Asia-Pacific*, edited by Ellis Krauss and T. J. Pempel. Stanford: Stanford University Press.

Hatch, Walter. 2000. Rearguard Regionalism: Protecting Core Networks in Japan's Political Economy. Ph.D. dissertation, University of Washington.

Hatch, Walter, and Kozo Yamamura. 1996. *Asia in Japan's Embrace: Building a Regional Production Alliance*. Cambridge, UK: Cambridge University Press.

Heaver, Richard. 2002. "Thailand's National Nutrition Program: Lessons in Management and Capacity Development." Health, Nutrition and Population Discussion Paper, World Bank, Washington, D.C.

Hedman, Eva-Lotta E. 2006. "The Philippines in 2005: Old Dynamics, New Conjuncture." *Asian Survey* 64(1): 187–93.

Henderson, J. Vernon, and Ari Kuncoro. 2004. "Corruption in Indonesia." National Bureau of Economic Research Working Paper no. 10674, Cambridge, Mass.

———. 2006. "Sick of Local Government Corruption? Vote Islamic." National Bureau of Economic Research Working Paper no. 12110, Cambridge, Mass.

Henning, C. Randall. 2002. *East Asian Financial Cooperation*. Washington, D.C.: Institute for International Economics.

Herberg, Mikkal. 2007. "The Rise of Asia's National Oil Companies," *The National Bureau of Asian Research*, Special Report No. 14.

Hewison, Kevin. 2003. "Crafting Thailand's New Social Contract." Unpublished manuscript, Southeast Asia Research Centre, University of Hong Kong.

———. 2004. "Crafting Thailand's New Social Contract." *Pacific Review* 17(4): 503–22.

———. 2005. "Neo-Liberalism and Domestic Capital: The Political Outcomes of the Economic Crisis in Thailand." *Journal of Development Studies* 41(2): 310–30.

———. 2006. "Boom, Bust, and Recovery." In *The Political Economy of Southeast Asia: Markets, Power and Contestation*, edited by Garry Rodan, Kevin Hewison, and Richard Robison. New York: Oxford University Press.

Hicken, Allen. 2001. "Parties, Policy and Patronage: Governance and Growth in Thailand." In *Corruption: The Boom and Bust of East Asia*, edited by José Edgardo L. Campos. Manila: Ateneo de Manila Press.

———. 2002. Parties, Pork and Policy: Policymaking in Developing Democracies. Ph.D. dissertation, University of California San Diego.

———. 2005. "Constitutional Reform and Budgetary Politics in Thailand." Paper presented at Annual MPSA meeting and 2005 Thai Studies Conference, Chicago, April.

———. 2007. "Party Fabrication: Constitutional Reform and the Rise of Thai Rak Thai." *Journal of East Asian Studies* 7(1): 149–58.

Hicken, Allen. forthcoming. "The 2007 Draft Constitution: A Return to Politics Past." *Crossroads.*

Higgott, Richard A. 2004. "US Foreign Policy and the 'Securitiztion' of Economic Globalization." *International Politics* 41: 147–75.

Hill, Hal. 1999. *The Indonesian Economy in Crisis: Causes, Consequences, and Lessons.* Singapore: Institute of Southeast Asian Studies.

Hohensee, Martin, and Kyungjik Lee. 2006. "A Survey on Hedging Markets in Asia: A Description of Asian Derivatives Markets from a Practical Perspective." *BIS Papers* 30(24): 261–81.

Holliday, Ian. 2000. "Productivist Welfare Capitalism: Social Policy in East Asia." *Political Studies* 48(4): 706–23.

Holliday, Ian, and Paul Wilding. 2003. *Welfare Capitalism in East Asia: Social Policy in the Tiger Economies.* New York: Palgrave Macmillan.

Holst, David Roland, and John Weiss. 2004. "ASEAN and China: Export Rivals or Partners in Regional Growth?" *World Economy* 27(8): 1255–74.

Hong Kong Trade Development Council. 2003. "Revised Forecast for Hong Kong Experts." Available from: http://www.tdctrade.com/econforum/tdc/tdc030803.htm.

Horiuchi, Akiyoshi. 2003. "The Big Bang Financial System Reforms: Implications for Corporate Governance." In *Japanese Governance: Beyond Japan Inc.*, edited by Jennifer Amyx and Peter Drysdale. London: RoutledgeCurzon.

Huang, Yasheng. 2003. *Selling China.* New York: Cambridge University Press.

Hutchcroft, Paul D. 1999. "Neither Dynamo nor Domino: Reforms and Crises in the Philippine Political Economy." In *The Politics of the Asian Economic Crisis*, edited by T. J. Pempel. Ithaca: Cornell University Press.

Hutchison, Jane. 2006. "Poverty of Politics in the Philippines." In *The Political Economy of Southeast Asia: Markets, Power and Contestation*, edited by Garry Rodan, Kevin Hewison, and Richard Robison. New York: Oxford University Press.

Ianchovichina, Elena, Sethaput Suthiwart-Narueput, and Min Zhao. 2004. "Regional Impact of China's WTO Accession." In *East Asia Integrates: A Trade Policy Agenda for Shared Growth*, edited by Kathie L. Krumm and Homi J. Kharas. Washington, D.C.: World Bank.

Ianchovichina, Elena, and Terrie Louise Walmsley. 2003. *The Impact of China's WTO Accession on East Asia.* Washington, D.C.: World Bank Poverty Reduction and Economic Management Network Economic Policy Division.

Ikenberry, G. John. 2001. *After Victory: Institutions, Strategic Restraint, and the Building of Order after Major Wars.* Princeton: Princeton University Press.

International Labour Organisation (ILO), Cross-Departmental Analysis and Reports Team. 1998. *The Social Impact of the Asian Financial Crisis.* Bangkok: ILO Regional Office for Asia and the Pacific Bangkok.

International Monetary Fund (IMF). 1998. "Government of Thailand Letters of Intent with the IMF (February [3rd Loi] and 26 May [4th Loi])." International Monetary Fund, Washington, D.C.

——. 2005a. *Indonesia: Selected Issues.* IMF Country Report no. 05/327. Washington D.C.: Asia and Pacific Department, International Monetary Fund.

——. 2005b. "Republic of Korea: 2004 Article IV Consultation—Staff Report; Staff Statement; and Public Information Notice on the Executive Board Discussion." International Monetary Fund, Washington, D.C.

——. 2007. "Japan: International Reserves and Foreign Currency Liquidity." August 10. Available from: http://www.imf.org/external/np/sta/ir/jpn/eng/curjpn.htm.

Jang, Ha Sung. 1999. "Corporate Governance and Economic Development: The Korean Experience." Paper presented at the Korea Development Institute—World Bank Conference on Democracy, Market Economy and Development, Seoul, February.

———. 2003. "Corporate Restructuring in Korea after the Economic Crisis." *Joint US-Korea Academic Studies* 13: 147–84.

Jayasuriya, Kanishka. 1998. "Introduction: A Framework for the Analysis of Legal Institutions in East Asia." In *Law, Capitalism and Power in East Asia: The Rule of Law and Legal Institutions*, edited by Kanishka Jayasuriya. London: Routledge.

———, ed. 1999. *Law, Capitalism and Power in Asia*. London: Routledge.

Job, Brian L. 2003. "Track 2 Diplomacy: Ideational Contribution to the Evolving Asian Security Order." In *Asian Security Order: Instrumental and Normative Features*, edited by Muthiah Alagappa. Stanford: Stanford University Press.

Johnson, Simon, and Todd Mitton. 2003. "Cronyism and Capital Controls: Evidence from Malaysia." *Journal of Financial Economics* 67(2): 351–82.

Joint Ministerial Statement of the 10th ASEAN+3 Finance Ministers' Meeting. 2007. Kyoto, Japan, May 5.

Jomo Kwame Sundaram, ed. 1998. *Tigers in Trouble: Financial Governance, Liberalisation and Crises in East Asia*. London: Zed Books.

———. 2001. "Capital Flows." In *Malaysian Eclipse: Economic Crisis and Recovery*, edited by Jomo Kwame Sundaram. London: Zed Books.

Jomo Kwame Sundaram, and Natasha Hamilton-Hart. 2001. "Financial Regulation, Crisis and Policy Response." In *Malaysian Eclipse: Economic Crisis and Recovery*, edited by Jomo Kwame Sundaram. London: Zed Books.

Jonsson, Gunnar. 2001. "Growth Accounting and the Medium Term Outlook in Thailand." In *Thailand: Selected Issues*, edited by IMF. Washington, D.C.: International Monetary Fund.

Kahler, Miles. 2000. "Conclusion: The Causes and Consequences of Legalization." *International Organization* 54(3): 661–83.

Kanjanaphoomin, Niwat. 2004. "Pension Fund, Provident Fund and Social Security System in Thailand." Paper presented at International Conference on Pensions in Asia, Hitotsubashi Collaboration Center, Tokyo, February 23–24.

Kaplan, Ethan, and Dani Rodrik. 2001. "Did the Malaysian Capital Controls Work?" National Bureau of Economic Research Working Paper No. 8142, Cambridge, Mass.

Katzenstein, Peter J. 2005. *A World of Regions: Asia and Europe in the American Imperium*. Ithaca: Cornell University Press.

———. 2006. *Beyond Japan: The Dynamics of East Asian Regionalism*. Ithaca: Cornell University Press.

Katzenstein, Peter J., and Takashi Shiraishi. 1997. *Network Power*. Ithaca: Cornell University Press.

Kawai, Masahiro. 2004. "Regional Economic Integration and Cooperation in East Asia." Paper presented at Experts' Seminar on the Impact and Coherence of OECD Country Policies on Asian Developing Economies, Paris, June 10–11.

———. 2005. "Reform of the Japanese Banking System." *International Economics and Economic Policy* 2(4): 307–35.

Keidanren. 2000. "Urgent Call for Active Promotion of Free Trade Agreements—Toward a New Dimension in Trade Policy." Available from: http://www.keidanren.or.jp/english/policy/2000/033/proposal.html [accessed November 5, 2001].

Kessler, Richard J. 1989. *Rebellion and Repression in the Philippines* New Haven: Yale Universit Press.

Kim, Byung-Kook, and Hyun-Chin Lim. 1999. "Labor against Itself: A Fundamental but Contentious Labor Movement and Structural Dilemmas of State Monism." In *Consolidating Democracy in South Korea*, edited by Larry Diamond and Byung-Kook Kim. Boulder: Lynne Rienner.

Kim, Byung-Tae. 2003. *Korea's Banking Law Reform: Post Asian Crisis*. The Hague: Kluwer Law International.

Kim, Dong-One, and Seongsu Kim. 2003. "Globalization, Financial Crisis, and Industrial Relations: The Case of South Korea." *Industrial Relations* 42(3): 356–61.

Kim, Il-Sup. 2000. "Financial Crisis and Its Impact on the Accounting System in Korea." Unpublished manuscript, Korea Accounting Standards Board, Seoul.

Klingner, Bruce. 2006. "South Korea's Economic Forecast: Partly Sunny, with Increasing Likelihood of Gloom in the Morning." Unpublished manuscript, Eurasia Group, New York.

Korea Labor Institute. 1999. *Korean Labor and Employment Laws*. Seoul: Korean Labor Institute.

Krauss, Ellis S. 2004. "The United States and Japan in APEC's EVSL Negotiations: Regional Multilateralism and Trade." In *Beyond Bilateralism: US-Japan Relations in the New Asia-Pacific*, edited by Ellis S. Krauss and T. J. Pempel. Stanford: Stanford University Press.

Krugman, Paul. 1998. "What Ever Happened to the Asian Miracle?" Available from: http://web.mit.edu/krugman/www/perspire.htm.

——. 1999. "Capital Control Freaks: How Malaysia Got Away with Economic Heresy." Available from: http://slate.msn.com/id/35534/ [accessed October 24, 2004].

Ku, Yeun-wen. 1997. *Welfare Capitalism in Taiwan*. New York: St. Martin's Press.

——. 2002. "Towards a Taiwanese Welfare State: Demographic Change, Politics and Social Policy." In *Discovering the Welfare State in East Asia*, edited by Christian Aspalter. New York: Praeger.

Kuhonta, Erik M. 2003. "The Political Economy of Equitable Development in Thailand." *American Asian Review* 21(4): 69–108.

Kuwajima, Kyoki. 2003. "Health Sector Management and Governance in Thailand." In *The Role of Governance in Asia*, edited by Yasutami Shimomura. Singapore: Institute for Southeast Asian Studies.

Kwon, Huck-ju. 1999a. "Inadequate Policy or Operational Failure?: The Potential Crisis of the Korean National Pension Programme." *Social Policy and Administration* 33(1): 20–38.

——. 1999b. *The Welfare State in Korea: The Politics of Legitimation* New York: St. Martin's Press.

Kwon, Soonman. 2002. "Globalization and Health Policy in Korea." *Global Social Policy* 2(3): 279–94.

——. 2003. "Pharmaceutical Reform and Physician Strikes in Korea: Separation of Drug Prescribing and Dispensing." *Social Science and Medicine* 57: 529–38.

Lall, Sanjaya, and Manuel Albaladejo. 2004. "China's Competitive Performance: A Threat to East Asian Manufactured Exports?" *World Development* 32(9): 1441–66.

Lane, Timothy, Atish R. Ghosh, Javier Hamann, Steven Phillips, Marianne Schulze-Ghattas, and Tsidi Tsikata. 1999. "IMF-Supported Programs in Indonesia, Korea, and Thailand: A Preliminary Assessment." Washington, D.C.: International Monetary Fund.

Laquian, Aprodicio A., and Eleanor R. Laquian. 2002. *The Erap Tragedy: Tales from the Snake Pit*. Manila: Anvil.

Lardy, Nicholas R. 1998. *China's Unfinished Economic Revolution*. Washington, D.C.: Brookings Institution.

——. 2002. *Integrating China into the Global Economy.* Washington, D.C.: Brookings Institution.

Laurence, Henry. 2001. *Money Rules: The New Politics of Finance in Britain and Japan.* Ithaca: Cornell University Press.

Lee, Cheol-Soo. 2002. "Law and Labor-Management Relations in South Korea: Advancing Industrial Democratization." In *Law and Labor Market Regulation in East Asia,* edited by Sean Cooney, Tim Lindsey, Richard Mitchell, and Ying Zhu. New York: Routledge.

Lee, Sook-Jong, and Taejoon Han. 2006. "The Demise of 'Korea, Inc.': Paradigm Shift in Korea's Developmental State." *Journal of Contemporary Asia* 36: 305–24.

Leung, Julia. 2006. "ABF2 Experience on Developing Bond Markets in Asia." Paper presented at FLAR-CEPAL Conference on The Role of Regional Funds in Macroeconomic Stabilization, Lima, Peru, July 17–18.

Levy-Yeyati, Eduardo, and Federico Sturzenegger. 2005. "Classifying Exchange Rate Regimes: Deeds vs. Words." *European Economic Review* 49: 1603–35.

Li, David. 2000. "Insider Control, Corporate Governance, and the Soft Budget Constraint: Theory, Evidence, and Policy Implications." In *Financial Market Reform in China: Progress, Problems, and Prospects,* edited by Baizhu Chen, J. Kimball Dietrich, and Yi Fang. Boulder: Westview Press.

Liddle, R. William. 1991. "The Relative Autonomy of the Third World Politician: Soeharto and Indonesian Economic Development in Comparative Perspective." *International Studies Quarterly* 35(4): 403–27.

——. 2001. "Indonesia in 2000: A Shaky Start for Democracy." *Asian Survey* 41(1): 208–20.

Lim, Hyun-Chin, and Jin-Ho Jang. 2006. "Neo-Liberalism in Post-Crisis South Korea: Social Conditions and Outcomes." *Journal of Contemporary Asia* 36(4): 442–63.

Lim, Wonhyuk, and Joon-Ho Hahm. 2006. "Turning a Crisis into an Opportunity: The Political Economy of Korea's Financial Sector Reform." In *From Crisis to Opportunity: Financial Globalization and East Asian Capitalism,* edited by Jongryn Mo and Daniel I. Okimoto. Washington, D.C.: Brookings Institution.

Lin, Kuo-min. 1997. From Authoritarianism to Statism: The Politics of National Health Insurance. Ph.D. dissertation. Yale University.

Ma, Guonan, and Eli Remolona. 2005. "Opening Markets through a Regional Bond Fund: Lessons from ABF2." *BIS Quarterly Review* (June): 81–92.

MacIntyre, Andrew J., ed. 1994. *Business and Government in Industrializing Asia.* Ithaca: Cornell University Press.

——. 2000. "Funny Money: Fiscal Policy, Rent-seeking and Economic Performance in Indonesia." In *Rents, Rent-Seeking and Economic Development: Theory and Evidence in Asia,* edited by Mushtaq H. Khan and Jomo Kwame Sundaram. Cambridge, UK: Cambridge University Press.

——. 2001. "Institutions and Investors: The Politics of the Financial Crisis in Southeast Asia." *International Organization* 55: 81–122.

——. 2003. *The Power of Institutions: Political Architecture and Governance.* Ithaca: Cornell University Press.

——. 2006. "Crony Capitalism in East Asia: Has Anything Changed?" Paper presented at the Conference on East Asia a Decade after the Crisis, Australian National University, Canberra, July 20–21.

MacIntyre, Andrew J., and Barry Naughton. 2005. "The Decline of a Japan-Led Model of the East Asian Economy." In *Remapping East Asia,* edited by T. J. Pempel. Ithaca: Cornell University Press.

MacKenzie, Donald. 2006. *An Engine, Not a Camera: How Financial Models Shape Markets.* Cambridge, Mass.: MIT Press.

Mackie, J. A. C. 1988. "Economic Growth in the ASEAN Region: The Political Underpinnings." In *Achieving Industrialization in East Asia,* edited by Helen Hughes. Cambridge: Cambridge University Press.

Mackie, Jamie, and Andrew MacIntyre. 1994. "Politics." In *Indonesia's New Order: The Dynamics of Socio-economic Transformation,* edited by Hal Hill. Honolulu: University of Hawaii Press.

Mahani Zainal Abidin. 2002. *Rewriting the Rules: The Malaysian Crisis Management Model.* Petaling Jaya, Selangor, Malaysia: Pearson Malaysia Sdn. Bhd.

Malley, Michael. 2002. "Indonesia in 2001: Restoring Stability in Jakarta." *Asian Survey* 42(1): 124–32.

Manger, Mark. 2005. "Competition and Bilateralism in Trade Policy: The Case of Japan's Free Trade Agreements." *Review of International Political Economy* 12(5): 804–28.

Martin, Will, and Elena Ianchovichina. 2001. "Implications of China's Accession to the World Trade Organization for China and the WTO." *World Economy* 24(9): 1205–19.

Martinez, Patricia. 2002. "Malaysia in 2001: An Interlude of Consolidation." *Asian Survey* 42(1): 133–40.

Mattli, Walter. 1999. *The Logic of Regional Integration: Europe and Beyond.* Cambridge, UK: Cambridge University Press.

McKinnon, Ronald I. 2005. *Exchange Rates under the East Asian Dollar Standard: Living with Conflicted Virtue.* Cambridge, Mass.: MIT Press.

McLeod, Ross. 2004. "Dealing With Bank System Failure: Indonesia, 1997–2003." *Bulletin of Indonesian Economic Studies* 40(1): 95–116.

———. 2006. "Indonesia's New Deposit Guarantee Law." *Bulletin of Indonesian Economic Studies* 42(1): 59–78.

McMillan, John, and Barry Naughton. 1992. "How to Reform a Planned Economy: Lessons from China." *Oxford Review of Economic Policy* 8(1): 130–43.

McMillan, John, and Christopher Woodruff. 2002. "The Central Role of Entrepreneurs in Transition Economies." *Journal of Economic Perspectives* 16(3): 153–70.

Milne, R. S., and Diane K. Mauzy. 1999. *Malaysian Politics under Mahathir.* London: Routledge.

Ministry of Finance and Economy (MOFE), Korea. n.d. "Purpose." Available from: http://english.mofe.go.kr/about/dpm.html.

Ministry of International Trade and Industry (MITI), Japan. 1999. "White Paper on International Trade 1999." Available from: http://www.meti.go.jp/english/report/data/gWP1999e.html [accessed February 24, 2002].

Mintorahardjo, Sukowaluyo. 2001. *BLBI Simalakama: Pertaruhan Kekuasaan Presiden Soeharto.* Jakarta: Penerbit RESI.

Mo, Jongryn, and Chung-in Moon. 2003. "Business—Government Relations under Kim Dae-jung." In *Economic Crisis and Corporate Restructuring in Korea: Reforming the Chaebol,* edited by Stephan Haggard, Wonhyuk Lim, and Euysung Kim. New York: Cambridge University Press.

Mo, Jongryn, and Daniel Okimoto, eds. 2006. *From Crisis to Opportunity: Financial Globalization and East Asian Capitalism.* Stanford: Walter H. Shorenstein Asia-Pacific Research Center.

Montinola, Gabriella, Yingyi Qian, and Barry Weingast. 1995. "Federalism, Chinese Style: The Political Basis for Economic Success in China." *World Politics* 48(1): 50–81.

Mujani, Saiful. 2006. "Mengkonsolidasikan Demokrasi Indonesia: Refleksi Satu Windu Reformasi." Working Paper, Lembaga Survei Indonesia, Jakarta.

Munakata, Naoko. 2002. "How Trade Agreements Can Reform Japan." Available from: http://www.brook.edu [accessed February 3, 2003].

———. 2006a. "Has Politics Caught Up with Markets?: In Search of East Asian Economic Regionalism." In *Beyond Japan: The Dynamics of East Asian Regionalism,* edited by Peter J. Katzenstein and Takashi Shiraishi. Ithaca: Cornell University Press.

———. 2006b. *Transforming East Asia: The Evolution of Regional Economic Integration.* Washington, D.C.: Brookings Institution.

Mundell, Robert. 2004. "Currency Area Formation and the East Asian Region." In *East Asia's Monetary Future: Integration in the Global Economy,* edited by Suthiphand Chirathivat, Emil-Maria Claassen, and Jürgen Schroeder. Northampton, UK: Edward Elgar.

Nakamura, Takeo, and Toshiaki Shinohara. 2007. "External Aspects of East Asian Economics and Finance: In Light of Growing Interest in Regional Integration." Bank of Japan Center for Monetary Cooperation in Asia Research Paper, Tokyo, January 19.

Naughton, Barry. 2000. "Financial Development and Macroeconomic Stability in China." In *Financial Market Reform in China: Progress, Problems, and Prospects,* edited by Baizhu Chen, J. Kimball Dietrich, and Yi Fang. Boulder: Westview Press.

Noble, Gregory, and John Ravenhill. 2000. "The Good, the Bad and the Ugly?: Korea, Taiwan and the Asian Financial Crisis." In *The Asian Financial Crisis and the Architecture of Global Finance,* edited by Gregory Noble and John Ravenhill. New York: Cambridge University Press.

Nolan, Peter. 2001. *China and the Global Business Revolution.* London: Palgrave.

Noland, Marcus. 2000. "The Philippines in the Asian Financial Crisis." *Asian Survey* 40(3): 401–12.

North, Douglass C., John Joseph Wallis, and Barry R. Weingast. 2006. "A Conceptual Framework for Interpreting Recorded Human History." National Bureau of Economic Research Working Paper no. 12795, Cambridge, Mass.

North, Douglass C., and Barry R. Weingast. 1989. "Constitutions and Commitment: The Evolution of Institutional Governing Public Choice in Seventeenth-Century England." *Journal of Economic History* 49(4): 803–32.

Nukul Commission. 1998. *Analysis and Evaluation on Facts behind Thailand's Economic Crisis: The Nukul Commission Report.* Bankok: Nation Multimedia.

O'Brien, Kevin, and Lianjiang Li. 2006. *Rightful Resistance in Rural China.* Cambridge, UK: Cambridge University Press.

Oatley, Thomas, and Robert Nabors. 1998. "Redistributive Cooperation: Market Failure, Wealth Transfers, and the Basle Accord." *International Organization* 52(1): 35–54.

Ogawa, Eiji, and Junko Shimizu. 2005. "A Deviation Measurement for Coordinated Exchange Rate Policies in East Asia." Discussion Paper No. 05-E-017, Research Institute of Economy, Trade and Industray (RIETI), Tokyo.

Oi, Jean C. 1992. "Fiscal Reform and the Economic Foundations of Local State Corporatism." *World Politics* 45(1): 99–126.

Oi, Jean C., and Andrew G. Walder, eds. 1999. *Property Rights and Economic Reform in China.* Stanford: Stanford University Press.

Okonjo-Iweala, Ngozi, Victoria Kwakwa, Andrea Beckwith, and Zafar Ahmed. 1999. "Impact of Asia's Financial Crisis on Cambodia and the Lao PDR." *Finance and Development* 36(3): 48–51.

Painter, Martin. 2005. "Thaksinocracy or Managerialization?: Reforming the Thai Bureaucracy." Southeast Asia Research Center Working Paper, City University of Hong Kong, Hong Kong.

Pakorn Malakul na Ayudhya. 2002. "Remarks by Mr. Pakorn Malakul na Ayudhya, Deputy Governor of the Bank of Thailand, on Occasion of The Inauguration of the Monetary Policy Committee, Bank of Ghana." September 10. Available from: http://www.bot.or.th.

Pangestu, Mari, and Manggi Habir. 2002. "The Boom, Bust and Restructuring of Indonesian Banks." IMF Working Paper 02/66, International Monetary Fund, Washington, D.C.

Pannarunothai, Supasit, Samrit Srithamrongsawat, Manit Kongpan, and Patchanee Thumvanna. 2000. "Financing Reforms for the Thai Health Card Scheme." *Health Policy and Planning* 15(3): 303–11.

Pasuk Phongpaichit, and Chris Baker. 1998. *Thailand's Boom and Bust.* Chiangmai: Silkworm Books.

——. 2000. *Thailand's Crisis.* Singapore: Institute of South East Asian Studies.

——. 2002. *Thailand: Economy and Politics.* New York: Oxford University Press.

——. 2004. *Thaksin: The Business of Politics in Thailand.* Chiangmai: Silkworm Books.

Pekkanen, Saadia M., Mireya Solís, and Saori N. Katada. 2006. "Gains for Control: Forum Choices in International Trade and Japanese Economic Diplomacy." Paper presented at International Studies Association Annual Convention, San Diego, March.

Pempel, T. J. 1999a. "Introduction." In *The Politics of the Asian Economic Crisis,* edited by T. J. Pempel. Ithaca: Cornell University Press.

——. 1999b. "Regional Ups; Regional Downs." In *The Politics of the Asian Economic Crisis,* edited by T. J. Pempel. Ithaca: Cornell University Press.

——. 2005a. "Firebreak: East Asian Institutionalizes Its Finances." Paper presented at Conference on Institutionalizing Northeast Asia: Making the Impossible Possible?, United Nations University and Aoyama Gakuin University, Tokyo, September 20–22.

——. 2005b. *Remapping East Asia: The Construction of a Region.* Ithaca: Cornell University Press.

——. 2006a. "A Decade of Political Torpor: When Political Logic Trumps Economic Rationality." In *Beyond Japan: The Dynamics of East Asian Regionalism,* edited by Peter J. Katzenstein and Takashi Shiraishi. Ithaca: Cornell University Press.

——. 2006b. "The Race to Connect East Asia: An Unending Steeplechase." *Asian Economic Policy Review* 1(2): 239–54.

Pempel, T. J., and Shujiro Urata. 2006. "Japan: A New Move toward Bilateral Trade Agreements." In *Bilateral Trade Agreements in the Asia-Pacific: Origins, Evolution and Implications,* edited by Vinod K. Aggarwal and Shujiro Urata. London: Routledge.

Pepinsky, Thomas B. 2007. Coalitions and Crises: Authoritarianism, Adjustment, and Transitions in Emerging Markets. Ph.D. dissertation, Yale University.

Pinto, Pablo. 2005. "The Politics of Investment: Partisanship and the Sectoral Allocation of Foreign Direct Investment." Paper presented at The American Political Science Association Annual Meeting, Washington, D.C., September 1–4.

Polsiri, Piruna, and Yupana Wiwattanakantang. 2004. "Corporate Governance of Banks in Thailand." Unpublished manuscript, Asian Development Bank Institute, Tokyo.

Powell, Bill. 2005. "Uncharted Waters," *Time,* July 11.

PricewaterhouseCoopers. 2006. "NPL Asia." Issue 7, Hong Kong.

Primorac, Marina. 2006. "Per Jacobsson Lecture: Will Asian Monetary Integration Ever Happen?" *IMF Survey* 35: 292.

Qian, Yingyi. 2003. "How Reform Worked in China." In *In Search of Prosperity: Analytic Narratives on Economic Growth,* edited by Dani Rodrik. Princeton: Princeton University Press.

Qian, Yingyi, and Chenggang Xu. 1993. "Why China's Economic Reforms Differ: The M-Form Hierarchy and Entry/Expansion of the Non-State Sector." *Economics of Transition* 1(2): 135–70.

Radelet, Steve, and Jeffrey Sachs. 1998. "The Onset of the East Asian Financial Crisis." Cambridge, Mass.: Harvard Institute for International Development.

Ramesh, M. 2000. *Welfare Capitalism in Southeast Asia: Social Security, Health and Education Policies.* New York: St. Martin's Press.

———. 2004. *Social Policy in East and South East Asia: Education, Health, Housing and Income Maintenance.* New York: Routledge Curzon.

Ravenhill, John. 2003. "The New Bilateralism in the Asia-Pacific." *Third World Quarterly* 24(2): 299–317.

———. 2006a. "Is China an Economic Threat to Southeast Asia?" *Asian Survey* 46(5): 653–74.

———. 2006b. "The Political Economy of the New Asia-Pacific Bilateralism: Benign, Banal or Simply Bad?" In *Bilateral Trade Agreements in the Asia-Pacific: Origins, Evolution and Implications,* edited by Vinod K. Aggarwal and Shujiro Urata. London: Routledge.

———. 2007. "China's 'Peaceful Development' and Southeast Asia: A Positive Sum Game?" In *China's Rule and the Balance of Influence in Asia,* edited by William W. Keller and Thomas G. Rawski. Pittsburgh: University of Pittsburgh Press.

Reyes, Celia M. 2002. "The Poverty Fight: Have We Made an Impact?" Discussion Paper series no. 2002-20. Philippine Institute of Development Studies, Manila.

Richter, Kaspar. 2006. "Thailand's Growth Path: From Recovery to Prosperity." World Bank Policy Research Working Paper 3912, Washington, D.C.

Riedinge, Jeffrey M. 1995. *Agrarian Reform in the Philippines: Democratic Transitions and Redistributive Reform.* Stanford: Stanford University Press.

Rigger, Shelley. 2001. *From Opposition to Power: Taiwan's Democratic Progressive Party.* Boulder: Lynne Rienner.

Robison, Richard, and Vedi R. Hadiz. 2004. *Reorganizing Power in Indonesia: The Politics of Oligarchy in an Age of Markets.* London: RoutledgeCurzon.

Rogoff, Kenneth S., Aasim M. Husain, Ashoka Mody, Robin Brooks, and Nienke Oomes. 2004. "Evolution and Performance of Exchange Rate Regimes." Occasional Paper 229, International Monetary Fund, Washington, D.C.

Root, Hilton. 1996. *The Key to the East Asian Miracle: Making Shared Growth Credible.* Washington, D.C.: Brookings Institution.

Ross, Andrew. 2006. *Fast Boat to China: Corporate Flight and the Consequences of Free Trade: Lessons from Shanghai.* New York: Pantheon Books.

Rozman, Gilbert. 2004. *Northeast Asia's Stunted Regionalism: Bilateral Distrust in the Shadow of Globalization.* Cambridge, UK: Cambridge University Press.

Rudra, Nita. 2007. "Welfare States in Developing Countries: Unique or Universal?" *Journal of Politics* 69(2): 378–96.

Samudavanija, Chai-Anan, Kusuma Snitwongse, and Suchit Bunbongkarn. 1990. *From Armed Suppression to Political Offensive.* Bangkok: Institute of Security and International Studies, Faculty of Political Science, Chulalongkorn University.

Schaede, Ulrike. 2006. "Competition for Corporate Control: Institutional Investors, Investment Funds and Hostile Takeovers in Japan." Working Paper, School of International Relations and Pacific Studies, University of California, San Diego.

Scollay, Robert, and John Gilbert. 2001. *New Regional Trading Arrangements in the Asia Pacific?* Washington, D.C.: Institute for International Economics.

Shambaugh, David. 2005. "The New Strategic Triangle: U.S. and European Reactions to China's Rise." *Washington Quarterly* 28(3): 7–25.

Sheng, Andrew. 2005. "Why Asia Needs to Integrate Financial Markets," *Financial Times,* 1 December.

———. 2006. "The Asian Way to Integration." *East Asian Bureau of Economic Research Newsletter,* November, 1–2.

Shirk, Susan. 1993. *The Political Logic of Economic Reform in China.* Berkeley: University of California Press.

Shleifer, Andrei, and Robert W. Vishny. 1993. "Corruption." *Quarterly Journal of Economics* 108(3): 599–617.

———. 1997. "A Survey of Corporate Governance." *Journal of Finance* 52(2): 737–83.

Shugart, Matthew Soberg, and Stephan Haggard. 2001. "Institutions and Public Policy in Presidential Systems." In *Presidents, Parliaments, and Policy,* edited by Stephan Haggard and Mathew D. McCubbins. Cambridge, UK: Cambridge University Press.

Siregar, Reza, and William James. 2006. "Designing an Integrated Financial Supervision Agency: Selected Lessons and Challenges for Indonesia." *ASEAN Economic Bulletin* 23(1): 98–113.

Sirivedhin, Tanya, and Rungsun Hataiseree. 2000. "Central Bank Independence: A Thai Perspective." Paper presented at the SEANZA Advisors' Meeting, 14 January.

Soedradjad Djiwandono. 2005. *Bank Indonesia and the Crisis: An Insider's View.* Singapore: Institute for South East Asian Studies.

Solis, Mireya. 2003. "Japan's New Regionalism: The Politics of Free Trade Talks with Mexico." *Journal of East Asian Studies* 3(3): 377–404.

Son, Annette Hye Kyung. 2001. "Taiwan's Path to National Health Insurance (1950–1995)." *International Journal of Social Welfare* 10(1): 45–53.

Standard Chartered Bank. 2005. "Standard Chartered and Korea First Bank to launch new brand identity as SC Jeil Eun Haeng." June 13. Available from: www.standardchartered.com/global/news/2005/grp_20050613.pdf.

Stasavage, David. 2002. "Credible Commitment in Early Modern Europe: North and Weingast Revisited." *Journal of Law, Economics, and Organization* 18(1): 155–86.

Steinfeld, Edward S. 1998. *Forging Reform in China: The Fate of State-Owned Industry.* Cambridge, UK: Cambridge University Press.

———. 1999. "Beyond the Transition: China's Economy at Century's End." *Current History* 98(629): 271–75.

———. 2004. "China's Shallow Integration: Networked Production and the New Challenges for Late Industrialization." *World Development* 32(11): 1971–87.

Stubbs, Richard. 1999. "War and Economic Development: Export-Oriented Industrialization in East and Southeast Asia." *Comparative Politics* 31(3): 337–55.

Suehiro, Akira. 2002. "Restructuring and Re-engineering of Local Commercial Banks in Thailand: From Family-Owned Bank to a Universal Bank." Paper presented at the 4th MDT Project, Institute of Social Science, University of Tokyo, July 22–24.

Supakankunti, Siripen. 2000. "Future Prospects of Voluntary Health Insurance in Thailand." *Health Policy and Planning* 15(1): 85–94.

Tang, Kwong-Leung. 2000. *Social Welfare Development in East Asia.* New York: Palgrave.

Tangcharoensathien, Viroj, Anuwat Supachutikul, and Jongkol Letiendumrong. 1999. "The Social Security Scheme in Thailand: What Lessons Can Be Drawn?" *Social Science and Medicine* 48: 913–23.

Tay, Simon S. C. 2005. "An East Asia Community and the United States." Paper presented at International Workshop organized by the Council on East Asian Community, Tokyo, June.

——. 2006. "An East Asia Community and the United States: A View from ASEAN." Paper presented at International Workshop organized by the Council on East Asian Community, Singapore, June 26.

Thun, Eric. 2006. *Changing Lanes in China*. Cambridge, UK: Cambridge University Press.

Tiberghien, Yves. 2004. "Policy-Making in the Era of Financial Globalization: The Battle for Japanese Corporate Reforms, 1996–2002." Unpublished manuscript, University of British Columbia.

Tiebout, Charles. 1956. "A Pure Theory of Local Expenditures." *Journal of Political Economy* 64(5): 416–24.

Tiwari, Rajnish. 2003. "Post-Crisis Exchange Rate Regimes in Southeast Asia: An Empirical Survey of De-Facto Policies." Unpublished manuscript, University of Hamburg.

Tocqueville, Alexis de. 1856/1998. *The Old Regime and the Revolution, Vol. 1: The Complete Text*. Translated by Alan S. Kahan. Chicago: University of Chicago Press.

Towse, Adrian, Anne Mills, and Viroj Tangcharoensathien. 2004. "Learning from Thailand's Health Reforms." *British Medical Journal* 328(10): 103–5.

Transparency International. 2006. "Corruption Perceptions Index." Available from: http://www.transparency.org.

United Nations Conference on Trade and Development (UNCTAD). 2006. *Foreign Direct Investment Online*, online database. Available from: http://www.unctad.org/Templates/Page.asp?intItemID=1923.

United Nations Conference on Trade and Development/World Trade Organization (UNCTAD/WTO), International Trade Centre. 2004. "Philippines." Available from: http://www.intracen.org/countries/toolpd03/phl_3.pdf [accessed January 26, 2007].

United Nations Development Programme and China Development Research Foundation (UNDP & CDRF). 2005. *China Human Development Report*. Beijing: United Nations Development Programme.

United Nations Educational, Scientific and Cultural Organization (UNESCO). 2000a. "Education for All: The Year 2000 Assessment, Thailand Country Report." Available from: http://www2.unesco.org/wef/countryreports/thailand/contents.html.

——. 2000b. "Education for All: The Year 2000 Assessment, Philippines Country Report." Available from: www2.unesco.org/wef/countryreports/philippines/contents.html#cont.

University of California Institute on Global Conflict and Cooperation. 1996. "Northeast Asia Cooperation Dialogue 5." Available from: http://igcc.ucsd.edu/regions/asia_pacific/NEACD05.php.

US-ASEAN Business Council. 2003. "The ASEAN Free Trade Area and Other Areas of ASEAN Economic Cooperation." Available from: http://www.us-asean.org/afta.asp.

U.S. Department of the Treasury. 2006. "Remarks by Under Secretary for International Affairs Timothy D. Adams at the World Economic Forum-East Asia Panel on Asian Financial Integration: A Miracle in the Making?" June 15. Available from: http://www.treas.gov/press/releases/js4323.htm.

Vogel, Steven K. 2006. *Japan Re-Modelled: How Government and Industry Are Reforming Japanese Capitalism*. Ithaca: Cornell University Press.

Volz, Ulrich. 2006. "Three Cases for Monetary Integration in East Asia." Working Paper FOX-04, Macmillan Center for International and Area Studies, Yale University, New Haven.

Wade, Robert. 1990. *Governing the Market: Economic Theory and the Role of Government in East Asian Industrialization*. Princeton: Princeton University Press.

Wade, Robert. 1992. "East Asia's Economic Success: Conflicting Perspectives, Partial Insights, Shaky Evidence." *World Politics* 44(2): 270–320.

———. 1998. "The Asian Debt-and-Development Crisis of 1997–?: Causes and Consequences." *World Development* 26(8): 1535–53.

———. 2007. "A New International Financial Architecture?" *New Left Review* 46: 113–29.

Wade, Robert, and Frank Veneroso. 1998. "The Asian Crisis: The High Debt Model versus
the Wall Street-Treasury-IMF Complex." *New Left Review* 1(/228): 3–23.

Walt, Stephen M. 2005. *Taming American Power: The Global Response to U.S. Primacy.* New
York: Norton.

Walter, Andrew. 2007. *Governing Finance: East Asia's Adoption of International Standards.*
Ithaca: Cornell University Press.

Warr, Peter G. 1998. "Thailand." In *East Asia in Crisis: From Being a Miracle to Needing
One?,* edited by Ross H. McLeod and Ross Garnaut. London: Routledge.

———. 2002. "Crisis Vulnerability." *Asian-Pacific Economic Literature* 16(1): 36–47.

Warr, Peter G., and Isra Sartinsart. 2004. *Poverty Targeting in Thailand.* Tokyo: Asian Development Bank Institute.

Weingast, Barry R. 1995. "The Economic Role of Political Institutions: Market-Preserving
Federalism and Economic Development." *Journal of Law, Economics, and Organization* 11(1):
1–31.

Weiss, John. 2004. *People's Republic of China and Its Neighbors: Partners or Competitors for
Trade and Investment?* Manila: Asian Development Bank.

Weiss, John, and Gao Shanwen. 2003. *People's Republic of China's Export Threat to ASEAN:
Competition in the US and Japanese Markets.* Manila: Asian Development Bank.

Welsh, Bridget. 2005. "Malaysia in 2004: Out of Mahathir's Shadow?" *Asian Survey* 45(1):
153–60.

Wibbels, Erik. 2006. "Dependency Revisited: International Markets, Business Cycles, and
Social Spending in the Developing World." *International Organization* 60: 433–68.

Williams, Jonathan, and Nghia Nguyen. 2005. "Financial Liberalisation, Crisis and Restructuring: A Comparative Study of Bank Performance and Bank Governance in South East
Asia." *Journal of Banking and Finance* 29(8–9): 2119–54.

Williamson, John. 1999. "The Case for a Common Basket Peg for East Asian Currencies."
In *Exchange Rate Policies in Emerging Asian Countries,* edited by Stefan Collignon, Jean
Pisani-Ferry, and Yung Chul Park. New York: Routledge.

———. 2005. *A Currency Basket for East Asia, Not Just China.* Washington, D.C.: Institute for
Internatioanl Economics.

Winters, Jeffrey A. 1999. "The Determinant of Financial Crisis in Asia." In *The Politics of
the Asian Economic Crisis,* edited by T. J. Pempel. Ithaca: Cornell University Press.

Witte, Johanna. 2000. "Education in Thailand after the Crisis: A Balancing Act between
Globalization and National Self-Contemplation." *International Journal of Educational Development* 20(3): 223–45.

Wong, John, and Sarah Chan. 2003. "China-ASEAN Free Trade Agreement: Shaping Future Economic Relations." *Asian Survey* 43(3): 507–26.

Wong, Joseph. 2003. "Resisting Reform: The Politics of Health Care in Democratizing Taiwan." *American Asian Review* 21(2): 25–56.

———. 2005. *Healthy Democracies: Welfare Politics in Taiwan and South Korea.* Ithaca: Cornell
University Press.

Woo, Jung-en. 1991. *Race to the Swift: State and FInance in Korean Industrialization.* New
York: Columbia University Press.

World Bank. n.d. *World Development Indicators*, online database. Available from: http://dev data.worldbank.org/dataonline.

———. 1993. *The East Asian Miracle: Economic Growth and Public Policy.* New York: Oxford University Press.

———. 1998a. *East Asia: The Road to Recovery.* Washington, D.C.: World Bank.

———. 1998b. "Philippine Social Expenditure Priorities." Report no. 18562-PH, Washington, D.C.

———. 2002. "Thailand: Country Development Partnership: Social Protection." Report no. 24378, Washington, D.C.

———. 2006. *East Asia Update.* Washington, D.C.: World Bank.

———. 2007. *East Asia and Pacific Update.* Washington, D.C.: World Bank.

World Bank Thailand Office. 1999a. "Thailand Social Monitor 1: Challenge for Social Reform." Bangkok: World Bank Thailand Office.

———. 1999b. "Thailand Social Monitor 2: Coping with the Crisis in Education and Health." Bangkok: World Bank Thailand Office.

World Economic Forum. 2002. *The Global Competitiveness Report 2001–2002.* New York: Oxford University Press.

———. 2004. *The Global Competitiveness Report 2003–2004.* New York: Oxford University Press.

———. 2006. *The Global Competitiveness Report 2006–2007.* Basingstoke, UK: Palgrave Macmillan.

World Trade Organization (WTO). 1998. "Regionalism: Article XXIV of GATT 1994 (2)." Available from: http://www.wto.org/english/thewto_e/whatis_e/eol/e/wto08/wto8_57.htm#note4 [accessed September 15, 2002].

Xu, Xiaonian, and Yan Wang. 1997. "Ownership Structure, Corporate Governance, and Firm's Performance: The Case of Chinese Stock Companies." Policy Research Working Paper 1794, Economic Development Institute, World Bank, Washington, D.C.

Yahuda, Michael. 2004. *The International Politics of the Asia-Pacific.* London and New York: RoutledgeCurzon.

Yam, Joseph C. K. 1997. *Asian Monetary Cooperation.* Washington, D.C.: Per Jacobsson Foundation.

Yang, Jae-jin. 2000. The 1999 Pension Reform and a New Social Contract in South Korea. Ph.D. dissertation, Rutgers University.

———. 2006. "Corporate Unionism and Labor Market Flexibility in South Korea." *Journal of East Asian Studies* 6(2): 205–32.

Yi, Sunny, and Chul-Joon Park. 2006. "Turbocharging Asian Turnarounds." *Harvard Business Review* 84(6): 30.

Yoo, Kil-sang, Jaeho Keum, Jai-joon Hur, Byung Hee Lee, and Jiyuen Chang. 2002. "Labor Market Trends and the Employment Insurance System in Korea." In *Active Labor Market Policies and Unemployment Insurance in Selected Countries,* edited by Kil-sang Yoo and Jiyuen Chang. Seoul: Korea Labor Institute.

Yoo, Seong-Min. 1999. "Corporate Restructuring in Korea: Policy Issues before and during the Crisis." Korea Development Institute Working Paper no. 9903, Seoul.

Yoon, Youngmo. 1999. "Chaebol Reform: The Missing Agenda in 'Corporate Governance'." Paper presented at the Conference on Corporate Governance in Asia: A Comparative Perspective, Seoul, Korea, March 3–5.

Yoshimatsu, Hidetaka. 2005. "Japan's *Keidanren* and Free Trade Agreements: Societal Interests and Trade Policy." *Asian Survey* 45(2): 258–78.

Yun, Mikyung. 2003. "Foreign Direct Investment and Corporate Restructuring after the Crisis." In *Economic Crisis and Corporate Restructuring in Korea: Reforming the Chaebol,* edited by Stephan Haggard, Wonhyuk Lim, and Eusung Kim. Cambridge, UK: Cambridge University Press.

Yuntho, Emerson. 2005a. "Korupsi BLBI dan Persidangan In Absentia." Available from: http://www.antikorupsi.org/mod.php?mod=publisher&op=viewarticle&artid=6351 [accessed June 1, 2006].

——. 2005b. "Tim Koordinasi Pemberantasan Korupsi: Antara Harapan dan Kekhawatiran." Available from: http://www.antikorupsi.org/docs/timtastipikoreson.pdf [accessed May 24, 2006].

Yusuf, Shahid. 2001. "The East Asian Miracle at the Millennium." In *Rethinking the East Asian Miracle,* edited by Joseph E. Stiglitz and Shahid Yusef. New York: Oxford University Press.

Yusuf, Shahid, Kaoru Nabeshima, and Dwight H. Perkins. 2005. *Under New Ownership: Privatizing China's State-Owned Enterprises.* Chicago: University of Chicago Press.

Contributors

Jennifer Amyx is assistant professor in the Political Science Department of the University of Pennsylvania.

Benjamin J. Cohen is the Louis G. Lancaster Professor of International Political Economy in the Department of Political Science at the University of California, Santa Barbara.

Peter Gourevitch is professor of political science at the Graduate School of International Relations and Pacific Studies at the University of California, San Diego.

Stephan Haggard is the Lawrence and Sallye Krause Professor of Korea-Pacific Studies at the Graduate School of International Relations and Pacific Studies at the University of California, San Diego.

Natasha Hamilton-Hart is assistant professor in the Department of Southeast Asian Studies at the National University of Singapore.

Allen Hicken is assistant professor in the Department of Political Science at the University of Michigan.

Andrew MacIntyre is professor of political science and director of the Crawford School of Economics and Government at the Australian National University.

Jongryn Mo is associate professor at the Graduate School of International Studies and director of the Center for International Studies at Yonsei University in Seoul.

T. J. Pempel is professor of political science at the University of California, Berkeley.

Thomas Pepinsky is assistant professor in the Department of Political Science at the University of Colorado at Boulder.

John Ravenhill is professor in the Department of International Relations in the Research School of Pacific and Asian Studies at the Australian National University.

Edward Steinfeld is associate professor in the Department of Political Science at the Massachusetts Institute of Technology.

Index

Page numbers followed by a "t" refer to tables. Page numbers followed by an "f" refer to figures.